continued on back

Digital Time Series Analysis

Digital Time Series Analysis

ROBERT K. OTNES
and
LOREN ENOCHSON

University Software Systems

A Wiley-Interscience Publication

JOHN WILEY & SONS
New York   London   Sydney   Toronto

Library of Congress Cataloging in Publication Data

Otnes, Robert K.
    Digital time series analysis.

    Bibliography: p. 455
    1. Electronic data processing—Time-series
analysis. I. Enochson, Loren D., joint author.
II. Title.

QA280.087   519.2'32   72-637
ISBN 0-471-65719-0

Printed in the United States of America

10 9 8 7 6 5 4 3 2

Preface

This monograph grew from the experience of the authors in the field of time series analysis and in particular the analysis of test data. The material presented here has been employed in practical situations and thus has the advantage of trial by fire.

This work was designed to fill two needs. First of all, it is intended as a tool and a reference for those actively engaged in digital data analysis in many fields: vibration, acoustics, medicine, seismology, communications, oceanography, etc.

Secondly, much of the material would be suitable for a graduate level course in time series analysis for students in engineering and related fields. With this in mind, some problems were included along with a first chapter which reviews much of the material required for reading the book.

There are some intended omissions, the principal topic not discussed being that of Walsh functions. While Walsh functions have aroused a great deal of theoretical interest, the number of applications for them is relatively small when compared to other procedures such as the Fourier transform.

The authors would like to thank Professor L. P. McNamee of UCLA for the assistance given during the writing of the book, Mrs. Judy Helbling and Miss Donna Kana for their help in its preparation, and Miss Beatrice Shube of Wiley for her editorial guidance.

Robert K. Otnes
Loren Enochson

Contents

Digital Time Series Analysis

CHAPTER 1
PRELIMINARY CONCEPTS

1.1 INTRODUCTION

The purpose of this chapter is to review the mathematics which will be used throughout the book, and to emphasize certain mathematical results or processes which are important to the understanding of the material. Chief among the latter are the following:

- Continuous Fourier transformations

- Discrete Fourier transformations

- The difference between the two transformations

- The Fourier transformation of the boxcar functions

- The concepts of mean, variance, and power

- The chi-square distributions, the normal distributions, and white noise

An understanding of the above concepts will greatly facilitate reading the remainder of the book. It is therefore recommended that this chapter be read and the examples and problems carefully examined if the reader is unfamiliar with the material.

Mathematical details are not the principal aim of this book. Therefore, many proofs in this chapter and the chapters following will be sketched or completely omitted. Should the reader require fuller mathematical details, he should refer to such works as Hannan (1960), Kuo and Kaiser (1966), or Parzen (1962).

Data reduction involves the processing of data records, usually referred to as time histories. A time history is simply the output of a measuring instrument recorded on some medium such as graph paper, punched paper tape, or magnetic tape. A record made of the daily closing price of a particular stock would be an example of a time history. In terms of the mathemati-

1

cal definitions usually associated with time histories, the price of the stock would be the dependent variable, whereas the time at which the price was quoted would be an independent variable. In the work that follows, the most frequently encountered independent variables are time and frequency. There are numerous other possible independent variables, such as position or velocity coordinates, but they are relatively uncommon in practice. However, the use of the word time for the independent variable in a recording of data should not be considered as restrictive. The techniques discussed are perfectly general, and the substitution of distance or depth, for example, in place of time is often done and only requires a consistent rearrangement of terms.

The precise definition of a function is not required for the ensuing discussion. Most of the functions employed may be thought of simply as processes that assign a single value to the dependent variable for each value of the independent variable. There are exceptions; in some cases functions will be used that have multiple dependent or independent variables.

The time histories to be discussed have a number of constraints placed on them by the nature of their origin. The four main limitations are:

1. Record length is finite

2. Range of the data is restricted

3. Data are sampled

4. Data are discrete (digitized to a finite precision)

Example 1.1. A recording digital voltmeter is used to monitor a certain experiment in which a transducer converts the physical quantity being observed into an electrical voltage. This voltage is the input to a voltmeter which records within a ±100 V range in one-digit steps, each step corresponding to one volt. It samples once per second, and the experiment consists of taking 100 samples--thus, the record length is limited to 100 sec. Values above 100 V or below -100 V

are not recorded, occurrences between the 1 sec samples are not observed, and fluctuations smaller than
1 V may be missed.

These values set definite limitations on what can
be observed with such a system. These limitations, as
will be seen in succeeding sections, carry over to
analyses done in a frequency domain.

Time functions will be denoted in the following
manner:

$x(t)$ = continuous function

and

x_i = sampled function

Usually the sampling increment is uniform and will be
denoted by Δt. In this case, we could write that

$$x_i = x(i\Delta t) \qquad\qquad (1.1)$$

The function x could be any physical quantity measured
during the course of a test and may be thought of as
any time in history being examined at some given point
in the data reduction process. If two time histories
must be considered at the same time, the first will be
denoted by x and the second by y.

Note that the following convention is used when
discussing time histories: A single letter x refers
to the function or process in general. The symbol $x(t)$,
on the other hand, is the particular numerical value
of the function x at time t.

1.2 MEAN VALUE

A host of problems arise when the time histories
under consideration are random processes. To avoid
continual rediscussion of these difficulties, an assumption is made: Unless explicitly stated otherwise,
the time histories, when they are random processes,
are stationary and ergodic. This topic is deferred to

Chapter 10, where the definition of these terms is more appropriate.

Under the above assumptions, the time average (mean value) of a function is equivalent to its ensemble average and may be used in place of it. The time average $\bar{x}$ is defined for continuous data by

$$\bar{x} = \lim_{T \to \infty} \frac{1}{2T} \int_{-T}^{T} x(t) \, dt \qquad (1.2)$$

Of course, only a finite portion of a record is available. Suppose the record starts at time $t = a$ and ends at time $t = b$. Then the time average over this piece of data would be

$$\bar{x} = \frac{1}{b-a} \int_{a}^{b} x(t) \, dt \qquad (1.3)$$

If the data are sampled, then (1.3) takes the form

$$\bar{x} = \frac{1}{N} \sum_{i=k}^{N-1+k} x_i \qquad (1.4)$$

where $k\Delta t = a$, and $(N - 1 + k)\Delta t = b$.

For convenience, k is usually taken to be zero, so (1.4) is usually written as

$$\bar{x} = \frac{1}{N} \sum_{i=0}^{N-1} x_i \qquad (1.5)$$

Subscripts could have been added to the last three definitions of $\bar{x}$ to indicate that the average was taken over the interval (a,b). However, $\bar{x}$ will always be a time average over the total record being discussed at the point at which it is used. Deviations from this convention will be duly noted when they occur.

1.3 VARIANCE

The variance of a time history under the assumptions discussed in Sections 1.2 is s_x^2, where

$$s_x^2 = \lim_{T \to \infty} \frac{1}{2T} \int_{-T}^{T} [x(t) - \bar{x}]^2 \, dt \qquad (1.6)$$

For finite record lengths, this is

$$s_x^2 = \frac{1}{t_2 - t_1} \int_{t_1}^{t_2} [x(t) - \bar{x}]^2 \, dt \qquad (1.7)$$

The standard deviation of x is the positive square root of the variance, s_x^2. Devices that compute s_x using a mechanization of (1.7) are called true root-mean-square (rms) meters. Other types of meters exist that give rms readings only for certain specific periodic functions, usually sine waves.

For sampled data, the definition of s_x^2 is

$$s_x^2 = \frac{1}{N - 1} \sum_{i=0}^{N-1} (x_i - \bar{x})^2 \qquad (1.8)$$

The mean square value of x in the continuous case, written Ψ_x^2, is

$$\Psi_x^2 = \lim_{T \to \infty} \frac{1}{2T} \int_{-T}^{T} x^2(t) \, dt \qquad (1.9)$$

As with the variance, both a record of finite length and discrete versions are employed where necessary.

Example 1.2. Suppose that x is a sinusoid

$$x(t) = A \sin(2\pi f_c t + \phi) \qquad\qquad -\infty < t < \infty \quad (1.10)$$

Then

$$s_x^2 = \lim_{T \to \infty} \frac{1}{T} \int_{T/2}^{T/2} A^2 \sin^2(2\pi f_c t + \phi) \, dt$$

$$= A^2 \lim_{T \to \infty} \frac{1}{T} \int_{-T/2}^{T/2} \sin^2(2\pi f_c t + \phi) \, dt$$

$$= A^2 \lim_{T \to \infty} \frac{1}{T} \left[\frac{T}{2} + \{\text{sine term} \leq 1\} \right] = \frac{A^2}{2} \qquad (1.11)$$

Note that Ψ_x^2 and s_x^2 are identical for those functions, since the mean is zero.

1.4   NORMAL AND CHI-SQUARE DISTRIBUTIONS

Suppose the variable x has mean μ and variance σ^2. Then it is *normally distributed* or has a *Gaussian distribution* if its probability density function $\phi(x)$ is given by

$$\phi(x) = \frac{1}{\sqrt{2\pi\sigma^2}} \exp\left[- \frac{(x - \mu)^2}{2\sigma^2} \right] \qquad (1.12)$$

The probability distribution function for such a Gaussian variable, $\Phi(x)$, is defined by

$$\Phi(x) = \int_{-\infty}^{x} \phi(\xi) \, d\xi \qquad (1.13)$$

In words:

$\Phi(x_o)$ = probability that $-\infty < x \leq x_o$

$\Phi(x_1) - \Phi(x_o)$ = probability that $x_o < x \leq x_1$

                                (provided $x_1 > x_o$)

$1 - \Phi(x_o)$ = probability that $x_o < x < \infty$ (1.14)

Some commonly used values of Φ for $\mu = 0$ and $\sigma = 1$ are

$$\frac{1}{\sqrt{2\pi}} \int_{-1}^{1} \exp\left(-\frac{x^2}{2}\right) dx = 0.682$$

$$\frac{1}{\sqrt{2\pi}} \int_{-2}^{+2} \exp\left(-\frac{x^2}{2}\right) dx = 0.954$$

$$\frac{1}{\sqrt{2\pi}} \int_{-3}^{3} \exp\left(-\frac{x^2}{2}\right) dx = 0.997 \qquad (1.15)$$

The concept of the normal distribution is a theoretical one; in actual practice it is not usually possible to have truly normal data. The principal problem is one of range. Most data functions have a finite range of values; normally distributed data must have an infinite range.

Example 1.3. Suppose a 2 cm rod is measured by a group of people, each using the same ruler, and that the resulting measurements are normally distributed. Let the true mean of the measurements be 2 cm and the variance be 0.25 cm. The probability of a measurement of −0.5 cm or less is

$$\frac{1}{\sqrt{2\pi\sigma^2}} \int_{-\infty}^{-0.5} \exp\left[-\frac{(x-\mu)^2}{2\sigma^2}\right] dx$$

Making the substitution $y = (x - \mu)/\sigma$ gives

$$= \frac{1}{\sqrt{2\pi}} \int_{-\infty}^{\frac{-0.5-2}{0.5}} \exp\left(-\frac{y^2}{2}\right) dy$$

$$= \Phi(-5.0) \approx 0.0000001 \qquad (1.16)$$

Thus, there is a finite (albeit small) probability of a negative measurement of the length of the rod. This, of course, is an absurdity. But, the normal distribution is entirely justified because it is a reasonable approximation to whatever the true distribution may be.

There are a number of reasons for assuming normality (i.e., that the data are normally distributed). The principal ones are:

1. There is a large body of knowledge about the normal distribution. This makes it easy to model a given situation and then make statements about the resulting statistics.

2. The *central limit theorem* (Cramer, 1946) shows that the sum of variables of any distribution whatsoever tends to be normally distributed if "enough of them" are added together. Filtering data (see Chapter 3) turns out to be the equivalent of adding a number of observations together so that filtered data "tends to be" normally distributed.

Some of the important properties of the normal distribution function are:

1. The density and distribution of the normal variable x are completely determined by the mean μ_x and variance σ_x^2.

2. The moments of x are

$$E[x^n] = \begin{cases} \mu & n = 1 \\ \mu^2 + \sigma^2 & n = 2 \\ \mu(\mu^2 + 3\sigma^2) & n = 3 \end{cases} \qquad (1.17)$$

. . .

The central moments are

$$E[(x-\mu)^n] = \begin{cases} 0 & n=1,3,\ldots \\ 1\cdot 3\cdots(n-1)\sigma^n & n=2,4,\ldots \end{cases} \tag{1.18}$$

A very important relation for fourth moments, provided $\mu = 0$, is

$$E[x_a x_b x_c x_d] = E[x_a x_b]\, E[x_c x_d] + E[x_a x_c]\, E[x_b x_d]$$

$$+ E[x_a x_d]\, E[x_b x_c] \tag{1.19}$$

Chi-Square Distribution

Suppose that $x_1, x_2, \ldots, x_n$ are independent, Gaussian variables with zero mean and unit variance. Define χ_n^2 by

$$\chi_n^2 = \sum_{i=1}^{n} x_i^2 \tag{1.20}$$

Then χ_n^2 is said to be a *chi-square* variable with n *degrees of freedom* (d.f.) and to have the *chi-square distribution*. The density function for χ_n is

$$p\left(\chi_n^2\right) = \left[2^{n/2}\ \Gamma(n/2)\right]^{-1} \left(\chi_n^2\right) \exp\left[-\chi_{n/2}^2\right]$$

$$\chi^2 \geq 0 \tag{1.21}$$

where $\Gamma(a)$ is the Gamma function.

The main use of the chi-square distribution in time series data analysis is in discussing the variability of sample variance and power spectral densities. If $\{x_i\}$ has zero mean, and N samples of $\{x_i\}$ are used to compute the sample variance s^2, then the probability is $(1 - \alpha)$ that the true variance is between two limits:

$$B_1 \leq \sigma^2 \leq B_2 \tag{1.22}$$

where the limits B_1 and B_2 are defined by

$$B_1 = \frac{ns^2}{\chi^2_{n;\ 1 - \frac{\alpha}{2}}}$$

$$B_2 = \frac{ns^2}{\chi^2_{n;\ \frac{\alpha}{2}}} \qquad\qquad n = N - 1 \tag{1.23}$$

Note that B_1 and B_2 are functions of s^2, α, and χ. The interval (B_1, B_2) is referred to as a *confidence interval*; and one speaks of the *[(1 - α)100]% confidence interval*.

As an example,* suppose N = 31 independent observations are taken from a normally distributed random variable, and that a 90% confidence interval on the sample variance is desired. Suppose further that the sample mean is $\bar{x}$ = 58.61 and the sample variance s^2 = 33.43. Then the theoretical variance σ^2 is bounded by

$$\text{Prob} \left[\frac{30\ s^2}{43.77} < \sigma^2 < \frac{30\ s^2}{18.49} \right] = 0.90$$

where

$$\chi^2_{30:0.05} = 43.77 = \chi^2_{30} \text{ such that } P(\chi^2_{30}) = 0.05$$

$$\chi^2_{30:95} = 18.49 = \chi^2_{30} \text{ such that } P(\chi^2_{30}) = 0.95$$

---

*Taken from Blackman and Tukey (1958).

When simplified, the above bounds become

$$22.91 \leq \sigma^2 < 54.22$$

Note that on the average the true variance will be outside such an interval once out of every ten tries.

1.5 FOURIER TRANSFORM

When speaking of the Fourier transform it should be kept in mind that there are four principal forms of it, each of which has its own variations. These latter minor differences are usually traceable to differences in multiplication constants used by different writers. The difference between the four basic forms, on the other hand, are due to the fact that different ranges and domains are employed. That is, the way in which the independent and dependent variables are defined is different in each of the four forms. Table 1.1 shows the four forms and their ranges.

While forms II and III are the ones that will be employed in the analysis of time series data, form I will be discussed first, as it is most familiar. It is the most common form for vibration analysis, communication theory, and many other physical application areas.

$$X(f) = \lim_{T \to \infty} \int_{-T}^{T} x(t) e^{-j2\pi ft} \, dt \qquad (1.24)$$

Here, X may be shown to exist if the square of x is integrable in the Lebesgue sense.* As usual, this restriction actually is far broader than it need be for practical applications. Also, it is only sufficient rather than necessary. Two notable exceptions to the requirement are the sine and cosine functions, which when squared and integrated, are unbounded. However, as will be seen, it is still possible to talk of their

---

*
See Wiener (1930) for details.

Table 1.1   The Four Forms of the Fourier Transform

Form	$x(f)$ or X_k	Range of f, or $k\Delta f$	$x(t)$ or x_i	Range of t, or $i\Delta t$
I	$\displaystyle\int_{-\infty}^{\infty} x(t)\,\exp(-j2\pi ft)\,dt$	$-\infty \le f \le \infty$ continuous	$\displaystyle\int_{-\infty}^{\infty} x(f)\,\exp(j2\pi tf)\,df$	$-\infty \le t \le \infty$ continuous
II	$\displaystyle\sum_{i=-\infty}^{\infty} x_i\,\exp(-j2\pi i\Delta tf)\Delta t$	$-\dfrac{1}{2\Delta t} \le f \le \dfrac{1}{2\Delta t}$ continuous repetitive	$\displaystyle\int_{-\frac{1}{2\Delta t}}^{\frac{1}{2\Delta t}} x(f)\,\exp(j2\pi fi\Delta t)\,df$	$-\infty \le i \le \infty$ discrete
III	$\displaystyle\sum_{i=0}^{N-1} x_i\,\exp\left(-j\dfrac{2\pi ik}{N}\right)\Delta t$	$0 \le k \le N-1$ discrete, repetitive	$\displaystyle\sum_{k=0}^{N-1} X_k\,\exp\left(j\dfrac{2\pi ik}{N}\right)\Delta f$	$0 \le i \le N-1$ discrete, repetitive
IV	$\displaystyle\int_{0}^{T} x(t)\,\exp(-j2\pi tk\Delta f)\,dt$	$-\infty \le k \le \infty$ discrete	$\displaystyle\sum_{k=-\infty}^{\infty} X_k\,\exp(j2\pi k\Delta ft)\,\Delta f$	$0 \le t < T$ continuous repetitive

Fourier transforms. It may also be shown that there is a function x_1 such that

$$x_1(t) = \lim_{F \to \infty} \int_{-F}^{F} X(f)e^{j2\pi tf} \, df \qquad (1.25)$$

The function x_1 is very much like x. In fact, the equation

$$x(t) - x_1(t) = 0 \qquad (1.26)$$

holds for most values of t. Technically, (1.26) is true almost everywhere. Thus, applying the operation defined by (1.25) is almost like reversing the procedure given in (1.24). Because the discrepancies are slight, and even nonexistent in most practical cases, the transformation defined by (1.25) is referred to as the inverse Fourier transform.

These operations may be denoted by $\mathcal{F}_I[x(t)]$ rather than the full integrals, the subscript denoting the particular form used. That is,

$$X(f) = \mathcal{F}_I[x(t)] = \int_{-\infty}^{\infty} x(t)e^{-j2\pi ft} \, dt$$

$$x(t) = \mathcal{F}_I^{-1}[X(f)] = \int_{-\infty}^{\infty} X(f)e^{j2\pi tf} \, df \qquad (1.27)$$

in the form I case.

The independent variable f will always be expressed in units of Hertz (Hz). Occasionally, it will be convenient to use two other related independent variables, ω and λ, where

$$\omega = 2\pi f$$

and

$$\lambda = 2\pi f \Delta t \qquad (1.28)$$

The unit impulse function I constantly occurs when dealing with various Fourier transforms. It is defined by the following integral equation:

$$y(t_0) = \int_{-\infty}^{\infty} y(t) I(t-t_0) \, dt \qquad (1.29)$$

where y is any bounded function. In this case, $I(t)$ is the Dirac delta function $\delta(t)$. The unit impulse functions for the other forms are shown in Table 1.2. This function δ may be viewed as one which is arbitrarily tall and narrow but of unit area. Serious problems arise from the use of delta functions. However, it has been shown (Lighthill, 1960) that the calculus of delta functions is consistent. Therefore, they will be used with no exploration of the extensive theory required to discuss them rigorously.

Applying (1.29) to a few simple expressions rapidly yields some very useful results:

$$\mathcal{F}^{-1}\left[\frac{I(f - f_0) + I(f + f_0)}{2}\right] = \cos 2\pi f_0 t \qquad (1.30)$$

$$\mathcal{F}^{-1}\left[\frac{I(f - f_0) - I(f + f_0)}{2j}\right] = \sin 2\pi f_0 t \qquad (1.31)$$

$$\mathcal{F}[I(t)] = \mathcal{F}^{-1}[I(f)] = 1 \qquad (1.32)$$

provided that f_0 is of the form $k/2\Delta t$.

Thus, the Fourier transform of a sine or cosine consists of two impulse functions. Also, suppose that the time function x is composed solely of sinusoids with varying amplitudes and phases,

$$x(t) = \sum_{n-1}^{N} A_n \cos(2\pi f_n t + \phi_n) \qquad (1.33)$$

Table 1.2 Convolution for the Four Domains, and the Corresponding Unit Impulse Functions

Form	$z = x*y$	Unit impulse $I(t)$	$z = X*Y$	Unit impulse $I(f)$
I	$\displaystyle\int_{-\infty}^{\infty} x(\tau)y(t-\tau)\,d\tau$	$\delta(t)$	$\displaystyle\int_{-\infty}^{\infty} x(v)Y(f-v)\,dv$	$\delta(f)$
II	$\displaystyle\sum_{i=-\infty}^{\infty} x_i y_{k-i}\,\Delta t$	$\dfrac{1}{\Delta t}$ $\;i=0$ 0 otherwise	$\displaystyle\int_{-\frac{1}{2\Delta t}}^{\frac{1}{2\Delta t}} x(v)Y(f-v)\,dv$ $(f-v)$ modulo $\dfrac{1}{2\Delta t}$	$\delta(f)$
III	$\displaystyle\sum_{i=0}^{N-1} x_i y_{k-i}\,\Delta t$ $[(k-i) \text{ modulo } N]$	$\dfrac{1}{\Delta t}$ $\;i=0$ 0 otherwise	$\displaystyle\sum_{k=0}^{N-1} X_k Y_{i-k}\,\Delta f$ $[(i-k) \text{ modulo } N]$	$\dfrac{1}{\Delta f}$ $\;k=0$ 0 otherwise
IV	$\displaystyle\int_{0}^{T} x(\tau)y(t-\tau)\,d\tau$ $[(t-\tau) \text{ modulo } T]$	$\delta(t)$	$\displaystyle\sum_{k=-\infty}^{\infty} X_k Y_{i-k}\,\Delta t$	$\dfrac{1}{\Delta f}$ $\;k=0$ 0 otherwise

Then X consists of a set of 2N impulse functions, as follows:

$$X(f) = \sum_{n=1}^{N} \frac{A_n}{2} \left[I(f - f_n)e^{j\phi_n} + I(f + f_n)e^{-j\phi_n} \right]$$

(1.34)

Example 1.4. Suppose x is defined by

$$x(t) = \begin{cases} 1 & 0 \le t < \frac{1}{2} \\ 0 & \frac{1}{2} + k \le t < \frac{3}{2} + k \\ 1 & \frac{3}{2} + k \le t < \frac{5}{2} + k \end{cases} \quad k = 0,2,4,\ldots \quad (1.35)$$

and x(t) = x(-t). This is a square wave of unit height. Another equivalent definition of x would be the trigonometric series obtained from the Fourier analysis or from the form IV transform given in Table 1.2:

$$x(t) = \frac{1}{2} + \frac{2}{\pi} \sum_{i=0}^{\infty} \frac{(-1)^i}{1 + 2i} \cos[\pi(2i + 1)t] \quad\quad (1.36)$$

The Fourier transform of x is

$$X(f) = \frac{1}{2}I(f) + \frac{1}{\pi} \sum_{i=0}^{\infty} \frac{(-1)^i}{1 + 2i} \left\{ I\left[f - \frac{1}{2}(2i + 1) \right] \right.$$

$$\left. + I\left[f + \frac{1}{2}(2i + 1) \right] \right\} \quad\quad (1.37)$$

This is shown graphically in Figure 1.1. The height of the arrow is equal to the coefficient of the corresponding impulse function. Because of the symmetry of x(t), X(f) is a real function.

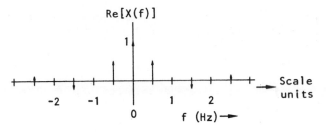

Fig. 1.1 Fourier transform of a square
wave with period one unit.

Suppose x, y, X, and Y are all known. What is the
relation between the product of x and y and the functions X and Y? It may be shown to be

$$\mathcal{F}_I[x(t)y(t)] = \int_{-\infty}^{\infty} X(f')\, Y(f-f')\, df'$$

$$= \int_{-\infty}^{\infty} X(f-f')\, Y(f')\, df' \qquad (1.38)$$

The above relation may be derived in the following
manner:

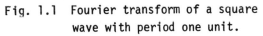

$$= \mathcal{F}_I\left\{\mathcal{F}_I^{-1}[X(f_1)]\,\mathcal{F}_I^{-1}[Y(f_2)]\right\}$$

$$= \int_{-\infty}^{\infty}\int_{-\infty}^{\infty}\int_{-\infty}^{\infty} X(f_1)Y(f_2)\,\exp[-j2\pi(ft-f_1 t-f_2 t)]\, df_1\, df_2\, dt$$

$$\mathcal{F}_I[x(t)y(t)]$$

$$= \int_{-\infty}^{\infty}\int_{-\infty}^{\infty} X(f_1)Y(f_2)\int_{-\infty}^{\infty} \exp[-j2\pi(f-f_1-f_2)t]\, dt\, df_1\, df_2$$

$$= \int_{-\infty}^{\infty} \int_{-\infty}^{\infty} X(f_1) Y(f_2) I(f-f_1-f_2) \, df_1 \, df_2$$

$$= \int_{-\infty}^{\infty} Y(f_2) \int_{-\infty}^{\infty} X(f_1) I(f-f_1-f_2) \, df_1 \, df_2$$

$$= \int_{-\infty}^{\infty} Y(f_2) X(f-f_2) \, df_2 \qquad\qquad (1.39)$$

The right-hand side of (1.39) is known as the convolution of X and Y, denoted by X * Y. Table 1.2 gives the forms of the convolutions for the four domains. In all four cases,

$$\mathcal{F}\,[x * y] = X \cdot Y$$

$$\mathcal{F}\,[x \cdot y] = X * Y \qquad\qquad (1.40)$$

Some general properties of convolution for all four forms are:

1. Commutativity

$$x * y = y * x \qquad\qquad (1.41)$$

2. Associativity

$$x * (y * z) = (x * y) * z \qquad\qquad (1.42)$$

3. Distributivity (for c = a constant)

$$c(x + y) * z = c(x * z) + c(y * z) \qquad\qquad (1.43)$$

4. Existence of an identity (namely the unit impulse function)

$$x * I = x \qquad\qquad (1.44)$$

Boxcar Function

The *boxcar function*, u_T, for the form I transform, is defined by

$$u_T(t) = \begin{cases} 0 & t < -T \\ 1 & -T \leq t \leq T \\ 0 & T < t \end{cases} \qquad (1.45)$$

Its Fourier transform is

$$U_T(f) = \int_{-\infty}^{\infty} u_T(t) e^{-j\omega t}\, dt = \int_{-T}^{T} e^{-j\omega t}\, dt$$

$$= \left. \frac{1}{-j\omega} e^{-j\omega t} \right|_{-T}^{T}$$

$$= -\frac{1}{j\omega} [\cos \omega T - j \sin \omega T \quad \cos(-\omega T) + j \sin(-\omega T)]$$

$$= \frac{2 \sin \omega T}{\omega} \qquad (1.46)$$

The transform is shown in Figure 1.2. This important function will occur repeatedly in subsequent analyses. Again, because of symmetry, $U_T(f)$ is a real function. There are three more forms of the boxcar function; these correspond to the three other forms of the Fourier transform, and will be discussed as they occur. They are, however, similar to $u_T(t)$ and $U_T(f)$ defined above. These equations can be extended to yield Table 1.3, which shows the relationship of some of the basic functions. It is apparent that there is a natural correspondence in Fourier transform pairs; a very narrow time function has a very broad transform. When such a narrow time function is widened, its Fourier transform becomes narrower. Thus, a function

of short time duration requires a Fourier transform
that is defined over a wide range of frequencies.
Conversely, a function that requires only a short
range of frequencies to define it will have a large
range in the time domain.

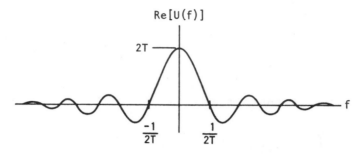

Fig. 1.2 Sine of x over x function.

Table 1.3 Comparison of Various Time Functions
and Their Fourier Transforms

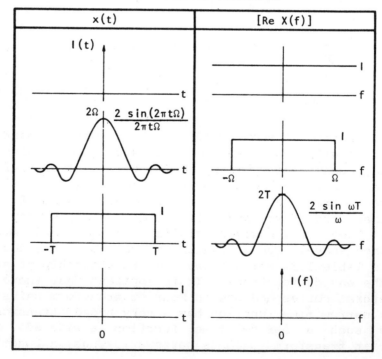

In actual practice, one cannot record the results of an experiment that is infinite in length. The question naturally arises as to what effect that has on the Fourier transform. One way of analyzing the problem is to regard the truncated record as being the function y, which is the product of two other functions,

x(t)   as usual

$$u_T(t) = \begin{cases} 1 & -T \le t \le T \\ 0 & \text{otherwise} \end{cases}$$ (1.47)

$$y(t) = x(t)\, u_T(t)$$

Thus, the Fourier transform of y is

$$Y(f) = \int_{-\infty}^{\infty} x(t) u_T(t) e^{-j\omega t}\, dt$$ (1.48)

It reduces to (using the convolution technique as discussed above)

$$Y(f) = \int_{-\infty}^{\infty} X(f') U_T(f - f')\, df'$$ (1.49)

The Fourier transform of $u_T(t)$ is given by (1.46) so that

$$Y(f) = \int_{-\infty}^{\infty} X(f') \frac{2 \sin[2\pi(f - f')T]}{2\pi(f - f')}\, df'$$ (1.50)

In the limit as T goes to infinity, $U_T(f)$ takes on the same characteristics as I(f), so that the right-hand side of (1.49) reduces to X(f). On the other hand, for finite T, the observed functions will be affected by the truncation. For example, if x were a cosine wave

$$x(t) = A \cos 2\pi f_0 t$$

then

$$X(f) = \frac{A}{2} [\delta(f - f_0) + \delta(f + f_0)]$$

and

$$Y(f) = \frac{A}{2\pi} \left\{ \frac{\sin[2\pi T(f - f_0)]}{f - f_0} + \frac{\sin[2\pi T(f + f_0)]}{f + f_0} \right\}$$

(1.51)

Note that the expression for $X(f)$ and $Y(f)$ become identical in the limit as T goes to infinity.

1.6 POWER SPECTRUM

In Section 1.3 the concept of the mean square is discussed, and an expression for the mean square is given:

$$\psi_x^2 = \frac{1}{t_2 - t_1} \int_{t_1}^{t_2} x^2(t) \, dt$$

Dimensionally, ψ_x^2 is proportional to the mean square energy per unit time, which is by definition, power.

The power spectral density of the function x, written $G_x(f)$ is an extension of this concept. The interpretation of $G_x(f)$ is that the integral

$$\psi_x^2(f_1, f_2) = \int_{f_1}^{f_2} G_x(f) \, df \qquad 0 \le f_1 \le f_2 \quad (1.52)$$

is the power between the frequencies f_1 and f_2. Thus

$$\psi_x^2 = \int_0^\infty G_x(f) \; df \tag{1.53}$$

It may be shown that an appropriate expression for G_x is given by

$$G_x(f) = 2 \lim_{T \to \infty} \frac{1}{T} \left| \int_{-T/2}^{T/2} x(t) e^{-j\omega t} \; dt \right|^2 \qquad f \geq 0 \tag{1.54}$$

Difficulties may arise if (1.54) is used without care. Statistically inconsistent estimates result when no frequency smoothing is performed. Also mathematical precautions are necessary, as pointed out in Korn and Korn (1968, p. 646). These two considerations, along with the fact that only inefficient computational procedures were available in the past, led to the dismissal of (1.54) as a suitable spectrum estimation procedure. However, the fast Fourier transform (see Chapter 4) eliminates the computational objection, proper frequency domain smoothing provides statistically consistent estimates, and finite record lengths eliminate the mathematical problems.

An equivalent expression, usually referred to as the Wiener-Khinchin theorem, is

$$G_x(f) = 2 \int_{-\infty}^\infty R_x(\tau) e^{-j\omega\tau} \; d\tau = 4 \int_0^\infty R_x(\tau) \cos 2\pi f \tau \; d\tau$$

$$f \geq 0 \tag{1.55}$$

where the term $R_x(\tau)$ the time-autocorrelation function of x, is defined as

$$R_x(\tau) = \lim_{T \to \infty} \frac{1}{T} \int_{-T/2}^{T/2} x(t) x(t + \tau) \; dt \tag{1.56}$$

Demonstration of the equivalence of these two methods for computing G_x is beyond the scope of this work but is discussed in several references (Bendat and Piersol, 1966; Wiener, 1949). A third method of defining G_x is available. However, it is based on the concept of filtering, and discussion must be postponed until after filtering has been introduced.

The function G_x is usually called the one-sided power spectral density (PSD). Thus, the PSD of x means G_x as defined by either (1.54) or (1.55). The function R_x requires further discussion. Under the condition of ergodocity assumed earlier, it is equal to

$$R_x(\tau) = E[x(t)x(t + \tau)] = \int_{-\infty}^{\infty} x(t)x(t + \tau)p(x,t,\tau)\, dx$$

(1.57)

where $p(x,t,\tau)$ is an appropriate joint probability density function.

Example 1.5. Suppose n(t) is uncorrelated random noise with a zero mean. Then its autocorrelation is given by

$$R_n(\tau) = \frac{N}{2}\, \delta(\tau)$$

and

$$G_n(f) = N$$

(1.58)

That is, the PSD of uncorrelated random noise is a constant. This type of data is known as white noise, because the power is uniform (flat) through any given band and, therefore, is like white light which is more or less uniform in the visible portion of the optical spectrum.

While useful as a mathematical tool for clarifying the concept of the PSD, it must be noted that true white noise is not physically realizable because its variance is infinite. Devices which supposedly generate white noise, in actuality produce noise whose PSD is flat out to some frequency and then drops off for higher frequencies.

Example 1.6. Suppose that x is a sine wave with frequency f_c, amplitude A, and phase ϕ. That is,

$$x(t) = A \sin(2\pi f_c t + \phi) \tag{1.59}$$

The autocorrelation function is computed as follows:

$$R_x(\tau) = \lim_{T\to\infty} \frac{1}{T} \int_{-T/2}^{T/2} A^2 \sin(2\pi f_c t + \phi)$$

$$\times \sin[2\pi f_c (t + \tau) + \phi] \, dt$$

$$= \lim_{T\to\infty} \frac{1}{T} \left(\frac{A^2}{2}\right) \int_{-T/2}^{T/2} [\cos 2\pi f_c \tau$$

$$- \cos(2\pi f_c \tau + 4\pi f_c t + 2\phi)] \, dt$$

$$= \lim_{T\to\infty} \frac{A^2}{2T} \left[t \cos 2\pi f_c \tau \right.$$

$$\left. + \frac{1}{4\pi f_c} \sin(2\pi f_c \tau + 4\pi f_c t + 2\phi) \right]_{-T/2}^{T/2}$$

$$= \lim_{T \to \infty} \left\{ \frac{A^2}{2} \cos 2\pi f_c \tau - \left(\frac{A^2}{8\pi f_c} \right) \left(\frac{1}{T} \right) \left[\sin(2\pi f_c \tau \right. \right.$$

$$\left. \left. + 2\pi f_c T + 2\phi) - \sin(2\pi f_c \tau - 2\pi f_c T + 2\phi) \right] \right\}$$

$$= \frac{A^2}{2} \cos 2\pi f_c \tau \qquad\qquad (1.60)$$

This is true because the term within the brackets is always less than 2. In the limit, this term must go to zero, since it is divided by T.

Note that the arbitrary phase angle ϕ has disappeared in the final result. As the phase angle was arbitrary, the function could just as well have been a cosine wave. Thus, the autocorrelation of a sinusoid, regardless of its phase, is always a cosine with zero phase. In general, phase information is lost in the autocorrelation process.

Applying (1.55),

$$G_x(f) = 4 \int_0^\infty \left(\frac{A^2}{2} \cos 2\pi f_c \tau \right) \cos 2\pi f \tau \; d\tau$$

$$= \frac{A^2}{2} I(f - f_c) \qquad\qquad f > 0 \qquad (1.61)$$

This is a major result. It says that the PSD of a sinusoid of frequency f_c is a single-impulse function at frequency f_c. The multiplier of the impulse function is equal to the power in the sinusoid. Recalling (1.53),

$$\psi_x^2 = \int_0^\infty G_x(f) \; df = \frac{A^2}{2} \int_0^\infty I(f - f_c) \; df = \frac{A^2}{2} \quad (1.62)$$

which is exactly the result obtained in Example 1.2.

Example 1.7. As a last example of power spectral density for this section, consider the case where the autocorrelation is a truncated cosine wave

$$R_x^*(\tau) = \begin{cases} \dfrac{A^2}{2} \cos 2\pi f_c \tau & \tau \leq T \\ \\ 0 & \tau > T \end{cases} \qquad (1.63)$$

This is precisely the type of function that might be obtained in some practical situation. It is trun- cated because the experiment cannot be continued indefinitely.

The following indicates a possible interpretation of R_x:

$$R_x^*(\tau) = R_x(\tau) u_T(\tau) \qquad (1.64)$$

where R_x is as defined in the previous case and $u_T(\tau)$ is as defined above. With this interpretation, we could find $G_x^*(f)$ using the convolution

$$G_x^*(f) = 2 \int_{-0}^{\infty} u_T(\tau) R_x(\tau) e^{-j2\pi f} \, d\tau$$

$$= \int_{-\infty}^{\infty} u_T(f - f') G_x(f') \, df'$$

$$= \int_{-\infty}^{\infty} \frac{2 \sin[2\pi T(f - f')]}{2\pi(f - f')} \frac{A^2}{2} I(f' - f_c) \, df'$$

$$= A^2 \left\{ \frac{\sin[T(\omega - \omega_c)]}{\omega - \omega_c} \right\} \qquad \text{for } f > 0 \quad (1.65)$$

This function is shown in Figure 1.3.

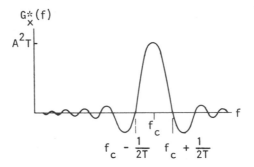

Fig. 1.3 Power spectral density of a
truncated sinusoidal function.

1.7 DIGITAL DATA FUNCTIONS

Digital data collected during a test may be thought
of as related to a hypothetical continuous function
x(t), defined for all t, by the equation

$$x_i = \int_{-\infty}^{\infty} I(t - i\Delta t)x(t) \, dt \qquad i = 0,\ldots,N \qquad (1.66)$$

There are a number of indexing conventions that could
be used besides the above. The other possibilities,
such as $i = 1,\ldots,N$ or $i = 0,\ldots,N - 1$, will be employed whenever they are convenient.

The question naturally arises as to how well the
sequence $\{x_i\}$ represents the function x. Put another
way, does the series of x_i values tell everything
about x? The asymptotic answer to this question is
given in the sampling theorem (Shannon, 1949), which
will be discussed below. The word asymptotic is used
because two hypotheses of the sampling theorem can be
met only in limiting cases.

Sampling Theorem

Hypotheses

1. x is a random variable defined for $-\infty < t < \infty$

2. PSD of x, $G_x(f)$, exists

3. $G_x(f) = 0$ for $f \geq B$

Conclusion

Let Δt be any sampling interval such that $\Delta t < 1/2B$. Given $\{x_i\}$ sampled at Δt intervals, $i = -\infty,\ldots,-1,0,1,$ ∞, then x(t) can be reconstructed uniquely (almost everywhere). Put another way, if the power of x is limited to a band less than $1/2\Delta t$ Hz, then sampling at interval Δt enables one to reconstruct the function x uniquely. There are some mathematical cases which must be excepted. One of these will be discussed in an example.

Proof of the Sampling Theorem

A precise (rigorous) proof will not be given, as it would necessitate more mathematics than is appropriate to this work. A heuristic (plausible but incomplete) proof may be given the following way: Hypotheses 2 and 3 of the theorem are sufficient to ensure that X the Fourier transform of x, exists and that $X(f) = 0$ for $|f| > B$. That is, X is a function defined for $-B \leq f \leq B$. Thus, X can be represented by a Fourier series. In particular, one could use the representation

$$X(f) = \frac{1}{2B} \sum_{k=-\infty}^{\infty} c_k \exp(-j2\pi kf/2B) \qquad -B \leq f \leq B \qquad (1.67)$$

where

$$c_k = \int_{-B}^{B} X(f) \exp(j2\pi fk/2B) \, df$$

$$\text{for } k = -\infty,\ldots,-1,0,1,\ldots,\infty \qquad (1.68)$$

This is the type II definition, as given in Table 1.1. The c_k term as defined above absorbs some of the coefficients encountered in other definitions.

Let

$$\Delta t = \frac{1}{2B} \qquad\qquad\qquad (1.69)$$

Also, note that the limits of integration of (1.68) could be extended from $(-B,B)$ to $(-\infty,\infty)$, as $X(f)$ is equal to zero on the extended interval. Thus, (1.68) could be rewritten as

$$c_k = \int_{-\infty}^{\infty} X(f)\ \exp(j2\pi fk\Delta t)df \qquad\qquad (1.70)$$

But the right-hand side of (1.70) is exactly equal to x_k. That is, the set $\{x_k\}$ uniquely represents $X(t)$.

The last question discussed is how to obtain x for values of t not equal to $k\Delta t$. There are two answers. If x is available, then $k\Delta t$ may be replaced with t, so that

$$x(t) = \int_{-B}^{B} X(f)\ \exp(j2\pi ft)df \qquad\qquad (1.71)$$

Alternatively, given only the x_k terms, one could write that

$$x(t) = \int_{-B}^{B} X(f)\ \exp(j2\pi ft)df$$

$$= \int_{-B}^{B} \frac{1}{2B} \sum_{k=-\infty}^{\infty} x_k\ \exp(-j2\pi fk\Delta t)\ \exp 2\pi ft\ df$$

$$= \frac{1}{2B} \sum_{k=-\infty}^{\infty} x_k \int_{-B}^{B} \exp[j2\pi f(t - k\Delta t)]\ df \qquad (1.72)$$

Using the results of Section 1.5, the integral term in
(1.72) may be evaluated and found to be

$$\int_{-B}^{B} \exp[j2\pi f(t - k\Delta t)]\, df = \frac{2\,\sin[2\pi B(t - k\Delta t)]}{2\pi(t - k\Delta t)}$$

(1.73)

Thus, for $t = k\Delta t$, (1.72) reduces to

$$x(k\Delta t) = \frac{1}{2B}(x_k 2B) = x_k$$

(1.74)

Note that (1.74) is valid only for values of k
which are integers. To recover x(t) for (t/Δt) not an
integer, the general expression in (1.72) must be used.
The integral within that equation may be replaced with
the sin x/x type of term given in (1.73), so that
(1.72) reduces to

$$x(t) = \sum_{k=-\infty}^{\infty} x_k \left\{ \frac{\sin[2\pi B(t - k\Delta t)]}{2\pi B(t - k\Delta t)} \right\}$$

(1.75)

Given $\{x_k\}$, (1.75) enables one to reconstruct x(t) for
any value of t.

The theorem holds only for infinite record lengths
and for band-limited functions. These requirements
cannot be met in actual practice. However, long record
lengths and the use of high-quality "lowpass" filters
(see Chapter 3) before the functions are sampled will
yield satisfactory results. The theorem breaks down
at B = 1/2Δt (called the Nyquist, folding, or aliasing
frequency when applied there. That is shown in
Example 1.8.

Example 1.8. Let x be given by

$$x(t) = A\,\sin(2\pi B t + \phi)$$

(1.76)

Where B = 1/2Δt, and $0 \le \phi < 2\pi$. That is, x is a sine
wave of arbitrary phase whose frequency is commensurate

with the sampling rate.   Then

$$x_k = x(k\Delta t) = A \sin(\pi k + \phi)$$

$$= A(\sin \pi k \cos \phi + \cos \pi k \sin \phi)$$

$$= A(-1)^k \sin \phi \qquad\qquad (1.77)$$

The last step is true because $\sin \pi k = 0$ for all k,
and $\cos \pi k = (-1)^k$.   Given only the sequence $\{x_k\}$, the
observer sees a term of magnitude $(A \sin \phi)$, which al-
ternates.   If ϕ is unknown, there is no way of recon-
structing the function. In fact, if $\phi = 0$, the observ-
er will see nothing!   In any case, as $0 < |\sin \phi| < 1$,
the observed sequence will have amplitudes which are
lower in value than A.   Calculations made using these
data will be biased.   An example of this is seen in
Figure 1.4.

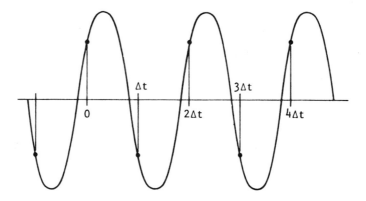

Fig. 1.4 Example: $x(t) = A \sin(2\pi Bt + \phi)$. Data
indicate when sampling takes place.

There is a folktale current in the engineering pro-
fession that a sampling rate of five times the highest
frequency to be observed is necessary for good, unbiased results.   This is pessimistic for most applications. Furthermore, use of the 5 sample/cycle criteria
is wasteful, since a 2.5 sample/cycle rule has been

found to give excellent results. This rule says that if f_c is the highest frequency to be observed, then set

$$B = \frac{5}{4} f_c$$

and   (1.78)

$$\Delta t = \frac{2}{5f_c}$$

Example 1.9. If $f = 1/2\Delta t$ is the highest frequency that can be observed in any case, what is the lowest frequency which can be observed? An answer to this question may be found by examining the PSD of sine waves. Suppose two sinusoid functions compose a data function, and that each has amplitude A. That is,

$$x(t) = A[\sin(2\pi f_1 t + \phi_1) + \sin(2\pi f_2 t + \phi_2)]$$

$$-\infty < t < \infty \quad (1.79)$$

The phases ϕ_1 and ϕ_2 are constant but arbitrary. The autocorrelation of this may be shown to be

$$R_x(\tau) = \frac{A^2}{2}(\cos 2\pi f_1 \tau + \cos 2\pi f_2 \tau) \quad (1.80)$$

and the PSD is then

$$G_x(f) = \frac{A^2}{2}[I(f - f_1) + I(f - f_2)] \qquad f \geq 0$$

Suppose that $R_x(\tau)$ is then limited to the range $-T < \tau < T$. Call this new function $R_x^*(\tau)$. That is,

$$R_x^*(\tau) = R_x(\tau) u_T(\tau)$$

and

$$u_T(\tau) = \begin{cases} 1 & -T < \tau < T \\ \\ 0 & \text{otherwise} \end{cases} \tag{1.81}$$

The Fourier transform of $u_T(\tau)$ is discussed in Section 1.4. The PSD corresponding to $R^*(\tau)$, $G^*(f)$, may be obtained in a manner similar to that of Example 1.7.

$$G_x^*(f) = 2 \int_{-\infty}^{\infty} R_x^*(\tau) e^{-j2\pi f\tau} \, d\tau$$

$$= 2 \int_{-\infty}^{\infty} R_x(\tau) u_T(\tau) e^{-j2\pi f\tau} \, dt \tag{1.82}$$

The convolution theorem may now be used:

$$G_x^*(f) = \int_{-\infty}^{\infty} G_x(f') \, U_T(f - f') \, df'$$

$$= \frac{A^2}{2} \int_{-\infty}^{\infty} [\delta(f' - f_1) + \delta(f' - f_2)]$$

$$\times \frac{2 \sin[2\pi T(f - f')]}{2\pi(f - f')} \, df'$$

$$= \frac{A^2}{2} \left\{ \frac{2 \sin[2\pi T(f - f_1)]}{2\pi(f - f_1)} + \frac{2 \sin[2\pi T(f - f_2)]}{2\pi(f - f_2)} \right\}$$

$$\tag{1.83}$$

Thus, the PSD $G_x^*(f)$ consists of two sin x/x terms, one
centered at f_1 and the other at f_2. When these sinusoids are close together, being able to resolve them
(being able to tell if there are one or two sinusoids)
parallels a similar problem in optics. Physicists use
Rayleigh's criterion in these circumstances, which
also applies to the case given in this example. Rayleigh's criterion (Jenkins and White, 1950) says that
the two sinusoids can be resolved if $\Delta f = |f_1 - f_2|$ is
as large as the following:

$$\Delta f = \frac{1}{2T} \text{ well resolved}$$

(1.84)

$$\Delta f = \frac{1}{4T} \text{ just resolved}$$

That is, if f_1 and f_2 are separated by 1/2T Hz or
more, then according to Rayleigh's criterion they may
be resolved easily.

Finally, to return to the original question, suppose there is only one sinusoid and it has a low frequency. Then in the range $0 \leq f \leq 1/2T$, it will be
very difficult to distinguish the frequency of the
sinusoid. Thus, if it is desired to examine a sine
wave with a frequency of approximately f, then the
length of record must be at least 1/2f units to be
able to say anything about its frequency.

Another problem arising from sampling data is that
of aliasing. If a sinusoid of frequency higher than
$1/2\Delta t$ Hz is sampled at a rate of $1/\Delta t$ samples per second, then the sinusoid will appear as a lower frequen-
cy. The frequency $f = 1/2\Delta t$ is called the folding
frequency. To illustrate, suppose that $x(t) = \sin 2\pi ft$,
and that $f = (1/2\Delta t)(n + p)$, where n is an integer and
$0 \leq p < 1$. Then

$$x(k\Delta t) = \sin 2\pi fk\Delta t = \sin 2\pi k\Delta t \frac{n + p}{2\Delta t}$$

$$= \sin[\pi k(n + p)]$$

$$= \sin \pi kn \cos \pi kp + \cos \pi kn \sin \pi pk \qquad (1.85)$$

Since $\sin \pi kn = 0$, (1.85) reduces to

$$x(k\Delta t) = [\cos \pi kn] \sin \pi kp = [(-1)^n]^k \sin \pi kp$$

$$= [(-1)^n]^k \sin 2\pi k\Delta t f' \qquad (1.86)$$

where

$$f' = \frac{p}{2\Delta t}$$

By definition,

$$0 \le f' < B \qquad (1.87)$$

If n is even, then the expression is simply

$$x(t) = \sin 2\pi t f' \qquad (1.88)$$

for $t = k\Delta t$. On the other hand, if n is odd, then

$$x(t) = \cos \pi k \sin \pi kp = \sin(\pi k - \pi kp)$$

$$= \sin[2\pi t(B - f')] \qquad (1.89)$$

for $t = k\Delta t$. This is a many-to-one mapping. In summary, if $f > B$, to find the frequency of the aliased sinusoid:

1. Divide f by B, and obtain n and p.

2. If n is even, the aliased frequency is simply pB.

3. If n is odd, the aliased frequency is (1 - p)B.

At least one example of aliasing is well known to all movie-goers; namely, the phenomenon of stagecoach wheels seeming to go backwards. In this case, one period would not be a complete revolution of the coach wheel, but rather a function of the spoke separation. If there are 12 spokes, one period is 1/12 of a revolution.

After the data function has been sampled, it may be necessary to obtain its PSD or to examine its Fourier transform. The Fourier transform is the most basic of these two frequency concepts, so its definition is examined first. Given $\{x_k\}$, $k = 0,\ldots,N-1$, the type III Fourier transform is

$$X(f) = \Delta t \sum_{k=0}^{N-1} x_k \exp(-j2\pi fk\Delta t) \qquad (1.90)$$

Note that $X(f)$ is also what would be obtained if the transform of $x_s(t)$ were taken, where

$$x_s(t) = \sum_{k=0}^{N-1} x(t)I(t - k\Delta t) = x(t) \sum_{k=0}^{N-1} I(t - k\Delta t)$$

$$(1.91)$$

Equation (1.90) is valid for all f in the range $(0,B)$. However, not all of these values need be considered. In fact, if the sequence $\{X_\ell\}$ is defined by

$$X_\ell = \Delta t \sum_{k=0}^{N-1} x_k \exp\left(\frac{-j2\pi\ell k}{N}\right) \qquad (1.92)$$

then $\{x_k\}$ can be obtained from $\{X_\ell\}$, $\ell = 0,\ldots,N$, using

$$x_k = \Delta f \sum_{\ell=0}^{N-1} X_\ell \exp\left(\frac{j2\pi\ell k}{N}\right) \qquad k = 0,\ldots,N-1 \quad (1.93)$$

The equivalence of (1.92) and (1.93) may be shown by inserting one of the relations into the other and applying the formulas given in Appendix B to reduce the resulting equation to a tautology.

The digital PSD may also be defined in several ways. The classical method, as popularized by Blackman and Tukey (1958), obtains the PSD in two steps. First, the sample autocorrelation function is computed:

$$R_r = \frac{1}{N - r} \sum_{k=o}^{N-r-1} x_k x_{k+r} \qquad r = 0,\ldots,m \quad (1.94)$$

The subscript r corresponds to the variable τ and is sometimes referred to as the lag value, whereas m, the largest lag value, is called, simply, the number of lags (calculated). The second step consists of taking the cosine transformation of the autocorrelation function, which yields

$$G_p = \Delta t \left[2R_0 + 4 \sum_{r=1}^{m} R_r \cos \frac{\pi p r}{m} \right] \qquad (1.95)$$

The alternative is to use the Fourier transform and obtain

$$G'_q = \frac{1}{N \Delta t} X^*_q X_q = \frac{1}{N \Delta t} |X_q|^2 \qquad q = 0,\ldots,N \quad (1.96)$$

where X^*_q is the complex conjugate of X_q. This version of the PSD may be shown to be the equivalent of using the following autocorrelation:

$$R'_r = \frac{1}{N} \sum_{k=0}^{N-r} x_k x_{k+r} \qquad r = 0,\ldots,m \quad (1.97)$$

As m→N and N→∞, G_p and G'_q will approach each other. However, for any given finite sequence, there may be differences. The Blackman-Tukey PSD was previously the standard, so that individuals using (1.96) attempted to rearrange that procedure so that the results it yielded were equivalent to the Blackman-Tukey PSD. This is difficult to do because of the difference in correlation functions. The direct method using (1.96) has important computational advantages, and the direct method with adjustments has become the standard usage.

Problems

1.1 What are the type I Fourier transforms of

(a) $x(t) = Ae^{-a|t|}$

(b) $x(t) = \begin{cases} t + 1 & [-1, 0] \\ -t + 1 & [0, 1] \end{cases}$

(c) $x(t) = \frac{1}{2}\left(1 + \cos\frac{\pi\tau}{\tau_{max}}\right)$ $[-\tau_{max}, \tau_{max}]$

1.2 What are the type II Fourier transforms of

(a) $x_i = A \sin \omega i\Delta t$

(b) $x_i = \begin{cases} 1 & |i| \le N \\ 0 & i > N \end{cases}$

(c) $x_i = 1$

1.3 Consider the function

$$R(\tau) = \begin{cases} 1 & |\tau| \le 1 \\ 0 & |\tau| > 1 \end{cases}$$

Assume this is an autocorrelation. Calculate the resulting PSD. Does this PSD make sense? Why?

1.4 Consider the function

$$R(\tau) = \begin{cases} 1 - |\tau| & |\tau| < 1 \\ 0 & |\tau| > | \end{cases}$$

Assume this is an autocorrelation. Calculate the
resulting PSD. Does this PSD make sense? Why?

CHAPTER 2
PREPROCESSING OF DATA

2.1 INTRODUCTION

The purpose of this chapter is to discuss the man-
ipulations of the data which take place after acquisition and before the analysis phase of the reduction.
This area includes:

- Data acquisition

- Analog-to-digital conversion

- Digital noise

- Conversion to engineering units

- Wild point editing

- Trend removal

- Plotting and tabulations

These topics are not as glamorous as some which follow, but they are quite important nonetheless.   Done
poorly, preprocessing can ruin data.

Many of the decisions made concerning preprocessing
are subjective in nature, or are peculiar to the type
of data being dealt with. It is difficult to treat
with them in a general manner. Therefore, this chapter
will only discuss many of the problems without at-
tempting to present general final solutions.

2.2 DATA ACQUISITION

There are a large number of data-acquisition system
configurations. It would be difficult to review them
all; and indeed such a project lies outside the scope
of this book. However, three common systems will be
outlined to illustrate the typical problems.

FM-FM Data-Collection System

The first of these, as shown in Figure 2.1, is the *FM-FM* data-acquisition system. In such a system, preliminary data processing is done in three stages. Figure 2.1a shows the basic collection systems. The electrical output of each transducer is input to an individual *voltage-controlled oscillator* (VCO), thus effectively converting the signal to a *frequency-modulated* (FM) signal. The allowable range of frequencies for each VCO is fixed and different, so that the VCOs, when added, produces a composite function whose spectrum is the sum of all the input spectra. This is *frequency multiplexing*. The multiplexed signal goes to an FM transmitter,from which arises the second "FM" in the "FM-FM" designators. After being received on the ground, the transmitted signal is *demodulated* (i.e., returned to the composite, multiplexed state) and recorded on analog magnetic tape. For a more complete description of these techniques along with Inter Range Instrumentation Group (IRIG) standards see Magrab and Blomquist (1971).

The second stage of this system usually involves a dedicated ground station, as shown in Figure 2.1b. The analog tape recorded in the first step is played back, the same identical signal going into a bank of *discriminators*. Discriminators perform the inverse operation of the VCOs; they select an individual channel and convert it from FM back to its original form. The multiplexor may be thought of as a rotating electronic switch which cycles through all of the outputs from the discriminators at a fixed rate, thus producing a serial train of samples of the data. This train of sampled data goes from the multiplexor to the *analog-to-digital converter* (ADC) or more simply, the *digitizer*, where it is converted from a voltage to a digital number, usually binary.

The *formatter* is usually some sort of small digital computer. Its purpose is to collect the digital numbers and form them into *words* and *records* for output onto digital tape. The speed at which the digital tape

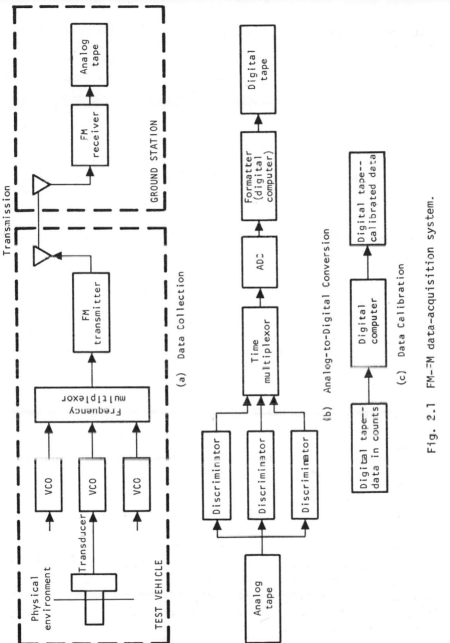

(a) Data Collection

(b) Analog-to-Digital Conversion

(c) Data Calibration

Fig. 2.1 FM-FM data-acquisition system.

can record the output of the formatter is usually the
parameter which puts the limit on the overall sampling
rate of the system.   There are ADCs available which
will run at a speed an order of magnitude faster than
that which the digital tape deck can record the information. Thus, it is necessary to be as efficient as
possible in the manner in which the data is put on
tape if one needs to attain very high digitization
rates. Also, the tape must be compatible with the digital computer further downstream which will be employed in processing the data. Such computers have
memories which oftentimes are organized in terms of
words.   A word is simply a set of binary digits or
bits. The number of bits per word varies considerably,
ranging from eight to sixty, depending on the manufac-
turer and model of the computer.

As an example, suppose that the computer to be used
has sixty bits per word, and that the numbers output
from the ADC are binary numbers, each having twelve
bits. Then the logical procedure is to pack five such
numbers into one word, so that maximum use is made of
word size and maximum data transfer rates can be
attained.

A digital magnetic tape *record* is a set of magnetic
images of whole words, each record separated by *end-
of-record* (eor) marks. Usually, the time to read or
write a record, t_r, is given by

$$t_r = nt_w + t_{eor}$$
(2.1)

where n is the number of words in the record, t_w is the
time to read or write a word, and t_{eor} is the time required to read or write an end-of-record mark. The
t_{eor} term is usually large compared to t_w, so that for
small records, say less than ten words, most of the
time spent reading or writing a record is spent with
the end-of-record gap. The total number of words read
per second, N, is given by

$$N = \frac{n}{t_r} = \frac{1}{t_w + (t_{eor}/n)}$$
(2.2)

where N increases with increasing n, and in the limit as n becomes large,

$$N \approx \frac{1}{t_w}$$ (2.3)

Thus, the speed at which the tape drive operates is ultimately a function of the record length, and to get the fastest data transmission to tape, fairly long records must be employed.

This in turn places a requirement on the formatter; because of the fact that the starting and stopping of the tape drive for each record is an asynchronous event relative to the arrival of the data from the ADC, it is necessary to be able to store the number of words equal to two record lengths.

Digital mini-computers have sufficient core storage for this type of function. Furthermore, they typically allow direct access from core storage to the tape drive with a minimum of program effort, thus speeding up the process of digitization. Because the access to core is direct, with only infrequent operations by the computer to continue the process, the computational power of the computer may be used for other purposes such as decoding time, performing checks, etc. Also, it can be used before the digitization run to check the equipment, and after the run to check the digital tape produced during the run to verify that data was processed correctly.

After the conversion to digital numbers on magnetic tape, the resulting tape is input to a computer, either the one used as the formatter, or a larger model, and the numbers on the tape are converted from digitizer counts to computer numbers which are interpretable at physical units. This is the data-calibration stage shown in Figure 2.1c.

The usual procedure is to make each digitized value into a single computer word in the *floating-point* format. The resulting calibrated data tape is usually much longer than magnetic tape from the digitizer, as there are many data values per computer word in the

latter, whereas there is only one value per word in
the floating-point format.

PCM Data-Collection System

The PCM data-collection system shown in Figure 2.2
is much more digital in orientation than the one discussed above. The PCM designation is the abbreviation
for *pulse code modulation*, which is the method of
electrical modulation during data transmission.

As shown in Figure 2.2a, the data goes immediately
from the transducer to the multiplexor and then to the
digitizer, so that the data are digital almost from
the beginning.

The parallel-to-serial converter turns the series
of digital values emerging from the digitizer into a
stream of bits. For example, suppose there are four
hundred channels, each of which is sampled 100 times
per second, each digitized value consisting of twelve
bits. Then there are

$$400 \times 100 = 40,000$$

words per second coming out of the digitizer, and

$$40,000 \times 12 = 480,000$$

bits per second output by the parallel-to-serial
converter.

The transmitter can send two frequencies; one frequency corresponds to a zero bit, the other to a one
bit. Thus, the transmitter sends frequency f_0 or f_1
for 1/480,000 of a second for each bit. Because the
transmission is made by changing frequency, it is referred to as FM.

At the ground station, the data is not *detected*
immediately, but usually shifted down in frequency and
recorded. This is referred to as *predetection*
recording.

Data formatting requires a special analog tape deck
to play back the previously recorded predetection
tape, a detection device to decide whether a zero or

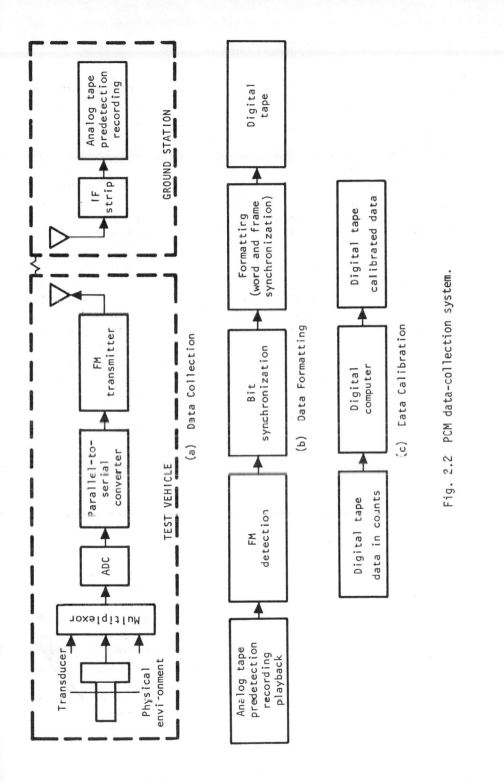

Fig. 2.2 PCM data-collection system.

one bit is present, and a bit synchronizer device to
detect the start and stop of the individual bits.
Thus, the output of the bit synchronizer is a stream
of bits.

The bit stream goes to the formatter, which is
either a hardwired or programmed digital computer.
The purpose of this device is to first break the bit
stream into words and then into *frames*. This is accomplished by making use of special bits which were injected into the bit stream at the ADC stage; if twelve
bits comprise a word, the first bit may be always set
to one, so that looking at a long sequence of bits, it
is possible to determine where the words start from
the repetitious nature of these bits. Having synchron-
ized the words, it is next required to synchronize the
frame,which may be taken as one complete sweep through
the data by the multiplexor. That is, if there are
400 channels being transmitted,one frame would consist
of 400 words of data, one from each channel. To facilitate frame synchronization, the first word in the
frame is not data, but always the same special number,
the *frame synchronization* word. After finding word
synchronization, the formatter uses the repetitivity
of the frame synchronization word to establish the
start and stop of the frame.

After this point, the PCM system is nearly identical to the FM-FM system.

Real-Time Analyzer

The third type of data-acquisition system of interest is the device referred to as a *real-time analyzer*.
Such a device might be used to monitor experiments,
compute PSDs, etc. The configuration shown in Figure
2.3 has the multiplexor and ADC in common with the
previous systems, but lacks a radio-frequency transmission link, magnetic tape recording devices, and is
in general much simpler.

After being digitized, the data are input to the
computer where the computations are performed, and the
results are output,typically on a plot display device.

The expression "real-time" means that there is no intermediate recording so that the computer analyzes the
data as it arrives.   There always is a time lag of
some sort in these devices,so that the results are not
really being displayed as soon as input. "Near real-
time" is sometimes used to describe such analyzers.

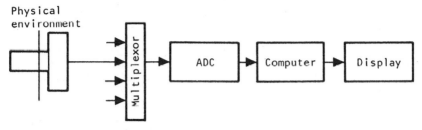

Fig. 2.3 Real-time analyzer.

2.3 ANALOG-TO-DIGITAL CONVERSION

All of the systems discussed in the previous sections have the conversion to a digital representation
in common.

Analog-to-digital convertors (ADCs) are usually
either *binary* or *binary coded decimal* (BCD) in nature.
Both of these terms refer to the way in which the input analog signal is represented as a number at the
output of the ADC. In both cases, the representation
is in *bits* (binary digits). A bit is simply a number
which can take on (only) the values 0 and 1.

The binary ADC is perhaps the easiest to under-
stand.   A "15-bit ADC" has 15 separate outputs which
when properly interpreted can be regarded as zeros or
ones. Collectively, these represent a binary number.
Suppose the 15 binary digits are labeled $\alpha_0,\ldots,\alpha_{14}$.
Usually, α_0 is a *sign* digit. Thus, the digits could
represent the number a as follows:

$$a = (-1)^{\alpha_0} \sum_{i=1}^{14} \frac{\alpha_i}{2^i} \qquad (2.4)$$

In this example it is assumed that the *binary point* is
to the left of digit α_1, so that the magnitude of a is
less than one. Typical outputs from such an ADC are:

Binary	Decimal
000000000000000	0
010000000000000	0.5
000000000000001	2^{-14} = 0.00006103515625
110000000000000	-0.5
111111111111111	$-(1.0 - 2^{-14})$ = -0.99993896484375

Note that while 14 decimal digits are required to represent the fifteen binary digit numbers in some cases, the range of the digitizer is only equivalent to 4-5 decimal digits insofar as precision is concerned.

The BCD type of ADC is most commonly found in digital voltmeters, where the output must be decimal. In such a device, there are four bits for each decimal digit on the meter. Any one of the sets of four bits can only take on values as follows:

0000	0
0001	1
0010	2
0011	3
0100	4
0101	5
0110	6
0111	7
1000	8
1001	9

After reaching 1001, the set recycles to 0000, sending over a carry to the next set of four bits.

Internal to the computer most BCD information is either on a six- or eight-bit basis. In such cases, it is common to add the required two or four extra zero bits onto each basic group of four, so that the numbers are compatible with the BCD system used in the particular computer. For example,

000001   001001   000000   000010   000111   001000

would be interpreted as 190278 on a machine which has six bits per BCD character.

Having the data in BCD has one large advantage: Properly done, it is possible to read a magnetic tape of BCD data in a FORTRAN program with much less effort than with a tape filled with binary data. This is because FORTRAN has an excellent capability insofar as BCD data manipulation is concerned, and a very poor one relative to binary data. Naturally, there is a price to pay for the simplified usage: Optimum use is not made of bits received by the computer; it takes fewer bits to send binary than decimal so that more binary than BCD numbers can be transmitted within the data-collection system for a fixed bit transmission rate.

In short, BCD is inexpensive to program but costly to run, while binary is costly to program, but efficient to process. Thus, BCD looks reasonable for low-volume or nonreoccurring projects, whereas binary coding is best employed where usage is voluminous and repetitious.

2.4 DIGITAL NOISE

Analog-to-digital convertors introduce a type of error known as quantization noise, shown by Figure 2.4. The relationship between the input quantity, here taken to be voltage, and the output in counts is

$$\alpha_e = R (e-e_1) = \alpha + n_d \tag{2.5}$$

The α_e term is the voltage e converted to counts including any fractional part; R is the conversion factor; e_1 is a system offset from zero volts; α is the rounded value of α_e in counts and has no fractional part. The n_d term is the quantization error which resulted from rounding α_e and is such that

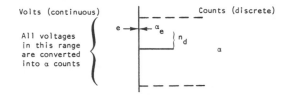

Fig. 2.4 The correspondence between volts and counts.

The quantization error n_d is the difference between α_e, voltage converted to counts without rounding of d fractional part, and α, the rounded value of α_e.

$$n_d = \alpha_e - \alpha \qquad (2.6)$$

It is reasonable to assume that n_d is uniformly distributed:

$$f(n_d) = \begin{cases} 1 & -\frac{1}{2} \le n_d \le \frac{1}{2} \\ \\ 0 & \text{otherwise} \end{cases} \qquad (2.7)$$

The mean and the variance of n_d are:

$$\mu_{n_d} = \int_{-1/2}^{1/2} n_d \, dn_d = 0$$

$$\sigma_{n_d}^2 = E\left[(n_d - \mu_{n_d})^2\right] = \int_{-1/2}^{1/2} n_d^2 \, dn_d = \frac{1}{12} \qquad (2.8)$$

The errors for any two readings are uncorrelated for most digitizers when the data are random. Thus, the digital autocorrelation of the noise is expected to be

$$R_{n_d}(i\Delta t) = \begin{cases} \dfrac{1}{12} & i = 0 \\[2ex] 0 & \text{otherwise} \end{cases} \qquad (2.9)$$

The PSD is therefore

$$G_{n_d}(f) = 2\Delta t\, \frac{1}{12} = \frac{\Delta t}{6} \qquad\qquad 0 \le f \le \frac{1}{2\Delta t} \quad (2.10)$$

The units of (2.10) are counts^2/Hz. If a range of C units goes into 2^N counts, then G_{n_d} can be given in terms of those units:

$$G_{n_d}(f) = \frac{\Delta t}{6}\, 2^{-2N}\, C^2 \qquad (2.11)$$

Thus, for a fixed range of the function being digitized, the PSD of the quantization noise decreases exponentially with the number of bits in the quantization word. For large N, say N greater than 10, the quantization noise tends to be negligible.

There are other digitizing errors. Their importance will vary with the particular application. In summary, they are:

1. Aperture error. This error arises from the fact that the sample is taken over a finite period of time rather than instantaneously. The aperture, which is the length of time over which the data averaged, should be small with respect to the sampling interval.

2. Jitter. If the length of the interval between samples varies slightly in some random manner, the resulting uncertainty is called jitter. Jitter can affect PSDs and may cause degradation of phase information at high frequencies.

3. Nonlinearities. This category covers a number
   of possible problems, usually traceable to the
   ADC being out of adjustment or to some parts
   actually being inoperative. Among the problems
   which can occur are (a) bit dropout--a portion
   of the circuitry corresponding to one of the
   bits is inoperative on an intermittent or regular basis; (b) spacing--the spacing between the
   levels may become nonuniform, resulting in some
   levels being more likely than others; and (c)
   zero discontinuity--if a digitizer has a range
   which includes both plus and minus, it is possible that misalignment of the ADC will result in
   a large discontinuity at the zero count value.

2.5 CONVERSION TO ENGINEERING UNITS

Two common procedures for converting to engineering
units will be discussed in this section. These are
step calibration and *sinusoidal calibration*.

In both cases it is assumed that prior to recording
of data the transducer is effectively disconnected
from the circuit, after which calibration voltages are
injected into it. This happens because it is usually
impossible to stimulate the transducer itself with the
exact force required for the standardization.

In the step calibrations, a series of voltage steps
are employed. For example, if the range of the voltage
applied to the transducer is 0-5 V, then steps of 0.0,
2.5, and 5.0 V could be employed.* Each step would
last a specified span of time, say 1 sec each. These
steps would each be digitized. For programming convenience, it would be best to arrange matters so that
they are clearly distinguishable. For example, the
steps could possibly be put in separate records if
digital magnetic tape is the recording media, the

---

* The actual procedure often is to replace the transducer with calibration resistors, one for each step.

starting and stopping of the record being accomplished by *interrupts* from the device producing the steps.

The first item in the computational procedure is to average each of the steps separately to arrive at a smoothed single value for the step. Label these $a_1, a_2, \ldots, a_N$ (N steps assumed).

Second, values in physical units for each of the steps would be input to the computer, one for each a_k. Label these $p_1, \ldots, p_N$.

Suppose that data are now input to be processed. The data will be in counts as output by the digitizer. Label these values $c_1, c_2, \ldots$. The calibrated data sequence $\{x_i\}$ is obtained by combining all of these sequences.

Linear interpolation is commonly used in calibration, and consists of the following: Find K such that

$$a_k \leq c_i < a_{k+1} \qquad\qquad (2.12)$$

provided $a_1 \leq c_i \leq a_N$. Then

$$x_i = p_k + (p_{k+1} - p_k)\, \frac{c_i - a_k}{a_{k+1} - a_k} \qquad\qquad (2.13)$$

For the cases where $c_i < a_1$, or $c_i > a_N$, then, extrapolation must be used. For example, suppose $c_i < a_1$. Then

$$x_i = p_1 + (p_2 - p_1)\, \frac{c_i - a_1}{a_2 - a_1} \qquad\qquad (2.14)$$

If $c_i > a_N$, then

$$x_i = p_{N-1} + (p_N - p_{N-1})\, \frac{c_i - a_{N-1}}{a_N - a_{N-1}} \qquad\qquad (2.15)$$

Sinusoidal calibration is done by injecting a sine wave of known amplitude into the system, and recording and digitizing many periods of it.

In processing it, the mean is computed as usual by

$$\bar{d} = \frac{1}{N} \sum_{i=1}^{N} d_i \qquad\qquad (2.16)$$

where the sequence $\{d_i\}$ is the digitized sine wave and $\bar{d}$ is the average of it. As before, the sample variance is

$$s_d^2 = \frac{1}{N-1} \sum_{i=1}^{N} (d_i - \bar{d})^2 \qquad\qquad (2.17)$$

These calculations yield three points:

$a_1 = \bar{d} + \sqrt{2}s_d$ Positive peak of the sine wave in counts

$a_2 = \bar{d}$ Zero of the sine wave in counts

$a_3 = \bar{d} - \sqrt{2}s_d$ Negative peak of the sine wave in counts

$$(2.18)$$

Physical units corresponding to these would be input, and the previous formulas would be used for interpolation or extrapolation.

This procedure would be exact if there were no noise and if only a set of whole cycles were digitized. It is usually impossible to eliminate the noise and start and end at the same place in the cycle. Therefore, many cycles have to be taken to eliminate or at least reduce these problems.

2.6 WILD POINT EDITING

Most data-acquisition systems will occasionally introduce spurious values into the data. This can occur for a variety of reasons: loss of signal in the transmission link, failure of the digitizer, failure of formatting equipment, etc. The wild points which could be generated by these failures can cause numer-

ous problems in subsequent analyses. A single wild
point,if at the digitizer maximum value, can seriously
bias a PSD by raising the overall noise level. Two
such points close to each other tend to produce a number of spurious frequencies into the PSD.

Because of this, it is best to include the detection and elimination of wild points in the overall
data-reduction scheme. Unfortunately, it is hard to
detect them adequately, and even more difficult to
properly replace them with reasonable values. There
are no general procedures for automatic elimination of
wild points.

Thus, it is prudent to have an editing program or
programs which facilitate manual correction, if such
is necessary. Such a set of computer programs would
operate as follows: A first pass would be made through
the data to detect wild points. Having found them,
descriptive information would be output on the printer
in the form of either a tabulation or a printer plot.
Having reviewed these printouts, the analyst would
then generate input into the next program to either
eliminate the bad points, replace them, or simply not
use them at all. The latter is preferable, if
possible.

A number of automatic editing schemes for removing
wild points have been proposed, none of which seem to
be entirely satisfactory. One such scheme is included
here as an illustration of the type of thing which is
done. The procedure is shown in Figure 2.5.

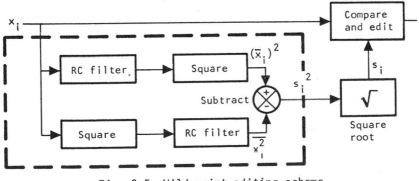

Fig. 2.5 Wild point editing scheme.

The scheme uses two digital RC filters for smoothing. These filters are discussed in detail in Chapter 3. Their object is to produce smoothed (lowpass filtered) data. The sequences $(\bar{x}_i)^2$ and $(\overline{x_i^2})$ are defined by the following operation

$(\bar{x}_i)^2$ results from smoothing the data and then squaring it

$(\overline{x_i^2})$ results from squaring the data and then smoothing it

The purpose of the operations within the area bordered by the dotted lines is to generate a continuously updated value of the sample variance, s_i^2. This is formed from $(\bar{x}_i)^2$ and $(\overline{x_i^2})$ as follows:

$$s_i^2 = \overline{x_i^2} - (\bar{x}_i)^2 \qquad\qquad (2.19)$$

The standard deviation is computed from s_i^2 by taking its square root.

The next step is to check the next data point, x_{i+1}. It is accepted as being good if

$$\bar{x}_i - ks_i < x_{i+1} < \bar{x}_i + ks_i \qquad\qquad (2.20)$$

The parameter k is set by the user to a value appropriate for the data. Typically, it would range from three to five, with four being a reasonable choice as a value with which to start.

The replacement for a bad x_{i+1}, labeled $\hat{x}_{i+1}$, could be calculated by the formula

$$\hat{x}_{i+1} = x_i + (x_i - x_{i-1}) \qquad\qquad (2.21)$$

This effectively amounts to linear extrapolation.

It is necessary to augment this procedure with additional complications. A preset limit for the number of successive extrapolations must be incorporated to avoid extrapolating forever. That is, after several bad point detections in succession, the extrapolation might wander far enough off track to reject good data when it finally arrives.

2.7 TREND REMOVAL

It is sometimes necessary to remove a linear or slowly varying trend from a particular time history. Such trends are likely to be found in the data, for example, when one or more of the components has been integrated. Integration introduces two types of errors. First of all, if the calibration zero point was incorrect, there will be a small error term with each time sample. When integrated, this constant term will become a straight line. Such a linear trend may produce large errors in PSD and related calculations.

The second type of error comes about because the integration procedure tends to amplify power corresponding to low-frequency noise. Such noise is usually present in the data. When integrated, it takes the form of a random but slowly varying trend. Just how rapidly the trend varies depends to some extent upon the sampling interval.

The varying trend can best be removed by using highpass filtering, a topic to be discussed in Chapter 3. Polynomial trends may be removed using least-square techniques. That is done in the following manner: Suppose, as usual, that x_i is a function sampled at the constant interval Δt for $i = 0,\ldots,N$, and that it is desired to fit a polynomial of the form

$$\hat{x}_i = \sum_{k=0}^{K} c_k (i\Delta t)^k \qquad (2.22)$$

The set of data points $\{x_i\}$ is an estimate of the polynomial content of x_i for polynomials of degree less or equal to K. The usual procedure consists of defining an intermediate function, G, of the polynomial coefficient terms:

$$G(c) = \sum_{i=0}^{N} \left[x_i - \sum_{k=0}^{K} c_k (i\Delta t)^k \right]^2 \qquad (2.23)$$

where G is always positive for any value of $c = (c_0, \ldots, c_k)$. It may be minimized using standard techniques from differential calculus. Taking derivatives of (2.23) with respect to c_j and setting them equal to zero,

$$\frac{\partial G}{\partial c_j} = \sum_{i=0}^{N} 2 \left[x_i - \sum_{k=0}^{K} c_k (i\Delta t)^k \right] [-(i\Delta t)^j] = 0 \quad (2.24)$$

Rearranging terms yields K equations of the form

$$\sum_{k=0}^{K} c_k \sum_{i=0}^{N} (i\Delta t)^{k+j} = \sum_{i=0}^{N} x_i (i\Delta t)^j$$

$$j = 0, \ldots, K \qquad (2.25)$$

For large K values, it becomes tedious to solve for c. Fortunately, the need for solutions for K larger than 3 or 4 are rare. If a program is only to remove low-order polynomials, then the computer memory that would be used to solve the above by means of matrix inversion techniques can be used for a direct calculation of the coefficients. For example, the solution for K = 0 is

$$c_0 = \frac{1}{N+1} \sum_{i=0}^{N} x_i \qquad (2.26a)$$

and for K = 1,

$$c_0 = \frac{2(2N + 1) \sum\limits_{i=0}^{N} x_i - 6 \sum\limits_{i=0}^{N} ix_i}{(N + 1)(N + 2)}$$

(2.26b)

$$c_1 = \frac{6 \left(2 \sum\limits_{i=0}^{N} ix_i - N \sum\limits_{i=0}^{N} x_i\right)}{\Delta t N (N + 1)(N + 2)}$$

For an odd number of points, a tremendous simplification in the formulas can be made. The procedure assumes that $i = -(N/2), \ldots, 0, \ldots, (N-1/2)$. Thus, the odd-power summation expressions in $(i\Delta t)$ will be zero, thereby eliminating many terms in the calculations. The formulas are, for $K = 1$,

$$c_0 = \frac{\Sigma x_i}{N+1}$$

$$c_1 = \frac{\Sigma i x_i}{\Sigma i^2 \Delta t}$$

where

$$\Sigma = \sum\limits_{i=-N/2}^{N/2}$$

for $K = 2$,

$$c_0 = \frac{\Sigma i^2 \, \Sigma i^2 x_i}{\left(\Sigma i^2\right)^2 - N\Sigma i^4}$$

$$c_1 = \frac{\Sigma i x_i}{\Sigma i^2 \, \Delta t}$$

$$c_2 = \frac{\Sigma i^2 \, \Sigma x_i - N\Sigma i^2 x_i}{\left[\left(\Sigma i^2\right)^2 - N\Sigma i^4\right]\left(\Delta t\right)^2}$$

for K = 3,

$$c_0 = \frac{\Sigma x_i \, \Sigma i^4 - \Sigma i^2 \, \Sigma i^2 x_i}{N \Sigma i^4 - (\Sigma i^2)^2}$$

$$c_1 = \frac{\Sigma i^4 \, \Sigma i^3 x_i - \Sigma i^6 \, \Sigma i x_i}{\left[\left(\Sigma i^4\right)^2 - \Sigma i^2 \, \Sigma i^6\right] \Delta t}$$

$$c_2 = \frac{\Sigma i^2 \, \Sigma x_i - N \Sigma i^2 x_i}{\left[\left(\Sigma i^2\right) - N \Sigma i^4\right] \left(\Delta t\right)^2}$$

$$c_3 = \frac{\Sigma i^4 \, \Sigma i x_i - \Sigma i^2 \, \Sigma i^3 x_i}{\left[\left(\Sigma i^4\right)^2 - \Sigma i^2 \, \Sigma i^6\right] \left(\Delta t\right)^3}$$

and for K = 4, (compute c_4 first, then c_3, etc.)

$$c_0 = \left(\Sigma x_i - c_2 \Sigma i^2 - c_4 \Sigma i^4\right) \Big/ N$$

$$c_1 = \left\{\Sigma_i x_i \left[\Sigma i^2 \Sigma i^6 - (\Sigma i^4)^2\right] - \left(\Sigma i^4 \, \Sigma i^2 \Sigma i^3 x_i\right.\right.$$

$$\left.\left. - \Sigma i^4 \Sigma i \, x_i\right)\right\} \Big/ \left(\left\{\Sigma i^2 \left[\Sigma i^2 \Sigma i^6 - (\Sigma i^4)^2\right]\right\} \ \Delta t\right)$$

$$c_2 = \left[\Sigma i^2 \Sigma x_i - N \Sigma i^2 \, x_i - c_4 \, (\Sigma i^2 \Sigma i^4 - N \Sigma i^6)\right] \Big/$$

$$\left\{\left[(\Sigma i^2)^2 - N \Sigma i^4\right] (\Delta t)^2\right\}$$

$$c_3 = \left(\Sigma i^2 \Sigma i^3 \, x_i - \Sigma i^4 \Sigma i \, x_i\right) \Big/ \left\{\left[\Sigma i^2 \Sigma i^6 - (\Sigma i^4)^2\right] (\Delta t)^3\right\}$$

$$c_4 = \left\{\left(N\Sigma i^4 x_i - \Sigma i^4 \Sigma x_i\right)\left[(\Sigma i^2)^2 - N\Sigma i^4\right] + \left(\Sigma i^2 \Sigma x_i\right.\right.$$

$$\left.- N\Sigma i^2 x_i\right)(\Sigma i^4 \Sigma i^2 - N\Sigma i^6)\right\} \bigg/ \left(\left\{\left[\Sigma i^2 \Sigma i^4 - N\Sigma i^6\right]^2\right.\right.$$

$$\left.\left.- \left[(\Sigma i^4)^2 - N\Sigma i^8\right]\left[(\Sigma i^2)^2 - N\Sigma i^4\right]\right\}(\Delta t)^4\right)$$

where

N = Number of equally spaced samples of x (N must be odd)

$$\Sigma i^2 = \frac{N(N^2 - 1)}{12}$$

$$\Sigma i^4 = \frac{N(N^2 - 1)(2N^2 - 7)}{240}$$

$$\Sigma i^6 = \frac{N(N^2 - 1)(3N^4 - 18N^2 + 31)}{1344}$$

$$\Sigma i^8 = \frac{N(N^2 - 1)(5N^6 - 55N^4 + 239N^2 - 381)}{11520}$$

$$\Sigma t_i = i\Delta t \qquad\qquad i = -\frac{N-1}{2},\ldots,\frac{N-1}{2} \quad (2.27)$$

Underflow or overflow is quite possible when computing terms of the form $\Sigma i^j x_i$, especially on machines with limited word size. The user should consider doing the summation portion of the calculation in double precision. To clarify the nature of the difficulty, consider the following example.

Suppose it is desired to calculate the sample mean of x_i where i varies from 1 to 2000. Furthermore, suppose that x_i is approximately unity for each i. The hypothetical computer on which this calculation is to be performed is assumed to have five decimal digits in each word. That is, the word, the basic unit of calculation, is composed of five individual decimal digits. However, to simplify the positioning of the decimal place, the hypothetical machine uses floating-point

arithmetic. In this mode, each such five-digit word
is broken into two parts. The first, with two digits,
is essentially an exponent of ten, while the second
part carries the significant digits. In this particular machine, the floating-point representation for x
would be

    xx   xxx

    A   B

    in   in

  2 digits   3 digits

$$x = B \cdot 10^{A-50} \qquad\qquad (2.28)$$

Thus, the five digits in storage 50100 would represent
1.00, and 46327 would be equivalent to 0.000327. If
these two numbers were added by the machine, using
special floating-point addition, the result would be
1.00. That is, the smaller number would effectively
be shifted out the low end of the add register. That
is termed underflow.

Continuing with the example, if 2000 units were
added to this machine, the result would not be 2000,
but 1000, because after summing up the first thousand,
the units thereafter would underflow. The computed
sample mean would be 0.5 rather than 1.0,a significant
error. If the summation were performed in double precision, there would have been no error in the mean
value computed in the example. Double precision is a
capability found in most machines (either in the hardware or in the software, usually the latter for small
computers), which combines two storage units into a
single one. This yields twice as many significant
digits and a considerably extended range for the exponent of the floating-point number.

2.8 PLOTTING AND TABULATION

Plotting is typically done using combinations of
software and a separate plotting device. There are
many of these machines. The digital incremental plot-

ting with ink on paper or on a cathode-ray tube (CRT) are perhaps the commonest.   Other types such as electrostatic printer-plotters are beginning to penetrate this market area.

Perhaps the topic of most concern in plotting is that of automatic scaling.   Automatic scaling procedures are used to pick "nice" limits for the plotting so that the plots are easier to read. There are a number of ways of accomplishing this.   The following is a fairly common example:

1. Suppose $\{x_i, y_i\}$, $i = 1, \ldots, N$, is to be plotted and that x_{max} and x_{min} are, respectively, the maximum and minimum of the sequence (only the x sequence will be considered; the y sequence would be handled in an identical manner).

2. Define I by

$$I = \left[\log_{10} \left\{ \frac{\left(x_{max} - x_{min} \right)}{S} \right\} \right] \qquad (2.29)$$

where the brackets here denote conversion to an integer without upwards rounding, and S is the number of even units (in inches, centimeters, etc.) of the size of the plot.

3. Compute

$$c = \frac{\left(x_{max} - x_{min} \right)/S}{10^I} \qquad (2.30)$$

The number c must be greater than one, but less than 10. For example, if $S = 10$, $x_{min} = 1001$, and $x_{max} = 9999$, then $I = 2$ and $c = 8.998$.

4. Pick D to be the smallest of the numbers 1.5, 2.0, 2.5, 5.0, and 10.0 such that

$$c \leq D$$

Then $D \cdot 10^I$ brackets the range of x_{min} and x_{max}. In the above example, $D = 10.0$.

5. Define J by

$$J = \left[\frac{x_{max}}{D \cdot 10^I} \right]$$

and

$$E = (D \cdot 10^I) \, J \qquad\qquad\qquad (2.31)$$

where E is the trial origin. In the example, J would be I and E would be 1000, which would be satisfactory.

6. The next step is to check to make sure that

$$x_{max} \leq E + D \cdot 10^I \, S \qquad\qquad\qquad (2.32)$$

If not, then D is replaced by the next larger of the values listed in Step 4. If D were already 10, then I is increased by one, and D is reduced to 2.0.

This procedure could be refined; one worthwhile addition is that of checking to see if x_{min} and x_{max} bracket zero, in which case it will look better if the plot is symmetric about the origin. The extra step to see if this is possible is usually worth the effort because of the better-looking aspect of the plot.

Problems

2.1 The functions $x(t) = \sin(2\pi f_c t + \phi)$, with f_c = 10 Hz, is digitized at the rate of 40 samples per second using an eleven-bit (including sign) digitizer. Denote x_i as the resulting sequence, x_i as $\sin(\frac{\pi i}{2} + \phi)$, and e_i as their difference. Discuss the relationship between these three sequences.

2.2 Show that sequences such as $\{c_i\}$ is Problem 2.1 are periodic or almost periodic (in the sense that the PSD of $\{c_i\}$ is not flat) for any f_c.

CHAPTER 3
RECURSIVE DIGITAL FILTERING

3.1 BASIC CONCEPTS

The principal use of filtering in data reduction is to smooth the data being analyzed. The first smoothing filters used were of the moving-average type. These were followed by polynomial filters, i.e., those which pass polynomials without change while attenuating jitter. Ormsby (1961b) introduced a lowpass filter that showed marked improvement over the polynomial type. Later writers have introduced recursive or feed back filters showing significant advancement in performance over previous filters. It is the recursive types that will be emphasized here. Digital filters are frequently analyzed using z-transform methods. This technique has not been used in this chapter because it does not describe filter action in terms familiar to the data user.

Broadly speaking, a filter is a device or a physical process that operates on a time history and (usually) changes the time history in some manner. This definition would include attenuation networks, amplifiers, nonlinear devices of all sorts, as well as the trivial filter that transmits the time history without change. Linear filters are the single, most important, category. There are a number of ways by which this type of filter could be defined. The most basic definition is through the unit impulse response function and the convolution integral. Let x be the unfiltered time history and y be the result of the action of the filter upon x. Suppose that if $x(t) = \delta(t)$, then $y(t) = h(t)$. That is, if the only input to the filter is a single delta function at time $t = 0$, then the output of the filter is the unique function $h(t)$, the unit impulse response function. The general relationship between the output from the filter, y, and the input to the filter for any x is then given by

$$y(t) = \int_{-\infty}^{\infty} h(\tau)\, x(t-\tau)\, d\tau \qquad\qquad (3.1)$$

This convolution of h(t) and x(t) produces y(t). The Fourier or Laplace transform of h(t) yields the system transfer function. For example, after taking the Fourier transform of (3.1) it becomes

$$Y(f) = H(f)\, X(f) \qquad\qquad (3.2)$$

The discrete representation of (3.1) is

$$y_i = \sum_{k=-\infty}^{\infty} h_k\, x_{i-k} \qquad\qquad (3.3)$$

The Fourier transform of this also yields (3.2); the meaning of Y, H, and X have to be reinterpreted, as in the second case they were based on digital rather than continuous functions. As discussed in Chapter 1, the domain of f is quite different for the two cases.

The filters Ormsby and others used were essentially implementations of (3.3) with finite though occasionally large values for k. Cases employing as many as 1000 $\{h_k\}$ terms have been routinely run in the processing of data. Filters of the type

$$y_i = \sum_{k=-K}^{K} h_k\, x_{i-k} \qquad\qquad (3.4)$$

are referred to as *simple* or *nonrecursive* filters.

Many types of filtering can be done more efficiently through the use of recursive filtering. A *recursive filter* is one which recirculates the output back into the input. Most of the filters to be discussed will be of the recursive form. In particular, this chapter considers first-order filters such as lowpass and highpass types, and integrators and their stability; the second-order filter, its unit response and stability; and higher-order filters of the pass band variety and their stability.

3.2 FIRST-ORDER RECURSIVE FILTERS

The most general form of the first-order recursive filter is

$$y_i = \alpha y_{i-1} + g(x_i) \tag{3.5}$$

If the Fourier transform of $g(x_i)$ exists, then the complex transfer function of the filter described by (3.5) is given by

$$H(f) = \frac{G(f)}{1 - \alpha \exp(-j2\pi\Delta tf)} \tag{3.6}$$

where $G(f)X(f)$ is the transform of $g(x_i)$.

A filter is defined to be stable if all of the roots of the denominator of the transfer function have positive imaginary parts. In particular, if f_k is a root, $\text{Im}[f_k]$ must be positive. In order for this filter to be stable, the parameter α must satisfy the condition

$$-1 < \alpha < 1 \tag{3.7}$$

Of the multitude of possible forms for (3.5), three are of particular interest: lowpass and highpass filters, and numerical integrators.

Lowpass Filters

The lowpass filter has the form

$$y_i = \alpha y_{i-1} + (1 - \alpha) x_i \tag{3.8}$$

where $g(x_i)$ is simply

$$g(x_i) = (1 - \alpha)x_i \qquad\qquad 0 \le \alpha < 1 \qquad (3.9)$$

The complex transfer function is therefore

$$H(f) = \frac{1 - \alpha}{1 - \alpha \exp(-j2\pi\Delta tf)} \qquad (3.10)$$

The absolute value squared of the transfer function is

$$|H(f)|^2 = \frac{(1 - \alpha)^2}{1 - 2\alpha \cos 2\pi f\Delta t + \alpha^2} \qquad (3.11)$$

The values of $|H(f)|^2$ for $f = 0$ and $1/2\Delta t$ are, respectively,

$$|H(0)|^2 = 1$$

$$|H\left(\frac{1}{2\Delta t}\right)|^2 = \left(\frac{1 - \alpha}{1 + \alpha}\right)^2 \qquad (3.12)$$

The half-power point of a lowpass filter is the frequency at which $|H(f)|^2$ has been reduced to one-half of the value it had at 0 Hz.

If the half-power point is at f_c Hz, then

$$\alpha = 2 - \cos 2\pi f_c\Delta t - \sqrt{\cos^2 2\pi f_c\Delta t - 4 \cos 2\pi f_c\Delta t + 3}$$

$$(3.13)$$

Highpass Filters

The highpass filter is very similar to the lowpass filter, the main difference being that α is replaced with a negative number. Equation (3.5) becomes

$$y_i = \beta y_{i-1} + (1 + \beta)x_{i-1} \qquad\qquad -1 \le \beta < 0 \qquad (3.14)$$

Then the complex transfer function is

$$H(f) = \frac{1 + \beta}{1 - \beta \exp(-j2\pi\Delta tf)} \qquad (3.15)$$

Thus,

$$\left|H(0)\right|^2 = \left(\frac{1 + \beta}{1 - \beta}\right)^2$$

and

$$\left|H\left(\frac{1}{2\Delta t}\right)\right|^2 = 1 \qquad (3.16)$$

Therefore, the transfer function attains its maximum for $f = 1/2\Delta t$, as would be expected for a highpass filter.

Integrators

Equation (3.5) may also be used for integration, in which case $\alpha = 1$. There are several possibilities for $g(x_i)$, the simplest being the rectangular scheme given by

$$y_i = y_{i-1} + \Delta tx_i \qquad (3.17)$$

This filter, like all integrators, is not stable. A constant input will be turned into an ever-increasing ramp output. White noise input will result in an output whose variance is linearly increasing with i. The transfer function of this integrator is

$$H(f) = \frac{\Delta t}{1 - \exp(-j2\pi\Delta tf)} \qquad (3.18)$$

By using the approximation

$$e^x \approx 1 + x$$

for small Δt, (3.18) reduces to

$$H(f) \approx \frac{\Delta t}{1 - (1 - j2\pi\Delta tf)} = \frac{1}{j2\pi f} \qquad (3.19)$$

The deterioration of (3.14) from perfect integration increases with increasing f both in amplitude and phase. This is shown in Figure 3.1. Note that the phase angle of the transfer function is not constant, but increases linearly with frequency.

3.3 FIRST-ORDER FILTERS--MISCELLANEOUS RELATIONS

A number of interesting parallels between digital first-order filters and their continuous counterparts may be drawn. This section discusses some of these equivalences along with other miscellaneous relations.

Unit Response Function

Suppose that the $g(x_i)$ term in (3.5) is given by

$$g(x_i) = \begin{cases} \gamma & i = 0 \\ 0 & \text{otherwise} \end{cases} \qquad (3.20)$$

Then a closed-form solution exists for $\{y_i\}$, namely,

$$y_i = \begin{cases} \gamma\alpha^i & i \geq 0 \\ 0 & i < 0 \end{cases} \qquad (3.21)$$

In the case of the lowpass filter, $g(x_i)$ is simply

$$g(x_i) = g_0 x_i = (1 - \alpha) x_i$$

$$0 < \alpha < 1; \quad x_i = \begin{cases} 1 & i = 0 \\ 0 & \text{otherwise} \end{cases} \qquad (3.22)$$

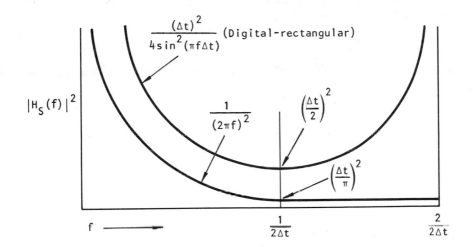

Fig. 3.1a The transfer function (absolute value squared) for continuous integration always falls below the digital rectangular transfer function.

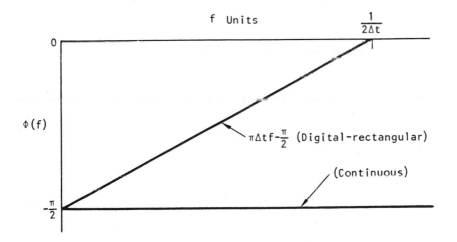

Fig. 3.1b The phase angle of the transfer function.

then the resulting response may be regarded as the *unit response function*, and be denoted by u_i:

$$u_i = \begin{cases} \alpha^i (1 - \alpha) & i \geq 0 \\ 0 & \text{otherwise} \end{cases} \qquad (3.23)$$

Thus $\{y_i\}$ for an arbitrary $\{x_i\}$ could be defined by

$$y_i = u_i * x_i$$

$$= \sum_{k = -\infty}^{i} x_k u_{i-k}$$

$$= \sum_{k = -\infty}^{i} x_k \alpha^{i-k} (1 - \alpha) \qquad (3.24)$$

where "$*$" indicates the *convolution operation*.

Averaging

The first-order lowpass filter makes a suitable averaging algorithm, as may be seen from the following deviation: Suppose $\{x_i\}$ is a stationary sequence with mean u_x and that $\{y_i\}$ is defined by (3.24). That is,

$$y_i = (1 - \alpha) \sum_{k = -\infty}^{i} x_k \alpha^{i-k} \qquad (3.25)$$

Then the expected value of y_i is the mean of $\{x_i\}$. This follows, as

$$E[y_i] = E\left\{(1 - \alpha) \sum_{k = -\infty}^{i} x_k \alpha^{i-k}\right\}$$

$$= \mu_x (1 - \alpha) \sum_{k = -\infty}^{i} \alpha^{i-k}$$

$$= \mu_x (1 - \alpha) \sum_{k = 0}^{\infty} \alpha^{k}$$

$$= \mu_x (1 - \alpha) \left[\frac{1}{1 - \alpha}\right] = \mu_x \qquad (3.26)$$

This presupposes very lenient conditions on $\{x_i\}$. On the other hand, in order to get usable results about the variance of $\{y_i\}$, some assumptions about $\{x_i\}$ need to be made. A simple and important case is the one where $\{x_i\}$ is uncorrelated with variance σ_x^2. It may be shown that

$$\sigma_y^2 = \frac{1 - \alpha}{1 + \alpha} \sigma_x^2 \qquad (3.27)$$

The variance of $\{y_i\}$, σ_y^2, is therefore a function of α for an uncorrelated stationary variable $\{x_i\}$. For values of α close to unity, the variance on the estimator becomes smaller, as would be expected.

Relation to the RC Filter

The lowpass filter described by (3.8) is analogous to an electrical filter of the form shown in Figure 3.2.

The differential equation governing this circuit is

$$RC\frac{dy}{dt} + y(t) = x(t) \qquad (3.28)$$

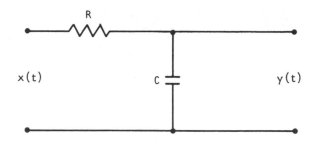

Fig. 3.2 Electrical RC filter.

where both x and y are taken to be voltages. If in
(3.5) the substitution

$$\alpha = e^{-\Delta t/RC} \qquad (3.29)$$

is made, and Δt is assumed to be small enough so that
the previous substitution for e^x may be made, then
(3.8) may be written as

$$y_i = \alpha y_{i-1} + (1 - \alpha)x_i$$

$$= \left(1 - \frac{\Delta t}{RC}\right) y_{i-1} + \left[1 - \left(1 - \frac{\Delta t}{RC}\right) x_i\right]$$

or

$$(y_i - y_{i-1}) + \frac{\Delta t}{RC} y_{i-1} = \frac{\Delta t}{RC} x_i$$

or

$$RC\left(\frac{y_i - y_{i-1}}{\Delta t}\right) + y_{i-1} = x_i \qquad (3.30)$$

which in the limit as Δt goes to zero is identical
with (3.28).

White Noise Response

Suppose $\{x_i\}$ is assumed to be uncorrelated with zero mean and variance σ_x^2. That is, $\{x_i\}$ is *white* noise. The one-sided PSD of $\{x_i\}$, denoted by $G_x(f)$, is defined in general in Bendat and Piersol (1966). It can be shown for this case that

$$G_x(f) = \sigma_x^2 \, 2\Delta t \qquad\qquad 0 \le f \le 1/2\Delta t \quad (3.31)$$

Thus, on the range $0 \le f \le 1/2\Delta t$, G_x is flat, which is an essential characteristic of white noise. The power spectra of $\{x_i\}$ and $\{y_i\}$ are related by the expression

$$
G_y(f) = |H(f)|^2 \, G_x(f)
$$

$$
= \frac{(1 - \alpha)^2 \, \sigma_x^2 \, 2\Delta t}{1 - 2\alpha \cos 2\pi f \Delta t + \alpha^2} \qquad\qquad (3.32)
$$

Finally, the variance of $\{y_i\}$, denoted by σ_y^2, is

$$
\sigma_y^2 = \int_0^{1/2\Delta t} G_y(f) \, df
$$

$$
= \int_0^{1/2\Delta t} \frac{(1 - \alpha)^2 \, \sigma_x^2 \, 2\Delta t}{1 - 2\alpha \cos 2\pi f \Delta t + \alpha^2} \, df
$$

$$
= \frac{1 - \alpha}{1 + \alpha} \, \sigma_x^2 \qquad\qquad (3.33)
$$

which is identical to the variance of $\{y_i\}$ when it is used as an estimator of the mean.

3.4 SECOND-ORDER RECURSIVE FILTERS

The most general form of the second-order filter is

$$y_i = h_1 \, y_{i-1} + h_2 \, y_{i-2} + g(x_i) \qquad (3.34)$$

As before, if $g(x_i)$ is a linear function of $\{x_i\}$ with Fourier transform $G(f)X(f)$, the transfer function of (3.34) is

$$H(f) = \frac{G(f)}{1 - h_1 \, \exp(-j2\pi\Delta tf) - h_2 \, \exp(-j4\pi\Delta tf)} \qquad (3.35)$$

The stability conditions for h_1 and h_2 are somewhat more complicated than in the first-order case. Figure 3.3 shows a triangular shape in the plane defined by h_1 and h_2. Values of h_1 and h_2 within the triangle result in stable filters. Values outside result in unstable filters, while those on the borders result in marginally stable filters, the latter being useful only for double integration or the generation of sequences of sines or cosines.

Stable second-order filters fall into two categories, depending on the position of the roots of the equation

$$z^2 - h_1 z - h_2 = 0 \qquad (3.36)$$

which was obtained by setting the denominator of (3.35) equal to zero, and substituting z for $\exp j2\pi\Delta tf$. If

$$h_1^2 + 4h_2 \geq 0 \qquad (3.37)$$

then the roots are real and unequal. If

$$h_1^2 + 4h_2 < 0 \qquad (3.38)$$

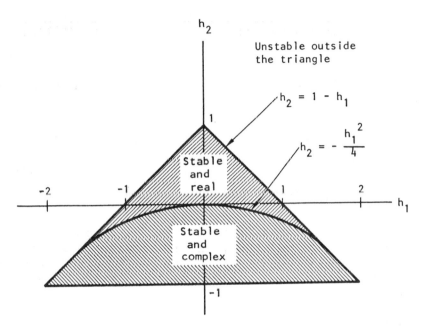

Fig. 3.3 Filter stability in terms of the coefficients h_1 and h_2.

then the roots are complex conjugates of each other.
In the first case, the filter can be regarded as two
first-order filters used in succession. Such a filter
will have the form

$$y_i = (\alpha + \beta)y_{i-1} - \alpha\beta y_{i-2} + g(x_i) \qquad (3.39)$$

The parameters α and β will be used in the remainder
of this chapter in several different ways, but always
as part of the second-order filter coefficients.   The
transfer function corresponding to (3.39) is

$$H(f) = \frac{G(f)}{1 - (\alpha + \beta)\exp(-j2\pi\Delta tf) + \alpha\beta\exp(-j4\pi\Delta tf)}$$

$$= \frac{G(f)}{[1 - \alpha\exp(-j2\pi\Delta tf)][1 - \beta\exp(-j2\pi\Delta tf)]}$$

$$(3.40)$$

The poles of this transfer function are both of the form

$$f_\alpha = \begin{cases} \dfrac{j}{2\pi\Delta t}\ln\alpha & 0 < \alpha < 1 \\[3ex] \dfrac{j}{2\pi\Delta t}[\ln\alpha + j\pi] & -1 < \alpha < 0 \end{cases} \qquad (3.41)$$

The case for α positive is like a lowpass filter, whereas for α negative, it is similar to a highpass filter. Various combinations of positive and negative α and β parameters can be used, resulting in a mixed form.

Complex Poles

When (3.38) holds, then roots of (3.36) are complex, and the original defining equation may be cast in yet another form:

$$y_i = 2\exp(-2\pi\Delta t\zeta f_n)\cos\left(2\pi\Delta tf_n\sqrt{1 - \zeta^2}\right)y_{i-1}$$

$$- \exp(-4\pi\Delta t\zeta f_n)\,y_{i-2} + g(x_i) \qquad (3.42)$$

That is,

$$h_1 = 2\exp(-2\pi\Delta t\zeta f_n)\cos\left(2\pi\Delta tf_n\sqrt{1 - \zeta^2}\right)$$

$$h_2 = -\exp(-4\pi\Delta t\zeta f_n) \qquad (3.43)$$

The ζ parameter is the *damping ratio*, whereas f_n is the *natural frequency*.

For convenience, the terms in (3.43) will sometimes be abbreviated to

$$h_1 = 2\alpha \cos \beta$$

$$h_2 = -\alpha^2$$

where

$$\alpha = \exp(-2\pi\Delta t\zeta f_n)$$

$$(3.44)$$

$$\beta = 2\pi\Delta t f_n \sqrt{1 - \zeta^2}$$

The poles of this form of the second-order digital filter are found from

$$z^2 - (2\alpha \cos \beta)z + \alpha^2 = 0 \qquad\qquad (3.45)$$

to be

$$z = \alpha[\cos \beta \pm j \sin \beta] = \alpha e^{\pm j\beta}$$

$$= \exp\left\{2\pi\Delta t f_n\left[-\zeta \pm j\sqrt{1 - \zeta^2}\right]\right\} \qquad\qquad (3.46)$$

As $z = \exp[j2\pi\Delta t f]$, the poles are

$$f_{1,2} = j\zeta f_n \pm \sqrt{1 - \zeta^2} f_n \qquad\qquad (3.47)$$

Note that it is f rather than $(j2\pi\Delta t)f$ that is being discussed. Converting to the latter form yields

$$(j2\pi\Delta t)f = (2\pi\Delta t)\zeta f_n \pm (j2\pi\Delta t)\sqrt{1 - \zeta^2} f_n \qquad (3.48)$$

This distinction is necessary so as to avoid confusion about the size of the *damping term* which is the real part (3.48). The reason for defining the h_1 and h_2 weights in terms of the ζ and f_n parameters is more apparent after looking at Figure 3.4.

As shown in Figure 3.4,

$$f_n = |f_i| \qquad\qquad i = 1,2$$

and

$$\zeta = \cos\theta = \frac{\zeta f_n}{f_n} \qquad (3.49)$$

Equation (3.42) reduces to the classical differential equation for small Δt. Defining

$$p = 2\pi\Delta t\zeta f_n$$

and

$$q = 2\pi\Delta t f_n \sqrt{1 - \zeta^2} \qquad (3.50)$$

and again using $e^x \approx 1 + x$ for x small, (3.42) becomes

$$y_i \approx 2\left(1 - p + \frac{p^2}{2}\right)\left(1 - \frac{q^2}{2}\right)y_{i-1} - (1 - 2p)y_{i-2} + g(x_i)$$

$$(3.51)$$

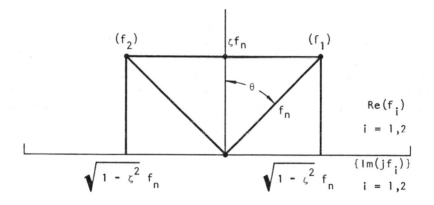

Fig. 3.4   The poles of (3.45) plotted using the two different
conventions.   The terms in braces refer to 3.48,
the others correspond to (3.44).

Recombining terms and dividing by $(\Delta t)^2$ yields

$$\frac{(y_i - 2y_{i-1} + y_{i-2})}{(\Delta t)^2} + \frac{2p}{(\Delta t)^2}(y_{i-1} - y_{i-2})$$

$$+ \frac{1}{(\Delta t)^2}\left\{q^2 - p^2 + \left[-pq^2 + \frac{p^2q^2}{2}\right]\right\}y_{i-1} + \frac{g(x_i)}{(\Delta t)^2}$$

$$(3.52)$$

Assuming that the third- and higher-order terms rapidly go to zero as Δt itself goes to zero, this becomes

$$\frac{d^2 y}{dt^2} + 2\pi f_n \zeta \frac{dy}{dt} + (2\pi f_n)^2 y = f(x) \qquad (3.53)$$

where $f(x)$ is the limiting form of $g(x_i)/(\Delta t)^2$.

The absolute value squared of the transfer func-
tion, $|H(f)|^2$, is somewhat more difficult to plot
than it would be for a first-order filter, although
its characteristics may be readily found. It has
minima at f equal to zero and 1/2 t Hz. Its maximum
occurs at f_p, where

$$\cos 2\pi\Delta t f_p = \frac{h_1(h_2 - 1)}{4h_2} \qquad (3.54)$$

Combining this with (3.43) yields

$$\cos 2\pi\Delta t f_p = \cos\left(2\pi\Delta t f_n \sqrt{1 - \zeta^2}\right)\cosh 2\pi\Delta t\zeta f_n \qquad (3.55)$$

Thus, if one knows the natural frequency f_n and damping factor ζ, it is easy to calculate the peak frequency f_p. The relation between f_p, f_n, and ζ is
approximately

$$f_n \approx \begin{cases} \dfrac{f_p}{\sqrt{1 - 2\zeta^2}} & f_p \text{ and } f_n\zeta \text{ small} \\[4ex] \dfrac{f_p}{\sqrt{1 - \zeta^2}} & f_p = 1/4\Delta t \end{cases} \qquad (3.56)$$

For f_p and f_n large, the equations cannot be simplified as much. For f_p near $1/2\Delta t$ and the product $f_n \zeta$ small, the following relation holds:

$$(\pi - 2\pi\Delta t f_n)^2 (1 - \zeta^2) - (2\pi\Delta t f_n)^2 \zeta^2 = (\pi - 2\pi\Delta t f_p)^2$$

(3.57)

Unit Response Function

If the second-order filter equation with complex roots is expressed as

$$u_i = (2e^{-\alpha} \cos \beta) u_{i-1} + (-e^{-2\alpha}) u_{i-2} + x_i \qquad (3.58)$$

and x_i is of the form

$$x_i = \begin{cases} 1 & i = 0 \\ 0 & \text{otherwise} \end{cases} \qquad (3.59)$$

then there is a general solution for u_i:

$$u_i$$

$$= \begin{cases} 0 & i < 0 \\ e^{-i\alpha} \left[\dfrac{\cos \beta \ \cos(i\beta - \beta) + (1 - 2\cos^2\beta) \cos i\beta}{1 - \cos^2\beta} \right] & i \geq 0 \end{cases}$$

(3.60)

For real poles, i.e., when the equation is

$$u_i = (\alpha + \beta) u_{i-1} - \alpha\beta u_{i-2} + x_i \qquad (3.61)$$

the solution for input such as (3.59) takes the form

$$u_i = \begin{cases} \dfrac{1}{\alpha - \beta} [\alpha^{i+1} - \beta^{i+1}] & \alpha \neq \beta \\[2em] (1 + i)\alpha^i & \alpha = \beta \end{cases} \qquad (3.62)$$

Clearly, (3.60) and (3.62) are the unit response functions, so that for arbitrary input $\{x_i\}$, the output $\{y_i\}$ from second-order filters with coefficients corresponding to those in (3.55) and (3.58) could be defined by

$$y_i = u_i * x_i \qquad (3.63)$$

as discussed for (3.24).

Response to White Noise

For the case with complex poles, the absolute value squared of the transfer function can be written as

$$|H(f)|^2$$

$$= 1 \bigg/ \left\{ \left(2e^{-\lambda_n \zeta}\right)^2 \left[\cos \lambda - \cos\left(\lambda_n \sqrt{1-\zeta^2} + j\zeta\lambda_n\right)\right] \right.$$

$$\times \left. \left[\cos \lambda - \cos\left(\lambda_n \sqrt{1-\zeta^2} - j\zeta\lambda_n\right)\right] \right\}$$

$$= 1 \bigg/ \left\{ \left(2e^{-\lambda}\right)^2 \left[\cos \lambda - \cos(\theta - j\gamma)\right] \left[\cos \gamma - \cos(\theta + j\gamma)\right] \right\}$$

$$\qquad (3.64)$$

where

$$\theta = \lambda_n \sqrt{1 - \zeta^2}$$

$$\gamma = \zeta\lambda_n$$

(3.65)

Note that there are four solutions to the equation obtained by setting the denominator of the right hand side of (3.64) equal to zero rather than the two which would be expected on first examination. If the input $\{x_i\}$ is white noise with variance σ_x^2, then σ_y^2, the variance of the output, is given by

$$\sigma_y^2 = 2\sigma_x^2 \, \Delta t \int_0^{1/2\Delta t} \left| \Pi^2(f) \right| \, df$$

(3.66)

$$= 2\sigma_x^2 \, \frac{\sinh 2\gamma}{\left(4e^{-2\gamma}\right)\left[1 + \left(\dfrac{\sinh \gamma}{\sin \theta}\right)^2\right]}$$

(3.67)

Though somewhat difficult to analyze, it can be shown that for fixed λ_n, σ_y^2 goes to zero as ζ goes to unity. Conversely, for ζ equal to zero, the output variance is simply one-half of the input.

The Second-Order Filter as Two Parallel First-Order Filters

Two of the three types of second-order filter can be implemented as two parallel first-order filters. In the complex case, where the denominator is

$$1 - (2\alpha \cos \beta) z^{-1} + \alpha^2 z^{-2}$$

$$= [1 - \alpha \exp(-j\beta) z^{-1}][1 - \alpha \exp(+j\beta) z^{-1}]$$

(3.68)

then the first-order filters are

$$u_i^{(1)} = u_{i-1}^{(1)} \alpha \exp j\beta + \frac{1}{1 - \exp(-2j\beta)} x_i$$

$$u_i^{(2)} = u_{i-1}^{(2)} \alpha \exp(-j\beta) + \frac{1}{1 - \exp 2j\beta} x_i$$

$$y_i = u_i^{(1)} + u_i^{(2)} \qquad\qquad (3.69)$$

where the superscripts denote a stage of the filter. While the filtering can now be done with only one delay time, there is an increase in computing time because the filter coefficients are complex. This could be diminished slightly by processing two functions at once; making one of the functions the real component, and the other the imaginary part.

The case of real but unequal roots can be dealt with in the same way. Here the denominator is

$$1 - (\alpha + \beta)z^{-1} + \alpha\beta z^{-2} \qquad\qquad (3.70)$$

so that the two first-order filters are

$$u_i^{(1)} = u_{i-1}^{(1)} \alpha + \frac{\alpha}{\alpha - \beta} x_i$$

$$u_i^{(2)} = u_{i-1}^{(2)} \beta + \frac{\beta}{\beta - \alpha} x_i$$

$$y_i = u_i^{(1)} + u_i^{(2)} \qquad\qquad \alpha \neq \beta \quad (3.71)$$

The filtering cannot be performed in one delay time if α is equal to β.

3.5 COMBINED, SERIAL, AND PARALLEL HIGHER-ORDER FILTER IMPLEMENTATIONS

There are three basic ways by which a higher-order filter can be implemented. It is possible, though probably not reasonable, to combine the three procedures and develop a much larger class of filter forms.

It is sufficient to discuss the more basic methods and leave the more esoteric implementations for specific applications where they might be appropriate.

The combined filter form is probably of greatest theoretical interest. In this case, the filtering equation is

$$y_i = \sum_{\ell=0}^{L} g_\ell x_{i-\ell} + \sum_{k=1}^{K} h_k y_{i-k} \qquad (3.72)$$

The filter is entirely defined by the parameters $\{g_\ell\}$ and $\{h_k\}$. After this point, in the absence of modifiers, this is the form to which reference is being made when filters are discussed.

The *serial* filter has M second-order filters of the form

$$y_i^{(m)} = \sum_{p=0}^{2} g_{mp} y_{i-p}^{(m-1)} + \sum_{q=1}^{2} h_{mq} y_{i-q}^{(m)}$$

$$m = 1,\ldots,M \qquad (3.73)$$

where

$$M \approx K/2 \qquad (3.74)$$

The superscript indicates the stage of the filter. By definition, $\{y_i^{(0)}\}$ is $\{x_i\}$ and $\{y^{(M)}\}$ is $\{y_i\}$ in terms of the previous formulation. The formulation is not unique in that the various stages may be commuted without affecting the transfer function of the filter. If K, the number of recursive terms, is odd, then one of the stages must have only a single g_{mp} term.

The parallel form also has M components:

$$u_i^{(m)} = \sum_{p=0}^{2} g_{mp} u_{i-p}^{(m)} + \sum_{q=1}^{2} r_{mq} x_{i-q} \qquad (3.75)$$

so that

$$y_i = \sum_{m=1}^{M} u_i^{(m)} \tag{3.76}$$

Note that the $\{g_{mp}\}$ terms are the same as those in the serial implementation of (3.73). While the combined or serial forms always require K delay times to perform the filtering operation, the parallel version performs it in two delay times. Indeed, if complex coefficients are allowed, then (3.75) and (3.76) can be replaced with a complex version in which all calculations are done in *one* delay time.

While the combined form can always be written in a serial manner and vice versa, the parallel version poses some problem. In particular, a necessary and sufficient condition for (3.72) or (3.73) to be implementable in the parallel mode of (3.75) is that all the roots of

$$1 - \sum_{k=1}^{K} h_k z^{-k} = 0 \tag{3.77}$$

be distinct (Guilleman, 1961). If such is the case, the $\{r_{mq}\}$ parameters can be obtained from the $\{g_{mp}\}$ and $\{h_{mq}\}$ terms in the following manner: Define

$$D_m(z) = (1 - h_{m1}z^{-1} - h_{m2}z^{-2}) \tag{3.78}$$

and

$$D(z) = \prod_{m=1}^{M} D_m(z) = 1 - \sum_{k=1}^{M} h_k z^{-k} \tag{3.79}$$

Similarly, suppose that

$$N_m(z) = (g_{m1} + g_{m2}z^{-1} + g_{m3}z^{-2}) \tag{3.80}$$

and

$$N(z) = \prod_{m=1}^{M} N_m(z) = \sum_{\ell=0}^{L} g_\ell z^{-\ell}$$ (3.81)

It is necessary to find the $\{r_{mq}\}$ terms. If there are no multiple roots of (3.77), then the following equation must hold:

$$\sum_{m=1}^{M} \frac{r_{m0} + r_{m1} z^{-1} + r_{m2} z^{-2}}{D_m(z)} = \frac{N(z)}{D(z)}$$ (3.82)

or

$$\sum_{m=1}^{M} \left[\frac{D(z)}{D_m(z)}\right] \left(r_{m0} + r_{m1} z^{-1} + r_{m2} z^{-2}\right) = N(z)$$ (3.83)

This may be rearranged to yield 3M equations in 3M unknowns and solved using numerical methods by equating the coefficients of like powers of z from each side of (3.83).

3.6 SINE VERSUS TANGENT FORMS, AND THE THEOREM OF HOLTZ AND LEONDES

The complex transfer functions of (3.72) is

$$H(f) = \frac{\sum_{\ell=0}^{L} g_\ell \exp(-j2\pi\Delta t\ell f)}{1 - \sum_{k=1}^{K} h_k \exp(-j2\pi\Delta t k f)}$$ (3.84)

Holtz and Leondes (1966) proved that the absolute value squared of H(f) may always be written in the form

$$|H(f)|^2 = \frac{\displaystyle\sum_{\ell=0}^{L} g_{\ell}' \cos^{2\ell} \pi\Delta tf}{\displaystyle\sum_{k=0}^{K} h_{k}' \cos^{2k} \pi\Delta tf} \tag{3.85}$$

where the $\{g_{\ell}'\}$ and $\{h_{k}'\}$ are, respectively, dependent on $\{g_{\ell}\}$ and $\{h_{k}\}$. Furthermore, any transfer function expression such as the right-hand side of (3.85) can be implemented with real coefficients as in (3.84).

Note that as the powers of the cosine in (3.85) are always even; an entirely equivalent expression, $|H(f)|^2$, could be written in terms of even powers of $\sin \pi\Delta tf$ by replacing $\cos^2 \pi\Delta tf$ terms with $(1 - \sin^2 \pi\Delta tf)$ throughout the equation.

One of the important features of this observation is that $\sin \pi\Delta tf$ behaves in a manner analogous to $(\pi\Delta tf)$ on the range $(0, 1/2\Delta t)$. This is shown in Figure 3.5.

Thus, filters designed in terms of powers of $\sin^2 \omega\Delta t/2$ are similar to those designed with powers of $(\omega\Delta t/2)^2$, or more simply ω^2, in the continuous-time domain. This means that many transfer function types can be carried over to the digital domain by replacing ω^2 with some form of $\sin^2 \omega\Delta t/2$.

Alternately, filters could be posed in the form

$$|H(f)|^2 = \frac{\displaystyle\sum_{\ell=0}^{L} g_{\ell}'' \tan^{2\ell} \pi\Delta tf}{\displaystyle\sum_{k=0}^{K} h_{k}'' \tan^{2k} \pi\Delta tf} \tag{3.86}$$

This could be reduced to a form similar to (3.85) by multiplying the right-hand side of (3.86) by

$$\frac{\cos^{2K} \pi\Delta tf}{\cos^{2K} \pi\Delta tf} \tag{3.87}$$

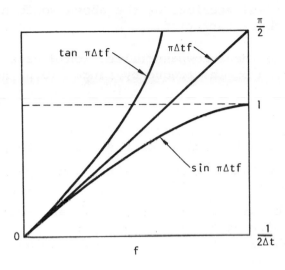

Fig. 3.5 Comparison of sine and cosine of (πΔtf) with the line
          (πΔtf).

After simplification, (3.86) could then be expressed
in terms of either sines or cosines in even powers.
   As tan ωΔt/2 increases more rapidly than sin ωΔt/2,
it would seem at first glance that filters designed
using tangents would be superior to those employing
sines. Indeed, such is the case if K is the same in
both filters. The improvement does not come without
cost, however.   There is a tendency for the tangent
formulation to require more numerator terms than do
equivalent sine filters, thus making their computational implementation more expensive.

3.7 IDEAL BASIC FILTERS

   By *basic filters* are meant the traditional forms
commonly used in processing of data or signals. The
ones of main concern are the lowpass, highpass, bandpass, or band-reject, the latter sometimes being referred to as the notch filter.

The ideal versions of the above would have the following characteristics:

1. The ideal lowpass filter would pass all information on the frequency range $(0,B)$ Hz, while rejecting all information on the range $(B,1/2\Delta t)$ Hz.

2. The ideal highpass filter would reverse the characteristics of the ideal lowpass filter.

3. The ideal bandpass filter would pass only information in the range $(f_c - B)$ to $(f_c + B)$ Hz.

4. The ideal band-reject filter would reject all information in the range $(f_c - B)$ to $(f_c + B)$ Hz, while retaining the information outside this range.

The widths of the pass bands are as follows:

Lowpass	B Hz
Highpass	B Hz
Bandpass	2B Hz
Band-reject	$\left(\dfrac{1}{2\Delta t} - 2B\right)$ Hz

The ideal forms are shown in Figure 3.6.

While such ideal filter responses are desirable, it turns out that perfect rejection or acceptance is not possible in practice. There are two reasons for this. The first is that only in the limit as K goes to infinity will it be possible to attain the ideal form, so that the filters actually used are only approximations to the ideal forms. Second, only finite amounts of data are present in practice, so that the true transfer function is actually the theoretical one convolved with a sin x/x term which arises from the truncations of the data. On the other hand, filters can be generated and applied which for all practical purposes are identical to their ideal counterparts.

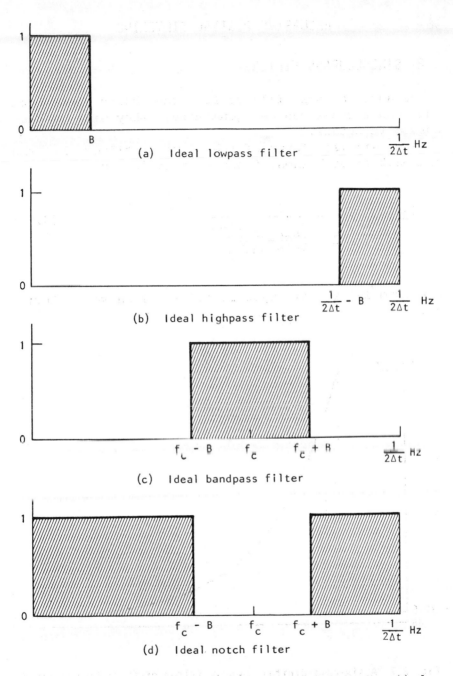

Fig. 3.6 The frequency response functions of the four ideal
filters. The cross-hatched areas indicate which
portions of the data are passed.

3.8 SINE LOWPASS FILTERS

Because lowpass filters form the basis upon which the other types can be generated, they will be discussed in detail.

The simplest form of the lowpass filter is the sine-Butterworth whose transfer function is:

$$|H(f)|^2 = \cfrac{1}{1 + \left(\cfrac{\sin \pi \Delta t f}{\sin \pi \Delta t B}\right)^{2K}} \qquad (3.88)$$

One example of this type of filter is shown in Figure 3.7.

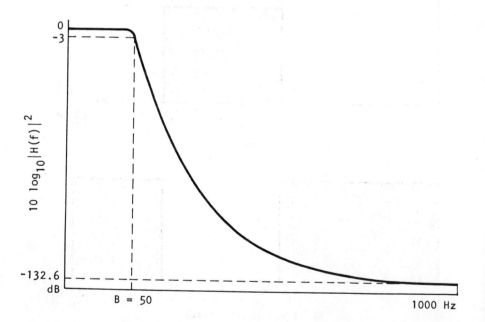

Fig. 3.7 A six-pole digital lowpass filter of the type described by (3.88). In this particular instance, K = 6, $\Delta t = 0.0005$ sec, and B = 50 Hz.

The performance of this filter could be discussed
in many ways.   One of the more fruitful techniques is
through the use of the *far point*, f_p, whose definition
for the lowpass case is

$$f_p = \frac{1}{2\Delta t} - B \qquad\qquad (3.89)$$

For f equal to f_p, the transfer function may be
simplified:

$$|H(f_p)|^2 = \cfrac{1}{1 + \left\{ \cfrac{\sin\left[\pi\Delta t \left(\frac{1}{2\Delta t} - B\right)\right]}{\sin \pi \Delta tB} \right\}^{2K}}$$

$$= \frac{1}{1 + \cot^{2K} \pi\Delta tB}$$

$$\approx \tan^{2K} \pi\Delta tB \qquad\qquad (3.90)$$

for small B.   Making the further simplification that
tan x = x for small x and expressing the relationship
in decibels (dB), then

$$10 \log_{10} |H(f_p)|^2 \approx 20K \log_{10} \pi\Delta tB \qquad\qquad (3.91)$$

Therefore, the number of dB that the transfer function
is down at the far point is proportional both to K,
the number of poles, and to the logarithm of $(\pi\Delta tB)$.
    The implementation problem consists of finding the
$\{g_\ell\}$ and $\{h_k\}$ terms which, when substituted in (3.84),
reduce to the form (3.88).   One straightforward approach, as discussed in Otnes (1968a), consists of the
following steps:

    1. Find the 2K complex roots of

$$1 + x^{2K} = 0 \qquad\qquad (3.92)$$

Only the set for which the imaginary part is positive is used, thus insuring stability. There are K of these. The roots take the form

$$\sin \pi \Delta f_k = \sin \pi \Delta t B \left[\sin \left\{ \pi \left[\frac{1}{2} + \frac{1}{K} \left(k - \frac{1}{2} \right) \right] \right\} \right.$$

$$\left. - j \cos \left\{ \pi \left[\frac{1}{2} + \frac{1}{K} \left(k - \frac{1}{2} \right) \right] \right\} \right]$$

$$= x_k \qquad\qquad k = 1, \ldots, K \qquad (3.93)$$

2. The next step is that of finding solutions to the equation

$$\sin \pi \Delta t f_k = x_k$$

Supposing that f_k and x_k of (3.92) are written in the form

$$\pi \Delta t f_k = \alpha_k + j \beta_k$$

$$x_k = a_k + j b_k \qquad\qquad (3.94)$$

where a_k, b_k, α_k, and β_k are real for all k, then (3.94) could be expressed as

$$\sin(\alpha_k + j \beta_k) = a_k + j b_k \qquad\qquad (3.95)$$

3. The solutions for α_k and β_k are[*]

$$\alpha_k = \arctan \left[\sqrt{\frac{D_k}{b_k^2} - 1} \, \operatorname{sgn}(a_k) \right]$$

$$\qquad\qquad\qquad (3.96)$$

$$\beta_k = \ln(E_k)$$

[*]Exceptions are noted below.

where

$$D_k = \frac{1}{2}\left[-C_k + \sqrt{C_k^2 + 4b_k^2} \right]$$

$$E_k = \sqrt{D_k + 1} + \sqrt{D_k}$$

and

$$C_k = 1 - (a_k^2 + b_k^2) \tag{3.97}$$

4. Thus, in terms of (3.73), the filter weights would be

$$h_{k1} = 2E_k b_k / \sqrt{D_k}$$

$$\tag{3.98}$$

$$h_{k2} = - E_k^2$$

5. If K is odd, there will be $\frac{K-1}{2}$ second-order sections and one first-order section, in which case the above mapping does not work properly for the odd weight. In this case, the single weight has the form

$$h_K = 2F^2 + 1 - 2F\sqrt{F^2 + 1} \qquad F = \sin \pi\Delta tB \tag{3.99}$$

6. The $\{h_{mp}\}$ weights could be used as above in the serial and parallel implementation, or the combined weights may be found from

$$h_k = \left[-\text{coefficient of } z^{-k} \text{ in} \right.$$

$$\left. \prod_{k=1}^{K/2} \left(1 - h_{k1} z^{-1} - h_{k2} z^{-2} \right) \right] \qquad (3.100)$$

7. There is only one $\{g_\ell\}$ coefficient, namely g_0:

$$g_0 = 1 - \sum_{k=1}^{K} h_k \qquad (3.101)$$

Chebyshev Lowpass Filter

The Chebyshev lowpass digital filter has a transfer function whose absolute value squared is of the form

$$|H(f)|^2 = \frac{1}{1 + \varepsilon\, T_K^2 \left(\dfrac{\sin \pi \Delta tf}{\sin \pi \Delta tB} \right)} \qquad (3.102)$$

where $T_K(x)$ is the Chebyshev polynomial of degree K as defined in Abramowitz and Stegun (1964). For example,

$$T_0(x) = 1$$

$$T_1(x) = x$$

$$T_2(x) = 2x^2 - 1$$

$$T_3(x) = 4x^3 - 3x \qquad (3.103)$$

There is a well-known recursive relationship by which these polynomials may be generated:

$$T_{K+1}(x) = 2x\, T_K(x) - T_{K-1}(x) \qquad (3.104)$$

The parameter ε in (3.102) affects the amount of ripple the filter will have in the pass band. Two standard values are

$$\varepsilon = \begin{cases} 10^{1/10}-1 & 1.0 \text{ dB ripple} \\ 10^{1/20}-1 & 0.5 \text{ dB ripple} \end{cases} \qquad (3.105)$$

As with the Butterworth lowpass filter, the Chebyshev filter is defined to within a constant by its poles. Finding the poles may be accomplished in a manner similar to the one described above. The principal difference is that a different set of poles must be employed, namely, the set x'_ℓ, $\ell = 1,\ldots,2K$, which are the roots of

$$1 + \varepsilon T_K^2 (x) = 0 \qquad (3.106)$$

The subset $\{x_k\}$ is selected where $\text{Im}(x_R) > 0$. This will ensure stability in the usual sense. The set of such roots required is fairly small; a table of 220 numbers will include the required roots of the first ten polynomials for two different values of ε. These roots could be precomputed and stored on many of the larger digital devices.

Next, the f_k poles must be found corresponding to the method discussed above at (3.93). Thereafter, the procedure is the same.

The performance of the Chebyshev filters at the far point is slightly different from the Butterworth filter:

$$|H(f_p)|^2 = \frac{1}{1 + \varepsilon T_K^2 (\cot \pi\Delta tB)} \qquad (3.107)$$

As

$$T_K(x) \approx 2^{K-1}x^K \qquad (3.108)$$

for large x, then (3.107) may be rewritten as

$$\left|H(f_p)\right|^2 \approx \varepsilon \ 2^{2K-2} \ \tan^{2K} \pi\Delta tB \qquad\qquad (3.109)$$

As large cot x implies small tan x, applying the approximation tan x $\approx$ x to (3.109) and expressing it in dB yields:

$$10 \ \log\left|H(f_p)\right|^2 \approx -10 \ \log_{10} \varepsilon - 6 \ (K - 1)$$

$$+ \ 20K \ \log_{10} \ \pi\Delta tB \qquad\qquad (3.110)$$

Comparing (3.110) with (3.91) shows that the Chebyshev filter has $[6(K - 1) + 10 \ \log \varepsilon]$ dB improvement over the Butterworth. Naturally, this is at the expense of the increased ripple.

Highpass Filters

Highpass filter generation is very similar to lowpass filter production. If (3.88) is modified slightly so as to become

$$\left|H(f)\right|^2 = \cfrac{1}{1 + \left[\cfrac{\sin\left(\pi\Delta tf - \dfrac{\pi}{2}\right)}{\sin \pi\Delta tB}\right]^{2K}} \qquad\qquad (3.111)$$

then the action is reversed, and the filter achieves its maximum at f = 1/2Δt, and its minimum at f = 0 Hz.

There are two ways by which the weight generation for the highpass filter may be accomplished:

1. Change the sign of the h_{kl} terms in (3.98) from plus to minus.

2. Generate a *lowpass* filter and then make all the weights negative.

These two statements are equivalent.

Highpass Chebyshev filters may be produced in a very similar manner. Rather than (3.111),

$$|H(f)|^2 = \cfrac{1}{1 + \varepsilon T_K^2 \left[\cfrac{\sin(\pi \Delta tf - \frac{\pi}{2})}{\sin \pi \Delta tB} \right]} \qquad (3.112)$$

would be used.   The actual route for calculating the weights would be the same as described above for the Butterworth case.

3.9 TANGENT FILTERS

As noted in Section 3.6, the tangent formulation is an alternative to that of the sine. In many cases, the tangent formulation may be specified merely by replacing sines with tangents wherever the sines occur. Thus, the tangent Butterworth lowpass filter has the form

$$|H(f)|^2 = \cfrac{1}{1 + \left(\cfrac{\tan \pi \Delta tf}{\tan \pi \Delta tB} \right)^{2K}} \qquad (3.113)$$

The right-hand side of (3.113) can be rewritten as

$$\cfrac{1}{1 + \left(\cfrac{\tan \pi \Delta tf}{\tan \pi \Delta tB} \right)^{2K}} = \cfrac{\cos^{2K} \pi \Delta tf}{\cos^{2K} \pi \Delta tf + \left(\cfrac{\sin \pi \Delta tf}{\tan \pi \Delta tB} \right)^{2K}}$$

$$(3.114)$$

When put in this form, it is clear that the tangent formulation of the lowpass filter has nonrecursive terms.   In particular, these turn out to be zeros at 0 Hz.

Setting aside the numerator problem for the moment, the denominator may be seen to cause somewhat more difficult problems than those arising from the numerator.   Rather than (3.93), the problem becomes that of solving

$$\tan \pi \Delta t f_k = \tan \pi \Delta t B \cdot \{\text{a root of unity}\}$$

$$= a_k + jb_k \tag{3.115}$$

Equation (3.115) can be squared and simplified to yield

$$\sin^2 \lambda_k = \sqrt{\frac{\left(a_k^2 - b_k^2\right) + 2ja_k b_k}{1 + \left(a_k^2 - b_k^2\right) + 2ja_k b_k}} \tag{3.116}$$

$$= a_k' + jb_k'$$

As a computational procedure, the tangent problem may thus be solved by first evaluating a_k' and b_k' as defined by (3.116), and then using them in place of a_k and b_k in the solution defined by (3.96) through (3.101).

The procedure described above will completely take care of finding the poles and hence the recursive weights as described in the preceding sections. There only remains the problem of finding the $\{g_\ell\}$ terms.

The latter terms turn out to be fairly straightforward. In the serial case they are, to within a constant, given by

$$g_{m0} = 1.0$$

$$g_{m1} = 2.0 \tag{3.117}$$

$$g_{m2} = 1.0$$

and for the combined case by

$$g_\ell = \binom{K}{\ell} \qquad \qquad \ell = 0, \ldots, K \tag{3.118}$$

The weights defined by (3.118) by themselves generate a filter, which is sometimes called a *binomial*
filter. The latter is a lowpass filter by itself.

A scale factor must be employed in order that the
filter transfer function is unity at 0 Hz. The scale
factor must multiply all the $\{g_\ell\}$ terms, or for the
serial case its effect may be split up over one or
more of the triplets defined by (3.117).

If there are an odd number of weights, the final
set of $\{g_{m\ell}\}$ terms corresponding to the odd term is

$$g_{m0} = 1.0$$

$$g_{m1} = 1.0 \hspace{4cm} (3.119)$$

$$g_{m2} = 0$$

Performance of the Tangent Lowpass Filter

The performance of the tangent Butterworth lowpass
filter may be examined in the same far point procedure
as with the sinc Butterworth lowpass filter in Section
3.8. In this case, (3.113) becomes

$$\left|H(f_p)\right|^2 = \frac{1}{1 + \left[\dfrac{\tan\left(\dfrac{\pi}{2} - \pi\Delta tB\right)}{\tan \pi\Delta tB}\right]^{2K}}$$

$$= \frac{1}{1 + \cot^{4K} \pi\Delta tB} \hspace{3cm} (3.120)$$

$$\approx (\pi\Delta tB)^{4K}$$

for small B. In dB, this is

$$10 \log_{10} \left|H(f_p)\right|^2 = 40K \log_{10} \pi\Delta tB \hspace{2cm} (3.121)$$

Comparing this with (3.91) reveals that the tangent Butterworth lowpass filter is down twice as many dB as its sine counterpart, thus showing a great deal of improvement. There is, however, one detail which should not be overlooked. Namely, that while the sine form of the filter has no nonrecursive terms, the tangent form does. This means that for equal K, while the tangent filter has improved performance, it also has increased complexity which requires more operations and/or hardware.

If the combined form of the filter is used in both cases, then the tangent formulation will require about twice as many arithmetical operations. A reasonable comparison (Otnes, 1968b) is to compare the filters when they each have an equal number of arithmetical operations. In this case, the tangent formulation will be seen to lose a great deal of apparent advantages. In particular, let

K = P (tangent filter)

K = 2P (sine filter)   (3.122)

Then the filters' transfer functions are exactly equal in three places:

$$
f = \begin{cases}
0 \text{ Hz} \\
B \text{ Hz} & \text{cutoff point} \\
\left(\dfrac{1}{2\Delta t}\right) - B \text{ Hz} & \text{the far point}
\end{cases}
\qquad (3.123)
$$

In between these three frequency points, the following relationships hold between the two transfer functions:

1. 0 to B Hz--the sine filter transfer function is greater than that of the tangent filter

2. B to [1/2Δt - B] Hz--the sine filter transfer function is less than that of the tangent filter

3. $[1/2\Delta t - B]$ to $[1/2\Delta t]$ Hz--the sine   filter
transfer function is greater than that of the
tangent filter

This is shown in Figure 3.8. The impact of this is
that for the conditions given above,the sine filter is
superior to the tangent filter on the range $[0,(1/2\Delta t - B)]$, which is probably the most important part for
most usages.

This result must be regarded as being asymptotic in
nature, for the nonrecursive portion may be done in a
simpler manner than would be indicated by the combined
form of the tangent filter,namely by a cascade of filters of the form

$$y_i^{(\ell)} = y_i^{(\ell - 1)} + y_{i-1}^{(\ell - 1)} \tag{3.124}$$

Exactly K of these cascading filters would be required; except for a scaling coefficient, no multipli-
cative operations are required, only K additions.

The gist of the above discussion is that both the
sine and tangent versions have good and bad points.
Superiority of one over the other will depend on the
particular application; that is, what the relative
speeds of the multiply and add devices on the hardware
are,and to some extent, the number of significant bits
in the computer words.

Other Tangent Filters

Highpass tangent Butterworth and highpass and lowpass tangent Chebyshev filters may be generated in
much the same manner as the tangent lowpass filter.
In the highpass Butterworth case, (3.111) becomes

$$|H(f)|^2 = \frac{1}{1 + \left(\dfrac{\tan \pi\Delta tf}{\cot \pi\Delta tB}\right)^{2K}} \tag{3.125}$$

The lowpass tangent Chebyshev filter has a transfer
function of the form

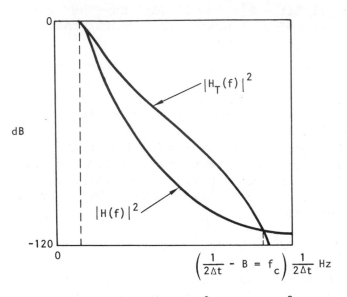

Fig. 3.8   Comparison of $|H_S(f)|^2$ and $|H_T(f)|^2$ for
$B = f_c = 1/8(1/2\Delta t)$.

$$|H(f)|^2 = \frac{1}{1 + \varepsilon \, T_k^2 \left(\dfrac{\tan \, \pi\Delta tf}{\tan \, \pi\Delta tB}\right)} \qquad (3.126)$$

The implementation of these follows the amended procedure discussed above.

3.10   BANDPASS AND BAND-REJECT FILTERS

Bandpass filters may be generated in all of the
different types discussed in preceding sections. That
is, all of the following are possible:

1. Bandpass sine Butterworth

2. Bandpass tangent Butterworth

3. Bandpass sine Chebyshev

4. Bandpass tangent Chebyshev

The sine Butterworth filter has the transfer function

$$|H(f)|^2 = \frac{1}{1 + \left(\dfrac{\cos 2\pi\Delta tf - C}{S}\right)^{2K}} \qquad (3.127)$$

where C and S are defined by

$$C = \cos 2\pi\Delta tf_c \; \cos 2\pi\Delta tB$$

and

$$S = \sin 2\pi\Delta tf_c \; \sin 2\pi\Delta tB \qquad (3.128)$$

In this case the filter has its maximum approximately at f_C Hz. At $(f_C - B)$ and $(f_C + B)$ Hz, it is exactly equal to one-half, so that it tends to follow the form of the ideal bandpass filter rather closely. The exact maximum occurs at frequency f_m Hz, defined by

$$\cos 2\pi\Delta tf_m = \cos 2\pi\Delta tf_c \; \cos 2\pi\Delta tB \qquad (3.129)$$

Minima of $|H(f)|^2$ occur at zero and $1/2\Delta t$ Hz.

One significant difference between (3.127) and the filter transfer functions discussed previously is that in the former all the trigonometric functions had arguments of the form $(\pi\Delta tf)$, whereas in the latter all such arguments are some form of $(2\pi\Delta tf)$. This difference of a factor of two changes the mappings discussed earlier by an equivalent factor. Other than this scale factor, the procedure defined by (3.92) through (3.101) holds.

A Chebyshev sine bandpass filter can be generated in much the same way. Equation (3.127) becomes

$$|H(f)|^2 = \frac{1}{1 + \varepsilon^2 T_K^2 \left(\dfrac{\cos 2\pi\Delta tf - C}{S}\right)} \qquad (3.130)$$

where C and S are as defined above and T_K is the Kth-order Chebyshev polynomial.

The tangent form of the Butterworth and Chebyshev bandpass filters are, as would be expected, somewhat more complicated than their sine counterparts. The butterworth filter has the form

$$|H(f)|^2 = \cfrac{1}{1 + \left(\cfrac{\cos\ 2\pi\Delta tf - D}{E\ \sin\ 2\pi\Delta tf}\right)^{2K}} \qquad (3.131)$$

The definitions of D and E are

$$D = \frac{\cos\ 2\pi\Delta tf_c}{\cos\ 2\pi\Delta tB}$$

$$E = \tan\ 2\pi\Delta tf_m \qquad (3.132)$$

As with the sine Butterworth form, the half-power points are at $(f_c - B)$ and $(f_c + B)$ Hz. The maximum occurs at f_m Hz, where

$$\cos\ 2\pi\Delta tf_m = D \qquad (3.133)$$

The Chebyshev version is much the same as defined in (3.112):

$$|H(f)|^2 = \cfrac{1}{1 + \varepsilon\ T_K^2 \left(\cfrac{\cos\ 2\pi\Delta tf - D}{E\ \sin\ 2\pi\Delta tf}\right)} \qquad (3.134)$$

Both types of the tangent filters require nonrecursive parameters when the filters are implemented. In both cases, the serial form has terms as follows:

$$y_i^{(\ell)} = c_\ell \left(y_i^{(\ell - 1)} - y_{i-2}^{(\ell - 1)}\right) + h_{1\ell}\ y_{i-1}^{(\ell)} + h_{2\ell}\ y_{i-2}^{(\ell)}$$

$$(3.135)$$

There are only two nonrecursive terms, but they are separated by two rather than one sampling interval. As usual, c_ℓ is a scaling parameter.

For a combined implementation, the nonrecursive weights would take the form

$$
g_\ell = \begin{cases} c\left(\dfrac{\frac{K}{2}}{\frac{\ell}{2}}\right)(-1)^{\ell/2} & \ell \text{ even} \\[2em] 0 & \ell \text{ odd} \end{cases} \tag{3.136}
$$

Alternative forms to those discussed above for bandpass filters may be found elsewhere. For example, Constantinides (1967) has developed a type which has its maximum exactly between the two half-power points.

Band-Reject Filters

One band-reject filter form is

$$
\left|H(f)\right|^2 = 1 - \frac{1}{1 + \left(\dfrac{\cos 2\pi \Delta tf - C}{S}\right)^{2K}}
$$

$$
= \frac{\left(\dfrac{\cos 2\pi \Delta tf - C}{S}\right)^{2K}}{1 + \left(\dfrac{\cos 2\pi \Delta tf - C}{S}\right)^{2K}} \tag{3.137}
$$

which is simply unity minus the transfer function of the bandpass filter.

The denominator of (3.137) is exactly the same as the transfer function of the bandpass filter used to generate. Thus, the recursive part of the band-reject filter will be the same as the recursive part of the bandpass filter. The latter has only one nonrecursive term. On the other hand, it is clear from (3.137) that the band-reject filter must have many nonrecursive terms. For each section of the serial implementation, the filter takes the form

$$y_i^{(\ell)} = c_\ell \left[y_i^{(\ell - 1)} - 2cy_{i-1}^{(\ell - 1)} + y_{i-2}^{(\ell - 1)} \right]$$

$$+ h_{1\ell} y_{i-1}^{(\ell)} + h_{2\ell} y_{i-2}^{(\ell)} \qquad (3.138)$$

That is, to within a constant, the nonrecursive serial weights are given by

$$g_{0\ell} = 1$$

$$g_{1\ell} = -2C$$

and

$$g_{2\ell} = 1 \qquad (3.139)$$

where C is as defined by (3.128). The combined form of the nonrecursive weights is given by

$$g_\ell = c \left[\text{coefficient of } z^{-\ell} \text{ in } (1 - 2C\, z^{-1} + z^{-2})^{K/2} \right] \qquad (3.140)$$

where the small c is an overall scaling constant which makes the transfer function unity for 0 Hz.

The tangent version of the Butterworth band-reject filter turns out to be given by a relation equivalent to its sine counterpart; the recursive part remains the same as for the tangent bandpass filter. The non-recursive weights in the serial form are given by

$$g_{0\ell} = 1$$

$$g_{1\ell} = -2E = -2 \tan 2\pi \Delta t B$$

$$g_{2\ell} = 1 \qquad (3.141)$$

3.11 NOISE AND INSTABILITY PROBLEMS DUE TO THE FINITE SIZE OF THE COMPUTER WORD

Until now, this chapter has implicitly assumed a perfect computer; that is, one which has no limitations on the number of bits in the computer word. In actual practice, all computers have a finite number of bits in their words, the current range being from eight to sixty. The purpose of this section is to discuss some of the problems which arise from the discreteness of the computer word. Much of the material to be given appeared in a paper by Otnes and McNamee (1970). The problems which come about from filter coefficient and data rounding fall into three categories:

1. Measurement of the deviation of the implemented filter from the ideal--for example, the mean square error criterion is employed in Knowles and Olcayto (1968) and Liu and Kaneko (1969).

2. Regarding the underflow (due to additions in the fixed-point case or to addition and multiplication in the floating-point case) as a noise source, and computing the spectrum of the output noise--this approach has been used in Gold and Rader (1966) and Knowles and Edwards (1965a-d), and more recently in Weinstein and Oppenheim (1969).

3. Examination of both the computer arithmetic and word format on the one hand, and the filter and its method of implementation on the other, for the purpose of determining at what point these variables will cause a filter (designed to be stable) to become unstable--it is this last area that Otnes and McNamee (1970) explore.

Kaiser, Kuo and Kaiser (1966) and Weinstein and Oppenheim (1965), and others (Weaver, et al., 1968) discuss the stability threshold problem for the combined filter. Kaiser's solution is of the form

$$m_b > 1 + \left[-\log_2 \left(\frac{5N}{2^{N+2}} \prod_{k=1}^{N} p_k T \right) \right] \qquad (3.142a)$$

where

  m_b = The minimum number of binary digits required to represent the word for a stable filter of the lowpass type

  N = The number of poles of the filter

  T = The sampling interval in seconds

  p_k = The kth pole of the transfer function in radians per second

Equation (3.142a) has the disadvantage of not giving a result directly in terms of bandwidth. As will be shown, a threshold for instability on a floating-point computer for the combined filter can be given in the form

$$m_b = \beta_N - N \log_2 2\pi BT \qquad (3.142b)$$

where

  B = Minimum attainable bandwidth in Hz

  β_N = The integer i such that

$$2^{i-1} \leq \binom{N}{[N/2]} < 2^i \qquad (3.143)$$

where the brackets [] indicate the integer part of the enclosed quantity.

In the cascade or serial form of implementation where N = 2, the filter has stages containing at most two poles, so that (3.142b) applies in the form

$$B_{cascade} \approx \frac{2^{(m_b-2)/2}}{2\pi T} \qquad (3.144)$$

for the cascade filter. It is thus possible to go much lower in filter bandwidth in the cascade implementation than with the combined.

The discussion which follows is essentially that in Otnes and McNamee (1970).

The argument will proceed in stages. The first stage to be examined will be a hypothetical computer which rounds only the filter coefficients at a given position, but otherwise does all of the computations perfectly. This device, hereafter referred to as the truncated coefficient perfect computer (TCPC), is a binary, fixed-point machine which rounds the filter coefficients at b places to the right of the binary point. That is, the weights (only) have the form

XXX.XXXXX...X000
$\underbrace{}$

   b digits

It is easiest to start with the second-order case. The filter expression is

$$y_i = g_o x_i + h_1 y_{i-1} + h_2 y_{i-2} \qquad (3.145)$$

and the transfer function is

$$H(\lambda) = \frac{g_o}{1 - h_1 \exp(-j\lambda) - h_2 \exp(-2j\lambda)} \qquad (3.146)$$

Setting the denominator of (3.146) equal to zero and solving for λ, one obtains

$$\lambda = -j \ln\left[\frac{h_1 \pm \sqrt{h_1^2 + 4h_2}}{2}\right] \qquad (3.147)$$

There are two cases.

1. If $h_1^2 + 4h_2 \geq 0$, the quantity within the brackets is always real. Then

$$
f + j\sigma = \begin{cases} -\dfrac{j}{2\pi\Delta t} \; \ln\underbrace{\left[\dfrac{h_1}{2} + \dfrac{1}{2}\sqrt{h_1^2 + 4h_2}\right]}_{\text{positive}} \\[2em] -\dfrac{j}{2\pi\Delta t} \; \ln\underbrace{\left[\dfrac{h_1}{2} - \dfrac{1}{2}\sqrt{h_1^2 + 4h_2}\right]}_{\text{positive or negative}} \end{cases} \tag{3.148}
$$

Without loss of generality, the lowpass case only is examined, so that

$$f = 0$$

$$
\sigma = -\frac{1}{2\pi\Delta t} \; \ln\left[\frac{h_1}{2} \pm \frac{1}{2}\sqrt{h_1^2 + 4h_2}\right] \tag{3.149}
$$

The filter is unstable on the line ($h_2 = 1 + h_1$). Therefore, for instability

$$
\sigma = -\frac{1}{2\pi\Delta t} \; \ln\left[(h_1 + 1) \text{ or } 1\right] \tag{3.150}
$$

The unit term always causes instability; the ($h_1 + 1$) term may add a second pole at zero. The conditions for causing this are a little more complicated than in the first-order case. The line defined by (3.149) may be subdivided into $(2 \cdot 2^b + 1)$ portions on the range ($-2 \leq h_1 \leq 0$). This is shown in Figure 3.9.

On the TCPC, the filter will be unstable for some values of h_1 and h_2 not on the ($h_2 = 1 + h$) border. The exact area is complicated, being of the exaggerated form shown in Figure 3.10. The dots shown in Figure 3.10 represent the second-order filters which could be implemented in a system with b = 2. Figure 3.11 illustrates the position in the frequency plane of the poles corresponding to these filters.

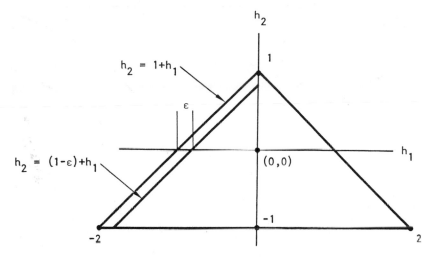

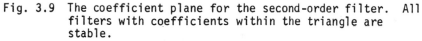

Fig. 3.9 The coefficient plane for the second-order filter. All filters with coefficients within the triangle are stable.

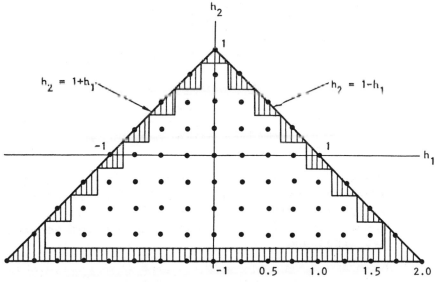

Fig. 3.10 Within the stability triangle, all perfect computer second-order filters are stable. On the other hand, for the TCPC with b = 2, the weights must originally have been within the area bounded by the shaded portion, and can in fact only take on values corresponding to the data shown in the figure.

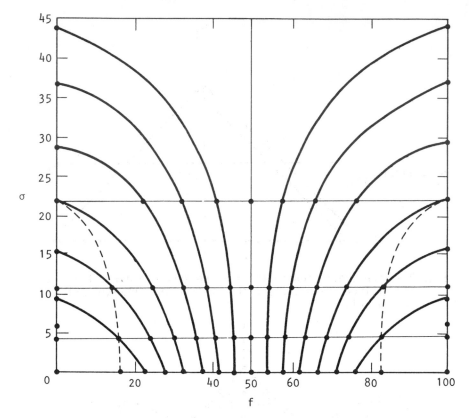

Fig. 3.11   Result of mapping second-order filter coefficient pairs
into the complex frequency plane. The dots correspond
to the truncated coefficients shown in Figure 3.10.
The sampling interval is taken to be 0.005 sec.

The shaded area bounded by ($h_2 = 1 + h_1$) and the
sawtooth line is tedious to describe mathematically, so a simpler approach will be taken.   The
space within the h-plane triangle between the
two lines and

$$h_2 = 1 + h_1 \tag{3.151}$$

$$h_2 = (1 - \varepsilon) + h_1 \tag{3.152}$$

where

$$\varepsilon = 2^{-b} \tag{3.153}$$

in an area where instability will occur for some values of h_1 and h_2. Thus, (3.152) may be regarded as a boundary condition for examining instability.

Recalling that (3.37),

$$4h_2 + h_1^2 = 0 \tag{3.154}$$

is a boundary in the triangle between real and imaginary roots, the intersection between it and (3.152) is given by

$$h_1 = -2 + 2\sqrt{\epsilon}$$

and

$$h_2 = -1 - \epsilon + 2\sqrt{\epsilon} \tag{3.155}$$

In terms of the frequency plane (f, σ), (3.153) maps into the line

$$f = 0$$

and

$$\sigma = \frac{1}{2\pi\Delta t} \ln\left[\frac{h_1 \pm \sqrt{h_1^2 + 4h_2 + 4(1-\epsilon)}}{2}\right] \tag{3.156}$$

2. If $h_1^2 + 4h_2 < 0$, there are complex roots. The relationship between f, σ, h_1, and h_2 is given by

$$f + j\sigma = \frac{1}{j2\pi\Delta t}\left[\frac{1}{2}\ln(-h_2) + j\arctan\left(\sqrt{-1-\frac{4h_2}{h_1^2}}\right)\right] \tag{3.157}$$

so that

$$f = \frac{1}{2\pi\Delta t} \arctan\left(\sqrt{-1 - \frac{4h_2}{h_1^2}}\right) \qquad (3.158)$$

and

$$\sigma = - \frac{1}{4\pi\Delta t} \ln(-h_2) \qquad (3.159)$$

Thus, the boundary curves for the left half of the complex portion of the triangle take on the following parametric forms:

(a) For the line parallel to the bottom of the triangle and $\varepsilon/2$ units above it,

$$\sigma = - \frac{1}{4\pi\Delta t} \ln(1 - 2^{-b-1}) \qquad (3.160)$$

$$f = \frac{1}{2\pi\Delta t} \arctan\left[\sqrt{-1 - \frac{4(1-2^{-b-1})}{h_1^2}}\right] \qquad (3.161)$$

the latter being valid only with the area of the h plane producing complex poles.

(b) For the boundary delimiting the sawtooth condition, these become

$$\sigma = - \frac{1}{4\pi\Delta t} \ln\left[- (1-2^{-b}) -h_1\right] \qquad (3.162)$$

and

$$f = \frac{1}{2\pi\Delta t} \sqrt{- \frac{h_1-1}{h_1} - \frac{4(1-2^{-b})}{h_1^2}} \qquad (3.163)$$

There is a substantial difference between the last two results in the second case. For large enough b, (3.160) approximately becomes

$$\sigma = \frac{2^{-b-1}}{4\pi\Delta t} \qquad\qquad (3.164)$$

which is seen to be relatively small.

For the sawtooth border, there are two boundary intersections which illuminate the situation. When the line $[h_2 = (1-\varepsilon) + h_1]$ intersects the line $(h_2 = -1)$, resulting in the point $(h_1 = -2 + \varepsilon, h_2 = -1)$, then using (3.158) and (3.159), the equivalent point in the frequency plane is

$$\sigma = 0$$

and

$$f = \frac{1}{2\pi\Delta t} \arctan \left[\sqrt{-1 - \frac{4h_2}{h_1^2}} \right]$$

$$= \frac{1}{2\pi\Delta t} \arctan \left[\sqrt{-1 - \frac{-4}{(-2 + 2^{-b})^2}} \right]$$

$$= \frac{1}{2\pi\Delta t} \arctan \left[\sqrt{\frac{-(4 - 4 \cdot 2^{-b} - 2^{-2b}) - 4}{(-2 + 2^{-b})^2}} \right]$$

$$\approx \frac{1}{2\pi\Delta t} \arctan 2^{-b/2}$$

$$\approx \left(\frac{1}{2\pi\Delta t} \right) 2^{-b/2} \qquad\qquad (3.165)$$

Similarly, the intersection of $[h_2 = (1 - \varepsilon) + h_1]$ with $(h_1^2 = 4h_2)$ results in h_2 having the value $(-1 -\varepsilon + 2\sqrt{\varepsilon})$ and the following values for (f,σ):

$$f = 0$$

$$\sigma = -\frac{1}{4\pi\Delta t} \ln(-h_2)$$

$$= -\frac{1}{4\pi\Delta t} \ln(1 - 2\sqrt{\varepsilon} + \varepsilon)$$

$$\approx \frac{\sqrt{\varepsilon}}{2\pi\Delta t} = \left(\frac{1}{2\pi\Delta t}\right) 2^{-b/2} \tag{3.166}$$

This last expression follows from the assumption that

$$\sqrt{\varepsilon} < 1 \tag{3.167}$$

which also means that

$$\varepsilon < \sqrt{\varepsilon} < 1 \tag{3.168}$$

so that for small enough ε, ε is negligible compared to $\sqrt{\varepsilon}$.

Equations (3.165) and (3.166) and further manipulation reveal that the line $[h_2 = (1 - \varepsilon) + h_1]$ between its intersections with $(h_2 = -1)$ and $(h_1^2 = 4h_2)$, approximately maps into the first quadrant section of the circle

$$f^2 + \sigma^2 = \frac{2^{-b}}{(2\pi\Delta t)^2} \tag{3.169}$$

which has a radius B_b of

$$B_b = \frac{2^{-b/2}}{2\pi\Delta t} \tag{3.170}$$

Some of these are shown in Figure 3.12.

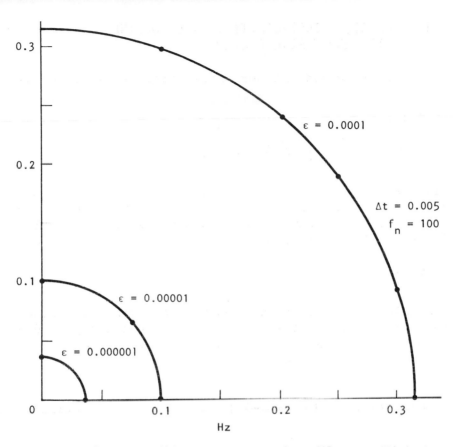

Fiq. 3.12 Instability areas for various filter coefficient
          lengths on the TCPC.

Thus, there are two important results for the TCPC:

1. Any second-order lowpass filter with its cutoff
   less than B_b may very well have instability
   problems due to its poles lying in the instability area.

2. As indicated by (3.164), the instability problems caused by approaching the line ($\sigma = 0$) are
   relatively   insignificant   as   compared   to
   approaching the points (0,0) or (1/2Δt,0).

3.12 NUMERICAL INSTABILITY IN THE COMBINED BUTTERWORTH SINE FILTER

The Butterworth filter whose transfer function is

$$|H(f)|^2 = \cfrac{1}{1 + \left[\cfrac{\sin(\lambda/2)}{\sin(\lambda_B/2)}\right]^{2K}} \tag{3.171}$$

will be investigated in detail. It is somewhat more amenable to analysis than other forms, and results obtained from it may be extended to more complicated filters. The filtering expression is

$$y_i = g_o x_i + h_1 y_{i-1} + \cdots + h_K y_{i-K} \tag{3.172}$$

The weights may be calculated from equations described earlier in the chapter. It will be necessary to develop closed-form expressions for both h_K and g_o. It is fairly easy to see that

$$h_K = (-1)^{K+1} \prod_{i=1}^{K} \exp(-\lambda_i) \tag{3.173}$$

where $\{\lambda_i\}$ are effectively the K damping ratios. The h_K terms may also be expressed as

$$h_K = (-1)^{K+1} \exp\left[-\sum_{i=1}^{K} \lambda_i\right] \tag{3.174}$$

from which it follows that

$$|h_K| \leq 1 \tag{3.175}$$

An exact expression for the $\{\lambda_i\}$ terms is

$$\lambda_i = 2 \ \arcsin \ \left\{ \left[\frac{1}{2} \left\{ - \cos^2\left(\frac{\lambda_B}{2}\right) + \left[\cos^4\left(\frac{\lambda_B}{2}\right) \right. \right. \right. \right.$$

$$\left. \left. \left. \left. + 4 \ \sin^2\left(\frac{\lambda_B}{2}\right) \sin^2 \ \theta_i \right]^{1/2} \right\}^{1/2} \right]^{1/2} \right\} \qquad (3.176)$$

where

$$\theta_i = \frac{\pi}{2K} \ (K + 1 - 2i) \qquad\qquad i = 1,\ldots,K \qquad (3.177)$$

This does not lend itself to easy evaluation.
    The expression for g_o is almost as involved, and will be shown to be

$$g_o = (2 \ \sin \ \pi\Delta tB)^K \ [\{(-1)^K\} \ h_K]^{\frac{1}{2}} \qquad (3.178)$$

This equation is demonstrated by making the following comparison: First, observe that the general expression for the absolute value squared of the transfer function has the form:

$$\left|H(f)\right|^2$$

$$= \left[g_o \Big/ \left(1 - h_1 z^{-1} - \ldots - h_K z^{-K}\right) \right] \left[g_o \Big/ \left(1 - h_1 z - \ldots - h_K z^K\right) \right]$$

$$= g_o^2 \Big/ \left[-h_K z^{-K} + (-h_{K-1} + h_K h_1) z^{-K+1} + \ldots \right.$$

$$\left. + (-h_{K-1} + h_K h_1) z^{K-1} - h_K z^K \right]$$

where as usual

$$z = \exp \ j2\pi\Delta tf \qquad\qquad (3.179)$$

Next, note that (3.171) may be expanded in the following manner:

$$|H(f)|^2$$

$$= \frac{1}{1 + \left[\dfrac{\sin(\lambda/2)}{\sin(\lambda_B/2)}\right]^{2K}}$$

$$= \frac{\sin^{2K}(\lambda_B/2)}{\sin^{2K}(\lambda_B/2) + \sin^{2K}(\lambda/2)}$$

$$= \frac{\sin^{2K}(\lambda_B/2)}{\sin^{2K}(\lambda_B/2) + \left[\dfrac{\exp(j\lambda/2) - \exp(-j\lambda/2)}{2j}\right]^{2K}}$$

$$= \frac{[2\sin(\lambda_B/2)]^{2K}}{[2\sin(\lambda_B/2)]^{2K} + (-1)^K \displaystyle\sum_{k=0}^{2K} \binom{2K}{k}(-1)^k \exp[-j\lambda(K-k)]}$$

$$= \frac{[2\sin(\lambda_B/2)]^{2K}}{[2\sin(\lambda_B/2)]^{2K} + (-1)^K \displaystyle\sum_{k=0}^{2K} \binom{2K}{k}(-1)^k z^{-K+k}}$$

$$(3.180)$$

After multiplying the numerator and denominator of this last expression by h_K and simplifying, the following expression may be obtained:

$$\frac{(-1)^{K+1} h_K \left[2 \sin(\lambda_B/2)\right]^{2K}}{-h_K \left[z^{-K} - Kz^{-K+1} + \ldots -Kz^{K-1} + z^K\right]} \qquad (3.181)$$

Comparing this with (3.179) shows that the numerators must be equal, so that

$$g_o^2 = (-1)^{K+1} h_K \left[2 \sin(\lambda_B/2)\right]^{2K} \qquad (3.182)$$

Finally, combining with this the expression for h_K given in (3.174),

$$g_o = \exp\left(-\frac{1}{2} \sum_{i=1}^{K} \lambda_i\right) (2 \sin \pi\Delta tB)^K \qquad (3.183)$$

as was to be shown.

For the lowpass filter, g_o is also given by

$$g_o = 1 - \sum_{k=0}^{K} h_K \qquad (3.184)$$

The reason for the g_o term being important enough to merit the above development comes from this last expression; the denominator of the complex transfer function has the form

$$1 - \sum_{k=0}^{K} h_k \exp(-2\pi\Delta tfk) \qquad (3.185)$$

If this expression is equal to zero for f equal to zero, then there is a pole at 0 Hz and the filter is unstable. This is exactly the same as saying that if g_o is (effectively) zero, then there is a pole at 0 Hz. On the TCPC, g_o will be zero if the summation is less than 2^{-b}. Hence, the critical value of frequency occurs when B is such that

$$\exp\left(-\frac{1}{2}\sum_{i=1}^{K}\lambda_i\right)(2\sin\pi\Delta tB)^K < 2^{-b} \qquad (3.186)$$

For small $(B\Delta t)$, the exponential is approximately one and the sine can be replaced with its argument, so that the threshold frequency B_b can be approximated by

$$(2\pi\Delta tB_b)^K \approx 2^{-b}$$

or

$$B_b = \frac{2^{-b/K}}{2\pi\Delta t} \qquad (3.187)$$

For $K = 2$, this is identical to the value obtained earlier for the second-order case.

The threshold frequency B_b is shown in Figure 3.13 plotted against b using (3.186) for several values of K. The graphs show the rapidity with which the combined form of the Butterworth lowpass filter becomes unstable as the number of filter weights increases.

In a comparison between the serial and the combined forms, the serial is clearly much less susceptible to instability, as its threshold is always computed with $K = 2$.

Equation (3.187) can be employed on actual machines with two additions to the model.

1. The number of binary digits m, is replaced with $(m_B-\beta_N)$, where m_B is the number of bits in the fixed-point word or the number of bits in the mantissa of the floating-point word on a given computer, and β_B is a corrective term; usually it is not possible to make use of all m_b bits; the corrective factor varies from machine to machine.

2. On an actual machine there will be underflow; in the case where fixed-point arithmetic is used, it may occur when numbers are multiplied; in floating-point arithmetic, it may occur both for

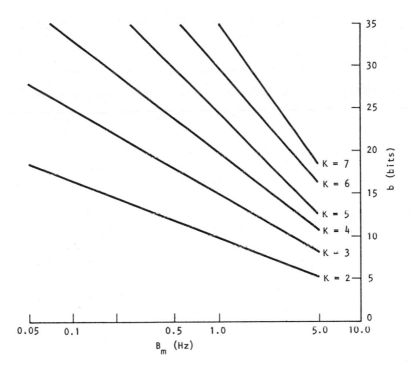

Fig. 3.13 Threshold frequencies for several values of K;
           Δt = 0.005.

addition   and   multiplication.   In either case,
this underflow may be   regarded as a noise term.
This   sort of   problem has   been investigated by
previously mentioned authors   and is outside the
scope of this work.

The fixed-point case   is the   easiest to   describe.
Suppose that the word on the fixed-point machine has t
bits as follows:

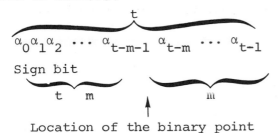

(3.188)

Location of the binary point

There are various methods for taking into account the position of the binary point when filtering is performed. Here it will be assumed that the maximum value for m is chosen that can be employed without danger of overflow, and that m does not vary during the calculations.

The question then becomes, what is the minimum number of bits which must be set aside for the integer portion of the computer word? A partial answer arises from the following. Many times the data being processed comes from an analog-to-digital converter having q bits. It will be assumed that $q \leq m-1$, if q includes a sign bit. Until it is converted to engineering units, these digitized quantities can be regarded as being on the range $\pm (1-2^{-m})$. The filtered numbers can be larger than one; for example, a square wave alternating between plus and minus the maximum input value may upon to nearly $4/\pi$ of that value after being acted upon by a lowpass filter which eliminates the higher harmonics.

Assume, however, that overshoot is not a problem. What remains is the question of how large m may be made as a function of the size of the weights. That is, the (t-m-1) bits used to express that part of the number greater than unity must be at least large enough to express the largest coefficient. It can be readily demonstrated that the coefficients of the lowpass filter are bounded as follows:

$$\left| h_k \right| < \binom{N}{k} \tag{3.189}$$

with equality being achieved for zero bandwidth. Define β_N by

$$2^{(\beta_{N-1})} < \binom{N}{\left[\frac{N}{2}\right]} \leq 2^{\beta_N} \tag{3.190}$$

Then the number of bits needed to express the maximum coefficient in magnitude is less than or equal to β_N. Near the threshold, (3.186) nearly becomes an equality, so that the threshold itself becomes

$$B_{t,N} \approx \frac{2^{-(t-1-\beta_N)/N}}{2\pi\Delta t} \qquad (3.191)$$

This approximately represents the lowest bound to which the threshold can be lowered on a t-bit machine. If the cascaded form is implemented, this becomes

$$B_{t,2} \approx \frac{2^{-(t-3)/2}}{2\pi\Delta L} \qquad (3.192)$$

Some values are shown in Table 3.1.

The floating-point case can have unusual characteristics. The floating-point word is made up of three parts; a sign, characteristic, and mantissa, usually in the following format:

$$t = 1 + P + Q \text{ bits}$$

$$\underbrace{\sigma}_{\substack{\uparrow \\ \text{Sign} \\ \text{bit}}} \qquad \underbrace{k_1 k_2 \ldots k_P}_{\substack{\text{Characteristic} \\ \text{bits}}} \qquad \underbrace{\mu_1 \mu_2 \ldots \mu_Q}_{\substack{\text{Mantissa} \\ \text{bits}}} \qquad (3.193)$$

On the IBM 704, 709, 7090, etc., t is 36, and the data word defined by (3.193) would be

$$(-1)^\sigma \left(\sum_{q=1}^{27} \mu_q 2^{-q} \right) 2^{\left[\sum_{p=1}^{8} k_p 2^{8-p} - 128 \right]} \qquad (3.194)$$

On the IBM 360 series there are 32 bits, and there is a subtle difference. The data word has the form

$$(-1)^\sigma \left(\sum_{q=1}^{24} \mu_2 2^{-q} \right) 16^{\left[\sum_{p=1}^{7} k_p 2^{7-p} - 64 \right]} \tag{3.195}$$

The fact that a power of 16 rather than a power of 2 is used as a scaling factor on the IBM 360 causes some difficulties.

The case for the IBM 704 format is a little easier to examine, so it will be discussed first. There are 27 bits used to express the number. As at least two of these must be used for the portion of the number greater than zero, the largest possible number of bits for the fractional portion is 25. For higher-order filters,

$$m \geq 27 - \beta_N \tag{3.196}$$

and the threshold becomes

$$B_{IBM\ 704,N} \approx \frac{2^{-(27-\beta_N)/N}}{2\pi\Delta t} \tag{3.197}$$

The IBM 360 cannot be simplified this easily. On the IBM 704, μ_1 is always a one bit, because floating-point numbers are always normalized, i.e., shifted so that the most significant digit is at position μ_1 and the characteristic is changed accordingly. In the IBM 360 floating-point word μ_1, μ_2 and μ_3 may be zero, as the normalizing is done in groups of four bits. This is consistent with using a power of 16 rather than 2. It thus turns out that p_N is a multiple of 4.

This difference shows up in Table 3.2, which has values of m_{max} tabulated for the two computers along with theoretical and actual thresholds.

The actual thresholds were found by filtering unit step functions and observing the output of the filter. If the output differed significantly from unity, the filter was assumed to be unstable. As m_{max} is generally greater than the actual number of bits required to represent the portion of the largest coefficient which is greater than one, the theoretical results are generally conservative.

Table 3.3 lists some fixed-point results obtained from a fixed-point arithmetic simulation program on an IBM 360 computer. Again, agreement is on the conservative side.

Table 3.1   Stability Threshold for Some
t-Bit Computers ΔT = 0.005

t(bits)	$B_{t,2}$(Hz)	$B_{t,6}$(Hz)
7	7.9	28
12	1.5	16
16	0.35	9.9
18	1.17	4.0

Table 3.2   Threshold Values (in Hz) for Several Values
of N for Two Computer Floating-Point Word Formats

N	$\binom{N}{[N/2]}$	IBM 704 format			IBM 360 format		
		M_{max}	$B_{m_{max}}$	B_{actual}	M_{max}	$B_{m_{max}}$	B_{actual}
2	2	25	0.0054	--	20	0.032	--
3	3	24	0.13	0.10	20	0.32	0.15
4	6	23	0.8	0.4	20	1.0	1.0
5	10	23	1.3	1.3	20	1.0	2.0
6	20	22	2.4	2.4	16-20	3.2-5.0*	3.8

*For N = 6 the threshold is difficult to calculate as $|b_3| \simeq 16$, thus causing a rapid change in the effective number of bits.

Table 3.3   Threshold Values (in Hz) for
Fixed-Point Arithmetic

N	$\binom{N}{[N/2]}$	Simulated m = 10		Simulated m = 12	
		B_{theory}	B_{actual}	B_{theory}	B_{actual}
2	2	1.0	0.9	0.5	0.4
3	3	3.12	3.2	2.0	1.8
4	6	5.66	5.7	3.97	3.8
5	10	7.95	8.2	6.10	6.1
6	20	10.0	10.4	8.95	9.1

Problems

3.1 What is the transfer function of the nonrecursive filter

$$y_i = \frac{1}{4} (x_{i-1} + x_i + x_{i+1})$$

What is the phase angle? Why?

3.2 A more general form of the filter in Problem 2.1 is

$$y_i = \frac{1}{2N} \sum_{n=-N}^{N} \binom{N}{n} x_{i - \frac{N}{2} + n}$$

where N is even. Show that its transfer function is

$$H(f) = \cos^N \pi \Delta t f$$

3.3 The recursive filter

$$y_i = \frac{\Delta t}{2} (x_i + x_{i-1}) + y_{i-1}$$

is often referred to as *rectangular integration*. Compute the filter transfer function and compare its plot with that of continuous integration.

3.4 Consider the simple filter

$$y_i = x_{i-m}$$

What is the phase angle of this transfer function?   Are there any problems in plotting it?

3.5   The transfer function

$$|H(f)|^2 = \cfrac{1}{1 + \left[\cfrac{\cot 2\pi\Delta tf - D}{E}\right]^{2K}}$$

where

$$D = \frac{\tan 2\pi\Delta tf_c \sec^2 2\pi\Delta}{\tan^2 2\pi\Delta tf_c - \tan^2 2\pi\Delta tB}$$

and

$$E = \frac{\tan 2\pi\Delta tB \sec^2 2\pi\Delta tf_c}{\tan^2 2\pi\Delta tf_c - \tan^2 2\pi\Delta tB}$$

was suggested by Otnes as a possible form for a
bandpass filter. Write a small program to evaluate the transfer function for one set of particular values of f_c, B, and Δt to see if the form is
correct, or analytically verify the shape by
showing that

$$|H(0)|^2 = 0$$

$$|H(f_c - B)|^2 = \frac{1}{2}$$

$$|H(f_m)|^2 = 1$$

$$|H(f_c + B)|^2 = \frac{1}{2}$$

$$|H(\tfrac{1}{2}\Delta t)|^2 = 0$$

where $2\pi\Delta tf_m$ = arccot D.

Applying Holtz's criterion, can this filter be implemented for all K? (Hint: Try K = 1 first.)

3.6 Derive (3.21).

3.7 Derive (3.23).

3.8 Fill in the missing steps between the first two lines of (3.26).

3.9 Derive (3.27).

3.10 Derive (3.31).

3.11 Relate highpass, bandpass, and band-reject filters to lowpass filters.

3.12 (a) Suppose that the sequence (1, 0, 0, 0, ... is input to the filter defined by (3.8). After how many intervals will the output be one-half of that of the first output value? (b) Supposing the same input as in part (a), after how many intervals will the sum of the output be one-half?

3.13 Derive (3.54).

3.14 Derive (3.56).

3.15 Derive (3.67).

3.16 In the sections on highpass filtering, two procedures for generating highpass filters are discussed. Show their equivalence.

3.17 Derive the expressions for the nonrecursive parts of the band-reject filters given in (3.139).

CHAPTER 4
FOURIER SERIES AND FOURIER TRANSFORM COMPUTATIONS

4.1 STANDARD FOURIER TRANSFORM AND FOURIER SERIES EVALUATION

Fourier series and, more generally, Fourier transforms arise repeatedly in the analysis of vibration, acoustic, seismic, economic, and many other time histories. In addition to simplifying theoretical analyses, certain data-analysis questions are answered via Fourier transforms. In the case of digitized data, the finite, discrete Fourier transform is most important. The classical Fourier series is, for all practical purposes, computationally identical to the Fourier transform, although they differ theoretically. Thus, attention may be directed toward the more general Fourier transform.

The continuous infinite-range transform as discussed in Chapter 1 is

$$X(f) = \int_{-\infty}^{\infty} x(t) e^{-j2\pi tf} \, dt$$

$$= \int_{-\infty}^{\infty} x(t) \cos 2\pi ft \, dt$$

$$- j \int_{-\infty}^{\infty} x(t) \sin 2\pi tf \, dt \qquad -\infty < f < \infty \qquad (4.1)$$

Attention shall be subsequently concentrated on the finite transform computed from discrete data:

$$Z(f) = \Delta t \sum_{i=0}^{N-1} z(i) e^{-j2\pi fi\Delta t} \qquad -\infty < f < \infty \qquad (4.2)$$

137

This differs from (4.1) in that the complex variable z
rather than the real variable x is used. The sequence
$\{z(i),\ i = 0,\ldots,N - 1\}$ is allowed to be a sequence of
complex variables.   For a real sequence $\{x_i,\ i = 0,$
$\ldots,N - 1\}$, the cosine and sine transforms will usually be evaluated separately:

$$C_x(f) = \Delta t \sum_{i=0}^{N-1} x_i \cos 2\pi f i \Delta t \qquad (4.3)$$

$$Q_x(f) = \Delta t \sum_{i=0}^{N-1} x_i \sin 2\pi f i \Delta t \qquad (4.4)$$

If no attention whatsoever is paid to computational
aspects, (4.2) is evaluated directly.   That is, a frequency value f is selected, and the summations are
evaluated with the necessary sines and cosines being
obtained.   The   basic   computational   loop is   the
following:

1. Evaluate $i \cdot \Delta t \cdot f \cdot 2\pi = \theta$.

2. Compute $\cos \theta$, $\sin \theta$.

3. Compute $x_i \cos \theta$, $x_i \sin \theta$.

4. Accumulate both sums.

5. Test for the $(N - 1)$th data point.

6. Increment i; return to step 1.

As an   illustration of computer time requirements in
the past, this basic loop would require about 542 µsec
on a typical 36 bit computer.   Thus, for $N = 10^3 =$
1000 data points, each value of the transform requires
310,000 µsec = 310 msec. For $N = 10^4$ = 10,000 data
points, the time is 3,100,000 µsec = 3.1 sec. If all
possible 5000 frequency points were evaluated, the
computing time would be over 4 hr.   The usual selection of frequency points at which to evaluate the Fourier transform or series is

$$f_k = k\Delta f = \frac{k}{T} = \frac{k}{N\Delta t} \qquad k = 0,\ldots,N/2 \quad (4.5)$$

The cosine transform then becomes

$$X_k = X(k\Delta f) = \sum_{i=0}^{N-1} x_i \cos 2\pi \frac{ik}{N} \qquad k = 0,1,\ldots,N/2$$

(4.6)

where Δt has been omitted for simplification. In order to reduce computational time, the sines and cosines can be evaluated recursively:

$$\begin{bmatrix} \cos \frac{2\pi k}{N}(i+1) \\ \sin \frac{2\pi k}{N}(i+1) \end{bmatrix} = \begin{bmatrix} \cos \frac{2\pi k}{N} & -\sin \frac{2\pi k}{N} \\ \sin \frac{2\pi k}{N} & \cos \frac{2\pi k}{N} \end{bmatrix} \begin{bmatrix} \cos \frac{2\pi k}{N}i \\ \sin \frac{2\pi k}{N}i \end{bmatrix}$$

$$i = 0,1,\ldots,N/2 \quad (4.7)$$

This method of computing sines and cosines will almost invariably be faster than utilizing "library" sine/cosine subroutines. Depending on the word length of the computer involved, this recursion must be re-initiated every few hundred iterations in order to avoid error buildup.

To illustrate, let $\Delta\theta = 2\pi/N$, and suppose $k = 1$ in (4.7) and we can compute $\cos \Delta\theta$ and $\sin \Delta\theta$ accurate to $n - 1$ bits so that an error $\varepsilon = \pm 1/2^n$ can appear in the result. Then we have

$$x = \cos \Delta\theta \pm 2^{-n}$$

$$y = \sin \Delta\theta \pm 2^{-n}$$

For $i = 1$,

$$\cos \frac{2\pi}{N}2 = x^2 - y^2 = \cos^2 \Delta\theta \pm 2^{-(n-1)} \cos \Delta\theta + 2^{-2n}$$

where the square sine terms are neglected. The quantity $\Delta\theta$ will be small, and therefore cos $\Delta\theta$ is close to unity. Thus the error in cos $(2\pi2/N)$ will be close to $\pm2^{-(n-1)}$. In the next iteration $\cos^2 \Delta\theta$ will appear multiplying the error; in subsequent iterations higher powers come into play. Thus, an additional error increment of approximately $\varepsilon = 2^{-n}$ will be added into the sine and cosine values for each iteration. Suppose 15-bit accuracy can be tolerated and that computations are being performed in floating-point on a 36-bit machine (1-bit for sign, 10-bits for exponent, 25-bits for magnitude). Assume that sin $\Delta\theta$ and cos $\Delta\theta$ have an error $\varepsilon = \pm 2^{-25}$. After $2^9 = 512$ iterations, the error is

$$\varepsilon' = \pm 2^{-25} 2^9 = \pm 2^{-16}$$

or the error has propagated to the sixteenth bit position and one has 15 bits of accuracy. One must restart the iteration at this point.

The computing procedure utilized in the recursion is:

1. Compute $\cos[2\pi(i + 1)/N]$ and $\sin[2\pi(i + 1)/N]$ recursively.

2. Compute $x_i \cos \theta$, $x_i \sin \theta$.

3. Accumulate both sums.

4. Test for the (N - 1)th data point.

5. Return to step 1.

6. Repeat steps 1 through 5 N/2 times.

In a carefully constructed machine language program on the 36-bit computer considered, the above algorithm takes about 71 machine cycles, or about 142 μsec. If 1000 data points are involved, then 14,200 μsec = 14.2 msec are necessary for each frequency point. If 500 frequency points are evaluated, the total time is

10^3 x 7100 μsec = 7.1 sec.   If 10,000 points are involved, then the time is   142,000 μsec = 142 msec for
each point and 710 sec for the total job. Hence, about
12 minutes is required in this nominal   case for just
basic computations.   Time requirements for data input,
printing, and plotting of results are additional.   The
computational time grows as N^2, and the time requirements can quickly become excessive.   Record lengths of
5 to 10,000 points are not unusual in time series data
analysis, hence the motivation for efficient computational techniques.

   The recursive formula   for sines and cosines can be
cast in the form of a complex exponential.   This leads
to a "nested" complex polynomial approach for a Fourier coefficient computation.   Although not as efficient in general   as the fast Fourier transform algorithms to be discussed,   it can be efficient if record
lengths are long and only a few Fourier coefficients
are desired:

$$e^{-j(i+1)\Delta\theta} = e^{-ji\Delta\theta} e^{-j\Delta\theta} \tag{4.8}$$

or, in terms of real and imaginary parts,

$$\cos(i+1)\Delta\theta - j \sin(i+1)\Delta\theta = (\cos i\Delta\theta - j \sin i\Delta\theta)$$

$$\times (\cos \Delta\theta - j \sin \Delta\theta) \tag{4.9}$$

   The complex form of the discrete Fourier transform
is

$$Z_k = \Delta t \sum_{i=0}^{N-1} z_i \, e^{-j \frac{2\pi ik}{N}} \tag{4.10}$$

This equation can be written as a polynomial by using
the notation

$$W = e^{-j\frac{2\pi}{N}} \tag{4.11}$$

and

$$W_k = e^{-j\frac{2\pi k}{N}}$$

(4.12)

Then (4.10) becomes (if the Δt is omitted)

$$Z_k = \sum_{i=0}^{N-1} z_i W_k^i$$

(4.13)

The classical near-minimum computational effort method of evaluating a polynomial is the "nesting" method, which is

$$Z_k = z_0 + \left\{ z_1 + \ldots + \left[z_{N-3} + \left(z_{N-2} \right. \right. \right.$$

$$\left. \left. \left. + z_{N-1} W_k \right) W_k \right] \underbrace{W_k \ldots \right\} W_k}_{\text{N-1 times}}$$

(4.14)

It is convenient to rearrange this, which allows work-ing with the data in the natural rather than the re-verse sequence. The desired reordering gives

$$Z_k = \left[z_{N-1} + \left(z_{N-2} + \left\{ \ldots + \left[z_2 + \left(z_1 \right. \right. \right. \right. \right.$$

$$\left. \left. \left. \left. + z_0 W_k^{-1} \right) W_k^{-1} \right] \underbrace{W_k^{-1} \ldots \right\} W_k^{-1} \right) \right] W_k^{N-1}}_{\text{N-1 times}}$$

(4.15)

The actual computational procedure involves partial sums, thus:

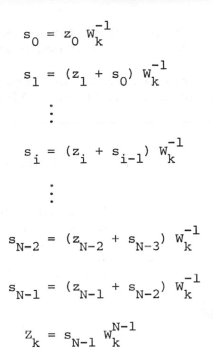

$$s_0 = z_0 \, W_k^{-1}$$

$$s_1 = (z_1 + s_0) \, W_k^{-1}$$

$$\vdots$$

$$s_i = (z_i + s_{i-1}) \, W_k^{-1}$$

$$\vdots$$

$$s_{N-2} = (z_{N-2} + s_{N-3}) \, W_k^{-1}$$

$$s_{N-1} = (z_{N-1} + s_{N-2}) \, W_k^{-1}$$

$$Z_k = s_{N-1} \, W_k^{N-1} \tag{4.16}$$

The computational time per each value of Z_k will be about the same as the method just described involving recursive sine cosine generation. An additional advantage is the simplicity of coding, especially FORTRAN, when complex arithmetic is available.

4.2 FAST FOURIER TRANSFORMS

In 1965, algorithms that reduce Fourier transform computational times by a startling degree came to light--the first widely noticed publication of a high-speed algorithm, the so-called fast Fourier transform (FFT), occurred (Cooley and Tukey, 1965). The crux of the procedure has been traced back to at least 1903 (Brigham and Morrow, 1967). With sufficient generalization, the FFT algorithms may be explained in a multitude of ways. The analytical explanations of Bergland (1967) and Gentleman and Sande (1966) will be heavily called upon here for expository purposes. In addition, a geometrical algebraic

method will be discussed in an attempt to further motivate the reader's intuition for understanding why
the FFT is, in fact, fast.

The algorithms are most simply designed for complex
sequences. Thus, the formula analyzed is the following:

$$z_k = \sum_{i=0}^{N-1} z_i \exp\left[-j \frac{2\pi ik}{N}\right] \quad k = 0,1,\ldots,N-1 \quad (4.17)$$

The factor Δt is omitted in the sequel to simplify notation. It serves as a scale factor and only become
important when the plotting and printing of results
are involved. Some further simplification in notation
is desirable.   The following notation for the complex
exponential is introduced as in (4.11):

$$W = \exp\left[-j \frac{2\pi}{N}\right] \quad\quad\quad\quad (4.18)$$

Then the complex exponentials in (4.18) become

$$W^{ik} = \exp\left[-j \frac{2\pi ik}{N}\right] \quad\quad\quad (4.19)$$

Equation (4.17) is then rewritten to become

$$z_k = \sum_{i=0}^{N-1} z_i W^{ik} \quad\quad\quad k = 0,1,\ldots,N-1 \quad (4.20)$$

The FFT algorithms are useful when the number of
data points is a nonprime (composite) integer.   Consider the simplest case, N = A x B. Equation (4.20)
can be rewritten as

$$z_{(c+dA)} = \sum_{b=0}^{B-1} \sum_{a=0}^{A-1} z_{(b+aB)} W^{(b+aB)(c+dA)} \quad\quad (4.21)$$

where

$i = b + aB$ time index

$k = c + dA$ frequency index

$a, c = 0,1,...,A - 1; b, d = 0,1,...,B - 1$

The exponents of W in (4.21) can be expanded to give

$$W^{(b+aB)(c+dA)} = W^{bc} W^{bdA} W^{acB} W^{adAB}$$

$$= W^{bc} W^{bdA} W^{acB} \qquad (4.22)$$

This is true since a and d are integers and the complex exponential W raised to any integral power is unity. A directly related fact used later is that

$$\exp\left[-j \frac{2\pi}{2}\right] = -1 \qquad (4.23)$$

This particular formula is often termed one of the most beautiful in mathematics since it relates the numbers, e, $j = \sqrt{-1}$, π, and 1. Equation (4.21) can now be rearranged, since portions of the complex exponential can be factored out from the innermost sum. Thus,

$$Z_{(c+dA)} = \sum_{b=0}^{B-1} \sum_{a=0}^{A-1} z_{(b+aB)} W^{bc} W^{bdA} W^{acB}$$

$$= \sum_{b=0}^{B-1} W^{bdA} \sum_{a=0}^{A-1} z_{(b+aB)} W^{acB} W^{bc}$$

$$c = 0,1,...,A = 1; d = 0,1,...,B - 1 \qquad (4.24)$$

This factoring of exponentials from the inner sum is tantamount to eliminating multiplication operations by factoring out equal coefficients in a linear combination. For example, it requires one less multiplication to compute

$$21 = (2 + 5)\ 3$$

rather than

$$21 = (2 \cdot 3) + (5 \cdot 3)$$

This is precisely what is being accomplished by factoring W^{bdA} from the inner sum.

Now, if it is assumed that the complex exponentials (sines and cosines) have been computed (and stored) in advance, then the number of complex multiply-add operations necessary to evaluate the double summation of (4.24) is $AB(A + B)$ rather than $(AB)(AB)$, as it would be if (4.20) were evaluated directly.

To evaluate this number of operations, first note that

$$W^{bdA} = \exp\left[-j\ \frac{2\pi}{B}\ bd\right] \quad b,d = 0,1,\ldots,B - 1$$

$$W^{acB} = \exp\left[-j\ \frac{2\pi}{A}\ ac\right] \quad a,c = 0,1,\ldots,A - 1 \qquad (4.25)$$

These are precisely the exponentials needed for a B-point and an A-point discrete transform, respectively. Equation (4.24) can be recognized as a sequence of two Fourier transforms applied to data sequences of length A and B, respectively. Redefine the original data as

$$a = 0,1,\ldots,A - 1$$

$$u_b(a) = z_{(b+aB)} \qquad\qquad (4.26)$$

$$b = 0,1,\ldots,B - 1$$

In terms of a digital computer core storage, the data have been relabeled as B sequences, each of length A. Figure 4.1 illustrates this for $A = 2$, $B = 5$, $N = 10$, where the data are being thought of as five sequences, each two points long.

Now, the B Fourier transforms of the $u_b(a)$ (each of length A) are computed:

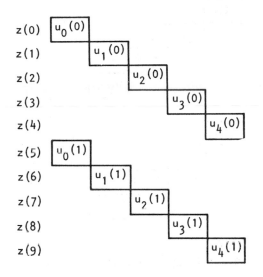

Fig. 4.1 Storage arrangement for ten points arranged as five sets of two points each.

$$U_b(c) = \sum_{a=0}^{A-1} u_b(a)\ W^{acB} \qquad \begin{matrix} b = 0,1,\dots,B-1 \\[6pt] \\[6pt] c = 0,1,\dots,A-1 \end{matrix} \qquad (4.27)$$

For the example $A = 2$, $B = 5$, the results are stored as shown in Figure 4.2. Now each value $U_b(c)$ must be multiplied by the quantity W^{bc}, termed a "twiddle factor" by Gentleman and Sande (1966). Multiplication by a complex exponential amounts to a rotation in the complex plane. This amounts to accounting for a time shift in the time domain. For example, the values $z(1)$ and $z(6)$ are transformed as if they had indices 0 and 5. Likewise, for $z(2)$ and $z(7)$, etc. This time shift by $(1/N)T$ is adjusted for with the twiddle factor. Define the new quantities

$$v_c(b) = U_b(c)W^{bc} \qquad\qquad (4.28)$$

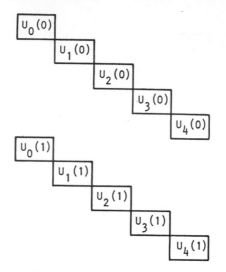

Fig. 4.2 Storage after the first operation.

Now, Fourier transforms (A of them) of length B are computed, namely

$$V_c(d) = \sum_{b=0}^{B-1} v_c(b)\, w^{bdA} \qquad \begin{array}{l} d = 0,1,\ldots,B-1 \\[4pt] c = 0,1,\ldots,A-1 \end{array} \qquad (4.29)$$

where

$$z_{(c+dA)} = V_c(d)$$

Hence, in two stages, the Fourier transform of the entire sequence has been computed. The final values are stored as shown in Figure 4.3. It should be noted that the arrangement of the Fourier-transformed values is not the same as that of the original data. To illustrate, consider

$$z_1 = z_{(1+0\cdot5)} = V_1(0)$$

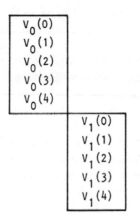

Fig. 4.3 Final storage arrangement where data is now
viewed as two sets of five points each.

which is not stored in the second memory position but
rather is the sixth, as illustrated in Figure 4.3.
This fact requires that the results be shuffled in
core storage to obtain the meaningful arrangement.
This will be illustrated in more detail in the discussion of the FFT for cases when $N = 2^P$.

The number of multiply-add operations is now noted
to be

$$B \cdot A \cdot A$$

operations for the B transforms of length A, plus

$$A \cdot B \cdot B$$

for the A transforms of length B. The total number of
multiply-add operations then is

$$B \cdot A \cdot A + A \cdot B \cdot B = AB(A + B)$$

In practice, programming the algorithm for N as a
power of two has special advantages. In this case, the
intermediate transforms are two elements, and the ex-

ponentials have values of +1 or -1. This allows complex multiplication operations to be avoided and saves
additional time. For $N = 4^p$, similar savings can sometimes be accomplished, since the values of the four
exponentials are +1, +j, -1, -j, and operations involving additions and subtractions of real and imaginary parts can be implemented. The power of two is the
smallest prime factor, however, and sequences can
usually be augmented with zero-value data points to
obtain an appropriate length with no insurmountable
problems.   In some applications, it is meaningful to
subdivide the record into shorter-length (possibly
overlapping) records and obtain averages of several
transforms.   Attention will now be directed to algorithms for sequences of length $N = 2^p$.

Two basic versions of the algorithm are fairly
easily derived, and the approach of Bergland (1967) is
followed.   First, write the indices i and k in the
binary notation

$$i = i_{p-1}\, 2^{p-1} + i_{p-2} 2^{p-2} + \ldots + i_0 = (i_{p-1}, \ldots, i_0)$$

$$k = k_{p-1}\, 2^{p-1} + k_{p-2} 2^{p-2} + \ldots + k_0 = (k_{p-1}, \ldots, k_0)$$

$$(4.30)$$

where each component i_v and k_v takes on only the
values 0 or 1. To simplify the relatively complicated
appearance of the indices, consider the case $N = 2^3 =$
8. Then, for example, the number 5 is

$$i = 5_{10} = 1 \cdot 2^2 + 0 \cdot 2 + 1 \cdot 2^0 = 101_2 = (1,0,1)$$

where the subscript indicates the number base.   Thus
the components i_v and k_v are the binary digits arranged from the most significant bit to the least significant bit.   The equation for the Fourier transform
(4.20) is now written below with the indices raised

and enclosed in parentheses due to the difficulty in typing such complicated subscripts:

$$Z(k_{p-1}, k_{p-2}, \ldots, k_0) = Z(k_{p-1}2^{p-1} + k_{p-2}2^{p-2} + \ldots$$

$$+ k_0)$$

$$= \sum_{i_0=0}^{1} \sum_{i_1=0}^{1} \cdots \sum_{i_{p-1}=0}^{1} z(i_{p-1}2^{p-1} + i_{p-2}2^{p-2} + \ldots$$

$$+ i_0)W^{ik}$$

$$= \sum_{i_0=0}^{1} \sum_{i_1=0}^{1} \cdots \sum_{i_{p-1}=0}^{1} z(i_{p-1}, i_{p-2}, \ldots, i_0)W^{ik}$$

$$(4.31)$$

where each successive summation consists of two terms. Now, as was done in (4.22) for two factors, the complex exponential can be expanded. When the exponent of W is expanded, it is seen that integral powers of exp-j2π may be factored out and thus disappear, since any integral power of exp-j2π is unity. For example, consider the product of only the $(k_{\ell-1})$-bit position in the k index with the entire i index:

$$W^{k_{\ell-1}2^{\ell-1}(i_{p-1}2^{p-1} + \ldots + i_0)}$$

$$= W^{k_{\ell-1}2^{\ell-1}(i_{p-1}2^{p-1} + \ldots + i_{p-\ell+1}2^{p-\ell+1})}$$

$$\times W^{k_{\ell-1}2^{\ell-1}(i_{p-\ell}2^{p-\ell} + \ldots + i_0)}$$

$$= W^{k_{\ell-1}2^{\ell-1}(i_{p-\ell}2^{p-\ell} + \ldots + i_0)} \qquad (4.32)$$

In the above equation, coefficients of bit positions of order $i_{p-\ell+1}$ or greater combine with the factor $2^{\ell-1}$. Since $2^{p-\ell+1} \cdot 2^{\ell-1} = 2^p = N$, the factor $N = 2^p$ in $\exp(-j2\pi/N)$ is cancelled, leaving integral powers of $\exp(-j2\pi)$. Hence, in each successive summation in (4.32), the dependence on the bit positions greater than $(p - \ell + 1)$ is eliminated. This allows successive portions of the complex exponential to be factored out of the inner summations as constants.

Recursive equations that have the ultimate effect of reducing the amount of arithmetic may now be directly obtained. Consider the innermost sum first, that is, for $\ell = 1$. Then (4.31) becomes

$$Z(k_{p-1}, \ldots, k_0)$$

$$= \sum_{i_0=0}^{1} \sum_{i_1=0}^{1} \cdots \sum_{i_{p-2}=0}^{1} \left[\sum_{i_{p-1}=0}^{1} z(i_{p-1}, \ldots, i_0) \right.$$

$$\left. \times W^{k_0 i_{p-1} 2^{p-1}} \right] W^{k(i_{p-2} 2^{p-2} + \ldots + i_0)} \tag{4.33}$$

The innermost sum is performed over the two values 0 amd 1 of the bit i_{p-1}. Thus, the bracketed quantity in (4.33) is a function of $i_{p-2}, i_{p-3}, \ldots, i_0$ and k_0 and may be written as

$$A_1(k_0, i_{p-2}, i_{p-3}, \ldots, i_0)$$

$$= \sum_{i_{p-1}=0}^{1} z(i_{p-1}, \ldots, i_0) W^{k_0 i_{p-1} 2^{p-1}} \tag{4.34}$$

The second stage in the recursion is

$$A_2(k_0,k_1,i_{p-3},\ldots,i_0)$$

$$= \sum_{i_{p-2}=0}^{1} A_1(k_0,i_{p-2},i_{p-3},\ldots,i_0) \; W^{(k_1 2+k_0)i_{p-2}2^{p-2}}$$

$$(4.35)$$

In general, for the ℓth stage is

$$A_\ell(k_0,k_1,\ldots,k_{\ell-1},i_{p-\ell-1},\ldots,i_0)$$

$$= \sum_{i_{p-\ell}=0}^{1} A_{\ell-1}(k_0,k_1,\ldots,k_{\ell-2},i_{p-\ell},\ldots,i_0)$$

$$\times \; W^{(k_{\ell-1}2^{\ell-1} + \ldots + k_0)i_{p-\ell}2^{p-\ell}} \qquad (4.36)$$

This is termed the "Cooley-Tukey" fast Fourier transform algorithm. Some observations are pertinent at this point. Note that a portion of the index in $A_{\ell-1}$, the sequence $k_0,k_1,\ldots,k_{\ell-1}$ appears in a reversed-bit form, namely $k_{\ell-1}2^{\ell-1} +\ldots + k_0$ in the exponent of W. Hence, when the index controlling an outer loop in a program is set to $k_0\,2^{p-1} + k_1\,2^{p-2} + \ldots + k_{\ell-1}\,2^{p-\ell}$ the argument required for W involves instead $(k_{\ell-1}2^{\ell-1} + k_{\ell-2}\,2^{\ell-2} + \ldots + k_0)\,2^{p-\ell}$. Thus, the necessary argument must be obtained by a bit-reversing procedure.

Suppose that instead of transforming $z(i)$, the sequence is transformed in reversed-bit address order. Then the first stage of the recursion becomes

$$C_1(i_{p-1},i_{p-2},\ldots,i_1,k_0)$$

$$= \sum_{i_0=0}^{1} z(i_0,\ldots,i_{p-1})W^{k_0 i_0 2^{p-1}} \qquad (4.37)$$

or

$$C_1(i_{p-1}, i_{p-2}, \ldots, i_1, k_0)$$

$$= \sum_{i_0=0}^{1} u(i_{p-1}, \ldots, i_0) \; W^{k_0 i_0 2^{p-1}}$$

where $u(i)$ is the rearranged $z(i)$:

$$u(i_{p-1}, \ldots, i_0) = z(i_0, \ldots, i_{p-1})$$

The second stage is

$$C_2(i_{p-1}, \ldots, i_2, k_1, k_0)$$

$$= \sum_{i_1=0}^{1} C_1(i_{p-1}, i_{p-2}, \ldots, i_1, k_0) \; W^{(k_1 2 + k_0) i_1 2^{p-2}}$$

$$(4.38)$$

and the ℓth stage is

$$C_\ell(i_{p-1}, \ldots, i_\ell, k_{\ell-1}, \ldots, k_0)$$

$$= \sum_{i_{\ell-1}=0}^{1} C_{\ell-1}(i_{p-1}, \ldots, i_{\ell-1}, k_{\ell-2}, \ldots, k_0)$$

$$\times W^{(k_{\ell-1} 2^{\ell-1} + \ldots + k_0) i_{\ell-1} 2^{p-\ell}}$$

$$(4.39)$$

The index bits of $z(i)$ have been reversed, but the exponent bits have also been reversed to ensure that the proper argument is used for the complex exponential. Finally, note that at the pth stage

$$Z(k_{p-1}, \ldots, k_0) = C_p(k_{p-1}, \ldots, k_0)$$

so that no bit reversal is required at the conclusion of the iterations. Further note that the necessary argument for the complex exponential is obtained in natural sequence rather than in a bit-reversed form. Thus, the data are operated on in a scrambled form rather than scrambling the results.

Before we consider some of the additional practical aspects of implementing (4.36) or (4.39) in a computer program, let us develop another version of the FFT.

As noted in Bergland (1967) and Gentleman and Sande (1966), an alternate form of the algorithm (the Sande-Tukey version) can be obtained if the roles of the indices are interchanged in (4.32). That is, instead of considering the product of the $k_{\ell-1}$ bit position of the k index with entire i index, consider the product of the $i_{\ell-1}$ bit position in the i index with the entire k index. The recursion is

$$\hat{A}_\ell (k_0, k_1, \ldots, k_{\ell-1}, i_{p-\ell-1}, \ldots, i_0)$$

$$= \sum_{i_{p-\ell}=0}^{1} \hat{A}_{\ell-1} (k_0, k_1, \ldots, k_{\ell-2}, i_{p-\ell}, \ldots, i_0)$$

$$\times W^{k_{\ell-1} 2^{\ell-1} (i_{p-\ell} 2^{p-\ell} + \ldots + i_0)} \qquad (4.40)$$

This recursion corresponds to the two-factor derivation appearing earlier in this section. For both cases, one begins with the original data,

$$A_0 (i_{p-1}, i_{p-2}, \ldots, i_0) = \hat{A}_0 (i_{p-1}, i_{p-2}, \ldots, i_0)$$

$$= z(i_{p-1}, i_{p-2}, \ldots, i_0) \qquad (4.41)$$

and ends   at the pth application of the recursion with
the Fourier coefficients,

$$Z(k_{p-1}, k_{p-2}, \ldots, k_0) = A_p(k_0, k_1, \ldots, k_{p-1})$$

$$= \hat{A}_p(k_0, k_1, \ldots, k_{p-1}) \qquad (4.42)$$

Notice that the final result has the binary components
of its index reversed. Thus, if data have been stored
in the memory location with the binary address corresponding to the index, a bit reversal must be performed to obtain the correct core memory address and
to rearrange the results in their natural sequence.
    Both recursions may be written in the form of a
Fourier transform multiplied by a twiddle factor. It
is simplest for the Sande-Tukey version, since the
portion involving the index $i_{p-\ell}$ appears in only one
segment of the index:

$$\hat{A}_\ell(k_0, k_1, \ldots, k_{\ell-1}, i_{p-\ell-1}, \ldots, i_0)$$

$$= W^{(i_{p-\ell-1}2^{p-\ell-1} + \ldots + i_0)k_{\ell-1}2^{\ell-1}}$$

$$\times \sum_{i_{p-\ell}=0}^{1} \hat{A}_{\ell-1}(k_0, k_1, \ldots, k_{\ell-2}, i_{p-\ell}, \ldots, i_0)$$

$$\times W^{k_{\ell-1}i_{p-\ell}2^{p-1}} \qquad (4.43)$$

The time variable is $i_{p-\ell}$ and the frequency variable
is $k_{\ell-1}$ for the two-term Fourier transform being computed at this stage of the recursion.
    The Cooley-Tukey version requires a modification of
the recursion. Let the first stage be

$$B_1(k_0, i_{p-2}, \ldots, i_0) = W^{k_0 i_{p-2} 2^{p-2}}$$

$$\times \sum_{i_{p-1}=0}^{1} A(i_{p-1}, \ldots, i_0) W^{k_0 i_{p-1} 2^{p-1}} \qquad (4.44)$$

The second stage is

$$B_2(k_0, k_1, i_{p-3}, \ldots, i_0)$$

$$= W^{(k_1 2 + k_0) i_{p-3} 2^{p-3}}$$

$$\times \sum_{i_{p-2}=0}^{1} B_1(k_0, i_{p-2}, \ldots, i_0) W^{i_{p-2} k_1 2^{p-1}} \qquad (4.45)$$

The ℓth stage of the recursion is

$$B_\ell(k_0, k_1, \ldots, k_{\ell-1}, i_{p-\ell-1}, \ldots, i_0)$$

$$= W^{(k_{\ell-1} 2^{\ell-1} + \ldots + k_0) i_{p-\ell-1} 2^{p-\ell-1}}$$

$$\times \sum_{i_{p-\ell}=0}^{1} B_{\ell-1}(k_0, k_1, \ldots, k_{\ell-2}, i_{p-\ell}, \ldots, i_0)$$

$$\times W^{i_{p-\ell} k_{\ell-1} 2^{p-1}} \qquad (4.46)$$

The quantity B_ℓ is related to A_ℓ in the other form of the recursion by

$$B_\ell(k_0, k_1, \ldots, k_{\ell-1}, i_{p-\ell-1}, \ldots, i_0)$$

$$= A_\ell(k_0, k_1, \ldots, k_{\ell-1}, i_{p-\ell-1}, \ldots, i_0)$$

$$\times W^{(k_{\ell-1}2^{\ell-1} + \ldots + k_0)i_{p-\ell-1}2^{p-\ell-1}} \qquad (4.47)$$

Substituting (4.47) in (4.46), it follows that

$$A_\ell(k_0, k_1, \ldots, k_{\ell-1}, i_{p-\ell-1}, \ldots, i_0)$$

$$\times W^{(k_{\ell-1}2^{\ell-1} + \ldots + k_0)i_{p-\ell-1}2^{p-\ell-1}}$$

$$= W^{(k_{\ell-1}2^{\ell-1} + \ldots + k_0)i_{p-\ell-1}2^{p-\ell-1}}$$

$$\times \sum_{i_{p-\ell}=0}^{1} A_{\ell-1}(k_0, k_1, \ldots, k_{\ell-2}, i_{p-\ell}, \ldots, i_0)$$

$$\times W^{(k_{\ell-2}2^{\ell-2} + \ldots + k_0)i_{p-\ell}2^{p-\ell}} W^{i_{p-\ell}k_{\ell-1}2^{p-1}}$$

$$= W^{(k_{\ell-1}2^{\ell-1} + \ldots + k_0)i_{p-\ell-1}2^{p-\ell-1}}$$

$$\times \sum_{i_{p-\ell}=0}^{1} A_{\ell-1}(k_0, k_1, \ldots, k_{\ell-2}, i_{p-\ell}, \ldots, i_0)$$

$$\times W^{(k_{\ell-1}2^{\ell-1} + k_{\ell-2}2^{\ell-2} + \ldots + k_0)i_{p-\ell}2^{p-\ell}} \qquad (4.48)$$

Thus, the recursions are equivalent except at the final stage where the twiddle factor is omitted.

It was noted on page 147 that the twiddle factor multiplication is a frequency rotation to account for a time shift. This can be clarified by viewing the data points as laid out on a unit circle in the complex plane. This is illustrated in Figure 4.4 for $N = 2^4 - 16$ data points. Note, for example, when $k = 1$ the data points for that Fourier coefficient must be multiplied by the complex exponential values at the corresponding points on the unit complex circle.

In equation form,

$$Z(1) = \sum_{i=0}^{15} z(i) \ \exp\left(-j\frac{2\pi}{16} \ i\right)$$

Note that this can be arranged as

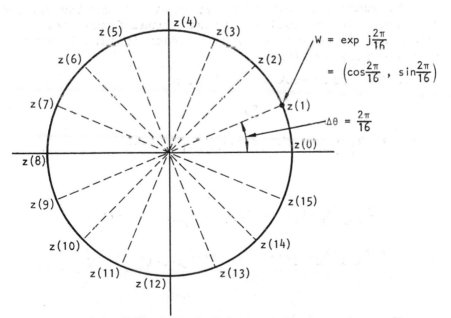

Fig. 4.4 Illustration of data points arranged on unit circle in complex plane.

$$Z(1) = [z(0) + z(8)] + [z(1) - z(9)]\exp\left(-j\frac{2\pi}{16}\right)$$

$$+ [z(2) - z(10)]\exp\left(-j\frac{2\pi}{16}\right)2 + [z(3) - z(11)]$$

$$\exp\left(-j\frac{2\pi}{16} 3\right) + \ldots$$

$$+ [z(7) - z(15)]\exp\left(-j\frac{2\pi}{16} 7\right) \qquad (4.49)$$

Now, (4.49) can be viewed as eight two-point transforms involving coefficient $\exp(0) = 1$ and $\exp(-j2\pi/2) = -1$. Then one multiplies by $\exp(-j2\pi/16i)$, $i = 0,1, \ldots,7$. This factor is analogous to the twiddle factor and is a rotation in the complex plane to account for the actual position of the points $z(i)$ and $z(i + N/2)$.

The summation appearing in both recursions can be written out in full to obtain final forms for programming. The most convenient form is (4.36) for the Cooley-Tukey version.

1. The Cooley-Tukey (C-T) version:

$$A_\ell(k_0,k_1,\ldots,k_{\ell-2},\overset{\overset{\textstyle k_{\ell-1}}{\downarrow}}{0},i_{p-\ell-1},\ldots,i_0)$$

$$= A_{\ell-1}(k_0,k_1,\ldots,k_{\ell-2},\overset{\overset{\textstyle i_{p-\ell}}{\downarrow}}{0},i_{p-\ell-1},\ldots,i_0)$$

$$+ A_{\ell-1}(k_0,k_1,\ldots,k_{\ell-2},1,i_{p-\ell-1},\ldots,i_0)$$

$$\times W^{(k_{\ell-2}2^{\ell-2} + \ldots + k_0)1 \cdot 2^{p-\ell}} \quad \overset{\overset{\textstyle i_{p-\ell}}{\downarrow}}{}$$

$$\ell = 1,2,\ldots,p \qquad (4.50a)$$

$$\overset{k_{\ell-1}}{\underset{\downarrow}{A_\ell(k_0,k_1,\ldots,k_{\ell-2},1,i_{p-\ell-1},\ldots,i_0)}}$$

$$= \overset{i_{p-\ell}}{\underset{\downarrow}{A_{\ell-1}(k_0,k_1,\ldots,k_{\ell-2},0,i_{p-\ell-1},\ldots,i_0)}}$$

$$- A_{\ell-1}(k_0,k_1,\ldots,k_{\ell-2},1,i_{p-\ell-1},\ldots,i_0)$$

$$\times W^{(k_{\ell-2}2^{\ell-2} + \ldots + k_0) \overset{i_{p-\ell}}{\underset{\downarrow}{1}} \cdot 2^{p-\ell}}$$

$$\ell = 1,2,\ldots,p \quad (4.50b)$$

The Sande-Tukcy version is implemented via (4.43).

2. The Sande-Tukey (S-T) version:

$$\overset{k_{\ell-1}}{\underset{\downarrow}{\hat{A}_\ell(k_0,k_1,\ldots,k_{\ell-2},0,1_{p-\ell-1},\ldots,i_0)}}$$

$$= [\overset{i_{p-\ell}}{\underset{\downarrow}{\hat{A}_{\ell-1}(k_0,k_1,\ldots,k_{\ell-2},0,i_{p-\ell-1},\ldots,i_0)}}$$

$$+ \hat{A}_{\ell-1}(k_0,k_1,\ldots,k_{\ell-2},1,i_{p-\ell-1},\ldots,i_0)]$$

$$\times W^{(i_{p-\ell-1}2^{p-\ell-1} + \ldots + i_0) \overset{k_{\ell-1}}{\underset{\downarrow}{(0)}} 2^{\ell-1}}$$

$$(4.51a)$$

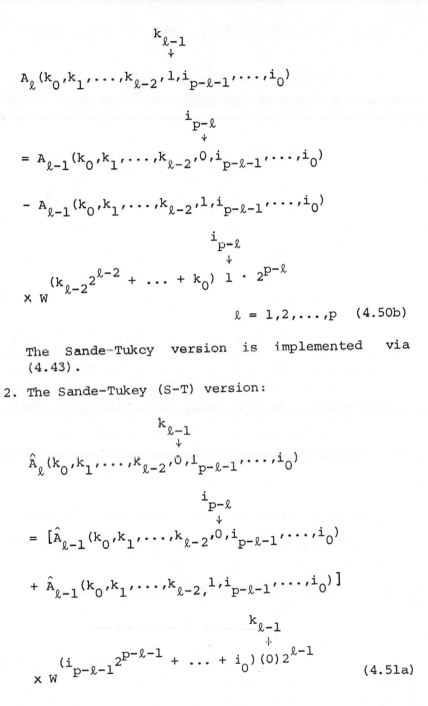

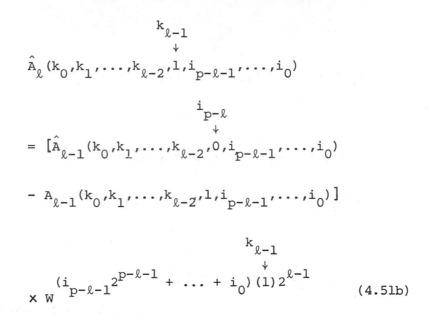

$$\hat{A}_\ell (k_0, k_1, \ldots, k_{\ell-2}, \overset{\overset{\displaystyle k_{\ell-1}}{\downarrow}}{1}, i_{p-\ell-1}, \ldots, i_0)$$

$$= [\hat{A}_{\ell-1}(k_0, k_1, \ldots, k_{\ell-2}, 0, \overset{\overset{\displaystyle i_{p-\ell}}{\downarrow}}{i}_{p-\ell-1}, \ldots, i_0)$$

$$- A_{\ell-1}(k_0, k_1, \ldots, k_{\ell-2}, 1, i_{p-\ell-1}, \ldots, i_0)]$$

$$\times W^{(i_{p-\ell-1}2^{p-\ell-1} + \ldots + i_0)(1)2^{\ell-1}} \overset{\overset{\displaystyle k_{\ell-1}}{\downarrow}}{} \qquad (4.51b)$$

In principal, the two versions require the same amount of arithmetic. In practice, the Sande-Tukey version is sometimes simpler for data arranged in natural order because of the exponent for W. Likewise, the C-T version can be simpler for scrambled data. In both the C-T and S-T versions, from (4.50) and (4.51) it is seen that the index required for A_ℓ or $\hat{A}_\ell$ can be broken into two parts:

Part 1

$$\overbrace{k_0 2^{p-1} + k_1 2^{p-2} + \ldots + k_{\ell-2} 2^{p-\ell-3} + k_{\ell-1} 2^{p-\ell-2}}$$

Part 2

$$\overbrace{+ i_{p-\ell-1} 2^{p-\ell-1} + \ldots + i_0} \qquad (4.52)$$

Note that exponent $(k_{\ell-1}2^{\ell-1} + \ldots + k_0)i_p 2^{p-\ell}$ in the C-T twiddle factor is a bit-reversed version of the first part of the index (4.52) multiplied by a power of two. In the S-T version, the exponent $(i_{p-\ell-1} \cdot 2^{p-\ell-1} + \ldots + i_0)2^{p-1}$ is the second part of the index (4.52)--not bit-reversed and multiplied by a power of two. Thus, in some instances it is easier to perform the tally necessary to obtain the complex exponential argument for the S-T version than for the C-T version.

The equations for the algorithms may appear simpler if some specific examples for the binary indices are illustrated. Consider the case when $p = 4$ and $N = 2^4 = 16$. Then the decimal and binary indices are

DECIMAL   BINARY

$$z(0_{10}) = z(0 \cdot 2^3 + 0 \cdot 2^2 + 0 \cdot 2 + 0) = z(0,0,0,0)$$

$$z(1_{10}) = z(0 \cdot 2^3 + 0 \cdot 2^2 + 0 \cdot 2 + 1) = z(0,0,0,1)$$

$$z(10_{10}) = z(1 \cdot 2^3 + 0 \cdot 2^2 + 1 \cdot 2 + 0) = z(1,0,1,0)$$

$$z(15_{10}) = z(1 \cdot 2^3 + 1 \cdot 2^2 + 1 \cdot 2 + 1) = z(1,1,1,1)$$

Further consider the indices involved in A_ℓ for the $\ell =$ second stage of the recursion. Equations (4.50a) and (4.50b) become, for this case,

$$A_2(k_0,0,i_1,i_0) = A_1(k_0,0,i_1,i_0) + A_1(k_0,1,i_1,i_0)$$
$$\times W^{(k_1 2+k_0)2^2}$$

$$A_2(k_0,1,i_1,i_0) = A_1(k_0,0,i_1,i_0) - A_1(k_0,1,i_1,i_0)$$
$$\times W^{(k_1 2+k_0)2^2}$$

The new results A_2 are stored as indicated in Figure 4.5.

In some respects, the programming necessary to implement the FFT algorithm reduces to a fairly straightforward procedure. First consider the diagram in Figure 4.6, which is an extension of Figure 4.5. This diagram is for the case $N = 2^3$, $p = 3$, and is taken from McGowan (1966). Solid lines indicate that the quantity in the location at the beginning of the solid line is multiplied by W, raised to the power in the circle, added to the quantity from the dashed line, and stored in the indicated location. For example, in the first iteration $x(1,0,0)$ is multiplied by W^0, added to $z(0,0,0)$, and stored in location with binary address $(0,0,0)$. In equation form,

$$z_{1(0)} = z_{0(0)} + z_{0(4)} \, W^0$$

This diagram is an implementation of (4.51a) and (4.51b). The relation $W^{N/2} = -1$ is used, as there are always pairs of exponentials differing by N/2. Thus, only one multiplication is performed, followed by an addition in one case and a subtraction in another. Note also the patterns that appear in the diagram, in that operations are performed on blocks of data whose lengths are divided by two at each stage of the recursion. Facts such as these simplify determining the locations in which data must be stored and in turn simplify the programming.

The following rules for the algorithm are due to C. M. Rader, according to McCowan (1966). The exponents of the complex exponential are determined from the following rule:

1. The number in the circle on the jth node in the
   ℓth array (for the ℓth recursion) is found by
   (a) writing the binary number j, (b) scaling
   (shifting) it by $(p - \ell)$ places to the right,
   and (c) reversing the order of the p bits. Thus,

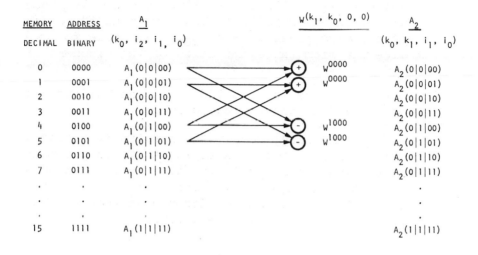

| MEMORY | ADDRESS | A_1 | | $W(k_1, k_0, 0, 0)$ | A_2 |
DECIMAL	BINARY	(k_0, i_2, i_1, i_0)			(k_0, k_1, i_1, i_0)
0	0000	$A_1(0\|0\|00)$		W^{0000}	$A_2(0\|0\|00)$
1	0001	$A_1(0\|0\|01)$		W^{0000}	$A_2(0\|0\|01)$
2	0010	$A_1(0\|0\|10)$			$A_2(0\|0\|10)$
3	0011	$A_1(0\|0\|11)$			$A_2(0\|0\|11)$
4	0100	$A_1(0\|1\|00)$		W^{1000}	$A_2(0\|1\|00)$
5	0101	$A_1(0\|1\|01)$		W^{1000}	$A_2(0\|1\|01)$
6	0110	$A_1(0\|1\|10)$			$A_2(0\|1\|10)$
7	0111	$A_1(0\|1\|11)$			$A_2(0\|1\|11)$
.	.	.			.
.	.	.			.
.	.	.			.
15	1111	$A_1(1\|1\|11)$			$A_2(1\|1\|11)$

Fig. 4.5   Illustration of storage at second stage of
recursion for p = 4.

INDEX	BINARY	ARRAY		W_3	REVERSED	INDEX
0	000	X(0)	0 0 0	A(0)	000	0
1	001	X(1)	0 0 4	A(1)	100	1
2	010	X(2)	0 4 2	A(2)	010	2
3	011	X(3)	0 4 6	A(3)	110	3
4	100	X(4)	4 2 1	A(4)	001	4
5	101	X(5)	4 2 5	A(5)	101	5
6	110	X(6)	4 6 3	A(6)	011	6
7	111	X(7)	4 6 7	A(7)	111	7

Fig. 4.6   Cooley-Tukey algorithm diagram, N = 8, p = 3
(McCowan, 1966).

in array 2, the last element, $B_2(7)$, has binary address $7_{10} = 111_2$. Scaling $(p - 2 + 1)$ place to the right gives 011, and reversing the order of the bits gives $110_2 = 6_{10}$. This rule follows directly from an examination of the exponent of W in (4.50a) and (4.50b).

The origin of the solid and dashed lines is determined by the following rule:

2. In the ℓth array, node j has a solid line from a node in array $(\ell-1)$ whose location is the same except that the bit in position $(p-\ell)$ must be a one. The dashed-arrow origin is determined similarly. The only difference is that the bit in position $(p-\ell)$ must be a zero.

These rules can be compared with (4.51a) and (4.51b), and their origins can be determined by careful inspection of the subscripts. The final iteration indicated in Figure 4.6 is the rearrangement obtained by reversing the order of the binary digits of an index. In an actual program, the bit-reversal procedure can be accomplished in various ways:

1. A reverse tally can be maintained where high-order bits, rather than low-order bits, are added in.

2. The following two-step recursive procedure can be employed.

    (a) Test leading bits to the previous index, setting them equal to zero until a zero bit is found. (b) Set this zero bit to a one bit, and this is the desired index. For example, when $p = 3$, we begin with $000_2 = 0_{10}$. Obtained from this is $100_2 = 4_{10}$, which is $001_2 = 1_{10}$ with bits reversed. Obtained next is $010_2 = 2_{10}$, etc. (The Author's have been told that computer instructions exist to accomplish this, but know of no specific computers.) Both the C-T and S-T versions require bit reversals to rearrange the final results in the natural method of implementing the algorithms. Recall, however, that tricks such as rearranging the order of the data according to bit-reversed addresses can result in alternative ways to implement the algorithms such as given by (4.39).

The complex exponentials can be determined in advance and stored in a table or computed as the calculations proceed. In generating in advance, the recursion of (4.8), slightly rewritten as

$$e^{-j\frac{2\pi ik}{N}} = e^{-j\frac{2\pi(i-1)k}{N}} \; e^{-j\frac{2\pi}{N}}$$

$$W^{ik} = W^{(i-1)k} \; W \tag{4.53}$$

should be used. In terms of sines and cosines, this is (4.7). If the complex exponentials are computed as required, standard sine/cosine subroutines are employed. This does not normally result in any significant loss of computational efficiency. This is true since only N complex exponentials are necessary. The computing time for the typical 36 bit computer system sine/cosine subroutine is about 250×10^{-6} sec. Thus, the time for an 8192-point case would be about

$$T = 8192 \times 250 \times 10^{-6} < 10^4 \times 250 \times 10^6 = 2.5 \; \text{sec}$$

Computational times of such magnitude are easily lost in the system overhead.

4.3 MATRIX FORMULATION OF ALGORITHM

In McCowan (1966), an alternate approach to a characterization of an FFT algorithm is presented. This explanation is in terms of factoring a matrix, and this approach is developed further in Theilheimer (1969). We can motivate the derivation in matrix terms by considering an analogous situation which is the decomposition of an aircraft maneuver into its roll, pitch, and yaw components. A rotation of plane coordinates through an angle θ can be written in matrix form as

$$\begin{pmatrix} x' \\ y' \end{pmatrix} = \begin{pmatrix} \cos\theta & -\sin\theta \\ \sin\theta & \cos\theta \end{pmatrix} \begin{pmatrix} x \\ y \end{pmatrix} \tag{4.54}$$

In three dimensions, any general rotation can be written in terms of three two-dimensional components (see Figure 4.7), roll [rotation in (y,z) coordinate plane], pitch [rotation in (x,z) coordinate plane], and yaw [rotation in (y,z) plane].

Thus, the total rotation is the product of three two-dimensional matrices

$$T(\theta_1, \theta_2, \theta_3)$$

$$= \overset{\text{Yaw}}{\begin{bmatrix} \cos\theta_3 & -\sin\theta_3 & 0 \\ \sin\theta_3 & \cos\theta_3 & 0 \\ 0 & 0 & 1 \end{bmatrix}} \overset{\text{Pitch}}{\begin{bmatrix} \cos\theta_2 & 0 & -\sin\theta_2 \\ 0 & 1 & 0 \\ \sin\theta_2 & 0 & \cos\theta_2 \end{bmatrix}}$$

Roll

$$x \begin{bmatrix} 1 & 0 & 0 \\ 0 & \cos \theta_1 & -\sin \theta_1 \\ 0 & \sin \theta_2 & \cos \theta_2 \end{bmatrix} \qquad (4.55)$$

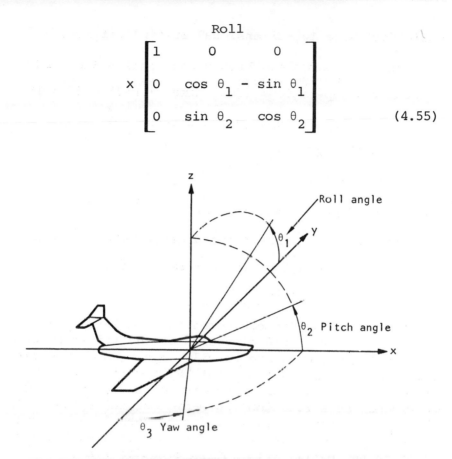

Fig. 4.7 Illustration of roll, pitch, and yaw components.

The actual computations necessary for performing a transformation of coordinates can thus be broken down into three two-dimensional matrix vector multiplications rather than one three-dimensional matrix vector multiplication. The number of operations for the single three-dimensional multiplication is

Number of operations (three-dimensional) $- 3^2 = 9$

while for three two-dimensional multiplications,

Number of operations (3 two-dimensional) = $3 \times 2^2 = 12$

Number of operations (four-dimensional) = $4^2 = 16$

Number of operations (4 two-dimensional)

$= 2^2 + 2^2 + 2^2 + 2^2$

$= 2(2+2+2+2) = 16$

For a five-dimensional rotation,

Number of operations (five-dimensional) = $5^2 = 25$

Number of operations (5 two-dimensional)

$= 2(2+2+2+2+2) = 20$

The time savings that can potentially materialize from this approach when the dimension of the transformation becomes large enough are readily seen. Roughly speaking, this is what happens for FFT algorithms. A discrete, finite Fourier transform of N data points may be viewed as a rotation in N-dimensional space. In mathematical terms, it is an orthogonal linear transformation. The exponent for W also specifies its position in the matrix. In matrix equation form,

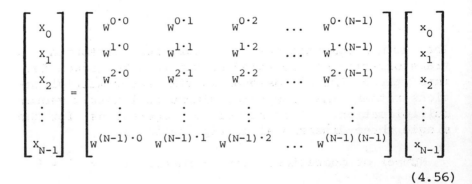

$$(4.56)$$

or in compact matrix notation,

$$X = Wx \qquad (4.57)$$

For the special case $N = 2^3 = 8$, $p = 3$, the explicit matrix is

$$
W = \begin{bmatrix}
1 & 1 & 1 & 1 & 1 & 1 & 1 & 1 \\
1 & w^1 & w^2 & w^3 & w^4 & w^5 & w^6 & w^7 \\
1 & w^2 & w^4 & w^6 & w^8 & w^{10} & w^{12} & w^{14} \\
1 & w^3 & w^6 & w^9 & w^{12} & w^{15} & w^{18} & w^{21} \\
1 & w^4 & w^8 & w^{12} & w^{16} & w^{20} & w^{24} & w^{28} \\
1 & w^5 & w^{10} & w^{15} & w^{20} & w^{25} & w^{30} & w^{35} \\
1 & w^6 & w^{12} & w^{18} & w^{24} & w^{30} & w^{36} & w^{42} \\
1 & w^7 & w^{14} & w^{21} & w^{28} & w^{35} & w^{42} & w^{49}
\end{bmatrix}
$$

This matrix can be factored into $(p + 1 = 4)$ matrices,

$$W = W_3\, W_2\, W_1\, W_0 \qquad (4.58)$$

or, in general, the factorization is

$$W = W_p\, W_{p-1}\, \cdots\, W_1\, W_0 \qquad (4.59)$$

The last matrix, W_p, is always a premutation matrix, which performs the reversed-bit memory location reordering.

Theilheimer (1969) gives rules for obtaining a factorization similar to (4.59). The matrices for the Cooley-Tukey factorization when $N = 2^p$ are easily developed. For the specific example of $N = 2^3$, the matrices are developed in McCowan (1966) and are:

$$
W_0 = \begin{bmatrix}
1 & 0 & 0 & 0 & w^0 & 0 & 0 & 0 \\
0 & 1 & 0 & 0 & 0 & w^0 & 0 & 0 \\
0 & 0 & 1 & 0 & 0 & 0 & w^0 & 0 \\
0 & 0 & 0 & 1 & 0 & 0 & 0 & w^0 \\
1 & 0 & 0 & 0 & w^4 & 0 & 0 & 0 \\
0 & 1 & 0 & 0 & 0 & w^4 & 0 & 0 \\
0 & 0 & 1 & 0 & 0 & 0 & w^4 & 0 \\
0 & 0 & 0 & 1 & 0 & 0 & 0 & w^4
\end{bmatrix}
$$

$$
W_1 = \begin{bmatrix}
1 & 0 & w^0 & 0 & 0 & 0 & 0 & 0 \\
0 & 1 & 0 & w^0 & 0 & 0 & 0 & 0 \\
1 & 0 & w^4 & 0 & 0 & 0 & 0 & 0 \\
0 & 1 & 0 & w^4 & 0 & 0 & 0 & 0 \\
0 & 0 & 0 & 0 & 1 & 0 & w^2 & 0 \\
0 & 0 & 0 & 0 & 0 & 1 & 0 & w^2 \\
0 & 0 & 0 & 0 & 1 & 0 & w^6 & 0 \\
0 & 0 & 0 & 0 & 0 & 1 & 0 & w^6
\end{bmatrix}
$$

$$W_2 = \begin{bmatrix} 1 & w^0 & 0 & 0 & 0 & 0 & 0 & 0 \\ 1 & w^4 & 0 & 0 & 0 & 0 & 0 & 0 \\ 0 & 0 & 1 & w^2 & 0 & 0 & 0 & 0 \\ 0 & 0 & 1 & w^6 & 0 & 0 & 0 & 0 \\ 0 & 0 & 0 & 0 & 1 & w^1 & 0 & 0 \\ 0 & 0 & 0 & 0 & 1 & w^5 & 0 & 0 \\ 0 & 0 & 0 & 0 & 0 & 0 & 1 & w^3 \\ 0 & 0 & 0 & 0 & 0 & 0 & 1 & w^7 \end{bmatrix}$$

$$W = \begin{bmatrix} 1 & 1 & 1 & 1 & 1 & 1 & 1 & 1 \\ 1 & w^1 & w^2 & w^3 & w^4 & w^5 & w^6 & w^7 \\ 1 & w^2 & w^4 & w^6 & w^8 & w^{10} & w^{12} & w^{14} \\ 1 & w^3 & w^6 & w^9 & w^{12} & w^{15} & w^{18} & w^{21} \\ 1 & w^4 & w^8 & w^{12} & w^{16} & w^{20} & w^{24} & w^{28} \\ 1 & w^5 & w^{10} & w^{15} & w^{20} & w^{25} & w^{30} & w^{35} \\ 1 & w^6 & w^{12} & w^{18} & w^{24} & w^{30} & w^{36} & w^{42} \\ 1 & w^7 & w^{14} & w^{21} & w^{28} & w^{35} & w^{42} & w^{49} \end{bmatrix}$$

The term w^0 is, of course, the same as unity. It was used rather than one to illustrate the symmetry. When the programming is specialized to take advantage of the specific forms of the matrices (i.e., do not multiply by zeros or ones), the time savings of the algorithm result.

The generalization of these matrices for any power
of two is obvious when one notes that the powers of W
are reversed binary numbers.   This is demonstrated by
noting the special case for N = 2^3.

Index		Reversed				
Decimal	Binary	Binary	Decimal	Stage 1	Stage 2	Stage 3
0	000	000	0	First 2		
1	001	100	4		First 4	
2	010	010	2			
3	011	110	6			All
4	100	001	1			
5	101	101	5			
6	110	011	3			
7	111	111	7			

Further note that the spacing between elements is
$N/2^{i+1}$ for the ith matrix, i = 0,1,2,...,p-1. Also,
the number of two-by-two submatrices is always N/2.
Finally, the number of different submatrices is $2^{(i+1)}$
for the ith stage, i=0,1,2,...,p.   Thus, p matrices
can always be constructed in this manner. The permutation matrix is obtained by placing a one in position
R(i) of row i, where R(i) is the bit-reversed version
of i.   As Theilheimer (1969) points out, the FFT is
not implemented by actually performing the matrix multiplications, but rather they are a device for
developing and understanding the FFT algorithms.

4.4 IMPORTANT RELATED FORMULAS

In the application of fast Fourier transforms to spectral and correlation analysis, a number of specialized relations regarding finite discrete Fourier transforms are useful. Many of these relations are noted here. A detailed discussion of their application to filtering, correlation, and spectra is left to Chapters 5 and 6.

The basic FFT algorithms are developed for complex data sequences. When applied to time series data analysis, real data are collected and, thus, transforms of real sequences are desired. Two real transforms may be computed simultaneously by inserting one time series in the real part and one in the imaginary part of the complex sequence to be transformed. In equation form,

$$z_i = x_i + jy_i \qquad\qquad i = 0,1,\ldots,N-1 \quad (4.60)$$

The transforms of x_i and y_i then are

$$X_k = \frac{Z_k + Z^*_{(N-k)}}{2} \qquad\qquad (4.61)$$

and

$$Y_k = \frac{Z_k - Z^*_{(N-k)}}{2j} \qquad\qquad k = 0,1,\ldots,N/2 \quad (4.62)$$

where $Z_N = Z_0$, since the transform of a real data sequence is periodic with a period equal to that of the Nyquist frequency. Equations (4.61) and (4.62) are only unique out to $k = N/2$. That is, in terms of discrete transforms, if N real data points are transformed to N frequency points at spacing $1/T$, the Nyquist frequency occurs at the $(N/2)$th frequency point.

When becoming involved in the programming of (4.61) and (4.62), it is important to note that $[(N/2)+1]$ instead of $(N/2)$ complex data points are obtained from the splitting of the single N-point complex transform. Actually, one begins with 2N values of two N-point real-valued data sequences. These are transformed to an N-point complex sequence which is still 2N real points. The splitting formula gives two complex sequences, each [(N/2)+1] points in length, and thus there are apparently (N+2) complex values. However, the values for k=0 and k=N/2 are each pure real numbers [the point for k=0 is merely the mean value (a real number) of the sequence]. Thus, 2N real data values are maintained. The storage of the data can become inconvenient at this stage, however. If it is desired to maintain all the results in only 2N positions of memory, then the value for k = N/2 must be stored in the imaginary part of the point for k=0. The other alternative is to reserve two additional (complex) memory cell positions for the extra data. This can be surprisingly inconvenient.

The derivation of (4.61) and (4.62) is straightforward. First, the transfer is

$$Z_k = \sum_{i=0}^{N-1} (x_i + jy_i) e^{-j\frac{2\pi i k}{N}} \qquad k = 0,1,\ldots,N-1 \qquad (4.63)$$

Note that

$$e^{-j\frac{2\pi i (N-k)}{N}} = e^{-j2\pi i} e^{j\frac{2\pi i k}{N}} = e^{j\frac{2\pi i k}{N}} \qquad (4.64)$$

since $e^{-j2\pi i} = 1$. Equation (4.61) is obtained directly:

$$Z_k + Z^*_{(N-k)} = \sum_{i=0}^{N-1} (x_i + jy_i)\, e^{-j\frac{2\pi ik}{N}}$$

$$+ \sum_{i=0}^{N-1} (x_i - jy_i)\, e^{-j\frac{2\pi ik}{N}}$$

$$= 2 \sum_{i=0}^{N-1} x_i\, e^{-j\frac{2\pi ik}{N}}$$

$$= 2X_k \qquad k = 0,1,\ldots,(N/2) - 1 \qquad (4.65)$$

Equation (4.51) is obtained similarly.

The FFT algorithms are naturally adapted to methods for doubling the length of data sequences that may be accommodated by the basic algorithm. For $N = 2^p$, each stage of the algorithm divides by two the number of points in the sequence upon which the corresponding final results depend. For example, the even-indexed results (before reverse-bit unscrambling) are stored in the first half of the memory allocated for data. Thus, the even-indexed results can be obtained from one pass through an algorithm based on half the storage. The odd-indexed results could be based on a second pass. As can be seen by analysis of the above statements, sequences decimated by two must be dealt with in order to obtain double-length transforms. The most convenient external storage therefore is a semi-random-access device, such as a disk or drum. A sequential device, such as a tape, is relatively inconvenient.

A double-length transform may be computed in the following manner. Suppose the algorithm is for N/2 data points where $N = 2^p$. Then, if the data are z_i, $i = 0,1,\ldots,N - 1$, and

$$W = \exp\left(\frac{-j2\pi}{N}\right)$$

the complex exponential for the algorithm of length N/2 is

$$W^2 = \exp\left(\frac{-j2\pi}{N/2}\right) \tag{4.66}$$

Two separate transforms of the even- and odd-indexed data points, respectively, can now be computed:

$$A_k = \sum_{i=0}^{(N/2)-1} z_{2i} (W^2)^{ik} \quad k = 0,1,\ldots,(N/2)-1 \tag{4.67a}$$

$$B_k = \sum_{i=0}^{(N/2)-1} z_{2i+1} (W^2)^{ik} \quad k = 0,1,\ldots,(N/2)-1 \tag{4.67b}$$

The full N-point transform of z_i is related to A_k and B_k by

$$Z_k = A_k + B_k W^k \quad k = 0,1,\ldots,(N/2)-1 \tag{4.68a}$$

$$Z_{(N/2)+k} = A_k - B_k W^k \quad k = 0,1,\ldots,(N/2)-1 \tag{4.68b}$$

The above procedure could be repeated to allow successive doubling of the number of data points.

The proof of (4.67a) and (4.67b) is as follows:

$$Z_k = A_k + B_k W^k$$

$$= \sum_{i=0}^{(N/2)-1} z_{2i} (W^2)^{ik} + \sum_{i=0}^{(N/2)-1} z_{2i+1} (W^2)^{ik} W^k$$

$$= \sum_{i=0}^{(N/2)-1} z_{2i} (W^2)^{ik} + \sum_{i=0}^{(N/2)-1} z_{2i+1} W^{(2i+1)k}$$

$$= z_0 \, W^{0 \cdot k} + z_2 \, W^{2 \cdot k} + \ldots + z_{N-2} \, W^{(N-2)k}$$

$$+ z_1 \, W^{1 \cdot k} + z_3 \, W^{3 \cdot k} + \ldots + z_{N-1} \, W^{(N-1)k}$$

$$= \sum_{i=0}^{N-1} z_i \, W^{ik} \qquad\qquad k = 0,1,\ldots,(N/2)-1$$

This gives (4.67a). To obtain (4.67b), note that

$$A_{\left(\frac{N}{2} + k\right)} = \sum_{i=0}^{(N/2)-1} z_{2i} \, (W^2)^{\left(i\frac{N}{2} + k\right)}$$

$$= \sum_{i=0}^{(N/2)-1} z_{2i} \, (W^2)^{ik} (W^2)^{i\frac{N}{2}}$$

$$= \sum_{i=0}^{(N/2)-1} z_{2i} \, (W^2)^{ik}$$

$$= A_k$$

since

$$(W^2)^{i\frac{N}{2}} = W^{iN} = \exp(-j2\pi i) = 1$$

Similarly, it can be shown that

$$B_{\left(\frac{N}{2} + k\right)} = B_k$$

Finally,

$$W^{\frac{N}{2} + k} = W^{\frac{N}{2}} W^k = -W^k$$

since

$$W^{\frac{N}{2}} = \exp\left(-j\,\frac{2\pi}{2}\right) = -1$$

Then (4.67b) follows directly, since

$$Z_{\left(\frac{N}{2} + k\right)} = A_{\left(\frac{N}{2} + k\right)} + B_{\left(\frac{N}{2} + k\right)} W^{\left(\frac{N}{2} + k\right)}$$

These formulas have direct application to the computation of spectral density functions and correlation functions to be discussed in Chapters 5 and 6.

Care must be taken if a factor of 1/N for an N-point Fourier transform has been employed in the basic definition. Then A_k and B_k, being (N/2)-point transforms, must have a factor of 2/N. But Z_k would require a factor of 1/N. Thus, the right-hand sides of (4.68a) and (4.68b) would be multiplied by 1/2 to account for this.

This doubling procedure is important since it provides an alternate derivation for the FFT when $N = 2^p$. One merely cascades the subdivision of the sequences back until the sequence length is N=2 points. A two-point transform requires two multiply-add operations. We have N/2 of these for a total of N operations. To proceed from two-point to four-point transforms requires the application of (4.68a) and (4.68b), which requires four operations repeated N/4 times, for a total of N operations. This sequence of N operations is repeated p times for $N = 2^p$, to finally arrive at an N-point transform derived from two transforms, each of length N/2.   Thus, we have performed N operations p times for a total of Np.

The paper by Danielson and Lanczos (1942) describes this doubling procedure and recognizes the fact that the amount of arithmetic essentially only doubles rather than quadrupling.   Thus, the authors had utilized the essence of the FFT algorithm without explicitly developing it to its fullest extent.

Two other useful formulas are (a) the transform of an N-point function, half of which are zeros, in terms of (M = N/2)-point transforms, and (b) the inverse transform of a Hermitian complex function. Both methods are important in the computation of noncircular (transient) correlation and convolution functions.

The first is derived by applying the two formulas just developed.

1. Let the input sequence be defined as

$$z_i = \begin{cases} x_{2i} + jx_{2i+1} & i = 0,1,2,\ldots,\dfrac{M}{2} - 1 \\[2ex] 0 & i = \dfrac{M}{2},\ldots,M-1 \end{cases} \qquad (4.69)$$

In a FORTRAN program, if a real-time history is read into M consecutive cells and M more cells are initialized to zero, then exactly the arrangement in (4.69) is obtained by merely redefining this area as an M-point complex array.

2. Now compute the M-point (complex) FFT of the z_i (4.17):

$$Z_k = \mathcal{F}(z_i) \qquad\qquad k = 0,1,2,\ldots,M-1$$

3. This complex sequence Z_k can now be split into two parts by (4.61) and (4.62) representing the first half of the Hermitian transform of the

even-indexed values, $X_k^e = \mathcal{F}(x_{2i})$, $k = 0,1,2,\ldots,$ $M/2-1$, and the first half of the Hermitian transform of the odd-indexed values,

$$X_k^o = \mathcal{F}(x_{2i+1}) \qquad\qquad k = 0,1,2,\ldots,\frac{M}{2} - 1$$

where

$$X_k^e = \frac{Z_k + Z_{M-k}^*}{2}$$

(4.70)

$$X_k^o = \frac{Z_k - Z_{M-k}^*}{2j} \qquad\qquad k = 0,1,2,\ldots,M/2$$

The Fourier transform of an M-point sequence is periodic with period M, hence $Z_0 = Z_M$. This implies that

$$X_0^e = \text{Re}(Z_0)$$

(4.71)

$$X_0^o = \text{Im}(Z_0)$$

Further, when (4.70) is evaluated at $k = M/2$, note that

$$X_{M/2}^e = \text{Re}(Z_{M/2})$$

(4.72)

$$X_{M/2}^o = \text{Im}(Z_{M/2})$$

An important and sometimes troublesome fact when programming is that two transforms of length $[(M/2)+1]$ are obtained from one of length M. There still exist only 2M real values, since

X_o^e, X_o^o, $X_{M/2}^e$, and $X_{M/2}^o$

are real values. However, either

$X_{M/2}^o$ and $X_{M/2}^e$

must be stored in the imaginary portions of

X_0^o and X_0^e,

or one additional complex memory location must be reserved.

4. At this stage, we have the transforms of the even- and odd-indexed portions of the series which were originally each half zeros. Now apply (4.68a) and (4.68b) to combine these two transforms into one transform of length $(N = 2 M)$. However, the transform of a real function is Hermitian (complex conjugate symmetric), so only the first $(M+1)$ points are required. This is emphasized by the fact that we only have X_k^e and X_k^o out to $k = M/2$. The equations are

$$X_k = X_k^e + X_k^o \, W^{k/2} \qquad k = 0,1,2,\ldots,M-1 \qquad (4.73a)$$

$$X_{M+k} = X_k^e - X_k^o \, W^{k/2} \qquad k = 0,1,2,\ldots,M-1 \qquad (4.73b)$$

where $W = \exp(-j2\pi/N)$ or $W^{1/2} = \exp(-j2\pi/M)$. In order to obtain just the first $(M+1)$ points from $[(M/2)+1]$-length transforms, take advantage of the relations

$$X_{N-k} = X_k^*$$

$$X_{M-k}^e = X_k^{o*}$$

$$X_{M-k}^o = X_k^{e*} \qquad\qquad k = 0,1,2,\ldots,M/2$$

Equation (4.73a) is used directly to obtain the first M/2 points, and a modified version for the second M/2 points is needed. Thus,

$$X_{k+\frac{M}{2}} = X_{k+\frac{M}{2}}^e - X_{k+\frac{M}{2}}^o \; W^{(k+\frac{M}{2})/2}$$

$$= X_{M-k-\frac{M}{2}}^{e*} - X_{M-k-\frac{M}{2}}^{o*} \; W^{k/2} \, W^{M/4}$$

$$= X_{\frac{M}{2}-k}^{e*} - j \, X_{\frac{M}{2}-k}^{o*} \; W^{k/2}$$

$$k = 0,1,2,\ldots,\frac{M}{2} - 1 \quad (4.74)$$

since

$$W^{M/4} = \exp\left(-j \, \frac{2\pi}{M} \, \frac{M}{4}\right) = \exp\left(-j \, \frac{2\pi}{4}\right) = -j$$

The final combination of equations required is

$$X_k = X_k^e + X_k^o \, W^{k/2} \qquad k = 0,1,2,\ldots,\frac{M}{2} - 1 \quad (4.75a)$$

$$X_{k + \frac{M}{2}} = X^{e*}_{\frac{M}{2} - k} - j \, X^{o*}_{\frac{M}{2} - k} \, W^{k/2}$$

$$k = 0,1,2,\ldots,\frac{M}{2} \qquad (4.75b)$$

Note that for $k = 0$, (4.72) must be used. By use of this method, given a single transform of length N, its (Hermitian) transform with an $(M = N/2)$-point FFT can be computed.

Consider now a closely related but slightly different problem of utilizing $(M = N/2)$-point FFTs to obtain the transform of an M-point (complex) function which has been augmented with M zeros (with the eventual objective of obtaining noncircular correlations or convolutions).

We shall term this the "half-zero procedure," and it proceeds as follows:

1. Read into memory an M-point (complex) sequence z_i, $i = 0,1,3,\ldots,M-1$.

2. Compute the M-point FFT of z_i and denote it by $Z^c_k = \text{FFT}(z_i)$, $k = 0,1,2,\ldots,M-1$.

3. Compute the M-point FFT of $z_i W^{i/2}$ and denote it by

$$Z^o_k = \text{FFT}(z_i \, W^{i/2}) \qquad k = 0,1,2,\ldots,M-1$$

We do this since the original N-point FFT of an N-point sequence (half of which is zeros) may be broken up by the following analysis:

$$Z_k = \sum_{i=0}^{N-1} z_i \, (W^{1/2})^{ik} = \sum_{i=0}^{M-1} z_i \, (W^{1/2})^{ik}$$

$$k = 0,1,2,\ldots,N-1 \qquad (4.76)$$

Now consider the even and odd parts of the index:

$$r = k/2 \qquad\qquad k = 0,2,4,6,\ldots,N-2$$
$$s = (k-1)/2 \qquad\qquad k = 1,3,5,7,\ldots,N-1 \qquad (4.77)$$

Then Z_k can be split as follows:

$$Z_r = \sum_{i=0}^{M-1} z_i \, (W^{1/2})^{i2r}$$

$$= \sum_{i=0}^{M-1} z_i \, W^{ir} \qquad\qquad r = 0,1,2,\ldots,M-1 \quad (4.78)$$

$$Z_s = \sum_{i=0}^{M-1} z_i \, (W^{1/2})^{i(2s+1)}$$

$$= \sum_{i=0}^{M-1} z_i \, (W^{1/2}) \, W^{is}$$

$$s = 0,1,2,\ldots,M-1 \quad (4.79)$$

Hence, to obtain Z_k for even values of k, compute the $(M = N/2)$-point transform of z_i, $i = 0,1,2,\ldots,M-1$. To obtain the odd values of Z_k, take the $(M = N/2)$-point transform of $z_i \, W^{i/2}$, $i = 0,1,2,\ldots,M-1$.

The inverse transform of a Hermitian (complex) function is of interest in doing convolutions via FFTs. In this case, if

$$u_k = \sum_{i=0}^{N-1} x_{(k-i) \bmod N} h_i \qquad\qquad k = 0,1,2,\ldots,N-1$$

then u_k is real, and therefore U_ℓ, $\ell = 0,1,2,\ldots,N-1$, is complex Hermitian, and only the first half U_ℓ, $\ell = 0,1,2,\ldots,M-1$, must be dealt with. Also, since the FFT generates a complex result, half the points of u_k can be stored in the real portion of the array and half the points in the imaginary position.

Let u_i'; $i = 0,1,3,\ldots,M-1$, represent the M-point inverse transform of a suitable function of U_k; $k = 0,1,2,\ldots,M-1$. Satisfy the conditions given above by the relations

$$u_i' + u_i'^* = 2\, u_{2i}$$

$$i = 0,1,2,\ldots,M-1 \quad (4.80)$$

$$u_i' - u_i'^* = 2\, ju_{2i+1}$$

if the even- and odd-indexed values of u_i are stored in the real and imaginary parts, respectively.

Now, u_i is defined as the inverse transform of U_k,

$$u_i = \frac{1}{N} \sum_{k=0}^{N-1} U_k \exp j\, \frac{2\pi}{N}\, ik \qquad i = 0,1,2,\ldots,N-1$$

Furthermore, by the relations (4.80),

$$u_i' = u_{2i} + j\, u_{2i+1} \qquad i = 0,1,2,\ldots,M-1$$

$$u_i' = \frac{1}{N} \sum_{k=0}^{N-1} U_k \exp j\, \frac{2\pi}{N}\, 2ik$$

$$+ \frac{j}{N} \sum_{k=0}^{N-1} U_k \exp \left(j\, \frac{2\pi}{N}(2i+1)k\right)$$

$$i = 0,1,2,\ldots,M-1 \quad (4.81)$$

Note that since U_k is Hermitian, $U_{N-k}^* = U_k$, (4.81) can further be reduced to

$$2Mu_i' = \sum_{k=0}^{M-1} U_k \exp j \frac{2\pi ik}{M} + \sum_{k=M}^{N-1} U_k \exp j \frac{2\pi ik}{M}$$

$$+ j \left[\sum_{k=0}^{M-1} U_k \exp j \frac{2\pi k}{N} \exp j \frac{2\pi ik}{M} \right.$$

$$\left. + \sum_{k=M}^{N-1} U_k \exp j \frac{2\pi k}{N} \exp j \frac{2\pi ik}{M} \right] \tag{4.82}$$

Now, if $k' = k-M$ and $W = \exp -j \frac{2\pi}{M}$, then

$$\sum_{k=M}^{N-1} U_k \exp j \frac{2\pi ik}{M} = \sum_{k=0}^{M-1} U_{k'+M} \exp \left[j \frac{2\pi i(k'+M)}{M} \right]$$

$$i = 0,1,2,\ldots,M-1 \tag{4.83}$$

Again recalling that $U_{N-k}^* = U_k$, note that

$$U_{k+M} = U_{N-k-M}^* = U_{M-k}^* \tag{4.84}$$

and also that

$$\exp \left[j \frac{2\pi i(k+M)}{M} \right] = \exp j \frac{2\pi ik}{M} \exp j2\pi i$$

$$= \exp j \frac{2\pi ik}{M}$$

Thus,

$$\sum_{k=M}^{N-1} U_k \exp j \frac{2\pi ik}{M} = \sum_{k=0}^{M-1} U_{M-k}^* W^{-ik}$$

$$i = 0,1,2,\ldots,M-1 \tag{4.85}$$

Similarly,

$$\sum_{k=M}^{N-1} U_k \exp\left(j\ \frac{2\pi k}{N}\right) W^{ik} = \sum_{k=0}^{M-1} U^*_{M-k} \exp\left[j\ \frac{2\pi(k+M)}{N}\right] W^{-ik}$$

$$i = 0,1,2,\ldots,M \quad (4.86)$$

Further note that

$$\exp\left[j\ \frac{2\pi(k+M)}{N}\right] = W^{-k/2} \exp j\ \frac{2\pi M}{N} = -W^{-k/2}$$

Substituting back, in (4.82),

$$2Mu'_i = \sum_{k=0}^{M-1} U_k\ W^{-ik} + \sum_{k=0}^{M-1} U^*_{M-k}\ W^{-ik}$$

$$+ j \sum_{k=0}^{M-1} U_k\ W^{-k/2}\ W^{-ik} - j \sum_{k=0}^{M-1} U^*_{M-k}\ W^{-k/2}\ W^{-ik}$$

$$= \sum_{k=0}^{M-1} \left[U_k + U^*_{M-k} + j(U_k - U^*_{M-k})\ W^{k/2} \right] W^{-ik}$$

$$i = 0,1,2,\ldots,M-1 \quad (4.87)$$

Thus, if an M-point inverse FFT is defined as

$$x_i = \frac{1}{M} \sum_{i=0}^{M-1} X_k \exp j\ \frac{2\pi ik}{N}$$

$i = 0,1,\ldots,M-1$, the Hermitian procedure is:

1. Compute

$$\left[U_k + U^*_{M-k} + j(U_k - U^*_{M-k})\ W^{-k/2} \right] = U'_k$$

$$k = 0,1,2,\ldots,M-1$$

noting that $U_M^* = U_{N-M} = U_M$ must be available.

2. Compute the M-point inverse FFT of U_k' and

$$u_i' = \frac{1}{2} \text{FFT}^{-1} (U_k')$$

3. Finally, the real part of u_i' is the even-indexed values of u_i, and the imaginary part is the odd-indexed values of u_i or

$$u_{2i} = \text{Re}(u_i')$$

$$u_{2i+1} = \text{Im}(u_i')$$

$$i = 0,1,2,\ldots,M-1$$

Thus, with the above method an inverse transform with half the storage that might otherwise seem to be necessary is computed.

4.5 FLOW CHARTS

The actual coding of the basic FFT algorithm reduces to a simple procedure (see Figure 4.8a-e). An inner loop is obtained which is executed first N/2 times, then N/4, etc. That is, the number of times through the loop is divided by two each time. An outer loop is also used, and the number of times through the loop is doubled each time, e.g., 1,2,4, etc. The computation of the twiddle factor is minimized, since it need only be computed once for each execution of the outer loop. These loops are illustrated in Figure 4.8. One point to note is that the innermost computation is a two-term, complex Fourier transform. However, only complex addition and subtraction need be used, rather than the much more time-consuming complex multiplication. This is true, since the only values of the complex exponential involved are +1 and -1.

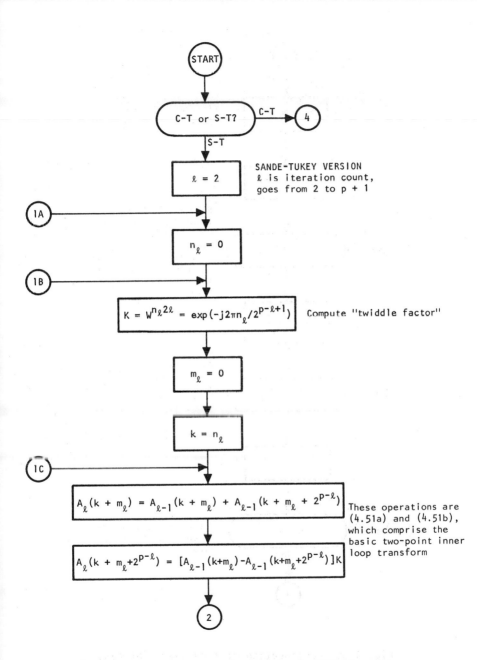

Fig. 4.8a   Flow chart for the basic FFT algorithm.

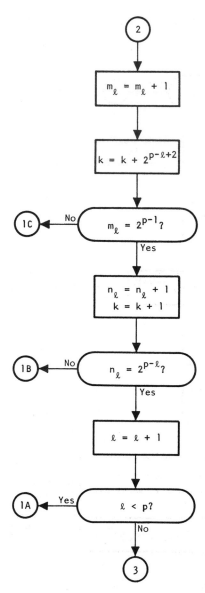

Increment k by N, N/2, N/4, ..., 1

For S-T version, this inner loop controlled by m_ℓ is executed first 1 time, then 2 times, 4,8, ...,N/2--this minimizes the number of different twiddle factor computations

Outer loop controlled by n_ℓ is executed first N/2 times, then N/4,...,1-- thus, twiddle factor is computed N/2 times in first iteration of recursion, N/4 times in second, N/8 times,...,1

ℓ controls the recursion which is performed p times

Fig. 4.8b Continuation of flow chart for basic FFT algorithm.

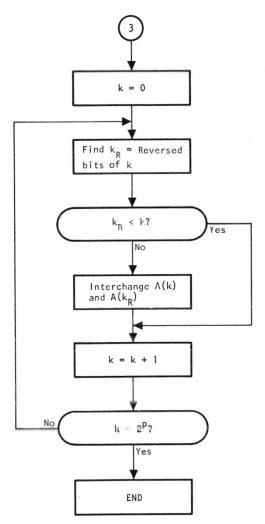

This portion of the program
is to perform the bit-reversed
address permutation

If $k_R < k$, then interchange has
already been accomplished

Fig. 4.8c Continuation of flow chart for basic
FFT algorithm.

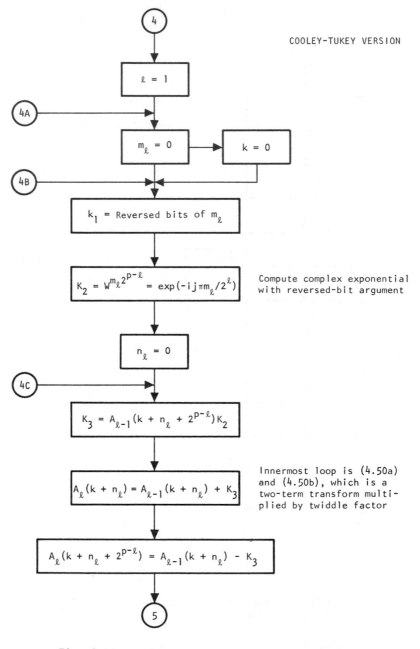

COOLEY-TUKEY VERSION

4

$\ell = 1$

4A

$m_\ell = 0$ → $k = 0$

4B

k_1 = Reversed bits of m_ℓ

$K_2 = W^{m_\ell 2^{p-\ell}} = \exp(-ij\pi m_\ell/2^\ell)$ Compute complex exponential with reversed-bit argument

$n_\ell = 0$

4C

$K_3 = A_{\ell-1}(k + n_\ell + 2^{p-\ell})K_2$

$A_\ell(k + n_\ell) = A_{\ell-1}(k + n_\ell) + K_3$ Innermost loop is (4.50a) and (4.50b), which is a two-term transform multiplied by twiddle factor

$A_\ell(k + n_\ell + 2^{p-\ell}) = A_{\ell-1}(k + n_\ell) - K_3$

5

Fig. 4.8d Continuation of flow chart for basic
FFT algorithm.

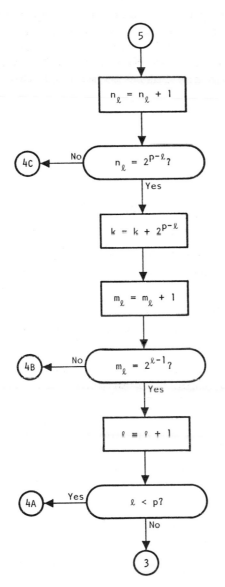

n_ℓ controls inner loop
done N/2 times, N/4,
N/8,...,1

m_ℓ controls outer loop
done 1 time, 2, 4,...,
N/2 times--complex
exponential factor is
thus computed 1 time, 2,
4, ,N/2 times

ℓ controls overall recursion performed p times

Fig. 4.8e Continuation of flow chart for basic
FFT algorithm.

In subsequent chapters we will describe computation
of power and cross spectra, correlation functions, and
convolutions (for filtering) with the use of discrete
Fourier transforms. Thus, the computational methods
discussed in this chapter are basic to much of the remainder of the book.

Problems

4.1 Consider (4.24),

$$Z_{(c+dA)} = \sum_{b=j}^{B-1} \sum_{b=j}^{A-1} Z_{(b+aB)}\, w^{bc}\, w^{bdA}\, w^{acB}$$

Suppose that instead of factoring w^{bdA} from under
the summation, we factor w^{acB}. Derive the results
from the FFT.

4.2 Suppose in (4.24) that A can be further factored
into two more factors A=CD. Continue the FFT derivation for these factors.

4.3 Show how the technique in Problem 4.2 can be continued in a cascaded manner to an arbitrary number
of factors.

4.4 In (4.37) verify that the exponent of w is the
proper one for the scrambled data.

4.5 Show that (4.40) for the power of two Sande-Tukey
FFT is equivalent to (4.27), (4.28), and (4.29) if
A=2 and $B=2^{p-1}$.

4.6 In (4.50a) and (4.50b), explain the origin of the
two-term summation and difference.

CHAPTER 5
GENERAL CONSIDERATIONS IN COMPUTING
POWER SPECTRAL DENSITY

5.1   INTRODUCTION

Power spectral densities (PSDs) may be computed by three methods. Each of the three methods is based on a different but asymptotically equivalent definition. These are:

1. The "standard" or Blackman-Tukey method. The procedure is first to compute the correlation function and then take its Fourier transform. That is, supposing $\{x_i\}$, $i = 1,\ldots,N$, to be the data (assumed zero mean); then R_r, $r = 0,\ldots,m$, is the correlation function

$$R_r = \frac{1}{N - r} \sum_{i=1}^{N-r} x_i x_{i+r} \qquad (5.1)$$

The PSD of $\{x_i\}$, labeled $G_k^{(1)}$, $k = 0,\ldots,m$, is computed from

$$G_k^{(1)} = 2\Delta t \left(R_0 + 2 \sum_{r=1}^{m-1} R_r \cos \frac{\pi k r}{m} + R_m \cos \frac{\pi k}{m} \right) \qquad (5.2)$$

where $G_k^{(1)}$ corresponds to the power near $k/2m\Delta t$ Hz.

The argument for the cosines in (5.2) arises as follows: The original angle is

$$\omega \tau = 2\pi f r \Delta t \qquad (5.3)$$

197

as both R_r and $\{x_i\}$ are at the interval Δt. The frequency interval $(0, 1/2\Delta t)$ is broken into m parts, so that each is separated by $(1/m)(1/2\Delta t)$ Hz from the next. The individual frequencies are therefore $0, 1/2\Delta tm, 2/2\Delta tm,\ldots,2m/2\Delta tm$. Thus,

$$\omega\tau = 2\pi\left(\frac{k}{2\Delta tm}\right)r\Delta t = \frac{\pi kr}{m} \tag{5.4}$$

One reason for computing as many PSD values as there are correlation values is to ensure that all of the information in the correlation is being utilized. That it is can be seen from the invertability of (5.2):

$$R_r = \frac{1}{4m\Delta t}\left[G_0^{(1)}+2\sum_{k=1}^{m-1}G_k^{(1)}\cos\frac{\pi kr}{m} + G_m^{(1)}\cos\frac{\pi r}{m}\right]$$
$$\tag{5.5}$$

There is more to computing this type of PSD than simply using (5.1) and (5.2); the details will be discussed in Chapter 6.

2. The direct Fourier transform method. In this procedure, the Fourier transform is first computed from the data:

$$X_k = \sum_{i=0}^{N-1}x_i e^{-j\frac{2\pi ik}{N}} \qquad k = 0,\ldots,N-1 \tag{5.6a}$$

The PSD is obtained from (5.6a) as follows:

$$G_k^{(2)} = \frac{2\Delta t}{N}\left|X_k\right|^2 \qquad k = 0,\ldots, \frac{N+1}{2} \tag{5.6b}$$

Here the frequency interval $(0, 1/2\Delta t)$ is broken into $N/2$ parts, so that the frequency increment is

$$\Delta f = \frac{1}{N\Delta t} \qquad\qquad (5.6c)$$

3. The third procedure utilizes filtering. In order to get $G_k^{(3)}$ for specific frequency index k, it is first necessary to assign frequencies $\{f_k\}$ and bandwidths $\{B_k\}$, both in Hz. Usually

$$0 < f_0 < f_1 < \ldots < f_k < \ldots \leq \frac{1}{2\Delta t}$$

in some consistent manner. Then, using techniques developed in Chapter 3, a bandpass filter for f_k and B_k is designed. In particular, the distance between the two half-power points is set at B_k Hz and then they are placed so that f_k is midway between them. Call the output of the filter $y_i^{(k)}$. That is,

$$y_i^{(k)} = \sum_{\ell=1}^{M} h_\ell^{(k)} y_{i-\ell}^{(k)} + \sum_{\ell=0}^{M} g_\ell^{(k)} x_{i-\ell} \qquad (5.7a)$$

There has to be one $\{y_i^{(k)}\}$ for each frequency being analyzed. The PSD is formed from these sequences from

$$G_k^{(3)} = \frac{1}{B_k N} \sum_{i=1}^{N} \left[y_i^{(k)}\right]^2 \qquad\qquad (5.7b)$$

In words, the data are passed through a bandpass filter, squared, and then summed, with a final normalization.

These methods produce results that are nearly the same, but in general they are not identical. If the effective bandwidths of all three procedures are the same at a given frequency, then the answers will usually be quite comparable. There are, however, certain

pathological cases in which the answers might be dras-
tically different, but these are usually not a problem
with real data.

There are two main problems which arise when employing these procedures: *statistical variability of
the PSD and leakage.* The remainder of this chapter
will be spent in discussing these two problems in a
general manner, with specifics in Chapters 6-8.

5.2 LEAKAGE

Leakage is caused by the manner of observation. Its
effect is to smear the PSD. There are procedures which
can significantly reduce leakage, and these will be
discussed after sufficient background techniques have
been developed.

It perhaps is easiest to visualize leakage in the
form it takes in the continuous domain. Suppose the
continuous autocorrelation function of $x(t)$ is $R_x(\tau)$.
Then the PSD, $S_x(f)$, would be obtained from

$$S_x(f) = \int_{-\infty}^{\infty} R_x(\tau) \exp(-j2\pi f\tau)\, d\tau \qquad -\infty < f < \infty \qquad (5.8)$$

The two-sided version is used for clarity of pre-
sentation. Suppose, however, that a second PSD is computed, where only a finite-length segment of $R_x(\tau)$ is
employed:

$$\hat{S}_x(f) = \int_{-T}^{T} R_x(\tau) \exp(-j2\pi f\tau)\, d\tau \qquad (5.9)$$

Only the interval $(-T,T)$ is employed. This is very
similar to the type of calculation done in the standard procedure. It turns out that the truncation of the
integral has a decided effect on $\hat{S}_x(f)$ and its relation to $S_x(f)$. Equation (5.9) can be rewritten as

$$\hat{S}_x(f) = \int_{-\infty}^{\infty} u_T(\tau) \; R_x(\tau) \; \exp(-j2\pi f\tau) \; d\tau \qquad (5.10)$$

where u_T is the boxcar function:

$$u_T(\tau) = \begin{cases} 1 & |\tau| \le T \\ 0 & |\tau| > T \end{cases} \qquad (5.11)$$

Use may now be made of the convolution theorem: If two functions are multiplied in the time domain, then their Fourier transforms are convolved in the frequency domain. Thus, we could rewrite (5.10) as

$$\hat{S}_x(f) = S_x(f) * U_T(f)$$

$$= \int_{-\infty}^{\infty} S(f') \; U_T(f - f') \; df' \qquad (5.12)$$

The symbol * denotes convolutions, and $U_T(f)$ is the Fourier transform of $u_T(\tau)$. In particular,

$$U_T(f) = 2 \; \frac{\sin 2\pi fT}{2\pi f} \qquad (5.13)$$

Thus, (5.9) finally may be rewritten as

$$\hat{S}_x(f) = \int_{-\infty}^{\infty} S_x(f') \; 2 \; \frac{\sin[2\pi T(f - f')]}{2\pi \; (f - f')} \; df' \qquad (5.14)$$

As an example, suppose that

$$R_x(\tau) = \frac{A^2}{2} \; \cos 2\pi f_0 \tau \qquad (5.15)$$

Then $S_x(f)$ is given by

$$S_x(f) = \frac{A^2}{4} \left[\delta(f - f_0) + \delta(f + f_0) \right] \qquad (5.16)$$

That is, $S_x(f)$ consists of peaks (delta functions) at frequencies f_0 and $-f_0$. When this particular expression for $S_x(f)$ is substituted into (5.14), the resulting $\hat{S}_x(f)$ is

$$\hat{S}_x(f) = \frac{A^2}{2} \frac{\sin\left[2\pi T(f - f_0)\right]}{2\pi(f - f_0)} + \frac{A^2}{2} \frac{\sin\left[2\pi T(f + f_0)\right]}{2\pi(f + f_0)}$$

$$(5.17)$$

For frequencies greater than zero, and for f_0 and T such that

$$0 \ll \frac{1}{T} \ll f_0 \qquad (5.18)$$

then

$$\hat{S}_x(f) \approx \frac{A^2}{2} \frac{\sin\left[2\pi T(f - f_0)\right]}{2\pi(f - f_0)} \qquad (5.19)$$

The maximum of this occurs at f_0, for which

$$\hat{S}_x(f_0) \approx \frac{A^2 T}{2} \qquad (5.20)$$

As T becomes larger, this peak becomes narrower and higher, and in the limit it goes to a delta function.

It is important to remember what has happened: Because of the finite value of T, what would have been a delta function for infinite T has become a sin x/x function centered about f_0. Thus, the power which was concentrated at a single point has been spread out over a much broader range. It is this spreading of the power that is termed *leakage*. Figure 5.1 shows the sin x/x function of (5.19).

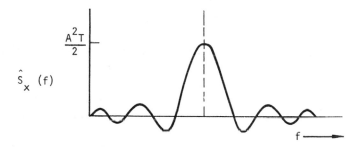

Fig. 5.1 Power spectral density of a sinusoid having a sin x/x form due to truncation.

The first zero crossing to the right of f_0 occurs at

$$2\pi T (f_r - f_0) = \pi$$

or

$$f_r = f_0 + \frac{1}{2T} \tag{5.21}$$

Similarly, the first zero crossing to the left of f_0 occurs at

$$f_\ell = f_0 - \frac{1}{2T} \tag{5.22}$$

The difference of these, f_w, is a function only of T:

$$f_r - f_\ell = f_w = \frac{1}{T} \tag{5.23}$$

Thus, the width of the sin x/x function is determined
solely by T. Note also that there are significant non-
zero portions of the sin x/x function on either side
of the main peak. These are referred to as *side lobes*.
These side lobes, in one form or another, will appear
in all finite PSD calculations.

The suppression of the side lobes (also referred to
as the reduction of leakage) is a serious problem and
one on which many papers have been written. For example, see Akaike (1962), Blackman and Tukey (1958),
Jenkins and Watts (1968), Parzen (1962), etc., for details of procedures summarized here.

The solutions are different for each of the PSD
procedures and for different assumptions on the nature
of the data.

The basic sin x/x function, or whatever form it is
altered .into by the calculation procedure and the
technique employed to reduce leakage, is commonly referred to as the *window*. That is, it is the limiting
(and irreversible) mechanism through which the PSD is
seen.*

The windows that are used in place of the basic
sin x/x window have less leakage at the expense of
broadening the main lobe. This is accomplished in a
variety of ways, the details of which will be discussed in the following chapters.

Table 5.1 lists the forms that the sin x/x functions take in the various f and t ranges.

---

*The analogy between this operation and the operation
which is performed on an object being viewed through a
telescope by the main objective lens of the telescope
makes the terminology much clearer. A star, which is
effectively a delta function insofar as intensity is
concerned, becomes a sort of two-dimensional sin x/x
function in the image plane of the telescope, with the
diameter of the main lobe of the resulting intensity
pattern being proportional to the reciprocal of the
diameter of the objective lens of the telescope.

Table 5.1 Window Functions Corresponding to the Four Forms of the Fourier Transform. The Record Length is Assumed to be T = NΔt. Additionally, Forms I and II are Taken to be Symmetric.

Form	Range of f, kΔf	Range of t, iΔt	$W(f)$ $\dfrac{\sin x}{x}$
I	$-\infty < f < \infty$ continuous	$-\infty < t < \infty$ continuous	$\dfrac{\sin \pi T f}{\pi f}$
II	$-\dfrac{1}{2\Delta t} \leq f \leq \dfrac{1}{2\Delta t}$ continuous repetitive	$-\infty \leq i < \infty$ discrete	$\Delta t \dfrac{\sin\left[(2m + 1)\pi f \Delta t\right]}{\sin \pi f \Delta t}$
III	$0 < K < N - 1$ discrete repetitive	$0 \leq i \leq N - 1$ discrete repetitive	$\Delta t \left[e^{-j\pi k \left(\frac{N - 1}{N}\right)} \right] \dfrac{\sin\left[\pi k\right]}{\sin\left[\dfrac{\pi k}{N}\right]}$
IV	$-\infty < k < \infty$ discrete	$0 \leq t \leq T$ continuous repetitive	$(e^{-j\pi k}) \left[\dfrac{\sin (\pi k)}{\pi k / T} \right]$

Types II and III are equivalent if:

1. The complex constant multiplying the type III form is ignored; its absolute value is unity, and in any event would disappear if the range of iΔt were redefined to be symmetric.

2. In the form II of (sin x/x), (2m + 1) must be replaced with N, and f with k/NΔt. When this is done, type II reduces to type III.

Table 5.2 shows the relationship between the sample PSDs produced by the three methods and the underlying PSD and Fourier-transformed time series.

It is difficult to visualize the lag windows as they become more complex. But their effects can be regarded as generally similar, with the following notable exceptions:

1. The correlation PSD procedure can produce negative values of the PSD due to the window. For example, as shown in Figure 5.1, the PSD of sine wave will have some negative values.

2. Both the Fourier transform and filter windows operate in some manner on x, while the correlation window operates on $R_x(\tau)$. The latter type of windowing turns out to have some conceptual advantages.

3. The filter PSD window seems to require the least corrections, assuming that the filter transfer function is reasonably strong; i.e., it already tends to act like the improvements to the correlation and filter windows which are described in Chapters 6 and 7. This presumes that the truncation takes place before the filtering. If the reverse is true, then leakage is more severe.

5.3   STATISTICAL ERROR

This section defines the statistical terms employed in discussing error, and applies them to the PSD. The error for the Fourier transform PSD of the Gaussian

Table 5.2   Summary of Three Forms of PSD

PSD type

Correlation

$$\hat{S}_x(f) = W_{II}(f) * S_x(f)$$

Fourier

$$\hat{S}_x\left(\frac{k}{N\Delta t}\right) = \left| W_{III}\left(\frac{k}{N\Delta t}\right) * X\left(\frac{k}{Nt}\right) \right|^2$$

Filter

$$\hat{S}_x(f) = \int_0^{\frac{1}{2\Delta t}} \left| \left[W_{II}(f') * X(f') \right] H(f,f') \right|^2 df'$$

In the table, $X(f)$ is assumed to be the Fourier transform of x_i, a form II process, whose PSD is $S_x(f)$;
$H(f_0,f)$ is the filter which passes power centered
about the frequency f_0. The expression for the correlation form of the PSD is slightly incorrect.
Another window type of term should be added to reflect
the truncation of the time series.

white noise case is shown to be quite large. Remedies
are discussed; they effectively involve averaging the
PSD or PSDs in some manner in order to reduce the variability of the original PSD.

Statistical error, as opposed to instrumentation
error, is the uncertainty in PSD measurements due to
the amount of data gathered, the underlying probabil-
istic nature of the data, and the method used in de-
riving the desired parameter. Suppose that the parameter Φ is being estimated and that the estimate of Φ
is $\hat{\Phi}$. Such an estimate is *unbiased* if

$$E[\hat{\Phi}] = \Phi \tag{5.24}$$

The *mean square* error of the *estimate* is defined by

$$\text{Mean square error} = E\left[(\hat{\Phi} - \Phi)^2\right] \tag{5.25}$$

The estimate $\hat{\Phi}$ will usually be a function of the record length T. If $\hat{\Phi}$ is a *consistent* estimate of Φ, then

$$\lim_{T\to\infty} E\left[(\hat{\Phi} - \Phi)^2\right] = 0 \tag{5.26}$$

This implies that as the record length becomes larger, the mean square error tends to decrease.

Consider the estimate of the PSD of x at the frequency f using the Fourier transform procedure:

$$\hat{G}_x(f) = \frac{2}{N\Delta t} \left[\Delta t \, X^*(f)\right] \left[\Delta t X(f)\right]$$

$$= \frac{2}{N\Delta t} \left(\Delta t \sum_{i=0}^{N-1} x_i e^{j2\pi fi\Delta t}\right) \left(\Delta t \sum_{k=0}^{N-1} x_k e^{-2\pi fk\Delta t}\right)$$

$$= \frac{2\Delta t}{N} \left(\sum_{i=0}^{N-1} \sum_{k=0}^{N-1} x_i x_k e^{-j2\pi f\Delta t(k-i)}\right) \tag{5.27}$$

By defining r to be equal to (k-i) and introducing a new variable ℓ, the above can be rearranged to yield

$$\hat{G}_x(f) = 2\Delta t \sum_{r=-(N-1)}^{N-1} \cos 2\pi fr\Delta t \left(\frac{1}{N} \sum_{\ell=0}^{N-|r|-1} x_\ell x_{\ell+r}\right) \tag{5.28}$$

Expectations may be taken of this, resulting in

$$E\left[\hat{G}_x(f)\right] = 2\Delta t \sum_{r=-(N-1)}^{N-1} \cos 2\Delta fr\pi t \left(\frac{N-|r|}{N} R_{xr}\right) \tag{5.29}$$

Suppose that $\{x_i\}$ is uncorrelated white noise. That is

$$R_{xr} = \begin{cases} \sigma^2 & r = 0 \\ 0 & \text{otherwise} \end{cases} \tag{5.30}$$

Then the PSD is a constant:

$$E[\hat{G}_x(f)] = 2\Delta t \sigma^2 \tag{5.31}$$

Note that this evaluation corresponds to a bandwidth of $(1/N\Delta t)$ Hz. If $N/2$ bands that do not overlap are formed, they will completely cover the frequency range. Thus, the integral with respect to f of $E[\hat{G}_x(f)]$ is σ^2. For white noise, at least, the estimate is therefore unbiased.

Next consider the normalized mean square error of $G_x(f)$ given by

$$\varepsilon^2 = \text{Mean square error}$$

$$= E[\hat{G}_x(f) - G_x(f)]^2 / G_x^2(f)$$

$$= E[\hat{G}_x^2(f) - 2G_x(f)\, \hat{G}_x(f) + G_x^2(f)] / G_x^2(f)$$

$$= \left\{ E[\hat{G}_x^2(f)] - 2G_x(f)\, E[\hat{G}_x(f)] + G_x^2(f) \right\} / G_x^2(f) \tag{5.32}$$

Suppose that white noise is again being discussed. Then

$$\varepsilon^2 = \left\{ E[\hat{G}_x^2(f)] - 4\Delta t \sigma^2 (2\Delta t \sigma^2) + (2\Delta t \sigma^2)^2 \right\} / G_x^2(f)$$

$$= \left\{ E[\hat{G}_x^2(f)] - 4(\Delta t)^2 \sigma^4 \right\} / 4\Delta t^2 \sigma^4 \tag{5.33}$$

Before this can be evaluated, another assumption about $\{x_i\}$ must be made. Up to now, the only assumptions required are that $\{x_i\}$ have a zero mean and be uncorrelated. The new assumption is that $\{x_i\}$ is Gaussian. The reason for making this assumption is to be able to employ a very useful feature of the Gaussian distribution; namely, that if x_a, x_b, x_c, x_d are any four samples from $\{x_i\}$, then

$$E[x_a x_b x_c x_d] = E[x_a x_b] E[x_c x_d] + E[x_a x_c] E[x_b x_d]$$

$$+ E[x_a x_d] E[x_b x_c] \tag{5.34}$$

This expression was introduced in Chapter 1. If $\{x_i\}$ is white noise, then using (5.34)

$$E[x_a x_b x_c x_d] = \begin{cases} 3\sigma^4 & a = b = c = d \\ \sigma^4 & a = b, \ c = d, \ a \neq c \\ \sigma^4 & a = c, \ b = d, \ a \neq b \\ \sigma^4 & a = d, \ b = c, \ a \neq b \\ 0 & \text{otherwise} \end{cases} \tag{5.35}$$

The expression for the expected value of the square of the sample PSD is

$$E[\hat{G}_x^2(f)]$$

$$= \left(\frac{2\Delta t}{N}\right)^2 E\left\{ \sum_{a=0}^{N-1} \sum_{b=0}^{N-1} \sum_{c=0}^{N-1} \sum_{d=0}^{N-1} x_a x_b x_c x_d \right.$$

$$\left. \exp[-j2\pi f\Delta t (a - b + c - d)] \right\} \tag{5.36}$$

This must be evaluated for each of the above four cases in which the expectation is not zero.

Case 1. (a = b = c = d). This holds in exactly N places. Therefore, the contribution is $3N\sigma^4$.

Case 2. (a = b, c = d, a ≠ c). There are $N^2 - N$ places where this occurs. As the exponent is zero, the contribution is $(N^2 - N)\sigma^4$.

Case 4. (a = c, b = d, a ≠ b). Same as Case 2. The contribution is $(N^2 - N)\sigma^4$.

Case 3. (a = d, b = c, a ≠ b). This case is more complex. Its contribution is

$$\sigma^4 \sum_{a=0}^{N-1} \sum_{b=0}^{N-1} \exp[-j4\pi f\Delta t(a - b)] - N\sigma^4$$

$$= \sigma^4 \left(\frac{1 - e^{-j4\pi f\Delta tN}}{1 - e^{-j4\pi f\Delta t}}\right)\left(\frac{1 - e^{+j4\pi f\Delta tN}}{1 - e^{+j4\pi f\Delta t}}\right) - N\sigma^4$$

$$= \sigma^4 \frac{2 - 2\cos 4\pi f\Delta tN}{2 - 2\cos 4\pi f\Delta t} - N\sigma^4$$

$$= \sigma^4 \left(\frac{\sin 2\pi f\Delta tN}{\sin 2\pi f\Delta t}\right)^2 - N\sigma^4 \qquad (5.37)$$

In summary

$$E[\hat{G}_x^2(f)]$$

$$= \left(\frac{2\Delta t}{N}\right)^2 \left[3N\sigma^4 + 2(N^2 - N)\sigma^4 + \sigma^4\left(\frac{\sin 2\pi f\Delta tN}{\sin 2\pi f\Delta t}\right)^2 - N\sigma^4\right]$$

$$= \left(\frac{2\Delta t}{N}\right)^2 \sigma^4 \left[2N^2 + \left(\frac{\sin 2\pi f\Delta tN}{\sin 2\pi f\Delta t}\right)^2\right] \qquad (5.38)$$

The mean square error therefore is

$$\varepsilon^2 = \left(\frac{2\Delta t}{N}\right)^2 \sigma^4 \left[2N^2 + \left(\frac{\sin 2\pi f \Delta t N}{\sin 2\pi f \Delta t}\right)^2 - N^2\right] \bigg/ 4\Delta t^2 \sigma^4$$

$$= 1 + \frac{1}{N^2}\left(\frac{\sin 2\pi f \Delta t N}{\sin 2\pi f \Delta t}\right)^2 \qquad\qquad (5.39)$$

Note that if $f = p/N\Delta t$, then

$$\varepsilon^2 = 1 \qquad\qquad\qquad\qquad\qquad\qquad (5.40)$$

This result is very important: If $\{x_i\}$ is uncorrelated Gaussian noise, then the value of the normalized stand-ard error for the estimate is greater than or equal to unity (the standard deviation of the estimate is greater than or equal to the quantity being estimated.

Furthermore, while it does decrease with increasing N, it does not vanish in the limit but goes to unity. Therefore, $G_x(f)$ is not a consistent estimate of $G(f)$. This result has been shown by many authors such as Hannan (1960), and is a fundamental limitation upon the PSD estimation process. As will be seen, this problem is overcome in practice if a sacrifice in re-solving power is made.

The Fourier transform PSD is usually computed for $f = p/N\Delta t$, $p = 0,\ldots,N/2$, so that the mean square error always unity.

Next, consider the random variable X_k, where, as usual

$$X_k = \sum_{i=0}^{N-1} x_i \exp(-j2\pi ki/N) \qquad k = 0,\ldots,N/2 \qquad (5.41)$$

If $\{x_i\}$ is Gaussian, then by an extension of the cen-tral limit theorem, so is X_k. Assuming $\{x_i\}$ to have a zero mean and to be uncorrelated, then

$$E[x_k] = E\left\{\sum_{i=0}^{N-1} x_i \exp(-j2\pi ki/N)\right\}$$

$$= \sum_{i=0}^{N-1} E(x_i) \exp(-j2\pi ki/N)$$

$$= 0$$

$$Var[x_k] = E[x_k^* x_k]$$

$$= N\sigma^2 \tag{5.42}$$

Furthermore, if $p \neq q$, then X_p and X_q are uncorrelated:

$$E[x_p^* x_q] = E\left\{\left[\sum_{i=0}^{N-1} x_i \exp(-j2\pi ip/N)\right]\left[\sum_{k=0}^{N-1} x_k \exp(j2\pi kq/N)\right]\right\}$$

$$= E\left\{\sum_{i=0}^{N=1}\sum_{k=0}^{N-1} x_i x_k \exp[-j2\pi(ip - kq)/N]\right\}$$

$$= \sum_{i=0}^{N-1}\sum_{k=0}^{N-1} E(x_i x_k) \exp[j2\pi(ip - kq)/N]$$

$$= \sigma^2 \sum_{i=0}^{N-1} \exp[-j2\pi i(p - q)/N]$$

$$= \sigma^2 \frac{1-\exp[-j2\pi(p - q)]}{1-\exp[-j2\pi(p - q)/N]}$$

$$= \begin{cases} N\sigma^2 & p = q \\ 0 & \text{otherwise} \end{cases} \tag{5.43}$$

The complex sequence X_k, $k = 0,\ldots,N/2$, can be broken down into real and imaginary parts. Define

$$Re(X_k) = \text{Real part of } [x_k]$$

$$= \sum_{i=0}^{N-1} x_i \cos \frac{2\pi ik}{N}$$

$$Im(X_k) = \text{Imaginary part of } [x_k]$$

$$= \sum_{i=0}^{N-1} x_i \sin \frac{2\pi ik}{N}$$

$$X_k = Re(X_k) + j\, Im(X_k) \qquad k = 0,\ldots,N/2 \qquad (5.44)$$

The expected value of the product of the real and imaginary parts may be shown to be zero for any p:

$$E[Re(X_k)\, Im(X_k)] = E\left[\sum_{p=0}^{N-1} \sum_{\ell=0}^{N-1} x_p x_\ell \cos \frac{2\pi pk}{N} \sin \frac{2\pi \ell k}{N} \right]$$

$$= \sigma^2 \sum_{p=0}^{N-1} \cos \frac{2\pi pk}{N} \sin \frac{2\pi pk}{N}$$

$$= \frac{\sigma^2}{2} \sum_{p=0}^{N-1} \sin \frac{4\pi pk}{N}$$

$$= \frac{\sigma^2}{2} \frac{\sin 2\pi k \sin \dfrac{N-1}{N} 2\pi k}{\sin \dfrac{2\pi k}{N}}$$

$$= 0 \qquad\qquad (5.45)$$

Thus, the $(N/2)$ values each of $\{\,Re(X_p)\,\}$ and $\{\,Im(X_p)\,\}$ are independent Gaussian random variables with zero mean and with variance $(\Delta t\sigma^2)$.

Now consider the following: An estimate of the power taken about the frequency f, where

$$f = \frac{2q + M - 1}{2N\Delta t} \tag{5.46}$$

can be made by taking an average of M of the absolute value squared components of X_k:

$$\hat{G}_x(f) = \frac{1}{M}\frac{2\Delta t}{N}\sum_{k=q}^{q+M-1}\left\{[Re\,(X_k)]^2 + [Im\,(X_k)]^2\right\} \tag{5.47}$$

The expectation of this estimate is

$$E[\hat{G}_x(f)] = 2\Delta t\sigma^2 \tag{5.48}$$

the same as that obtained from the previous formulation of $\hat{G}_x(f)$ in (5.31). The bandwidth is broader, because it now covers $(M/N\Delta t)$ Hz. On the other hand, because it is estimated using 2M rather than the basic two estimates, the variability will be found to be much less.

The variability may be discussed in either of two manners: In the first, the normalized standard error will be found simply by dividing the original normalized error by the number of estimates; the second interpretation is to view the sum of the absolute value squared terms in (5.47) as a χ^2-variable, and to make use of that distribution to find a confidence interval for the estimate.

The first of these procedures is the simplest: the standard error, ε_0, is simply

$$\varepsilon_0^2 = \frac{\varepsilon^2}{M} \tag{5.49}$$

or

$$\varepsilon_0 = \sqrt{\frac{1}{M}}$$ (5.50)

as ε^2, the mean square error, is unity. Clearly, as M increases, ε_0 decreases. For example, if M is equal to 81, then 81 PSD values are averaged, and the ε_0 is 1/9.

Define B_e as the bandwidth of the estimate. Then

$$B_e = M\Delta f$$

$$= M \left(\frac{1}{N\Delta t}\right)$$

$$= \frac{M}{T}$$ (5.51)

Thus,

$$M = B_e T$$ (5.52)

The expression for the normalized standard error can therefore be put in the form

$$\varepsilon_0^2 = \frac{1}{B_e T}$$ (5.53)

The second way of discussing the error is through the χ^2-distribution discussed in Chapter 1. It is applied in the following manner: If $\hat{G}(f)$ is an estimate of the PSD around the frequency f, then the confidence limits take the form

$$\text{Prob}[A < G(f) \leq B] = p$$ (5.54)

The parameter p is a fixed confidence level, which commonly is either 0.80,0.90, or 0.95. Equation (5.54) may be interpreted as, "with 100p% confidence, the true value of G(f) lies between A and B."

The value for p is chosen before tests are made. A related parameter α, where

$$\alpha = 1 - p \tag{5.55}$$

is sometimes also used with p. Having obtained $\hat{G}(f)$, the A and B parameters known as the confidence limits, are

$$A = \frac{n\hat{G}(f)}{\chi^2_{n;\alpha/2}}$$

$$B = \frac{n\hat{G}(f)}{\chi^2_{n;1 - \alpha/2}} \tag{5.56}$$

The $\chi^2_{n;\alpha}$ expression is based on the χ^2-distribution. Its definition is

$$\chi^2_{n;\alpha} = \left[b \text{ such that } \int_b^\infty p(\chi^2_n) \, d\chi^2_n = \alpha \right] \tag{5.57}$$

The number of degrees of freedom, n, is twice the number of X_k terms that appear within the bandwidth of the estimate. Thus,

$$n = 2B_e T \tag{5.58}$$

which can be interpreted as the total number of real and imaginary components within the bandwidth B_e. As shown above, each of these components is in itself a Gaussian random variable, so that squaring and adding them does indeed produce a χ^2-variable.

These results were derived for the Fourier transform PSD case, but using (5.58), they can be applied
to the other two procedures.

In the correlation case,

$$B_e = \frac{2}{m\Delta t} \qquad (5.59)$$

so that

$$n = 2 \left(\frac{1}{m\Delta t}\right) N\Delta t = \frac{2N}{m} \qquad (5.60)$$

That is, for the correlation PSD the number of degrees
of freedom is the ratio of two times the number of
original data points to the number of autocorrelation
lags. Similarly, the standard error may be written as

$$\varepsilon_0 = \sqrt{\frac{m}{N}} \qquad (5.61)$$

In the filter case, the formulas are

$$\varepsilon_0 = \sqrt{\frac{1}{B_k T}}$$

and

$$n = 2B_k T \qquad (5.62)$$

where B_k is the bandwidth of the filter. These results
are compared in Table 5.3.

An example will illustrate the formulas, given in
Table 5.3. Suppose $\Delta t = 1/2000$, the desired bandwidth
is $B_e = 10$ Hz, and $N = 4000$, i.e., 4000 data points
are used. Then

Table 5.3 Degrees of Freedom and Standard Error
Formulas for the Three PSD Methods

PSD type	Degrees of freedom, $n = 2B_eT$	Standard error, $\varepsilon_0 = \sqrt{\dfrac{1}{B_eT}}$
Correlation	$\dfrac{2N}{m}$	$\sqrt{\dfrac{m}{n}}$
Fourier	$2M$	$\sqrt{\dfrac{1}{M}}$
Filter	$2B_kT$	$\sqrt{\dfrac{1}{B_kT}}$

*Legend: n = Number of degrees of freedom; N = Total
number of data points; m = Number of autocorrelation
lags; M = Number of complex Fourier components averaged; B_k = Bandwidth of the filter employed; $T = N\Delta t$ =
Length of record.

$$\text{Folding frequency} = \frac{1}{2\Delta t} = 1000 \text{ Hz}$$

$$T = \text{Record length} = N\Delta t = 2 \text{ sec}$$

$$\varepsilon = \text{Standard error} = \sqrt{\frac{1}{B_eT}} = \sqrt{\frac{1}{20}} = \sqrt{0.05} \approx 0.$$

$$n = \text{Degrees of freedom} = 2B_eT = 40$$

If the correlation procedure were employed,

$$m = \text{Number of autocorrelation lags} = \frac{2N}{n} = 200$$

If the Fourier procedure were used,

$$M = \text{Number of } |X_k|^2 \text{ values to average}$$

$$= \frac{B_e}{1/N\Delta t} = \frac{n}{2} = 20$$

The 95% confidence bands are found in the following manner: $\chi^2_{40;0.975}$ and $\chi^2_{40;0.025}$ are found from Table 5.4.

$$\chi^2_{40;.975} = 24.43$$

$$\chi^2_{40;0.025} = 59.34 \qquad\qquad (5.63)$$

Then if $\hat{G}(f)$ is a particular sample value, then the 95% confidence bounds on G(f) are

$$\frac{40}{59.34} \hat{G}(f) \le G(f) \le \frac{40}{24.43} \hat{G}(f) \qquad\qquad (5.64)$$

In words, "with 95% confidence, the true spectrum G(f) lies in the interval $[0.68\ \hat{G}(f), 1.64\ \hat{G}(f)]$."

All of the above analysis was done on the assumption that the data were both Gaussian and white. With actual data, the premise which is most often violated is that of whiteness. Usually, the data are colored (i.e., correlated) in some manner. This has the effect of reducing n, the number of degrees of freedom. The maximum for n is N, the total number of data points. This may be reduced to nearly zero. For example, if the data examined is the result of passing white noise through a bandpass filter of width 1 Hz, and 1 sec of the data is recorded, then the total degrees of freedom, using the $2B_eT$ formula is two. This figure is for the total in the record; it does not matter if the sampling rate were 10,000 samples per second so that 10,000 data points were taken, the number of total degrees of freedom would still be only two.

Standard practice is to use the white noise results as guidelines. As long as this is done with care, they are useful, particularly in planning. If they are employed where their use is not warranted, then they may give very erroneous answers.

We will discuss more detailed aspects of the computational methods in Chapters 6 and 7. Special aspects

Table 5.4 Percentage Points of Chi-Square Distribution

Value of $\chi^2_{n;a}$ such that $\text{Prob}[\chi^2_a > \chi^2_{n;a}] = \alpha$

n	α									
	0.995	0.990	0.975	0.950	0.900	0.10	0.05	0.025	0.010	0.005
1	0.000039	0.00016	0.00098	0.0039	0.0158	2.71	3.84	5.02	6.63	7.88
2	0.0100	0.0201	0.0506	0.103	0.211	4.61	5.99	7.38	9.21	10.60
3	0.0717	0.115	0.216	0.352	0.584	6.25	7.81	9.35	11.34	12.84
4	0.207	0.297	0.484	0.711	1.06	7.78	9.49	11.14	13.28	14.86
5	0.412	0.554	0.831	1.15	1.61	9.24	11.07	12.83	15.09	16.75
6	0.676	0.872	1.24	1.64	2.20	10.64	12.59	14.45	16.81	18.55
7	0.989	1.24	1.69	2.17	2.83	12.02	14.07	16.01	18.48	20.28
8	1.34	1.65	2.18	2.73	3.49	13.36	15.51	17.53	20.09	21.96
9	1.73	2.09	2.70	3.33	4.17	14.68	16.92	19.02	21.67	23.59
10	2.16	2.56	3.25	3.94	4.87	15.99	18.31	20.48	23.21	25.19
11	2.60	3.05	3.82	4.57	5.58	17.28	19.68	21.92	24.73	26.76
12	3.07	3.57	4.40	5.23	6.30	18.55	21.03	23.34	26.22	28.30
13	3.57	4.11	5.01	5.89	7.04	19.81	22.36	24.74	27.69	29.82
14	4.07	4.66	5.63	6.57	7.79	21.06	23.68	26.12	29.14	31.32
15	4.60	5.23	6.26	7.26	8.55	22.31	25.00	27.49	30.58	32.80
16	5.14	5.81	6.91	7.96	9.31	23.54	26.30	28.85	32.00	34.27
17	5.70	6.41	7.56	8.67	10.08	24.77	27.59	30.19	33.41	35.72
18	6.26	7.01	8.23	9.39	10.86	25.99	28.87	31.53	34.81	37.16
19	6.84	7.63	8.91	10.12	11.65	27.20	30.14	32.85	36.19	35.58
20	7.43	8.26	9.59	10.85	12.44	28.41	31.41	34.17	37.57	40.00
21	8.03	8.90	10.28	11.59	13.24	29.62	32.67	35.48	38.93	41.40
22	8.64	9.54	10.98	12.34	14.04	30.81	33.92	36.78	40.29	42.80
23	9.26	10.20	11.69	13.09	14.85	32.01	35.17	38.08	41.64	44.18
24	9.89	10.86	12.40	13.85	15.66	33.20	36.42	39.36	42.98	45.56
25	10.52	11.52	13.12	14.61	16.47	34.38	37.65	40.65	44.31	46.93
26	11.16	12.20	13.84	15.38	17.29	35.56	38.88	41.92	45.64	48.29
27	11.81	12.88	14.57	16.15	18.11	36.74	40.11	43.19	44.96	49.64
28	12.46	13.56	15.31	16.93	18.94	37.92	41.34	44.46	48.28	59.99
29	13.12	14.26	16.05	17.71	19.77	39.09	42.56	45.72	49.59	52.34
30	13.79	14.95	16.79	18.49	20.60	40.26	43.77	46.98	50.89	53.67
40	20.71	22.16	24.43	26.51	29.05	51.81	55.76	59.34	63.69	66.77
60	35.53	37.48	40.48	43.19	46.46	74.40	79.08	83.30	88.38	91.95
120	83.85	86.92	91.58	95.70	100.62	140.23	146.57	152.21	158.95	163.65

For $n > 120$, $\chi^2_{n;a} \approx n\left[1 - \dfrac{2}{9n} + z_a\sqrt{\dfrac{2}{9n}}\right]^3$ where z_a is the desired percentage point for a standardized normal normal distribution.

of the computations will have some effect on degrees
of freedom and bias, but the principles discussed in
this chapter substantially hold.

Problems

5.1   Explain the factor $1/4m\Delta t$ in (5.5).

5.2   Prove

$$\hat{G}_x(f) = \frac{2\Delta t}{N} \sum_{i=0}^{N-1} \sum_{k=0}^{N-1} x_i x_k \, e^{-j2\pi f\Delta t(k - i)}$$

$$= 2\Delta t \sum_{r=-(N-1)}^{N-1} \cos 2\pi fr\Delta t \, \frac{1}{N}\left(\sum_{\ell=0}^{N-|r|-1} x_\ell x_{\ell + r} \right)$$

[Hint: Arrange terms of double summation in
matrix form.]

5.3   Explain the origin of the factor $2\Delta t/N$ in the
formula for $G_x(f)$ in Problem 5.1.

5.4   What is

$$E\left[\frac{1}{N} \sum_{\ell=0}^{N-r-1} x_\ell x_{\ell + r} \right]$$

equal to? For white noise?

5.5   What is the width of the main lobe (in Hz) of

$$\mathcal{F}[u(f)]$$

5.6   Why is the term "window" reasonable when applied
to spectrum estimates?

5.7   Derive (5.36) based on $\hat{G}_x(f)$ from (5.27).

5.8   Why does

$$E \sum_{p=0}^{N-1} \sum_{\ell-1}^{N-1} X_p X_\ell \cos \frac{2\pi pk}{N} \sin \frac{2\pi \ell k}{N}$$

$$= \sigma^2 \sum_{p=0}^{N-1} \cos \frac{2\pi pk}{N} \sin \frac{2\pi pk}{N}$$

for white noise.

5.9   Equation (5.31) states that the PSD of white noise with variance σ^2 is $G(f) = 2\Delta t \sigma^2$. Prove this.

5.10   Explain the last step in (5.45).

CHAPTER 6
CORRELATION FUNCTION AND BLACKMAN-TUKEY
SPECTRUM COMPUTATIONS

6.1 BASIC CONCEPTS

This chapter contains a discussion of autocorrelation and cross-correlation functions. The autocorrelation is a natural specialization of the cross-correlation, and thus the computational considerations are nearly identical.

Correlation functions have wide applications in shock and vibration analysis, communication problems, radar detection, control systems, oceanographic data analysis, and in fact any field where spectral analysis is pertinent due to the relationship via Fourier transforms. When power or cross spectra can be applied to the analysis of a problem, the corresponding correlation functions can, in principle, be used in an equivalent manner, since they are Fourier transform pairs. In practice, there may be a strong reason for choosing one or the other. For example, the time delay between two signals can be determined from the phase of a cross spectrum, but would often show up in a more natural manner in the cross-correlation function.

The computation of correlation functions has in the past required large amounts of computer time. The primary computational loop involved is a multiply-add sequence which often must be executed on the order of 10^7 times. This means, for example, that on a modern high-speed, large-scale digital computer where a fixed-point, multiply-add loop could be executed in, say, 20 μsec, a total of 200 sec, or 3 minutes and 20 sec, would be required for just the execution of this loop. That would be the computational time required for just one single data record. In many physical applications, the number of data records to be analyzed both individually and jointly can run into fairly large numbers. Hence, there has been a real need to give attention to this correlation computation loop to make it less time-consuming and more efficient.

It has been shown by Sande (1965) that the computational speed for the correlation functions can sometimes be reduced via the indirect route of using FFTs. Many other specialized methods, based on other considerations, have been developed and may be more economical than the FFTs from one standpoint or another, depending on specific circumstances. For example, if one has invested in a high-speed, special-purpose, multiply-add unit, such as those which have been available from many computer manufacturers, straightforward computations may be the most economical. Direct programming of the correlation equation may be by far the simplest. Also, the adaptation of the computational procedures to more than a coreful of data is probably simplest for the basic correlation equation.

The equation to be evaluated is

$$\hat{R}_{xyr} = \frac{1}{N-r} \sum_{i=1}^{N-r} x_i y_{i+r} \qquad r = -m, \ldots, -1, 0, 1, \ldots, m$$

(6.1)

where

$$\hat{R}_{xyr} \equiv \hat{R}_{xy}(r\Delta\tau)$$

$$x_i \equiv x(i\Delta t)$$

$$y_i \equiv y(i\Delta t)$$

and usually,

$$\Delta\tau = \Delta t$$

It is this equation that will form the basis of all correlation computations. There are sometimes reasons for preferring a divisor of N instead of (N - r) in certain instances. The equation is

$$\hat{R}'_{xyr} = \frac{1}{N} \sum_{i=1}^{N-r} x_i y_{i+r} \qquad r = -m,\ldots,-1,0,1,\ldots,m \qquad (6.2)$$

It can be shown (Parzen, 1961) that the variance of $\hat{R}'_{xyr}$ is less than that of $\hat{R}_{xyr}$, although it is a biased estimate while $\hat{R}_{xyr}$ is not. For large lag values of m close to N, a disconcerting characteristic of $\hat{R}_{xyr}$ is that the correlation coefficient derived from it will not necessarily lie between plus and minus one. This would occur only rarely for typical lag values of m not exceeding 10 or 20% of N and normalized data.

As has been pointed out previously, two different types of time series data arise that are to be processed by a digital computer. Some processes are discrete by their very nature, say, for example, the daily closing prices of a given stock. On the other hand, some data arise naturally as a continuous record such as the continuously recorded output of an accelerometer mounted on the skin of a missile structure which is intended to give a measure of the vibration at that point. The continuous record is digitized for digital analysis by an analog-to-digital conversion procedure. In either case, an important observation to make is that only a finite number of bits in a binary digital computer are required to represent any given individual data point. In actual practice, many analog-to-digital converters present their output at a precision of 8 to 10 bits (including the sign bit). For almost all applications, the recording instruments are no more accurate than one part in 256 to 1024, and hence, that quantization is fine enough. The dynamic range in terms of decibels (dB) is from about 42 dB for 8 bits to 54 dB for 10 bits. In some legitimate applications, greater dynamic ranges can exist in the data and transducers, but not usually.

As it turns out, for many time series of interest, much coarser quantization is often acceptable. In the extreme case, one can quantize to a single bit. That is, if the value of a signal is larger than or equal to zero, set the bit equal to zero; if the value of the signal is less than zero, set the bit equal to one. In simpler terms, the sign bit of the data point is the only information retained. Applications of this concept will be discussed in Section 6.5. In mathematical terms, if $x(t)$ is the original signal, then the one-bit quantized (hard-clipped) signal $y(t)$ is defined by the relation

$$
y(t) = \text{sgn } x(t) = \begin{cases} 1 & x(t) \geq 0 \\ \\ -1 & x(t) < 0 \end{cases} \tag{6.3}
$$

A very important observation is that when 8 to 10 bits or less are employed for the level of quantization, the number of unique values that a data point can have is not too great, namely, $2^8 = 256$ to $2^{10} = 1024$ different values. By proper development of this concept, certain time-saving procedures can be implemented and are discussed in Sections 6.3, 6.4, 6.5, and 6.6.

In Sections 6.2-6.7, different procedures for computing the correlation function are discussed. First, the basic direct method of implementing (6.1) is described along with an indication of the number of operations necessary for its implementation. The other methods are:

1. One that expands the summation and collects like terms so that they may be factored out to eliminate multiplications

2. A method that involves relatively coarse quantization so that advantage may be taken of one of the special instructions in certain machines which in effect perform a fairly involved table look-up

3. So-called hard clipping methods which are based on the one-bit quantization

4. A "quarter-square" method that takes advantage of the fact that a cross product can be expanded as a linear combination of squares, which can then be efficiently obtained by table look-up procedures

5. A direct Fourier transformation of the original time history to obtain the power spectrum and then an inverse Fourier transform to obtain the correlation function

   The Fourier transform method undoubtedly holds the most appeal for a contemporary general-purpose program. However, the specialized methods definitely still have their place in particular applications, especially when smaller special computers are involved and are not to be ignored. These methods will now be described.

6.2 BASIC CORRELATION FUNCTION COMPUTATIONAL METHOD

   The fundamental correlation computational procedures consist of implementing (6.1) directly. Since $\hat{R}_{xy}(\tau) = \hat{R}_{yx}(-\tau)$, the two parts of the cross-correlation function can be computed for positive time delays. That is,

$$\hat{R}_{xyr} = \frac{1}{N - r} \sum_{i=1}^{N-r} x_i y_{i+r} \qquad r = 0,1,\ldots,m \quad (6.4a)$$

$$\hat{R}_{yxr} = \frac{1}{N - r} \sum_{i=1}^{N-r} y_i x_{i+r} \qquad r = 0,1,\ldots,m \quad (6.4b)$$

For an autocorrelation function, $\hat{R}_x(\tau) = \hat{R}_x(-\tau)$. Hence, only (6.4a) need be evaluated in this case:

$$\hat{R}_{xr} = \frac{1}{N - r} \sum_{i=1}^{N-r} x_i x_{i+r} \qquad\qquad r = 0,1,\ldots,m \quad (6.5)$$

Thus, although the basic computational method is identical for autocorrelation or cross-correlation functions, there is essentially half the amount of computation required for the autocorrelation function.

The number of multiply-add operations required for the computation of $R_{xy}(r)$ is roughly $(m + 1)(N - m/2)$ $\approx mN - (m2/2)$. This essentially defines the required computation time. In order not to make the discussion machine-dependent, the examples will be worked out for a hypothetical computer having a basic machine cycle time of 1.4 μsec. Thus, for a typical program operating on N = 10,000 data points for m = 1000 lags, the computation time could be estimated at

$$T_a = ncT_1$$

$$= \left[mN - \frac{m^2}{2} \right] \left[12 \right] \left[1.4 \times 10^{-6} \right]$$

$$= \left[10^4 \times 10^3 - \frac{10^6}{2} \right] \left[12 \right] \left[1.4 \times 10^{-6} \right] = 160 \text{ sec}$$

where

T_a = Total computation time

n = Number of multiply-add operations

c = Number of machine cycles per multiply-add operation

T_1 = Time for one machine cycle

If the sampling interval is t = 0.1 msec, then the parameters in the example correspond to an analysis bandwidth of 10 Hz, performed in the frequency band 0-5000 Hz.

6.3   BASIC METHOD FOR LONG RECORD LENGTHS

The basic correlation computation method requires some adaptation if it is desired to compute correlation functions for record lengths that exceed the memory capacity of the computer.

An autocorrelation function can be computed as data are read into the digital computer to eliminate any record length restrictions. To illustrate this, suppose an autocorrelation function with $m = 5$ lag values is to be computed. All lag values can be determined by reading only $2(m + 1) = 12$ data points at a time into the computer storage. The process is as follows:

1. Read in data points $x_1, \ldots, x_6$

2. Compute and accumulate products:

R_{x0}	R_{x1}	R_{x2}	R_{x3}	R_{x4}	R_{x5}
x_1^2	$x_1 x_2$	$x_1 x_3$	$x_1 x_4$	$x_1 x_5$	$x_1 x_6$
$+x_2^2$	$+x_2 x_3$	$+x_2 x_4$	$+x_2 x_5$	$+x_2 x_6$	
$+x_3^2$	$+x_3 x_4$	$+x_3 x_5$	$+x_3 x_6$		
$+x_4^2$	$+x_4 x_5$	$+x_4 x_6$			
$+x_5^2$	$+x_5 x_6$				
$+x_6^2$					

The above products are summed by column to obtain partial sums that will eventually make up points on the correlation function.

3. Read in data points $x_7, \ldots, x_{12}$; save $x_1, \ldots, x_6$.

4. Compute and accumulate the products:

R_{x0}	R_{x1}	R_{x2}	R_{x3}	R_{x4}	R_{x5}
					$x_2 x_7$
				$x_3 x_7$	$+x_3 x_8$
			$x_4 x_7$	$+x_4 x_8$	$+x_4 x_9$
		$x_5 x_7$	$+x_5 x_8$	$+x_5 x_9$	$+x_5 x_{10}$
	$x_6 x_7$	$+x_6 x_8$	$+x_6 x_9$	$+x_6 x_{10}$	$+x_6 x_{11}$
x_7^2	$+x_7 x_8$	$+x_7 x_9$	$+x_7 x_{10}$	$+x_7 x_{11}$	$+x_7 x_{12}$
$+x_8^2$	$+x_8 x_9$	$+x_8 x_{10}$	$+x_8 x_{11}$	$+x_8 x_{12}$	
$+x_9^2$	$+x_9 x_{10}$	$+x_9 x_{11}$	$+x_9 x_{12}$		
$+x_{10}^2$	$+x_{10} x_{11}$	$+x_{10} x_{12}$			
$+x_{11}^2$	$+x_{11} x_{12}$				
$+x_{12}^2$					

These products are added to the previous partial sums by column.

5. The next set of six data values would be read into the storage space occupied by the first six. By proper programming, the appropriate cross products can be computed and the partial sums accumulated as the process goes along, so that when the data have been read, all points on

the correlation function will have been determined. This can easily be generalized to handle
an arbitrary number of variables if the data are
multiplexed. Denote the variables by $x_1(t), x_2(t),$
$\ldots, x_p(t)$. The N digitized values of $x_1(t)$ are
denoted by $x_{11}, x_{12}, x_{13}, \ldots, x_{1N}$. For the remainder of the variables, the data are then arranged
on the digital input tape in the sequence

$$x_{11}, x_{21}, \ldots, x_{p1}; \quad x_{12}, x_{22}, \ldots, x_{p2};$$

$$x_{13}, x_{23}, \ldots, x_{p3}; \ldots; \quad x_{1N}, x_{2N}, \ldots, x_{pN}$$

All autocorrelation and cross-correlation functions
can then be computed in parallel with the required
storage being $3p(m + 1)$ cells. More than this amount
of storage can, of course, be employed. That is merely
the minimum requirement.

Performing the input of a subsequent section of
data while computations are in progress requires some
care in programming. A minimum of three buffer areas
must be established in the core storage for an autocorrelation computation to avoid reading new data in
on top of data that is still in use. Six input areas
are necessary for cross-correlation computations involving two sequences. The buffering procedure must
progress as follows:

1. Read first set of data into buffer 1.

2. Read second set of data into buffer 2.

3. Initiate reading of next set of data into buffer
   3.

4. Wait for termination of read operation into
   buffer 2.

5. Perform partial product accumulations on data in
   buffer 1, overlapping as necessary into buffer 2
   to obtain lagged products.

6. Initiate reading of next set of data into
   buffer 1.

7. Wait for termination of read operation into buffer 3.

8. Perform partial product accumulations on data into buffer 2, overlapping into buffer 3 as necessary to obtain lagged products.

9. Initiate reading of next set of data into buffer 2.

10. Wait for termination of read operation into buffer 1.

11. Perform partial product accumulation on data in buffer 3, overlapping into buffer 1 as necessary to obtain lagged products.

The computation in step 11 is slightly more involved than in steps 5 and 8 if the buffer areas are contiguous and in sequence. To obtain the core memory address for the data in buffer 1, a factor of $3N_b$, where N_b = buffer size, must be subtracted from the index for the lagged data obtained from buffer 1. At the first pass through step 11, lagged products are being accumulated:

$$P_r = \sum_{i=2N_b+1}^{3N_b} x_i x_{i+r} \qquad\qquad r = 0,1,\ldots,m \quad (6.6)$$

However, for $i + r$ $3N_b$, the data is located at $i + r - 3N_b$. Thus, (6.6) must be broken into two parts:

$$P_{1r} = \sum_{i=2N_b+1}^{3N_b-r} x_i x_{i+r} \qquad\qquad\qquad (6.7a)$$

$$P_{2r} = \sum_{i=3N_b-r+1}^{3N_b} x_i x_{i+r-3N_b} \qquad\qquad (6.7b)$$

The diagrams presented for partial cross products for m = 6 form the basis for the long record length computations. One should be able to program from them letting m be an arbitrary value. An individual programmer on a specific machine can then implement the method in the way that is optimum or easiest for him. When programming in FORTRAN, the input buffering might be handled by the operating system software. In such a case, the programming considerations described above will change. One only has to be sure he computes all the partial cross product sums required.

6.4 FACTORING OF COMMON TERMS

A method employed in connection with seismic data analysis is described by Simpson (1961). This method includes scanning the data to factor out common terms that appear in the summation for the evaluation of the correlation function. This procedure can only be efficiently accomplished if a relatively small number of data quantization levels, as compared to the total number of data points, are possible so that relatively large numbers of common factors exist on the average. For example, suppose a sequence of data is obtained, as indicated below:

i: 1 2 3 4 5 6 7 8 9 10 11 12 13 14 15 16 17 18 19 20

x_i: 3 -2 1 4 2 2 3 4 1 0 1 -1 3 2 -4 0 3 4 1 -2

Equation (6.1) can be expanded in the form

$$
\begin{aligned}
R_{xyr} = 1 \cdot & [x_{3+r} + x_{9+r} + x_{11+r} + x_{19+r} - x_{12+r}] \\
+ 2 \cdot & [x_{5+r} + x_{6+r} + x_{14+r} - (x_{2+r} + x_{20+r})] \\
+ 3 \cdot & [x_{1+r} + x_{7+r} + x_{13+r} + x_{17+r}] \\
+ 4 \cdot & [x_{4+r} + x_{8+r} + x_{18+r} - x_{15+r}] \qquad (6.8)
\end{aligned}
$$

Note that when (6.1) has been rewritten in this form, only four instead of twenty multiplications are necessary. Because of the reduction in the number of multiplications, the evaluation of (6.8) can be performed considerably faster than that of (6.1). This is where the potential advantage lies.

Note that (6.8) is a function of the specific data being used. Therefore, the particular record of data being analyzed must be examined in order to generate the computational form given by (6.8). A complicated "program-writing program" is required; that is, a program that will generate a computational program of the form of (6.9) for each given input data record.

A correlation function program involved in this procedure was written for the data analysis procedures described by Simpson (1961). A quantization of 100 levels (between 6 and 7 bits) was assumed and empirical speed advantage factors were determined, which are a function of the length of the data, as indicated in Table 6.1.

TABLE 6.1   Speed Advantage Ratio of Computing
Time of Normal Method to Factoring Method

Speed advantage ratio	Normal method
3.6	500
5.7	1000
8.1	2000
10.9	5000
12.4	10000

Hence, for the particular data involved in this application, a considerable saving in time resulted from this highly specialized computational method. Considerable programming effort is required to develop the necessary program-writing program as opposed to merely coding the direct or FFT computational methods. This is a disadvantage that has to be balanced against the computational time savings.

6.5 EIGHT-LEVEL QUANTIZATION METHOD

A method based on a four-bit quantization level can be useful; that is, plus or minus eight levels of quantization are allowed, which corresponds to roughly plus or minus one decimal digit. The advantage of this coarse quantization is that if a few enough number of levels is used, then table look-ups can be used rather than multiplication operations to determine the products between a pair of data values. Of course, when the number of potential products between two arbitrary data values is too large, then it is likely that the core storage is not large enough to contain the necessary table, and this procedure cannot be used. Many of the fast correlation computation methods are based on being able to employ a table look-up procedure instead of direct multiplication. As will be shown in Section 6.6, data can be quantized all the way to only one bit and reasonable results can still be obtained by a final functional adjustment of the results.

The method under discussion was programmed on a computer with an automatic table look-up feature, which may be used for performing the multiplications automatically. By properly constructing the multiplication table of possible products between two data points and by properly placing the two sets of data to be multiplied, this conversion instruction can be used to perform the table look-up to obtain the desired products between two sets of data. Similar procedures are used for the conversion instructions to convert from binary to binary coded decimal format. The data must be preprocessed in order to properly pack several data points into one computer word. The conversion instruction essentially adds in sequence the six, six-bit characters in a computer word to some predetermined value and then accumulates the contents of this location in the accumulator. Hence, six pairs of data points can be multiplied in one instruction, which is accomplished mush faster than regular multiplication operations.

The results of this procedure, based on both experimental and analytical results, indicate that very little precision is lost because of coarse quantization. That is to be intuitively expected, since the correlation function is an averaged result, and results with more precision than the original data are often not of any particular interest. But when many numbers of a given accuracy are added, the effect is to gain significant digits of precision. That is, the resulting mean values contain more accuracy than the original data. The additional accuracy may or may not be of value. One disadvantage encountered in employing such a procedure, and, as a matter of fact, the reason many engineers to not like the results of the four-bit or other quantization methods, is that the dynamic range is less. There is a fundamental quantization noise floor, which increases in proportion to the minimum level of quantization. Also, care must be utilized in the analog-to-digital (A/D) conversion process to ensure that all of the quantization levels are actually used.

The eight-level method has an inner computational loop requiring 24 machine cycles to obtain the sum of six products. As an estimate, an additional two machine cycles might be required on the average to prepare the data in the necessary format of six data points per computer word. The total is then 26/6 cycles per multiply-add operation. For the previous example of N = 10,000 and m = 1000, the time is approximately

$$T = \frac{160}{12} \cdot \frac{26}{6} = 57.8 \text{ sec}$$

6.6 ONE-BIT QUANTIZATION, OR EXTREME CLIPPING METHOD

A relation between the correlation function of the extremely clipped signal (6.3) and an original Gaussian zero mean process from which it is obtained gives the normalized correlation function (correlation coefficient $\rho_x(\tau)$ in terms of the correlation coefficient function of the clipped signal $\rho_y(\tau)$. It is

$$\rho_x(\tau) = \sin\left[\frac{\pi}{2} \rho_y(\tau)\right] \tag{6.9}$$

where $\rho_x(\tau)$ and $\rho_y(\tau)$ are defined as

$$\rho_x(\tau) = \frac{R_x(\tau)}{R_x(0)} \qquad \rho_y(\tau) = \frac{R_y(\tau)}{R_y(0)} \tag{6.10}$$

See Weinreb (1963) for a derivation of this relation and Hinich (1967) for theoretical work on the spectrum estimation question. The original derivation of this dates back to 1898, however, according to Kendall and Stuart (1961). Clearly, when the one-bit quantization is performed, the multiplications that need be accom- plished become trivial in that only plus or minus one is involved. Various ways exist for taking advantage of this trivial multiplication. One method employed is to again use a conversion instruction. In this case, the data are packed, as many points per computer word as there are binary digits by an initial examina- tion of the input record. Then by properly generating the table look-up procedure and by employing the ap- propriate table, all products corresponding to one word can in effect be looked-up with one instruction by using a conversion operation.

Procedures other than the use of the conversion in- struction might prove to be just as efficient for evaluating a sum of one-bit products. Simple counters can be set up in which a point, say x_i, is selected. Then all the products of x_i with each data point y_{j+r},

$j = 1,\ldots,N - r$, can be determined by a simple examination of the data. The problem is not one that can be
solved in any general manner, because it depends on
the characteristics of the particular computer being
used for the problem at hand.

There are certain problems connected with the use
of the clipping methods for correlation computations.
The problem is that requirements for increased record
length are traded for computational speed, assuming a
constant statistical accuracy is desired. Weinreb
(1963) shows that the variance of an autocorrelation
function estimate is increased by a maximum factor of
roughly $\pi^2/4 \approx 2.5$. This variance is proportional to
T, so if the variance is to be kept constant, record
lengths are required that are two-and-a-half times as
long as those needed if all the information available
in the data is to be used. The work of Hinich (1967)
extended the results and is applicable to spectrum
computations. The theoretical results of Hinich show
that the wide band (uncorrelated data points) is a
worst case. For narrow-band data, he shows less increase in variance. This result was experimentally
verified at the University of Arizona prior to the
availability of the theory. In the Electrical Engineering Department, experiments to test the variability of methods employing quantized data rarely showed
over a 150% increase in the variability of autocorrelation function estimates. The theoretical bound of
250% assumes uncorrelated data samples. In a typical
time series, there is considerable correlation between
the 250% maximum. Hinich demonstrates that and gives
a narrow-band (high-correlation) example of a 128%
value.

Note that certain assumptions are involved in the
use of the hard clipping method: either (a) a Gaussian
distribution, or (b) a sinusoid, or (c) a sinusoid plus
Gaussian noise is assumed. Equation (6.9) applies to
data with these characteristics. Note that any periodic (i.e., the same zero crossings) would give the
same clipped correlation function as that of a sine

wave whose clipped correlation function is a triangular wave prior to applying (6.9). Consider, for example, Figure 6.1 to illustrate this idea. Thus,
caution must be used when applying the clipped correlation ideas to various types of data.

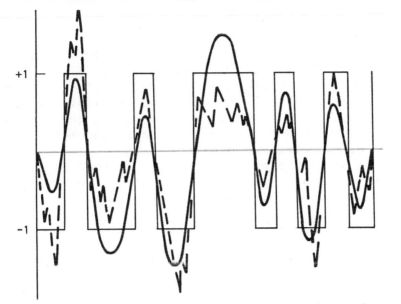

Fig. 6.1 Two time series having an identical extremely
          clipped version.

Only normalized correlation functions are directly
obtained by this method. Hence, the mean square value
must be calculated separately for use as a scale factor. Also, the nonlinear effects that distort probability density functions to non-Gaussian shapes will
be masked completely when such a computing method is
used.

An alternative to applying the clipping idea to
correlation function computations is clipping only one
of the components of the product being computed. For
example, if the cross-correlation function is to be
computed between x(t) and y(t), then clip only y(t).
In that case, multiplications are again traded for additions, since the sequence y_i is merely added after

adjustment for the proper sign of the point x_i that is multiplying it. In that case, the correlation function can be shown to be

$$R_{xy}(\tau) = \sqrt{\frac{\pi}{2}}\, R_{yy}(0)\, R_{xsgny}(\tau)$$ (6.11)

where $R_{xsgny}(\tau)$ denotes the correlation function of $x(t)$ with the hard clipped version of $y(t)$.

Relative time estimates for this method are given in Bordner et al. (1964). For the IBM 7044, it is indicated that the computing time can be reduced at a ratio of about 6 to 1. The full clipping method would take proportionately less time. One could expect to perform 36 multiply-add operations in roughly the same amount of machine time. However, more time is required to prepare the data in the proper format.

6.7 SUM OF SQUARES METHOD

An additional technique that has been suggested (Schmid, 1965) takes advantage of the finite quantization of the data and expresses the product as a sum of squares. The relation employed here expresses the fact that a cross product may be expressed as a linear combination of squares by the following relation:

$$xy = \frac{1}{2}[(x + y)^2 - x^2 - y^2]$$ (6.12)

This is very similar to the fairly well-known "quarter-square" method used in construction of analog multipliers. (See Kelly et al., 1966, Section 3.1.2.) The quarter-square multipliers are based on the relation

$$xy = \frac{1}{4}[(x + y)^2 - (x - y)^2]$$ (6.13)

Equation (6.12) may be modified into a form involving the correlation function immediately:

$$\hat{R}_{xyr} = \frac{1}{2N}\left[\sum_{i=1}^{N-r}(x_i + y_{i+r})^2 - \sum_{i=1}^{N-r}x_i^2 - \sum_{i=1}^{N-r}y_{i+r}^2\right] \quad (6.14)$$

The key point in using such an indirect relation is that products may now be obtained by table look-up procedures. Tables of squares of two sets of data take up much less storage space than tables of cross products for the same number of data points. For example, say ten-bit quantization is being used so that a table of size 2^{20} cells could be required if all possible cross products were to be stored. The same table of squares of the sum of the data points would only take up 2^{11} cells; 2^{11} might be a very reasonable size, whereas 2^{20} is not. The second and third sums of squares on the right-hand side of (6.14) are evaluated by simple recursion relations. A separate initial pass through the data is required to evaluate the sums of squares of all the data. Then the partial sums of squares are obtained from

$$\sum_{i=1}^{N-r}x_i^2 = \sum_{i=1}^{N-r+1}x_i^2 - x_{N-r+1}^2 \qquad (6.15a)$$

$$\sum_{i=1}^{N-r}y_{i+r}^2 = \sum_{i=1}^{N-r+1}y_{i+r-1}^2 - y_r^2 \quad r = 0,1,2,\ldots,m \quad (6.15b)$$

Since only one pass through the data is required initially plus one subtraction operation for each correlation function point, the amount of time required is negligible compared with that of the overall correlation function evaluation.

The other portion of (6.14) requires a more complicated method of evaluation. One possible method of programming is given in Schmid (1965). This method requires one pass through the data to set it up in a special tabular format. Then, with the aid of a table of squares, the quantity

$$\sum_{i=1}^{N-r} (x_i + y_{i+r})^2$$

can be generated in a computational loop requiring six machine cycles. The time required is about half that for a straightforward evaluation of the direct sum of products. For this method, the data must be in fixed-point arithmetic. When the amount of data is too large to fit into the core memory simultaneously, more complicated approaches are required to apply this technique. In the case of a small machine with no hardware multiplication and division functions, this might be a valuable approach. However, in view of the potential speed of FFT approaches to correlation function evaluation, it is unlikely that there would be a need to apply this technique in large-scale computers except in very special circumstances.

6.8 CORRELATION FUNCTIONS VIA FAST FOURIER TRANSFORMS

The autocorrelation or cross-correlation function can be obtained from the power or cross spectral density function. The Wiener-Khinchine relations are applied for this approach. Since spectra can be obtained from Fourier transforms of time histories, the FFT can be applied to obtain correlation functions. Even though this appears to be a roundabout method, it proves to be from 5 to 100 times faster, depending on the maximum lag value desired. One can always obtain N lags of the correlation function nearly as fast as m lags, even though m is considerably smaller than N. Considerable detail is given in Sande (1965) concerning this procedure.

Basic Method

The basic method is as follows:

1. Compute the transform X_k of time series x_i; i,k = 0,1,...,N - 1.

2. Compute the "raw" spectrum $\hat{S}_{xk} = (\Delta t/N) |X_k|^2$.

3. Compute the inverse FFT to obtain the autocorrelation function

$$R_{xr} = \mathcal{F}^{-1}[S_{xk}]$$

Considerable amplification is necessary to illustrate the problems with this procedure. Some explanation is given here that applies to spectrum computations discussed in Section 6.2. Since correlation functions and spectra are Fourier transform pairs, related considerations apply to each function. Thus, the discussion in this section is highly correlated with the comments in Section 6.3.

Certain modifications that are not obvious must be made to this approach. It is shown in Sande (1965) that the usual correlation function is not obtained after step 3 above, but rather a "circular" autocorrelation function $\hat{R}_{xr}^c$ defined by the relation

$$\hat{R}_{xr}^c = \frac{N-r}{N} [\hat{R}_{xr} + \hat{R}_{x(N-r)}] \qquad (6.16)$$

which is illustrated in Figure 6.2.

The effect on the correlation function of adding zeros to the data is to spread apart the two portions of the circular correlation function. If N zeros are attached, the two pieces spread as illustrated in Figure 6.3.

The preceding computational sequence can easily be modified to obtain the noncircular correlation function. If the length of the original sequence of data is a power of 2, $N = 2^p$, then N zeros would be added to obtain all N lags. If the sequence length is not a power of 2, then the sequence could be filled with N_z zeros until the first power of 2 was reached. The number of unbiased lag values obtained would be N_z in this case. If more were necessary, the sequence length

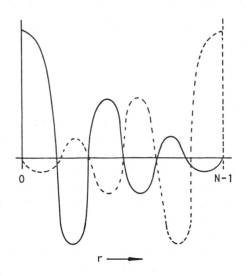

Fig. 6.2   Two parts of a correlation function obtained
if zeros are not added.

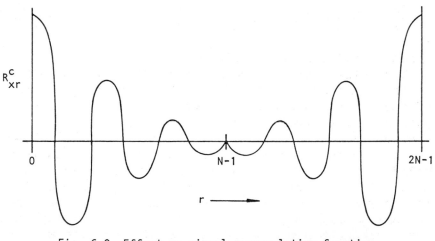

Fig. 6.3   Effect on circular correlation function
when N zeros are added.

would have to be doubled by augmenting with 2^P additional zeros. The modified computational sequence is

1. Augment original time series x_i', $i = 0,1,\ldots,$ $N - 1$, with N zeros to obtain sequence x_i, $i = 0,$ $1,\ldots,2N - 1$.

2. Compute the 2N-point FFT, X_k, $k = 0,1,\ldots,2N - 1$.

3. Compute the "raw" spectrum $\hat{S}_{xk} = (\Delta t/N)|X_k|^2$, for $k = 0,1,\ldots,2N - 1$.

4. Compute the inverse FFT of $\hat{S}_{xk}$ and multiply by $N/(N - r)$ to obtain the correct divisor $\hat{R}_{xr}$ $= N/(N - r)\mathcal{F}^{-1}[\hat{S}_{xk}]$, $r = 0,1,\ldots,2N - 1$.

5. Discard the last half of $\hat{R}_{xr}$ to obtain N correlation function points.

For cross-correlation functions, the same approach applies. In this case, (6.16) generalizes to

$$\hat{R}_{xyr}^c = \frac{N - r}{N}[\hat{R}_{xyr} + \hat{R}_{yx(N-r)}] \qquad (6.17)$$

Hence, when zeros are used to augment the sequence, the $\hat{R}_{yxr} = 0$ is included and $\hat{R}_{yx0} = \hat{R}_{xy0}$ does not appear. If the two sequences are arranged as follows

$$x_0,x_1,x_2,\ldots,x_{N-1},0_N,0_{N+1},\ldots,0_{2N-1}$$

$$y_0,y_1,y_2,\ldots,y_{N-1},0_N,0_{N+1},\ldots,0_{2N-1}$$

then the cross-correlation result obtained via FFTs is

$$R_{xy0},R_{xy1},\ldots,R_{xy(N-1)},R_{yx(N)},R_{yx(N-1)},\ldots,R_{yx1}$$

If the arrangement of zeros is modified so that the x sequence has trailing zeros and the y sequence has leading zeros, then the entire cross-correlation function from R_{yxN} to $R_{xy(N-1)}$ is obtained. If the sequence is arranged as

$$x_0, x_1, x_2, \ldots, x_{N-1}, 0_N, 0_{N+1}, \ldots, 0_{2N-1}$$

$$0_0, 0_1, 0_2, \ldots, 0_{N-1}, y_0, y_1, y_2, \ldots, y_{N-1}$$

then the cross-correlation result obtained is

$$R_{yxN}, R_{yx(N-1)}, \ldots, R_{yx1}, R_{xy0}, R_{xy1}, \ldots, R_{xy(N-1)}$$

Since $R_{yxr} = R_{xy(N-1)}$, the entire cross-correlation function is obtained in proper sequence from $r = -N$ to $r = (N - 1)$.

The computation of the correlation function can become moderately involved. Also, even though the cross-correlation is the inverse transform of the cross spectral density function, the computation of these two functions actually are carried out in quite distinct ways. A useful spectral density function estimate will often be one that has had its Fourier transform modified (either a tapering function applied to the time history or a smoothing operation on the raw Fourier transforms). Then after $\tilde{S}_{xyk} = (\Delta t/N) X_k^* Y_k$ is computed, a further smoothing will be performed. Neither of these operations are utilized in computing the correlation function.

Likewise, the augmentation with zeros is not required to obtain a useful spectral density estimate. Hence, when computer programs are generated for spectra and correlation functions, one finds that it is most convenient to keep them as distinct and separate routines.

Some of the special formulas discussed in Section 4.4 can be applied in a useful way to the computation of noncircular correlation functions. Instead of actually augmenting the data sequence with zeros, the special "half-zero procedure" described beginning on page 185 and with (4.76) is utilized. The discussion will be in terms of a cross-correlation function.

The cross-correlation function is obtained from the cross spectral density function. Hence, two FFTs are involved rather than one. The computational steps for the cross-correlation are as follows:

1. Store x_i in the real part and y_i in the imaginary part, $z_i = x_i + jy_i$; $i = 0,1,...,M - 1$.

2. Compute the M-point FFT of z_i and denote it by z_k^e,

$$z_k^e = \text{FFT}[z_i] \qquad k = 0,1,2,...,M - 1 \quad (6.18)$$

3. Read z_i; $i = 0,1,2,...,M - 1$ and multiply by $W^{i/2}$ where

$$W = \exp(-j2\pi/M) \qquad\qquad\qquad (6.19)$$

4. Compute the M-point FFT of $z_i W^{i/2}$,

$$z_k^0 = \text{FFT}[z_i W^{i/2}] \qquad k = 0,1,2,...,M - 1 \quad (6.20)$$

5. The full N-point FFT is given by

$$Z_{2k} = Z_k^e$$

$$\qquad\qquad\qquad k = 0,1,2,...,M - 1 \quad (6.21)$$

$$Z_{2k+1} = Z_k^0$$

6. Compute the "raw" cross spectrum:

$$\tilde{S}_{ryk} = \frac{\Delta t}{N} X_k^* Y_k$$

$$= \frac{\Delta t}{N} \left[\frac{Z_k + Z_{N-k}^*}{2}\right]^* \left[\frac{Z_k - Z_{N-k}^*}{2j}\right]$$

$$k = 0,1,2,...,N - 1 \quad (6.22)$$

which is an application of (4.61) and (4.62). This can be further simplified to obtain

$$\tilde{S}_{xyk} = \frac{\Delta t}{N} \frac{|Z_k|^2 - |Z_{N-k}|^2 + 2j \ \text{Im}[Z_k Z^*_{N-k}]}{2j}$$

$$k = 0,1,2,\ldots,N - 1 \quad (6.23)$$

and $Z_N = Z_0$. Equation (6.23) may or may not be more efficient computationally. From Z_k^e we obtain

$$\tilde{S}_{xy2k} = \frac{\Delta t}{N} \frac{|Z_{2k}|^2 - |Z_{N-2k}|^2 + 2j \ \text{Im}[Z_{2k} Z^*_{N-2k}]}{2j}$$

or

$$\tilde{S}^e_{xyk} = \frac{\Delta t}{N} \frac{|Z^e_k|^2 - |Z^e_{M-k}|^2 + 2j [\text{Im} \ Z^e_k Z^{e*}_{M-k}]}{2j}$$

$$k = 0,1,2,\ldots,\frac{M}{2} \quad (6.24)$$

and $Z_M = Z_0$. From Z_k^o we obtain

$$\tilde{S}_{xy(2k+1)}$$

$$= \tilde{S}^o_{xyk} = \frac{\Delta t}{N} \frac{|Z^o_k|^2 - |Z^o_{M-k}|^2 + 2j [\text{Im} \ Z^o_k Z^{o*}_{M-k}]}{2j}$$

$$k = 0,1,2,\ldots,\frac{M-1}{2} \quad (6.25)$$

In both cases we note $Z^o_0 = Z^o_M$ and $Z^e_0 = Z^e_M$.

7. The full first half of the cross spectrum, which is a Hermitian function, is

$$\tilde{S}_{xy2k} = S^e_{xyk}$$

$$k = 0,1,2,\ldots,\frac{M}{2}-1 \quad (6.26)$$

$$\tilde{S}_{xy(2k+1)} = S^o_{xyk}$$

8. We now obtain the N-point noncircular cross-correlation function by implementing (4.87) and the procedure described on page 189. Compute

$$S'_{xyk} = \tilde{S}_{xyk} + \tilde{S}^*_{xy(M-k)} + j(\tilde{S}_{xyk} - \tilde{S}^*_{xy(M-k)})W^{-k/2}$$

$$k = 0,1,2,\ldots,M-1 \quad (6.27)$$

Note that this computation must be done in pairs for locations k and (M - k) simultaneously in order to avoid the necessity for extra memory.

9. Compute the M-point inverse FFT of S'_{xyk}:

$$R_{xyr} = FFT^{-1}[S'_{xy}] \quad r = 0,1,2,\ldots,M-1 \quad (6.28)$$

10. Finally, we have the N-point noncircular correlation function

$$\hat{R}_{xy2r} = \frac{N}{N-r} Re[R'_{xyr}]$$

$$\hat{R}_{xy(2r+1)} = \frac{N}{N-r} Im[R'_{xyr}]$$

$$r = 0,1,2,\ldots,M-1 \quad (6.29)$$

Note that in the usual way of computer storage of complex numbers in a FORTRAN program R_{xyr} is obtained in natural order without any rearranging.

The method described above limits storage requirements to the length of the data sequence input. One
can simplify the method by actually augmenting the
data with zeros, and computing a double-length transform in both directions which will require more time
and storage.

6.9 NORMALIZATION OF CORRELATION FUNCTIONS

In classical statistics, it is common to describe
correlation in terms of a normalized quantity $\rho(t)$
where

$$|\rho(\tau)| = \left|\frac{C(\tau)}{C(0)}\right| \leq 1$$

The unnormalized quantity $C(\tau)$ is usually termed a covariance function with the tacit assumption that the
mean value is zero. In the early development of statistical communication theory, the term correlation
function was generally applied to the lagged cross
product of two variables without regard to their mean
values and without normalization. Special notation is
therefore required, and the notation here is patterned
after that of Bendat and Piersol (1966). The correlation function is defined without restriction on the
mean value and without normalization:

$$\hat{R}_{xyk} = \frac{1}{N-r} \sum_{i=1}^{N-r-1} x_i y_{i-r} \qquad r = 0,1,\ldots,m$$

The covariance function has the mean value removed:

$$\hat{C}_{xyk} = \frac{1}{N-r} \sum_{i=1}^{N-r-1} (x_i - \bar{x})(y_{i-r} - \bar{y}) \qquad (6.30)$$

In practice, the mean value usually has been subtracted from the data. Finally, the normalized quantity

is termed the correlation coefficient function and is defined by

$$\rho_{xyk} = \frac{C_{xyk}}{\sigma_x \sigma_y} \qquad (6.31)$$

where

$$\sigma_x = \sqrt{C_x(0)}$$

and

$$\sigma_y = \sqrt{C_y(0)}$$

The primary digital computer use of this quantity is as a plotting convenience. Also, in many cases it provides a convenient interpretation of the degree of (linear) correlation between two variables. The use of ρ_{xyk} simplifies a plotted output in that the scale of the function is guaranteed to be between minus one and plus one.

The normalization may be accomplished by an alternative method. If the sample mean $\bar{y}$ and sample variance s_y^2 have been computed, it is often convenient to transform the data to unit variance in addition to zero mean:

$$x_i = \frac{y_i - \bar{y}}{s_y} \qquad (6.32)$$

This process is termed "standardizing" the data by statisticians.

6.10 COMPUTATIONAL TIME COMPARISONS

The straightforward implementation of (6.1) requires Nm (real) multiply-add operations for m lags of an autocorrelation function and 2Nm for a cross-correlation function. An FFT of an ($N = 2^p$)-point sequence requires Np complex multiply-add operations if it is assumed that the necessary complex exponentials have been computed in advance. If the necessary sines and cosines are to be computed, $N/2$ of each are required with a total of about 10 real multiply-add operations each. If two transforms are computed simultaneously, an additional 2N real multiply-add operations are required if it is assumed that multiplication by 1/2 is performed.

Obtaining a cross-correlation requires the following:

Computation	Number of real operations
1. One 2N-point transform	4 · 2N · 2p
2. Sines and cosines	10 · 2N
3. Split apart X(k) and Y(k)	4 · N
4. Cross product	N
5. Inverse 2N-point transform	4 · 2N · 2p
TOTAL	$T_0 = (32p + 25)N$

Hence, if $(32p + 25) < 2m$, then the FFT route is quickest and all possible $(2N - 1)$ lag values are always obtained. A typical specific example might be $N = 2^{12} = 4096$. Then

$$T_0 = (32 · 12 + 25)N = 409N \text{ operations}$$

A typical choice of m is 0.1N, so that the direct route requires about $2 · T_0$ operations.

6.11 BLACKMAN-TUKEY SPECTRUM COMPUTATIONS

The works of Khinchine (1934) and Wiener (1930) showed that the autocorrelation transform method was equivalent to the Fourier transform method for comput-

ing spectra (discussed in Chapter 7). These works
provided a firm mathematical foundation, since transforms of correlation functions will usually exist
mathematically where transforms of the time history do
not. Bandwidth requirements permitting, the correlation PSD was much cheaper to obtain (prior to the FFT)
than the Fourier transform PSD. It should be noted,
however, that correlations themselves were extremely
difficult to compute with reasonable amounts of computer time until the mid-1950s. Computing power has
dropped in price every year because of the successive
improvements that have been made in computer hardware
and software, steadily making correlation PSD calculations less expensive. The credit for developing the
correlation PSD into a firmly established, practical,
and available technique belongs to Blackman and Tukey
(1958), whose work is a milestone in the data-analysis
field. Their contributions will be referred to constantly in this section.

Analog mechanizations of the PSD techniques usually
have been some form of the third method which is discussed in detail in Chapter 8. This type of machine
can be visualized as a bank of bandpass filters. The
data to be analyzed are the input to each filter, and
the output of each filter is squared and integrated
(averaged). When the entire record has been processed
in this manner, the machine stops and the PSD is read
out as the final output of the integrators. Because
of the expense of the filters, many machines use a
single filter with an effectively variable center frequency. In this case, the data are fed through the
filter many times while the center frequency of the
filter is either slowly changed in a continuous fashion or stepped in discrete increments after each time
the data pass through.

At one time the correlation PSD was the standard
method if a digital computer was to be used, while
filtering was the traditional analog technique. Times
and equipment change, however. There now exist excellent analog and hybrid instruments for computing the

correlation function, and digital bandpass filters
suitable for PSD analysis have been derived. Thus, it
is possible and practical to compute a correlation PSD
on analog* equipment and a filter PSD on a general-
purpose digital computer.

With the advent of FFT algorithms, PSD calculations
using the second method have become practical. While
not all problems inherent in this method have been
solved, the procedure has been implemented both on
general-purpose digital computers and in analog equipment. On the surface, the high speed of the FFT approach might seem to render all others obsolete. However, this is not always the case. For example, many
special-purpose high-speed, multiply-add units that
permit very rapid correlation computations have been
developed for digital computers.

All three methods have the same problems related to
bandwidth, leakage, and statistical variability discussed in Chapter 5. Leakage varies somewhat from
method to method and so must be accounted for specifi-
cally when implementing each of them. The remainder
of this section will be spend on the correlation PSD
and the leakage problems peculiar to it.

The previous sections in this chapter showed various ways by which the correlation function can be obtained. Therefore, let it be assumed that the correlation function of the random variable x is available.
Furthermore, for present purposes, suppose that $R_x(\tau)$,
the correlation function, is continuous and defined
over the interval $-\infty$ to ∞. The one-sided PSD** of x is

---

* It should be noted that the term analog as used
  herein really refers to a special-purpose machine,
  that is, one designed mainly to provide PSDs. In-
  ternally, many of these devices are digital or pulse
  processing in nature.

**When the term PSD is used, it is implicit that it is
  one-sided.

$$G_x(f) = 4 \int_0^\infty R_x(\tau) \cos 2\pi f\tau \, d\tau$$

$$= 2 \int_{-\infty}^\infty R_x(\tau) \cos 2\pi f\tau \, d\tau$$

$$= 2 \int_{-\infty}^\infty R_x(\tau) e^{-j2\pi f\tau} \, d\tau \qquad f \geq 0 \quad (6.33)$$

All three of these formulations are equivalent. The complex part of the third form drops out because of the symmetry of the autocorrelation function and the antisymmetry of the imaginary part of the exponential.

The top line of (6.33) is implemented [with the boxcar function $u_T(\tau)$ tacitly involved] in the Blackman-Tukey (B-T) computational method which is defined in (5.2)

$$\hat{G}_k = 2\Delta t \, R_0 + 2 \sum_{r=1}^{m-1} R_r \cos \frac{\pi kr}{m} + R_m \cos \frac{\pi k}{m} \qquad (6.34)$$

If a maximum lag value m (where $T_m = m\Delta t$) is selected regardless of record length $T = N t$, then the analysis bandwidth, $B_e \approx 1/m\Delta t$, is fixed. Thus, consistency of the estimate is assured, since degrees of freedom approximately equal to $2B_e T$ increase as record length increases and statistical variability in turn decreases.

However, the undesirable side lobe characteristics of the boxcar function will exist in the estimate. This is illustrated by the PSD of a sine wave at frequency f_0. As shown in (5.19), a good approximation when f_0 is not near zero is

$$\hat{G}_x(f) = A^2 T_m \frac{\sin[2\pi T_m(f-f_0)]}{2\pi T_m(f-f_0)} \qquad f > 0 \quad (6.35)$$

Thus, instead of obtaining a single delta function as would be the case for the PSD of a sine wave, the truncation spreads the result considerably. The width of the basic lobe of $G_x(f)$ is $1/T_m$ between zero cross-ings. This is shown in Figure 5.1.

Besides the spreading in the main lobe, there is an infinite number of smaller lobes added to the PSD by the truncation. Not only does the magnitude of these side lobes decrease slowly, but half of them are nega-tive, a most displeasing result, since average power is positive by definition. The height of the first two negative lobes is about one-fifth that of the main lobe.

A number of ideas have been suggested to alleviate this problem. The three procedures discussed below are all candidates for a solution to it.* None of the three stands out as being obviously the best. Their good and bad points must be considered by the user, and an engineering judgment made as to which is most suitable for a particular application.

All three do have a common property: They obtain their improvement by modifying the boxcar function in the time domain (or by an equivalent operation in the frequency domain) and by so doing, broaden the princi-pal lobe of the window function in the frequency domain.

The Hann Window

The first of these modified spectral windows, or lag windows, is called the Hann** window:

---

* Several other less important ones are discussed in Appendix B, Section 5 of Blackman and Tukey (1958).

**After Julius von Hann, according to Blackman and Tukey (1958).

$$
u_{T_m}^{(1)} (\tau) = \begin{cases} 0 & \tau < -T_m \\ \dfrac{1}{2}\left(1 + \cos \dfrac{\pi \tau}{T_m}\right) & -T_m \leq \tau \leq T_m \\ 0 & \tau > T_m \end{cases} \qquad (6.36)
$$

The Fourier transform of this is

$$
U_{T_m}^{(1)} (f)
$$

$$
= \frac{1}{2} U_{T_m} (f) + \frac{T_m}{2}\left\{\frac{\sin\left[T_m\left(2\pi f - \dfrac{\pi}{T_m}\right)\right]}{T_m\left(2\pi f - \dfrac{\pi}{T_m}\right)} + \frac{\sin\left[T_m\left(2\pi f + \dfrac{\pi}{T_m}\right)\right]}{T_m\left(2\pi f + \dfrac{\pi}{T_m}\right)}\right\}
$$

$$
= \frac{1}{2} U_{T_m} (f) + \frac{1}{4} U_{T_m}\left(f - \frac{1}{2T_m}\right) + \frac{1}{4} U_{T_m}\left(f + \frac{1}{2T_m}\right) \qquad (6.37)
$$

The Hann window turns out to be the summation of three sin x/x functions! This function is shown in Figure 6.4. As the lobes are spaced $1/2T_m$ Hz apart, this window has the effect of averaging three adjacent lobes, giving the center one twice as much weight as the side ones. Thus, there will be a tendency to greatly decrease the size of the side lobes. The main lobe is reduced to one-half of its previous height, and its width is doubled. The reduction in leakage therefore results in a corresponding widening of the bandwidth of analysis. The distance between the first zero crossings on either side of the main lobe is $2/T_m$

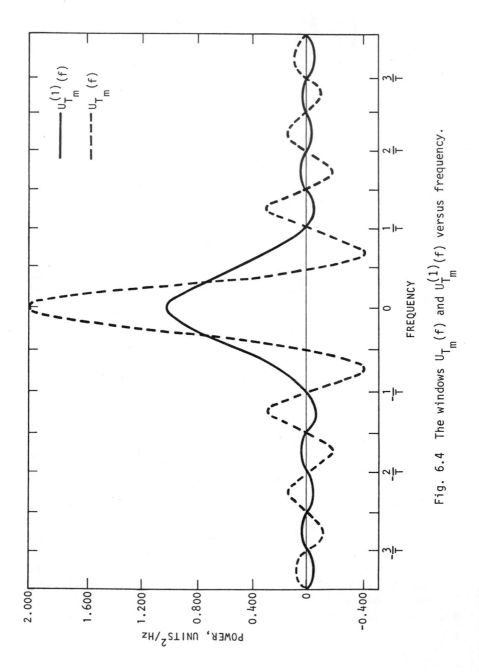

Fig. 6.4 The windows $U_{T_m}(f)$ and $U_{T_m}^{(1)}(f)$ versus frequency.

Hz. The distance between the half-power points, however, is $1/T_m$. This value usually is taken to the effective resolution bandwidth B_e of the analysis. Note
that T_m refers to the length of autocorrelation used
rather than the length of the data record.

It is noted in Chapter 7 that this window is a special case of a general type of cosine taper given by
(7.5).

The Hamming Window

The second spectral window is called the Hamming*
window and is given by

$$u_{T_m}^{(2)}(\tau) = \begin{cases} 0 & \tau < -T_m \\ 0.54 + 0.46 \cos \dfrac{\pi \tau}{T_m} & -T_m < \tau < T_m \\ 0 & \tau > T_m \end{cases} \qquad (6.38)$$

The Fourier transform of (6.38) is

$$U_{T_m}^{(2)}(f) = 0.54 \ U_{T_m}(f) + 0.23 U_{T_m}\left(f + \frac{1}{2T_m}\right) + 0.23 \ U_{T_m}\left(f - \frac{1}{2T_m}\right)$$

$$(6.39)$$

The Hamming window is similar to the Hann window. In
detail, there are differences. A comparison of the
two windows is made in Figure 6.5. As indicated in
Blackman and Tukey (1958), their differences can be
summarized by the following two observations:

---

*
After R. W. Hamming, according to Blackman and Tukey
(1958).

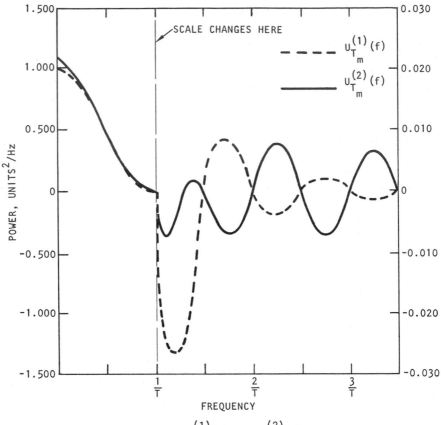

Fig. 6.5 The windows $U_{T_m}^{(1)}(f)$ and $U_{T_m}^{(2)}(f)$ versus frequency.

1. The height of the maximum side lobe for the Hamming window is approximately one-fifth that of the Hann window.

2. The heights of the side lobes of the Hann window tend to drop more rapidly than those of the Hamming window.

Both of these windows reduce the height of the side lobes after the first to less than 2% of the height of the main lobe, and even there the Hann window is almost within the 2% bound.

The Parzen Window

The third window is one of several attributable to Parzen (1961). It takes the form

$$
u_{T_m}^{(3)}(\tau) = \begin{cases} 1 - 6\left(\dfrac{|\tau|}{T_m}\right)^2 \left(1 - \dfrac{|\tau|}{T_m}\right) & \tau < T_m/2 \\[3ex] 2\left(1 - \dfrac{|\tau|}{T_m}\right)^3 & |\tau| > T_m/2 \end{cases} \qquad (6.40)
$$

It is shown in Figure 6.6a along with the Hann window for comparison. The Fourier transform of the Parzen window is

$$
U_{T_m}^{(3)}(f) = \frac{3}{4} T_m \left[\frac{\sin(\pi f T_m/2)}{\pi f T_m/2}\right]^{?} \qquad (6.41)
$$

Thus, the Parzen window has a very simple relation to the basic sin x/x window, $U_{T_m}(f)$. The Parzen window is plotted in Figure 6.6b, again with the Hann window for comparison. The Parzen is wider (about 30%) than either the Hann or the Hamming window. Hence, the simple relation giving B_e as $1/T_m$ for the Hann and Hamming windows must be modified for the Parzen window. The effective bandwidth is about

$$
B_c(\text{Parzen}) = \frac{1.3}{T_m}
$$

Thus, resolution is decreased when using the Parzen window and statistical variability is correspondingly reduced.

Another feature of the Parzen window is that, as $U_{T_m}^{(3)}(f)$ is never negative, the PSD generated using it must also be nonnegative. This is a great comfort for

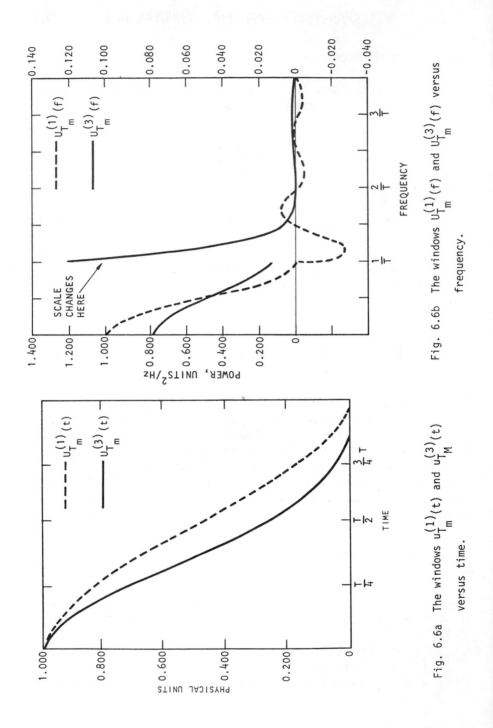

Fig. 6.6b The windows $U_{T_m}^{(1)}(f)$ and $U_{T_m}^{(3)}(f)$ versus frequency.

Fig. 6.6a The windows $u_{T_m}^{(1)}(t)$ and $u_{T_M}^{(3)}(t)$ versus time.

those who are squeamish about seeing negative power indicated on their PSD calculation printouts. This is viewed as an advantage by many engineers. However, negative spectral estimates are not necessarily bad and in fact provide qualitative information about the spectrum. Let us view the relative effects of the Hann and Parzen windows on band-limited white noise (the spectrum is constant) with respect to leakage.

Consider the general characteristics of the side lobes of the two windows:

1. Hann window--side lobes oscillate between positive and negative values. Two consecutive side lobes contribute more or less equally to leakage.

2. Parzen window--side lobes are rippling but always remain positive.

With these characteristics in mind and white noise being considered, it can be seen that roughly constant power coming in through Hann side lobes will be given alternate positive and negative signs. Thus, the contribution from a consecutive pair of side lobes will tend to cancel out. This means that leakage will be minimized for the Hann window. The Parzen window, on the other hand, *always* gives positive weight to power coming in through its side lobes and hence leakage can never cancel. Thus, the Parzen window gives of necessity a biased estimate of the PSD for white noise, whereas the Hann estimates are very nearly unbiased.

Consider now what happens if the PSD is not constant. If the spectrum has a varying shape that happens to oscillate in "resonance" with the Hann side lobes, then the leakage can be magnified. In fact, substantial negative leakage can occur, and if the power coming in through the main lobe is small (i.e., the PSD is of low magnitude in this bandwidth) then the PSD estimate can be negative. Hence, if a negative spectral estimate is obtained, one knows that the spectrum is of low power and probably of an oscillating nature in the immediate vicinity.

Spectral Window Characteristics

All three of these lag windows share an important property. The value of the correlation function at the zero lag is the variance, i.e., the total power. As all three windows are equal to unity at τ equal to zero, the variance is unchanged by any of the three operators. This means that the total amount of power shown by the PSD (the area under the PSD) is invariant. That is a desirable characteristic.

Up to this point in the discussion, only continuous correlation functions have been employed. When making the switch to discrete data, it is frequently assumed that the results are identical. As will be seen, the use of the continuous correlation function results in an approximation, though admittedly a very good one.

Suppose that R_{xr} is defined by

$$R_{xr} = E[x_i x_{i+r}] \qquad\qquad -\infty \le r \le \infty \quad (6.42)$$

The two-sided PSD is then

$$S_x(f) = \Delta t \sum_{r=-\infty}^{\infty} R_{xr} \cos 2\pi fr\Delta t \qquad\qquad (6.43)$$

Suppose that it is truncated in a manner similar to truncation of the continuous case. That can be accomplished by using only the values of r for r = 0,1...,m,

$$\hat{S}_x(f) = \Delta t \sum_{r=-m}^{m} R_{xr} \cos 2\pi fr\Delta t \qquad\qquad (6.44)$$

As before (6.19) could be written using a form of the boxcar function,

$$\hat{S}_x(f) = \Delta t \sum_{r=-\infty}^{\infty} u_{mr} R_{xr} \cos 2\pi fr\Delta t \qquad\qquad (6.45)$$

The definition given to u_{mr} is

$$
u_{mr} = \begin{cases} 1 & |r| \leq m \\ \\ 0 & |r| > m \end{cases} \tag{6.46}
$$

As before, $\hat{S}_x(f)$ can be interpreted as the convolution of $S_x(f)$ and $U_m(f)$, the Fourier transform of u_{mr}. Naturally, this implies that $U_m(f)$ should be calculated and examined. Its definition is

$$
U_m(f) = \Delta t \sum_{r=-m}^{m} \cos 2\pi f \Delta t
$$

$$
= \Delta t \; \frac{\sin[\pi f(2T_m + \Delta t]}{\sin \pi f \Delta t} \tag{6.47}
$$

Here, T_m means $m\Delta t$. Recall that, for the continuous case,

$$
U_{T_m}(f) = 2T_m \; \frac{\sin 2\pi f T_m}{2\pi f T_m} \tag{6.48}
$$

The graphs of these two functions look very much alike for the range of values $0 \leq f \leq 1/2\Delta t$, the principal domain for the digital analysis. In that interval, $\sin \pi f \Delta t$ behaves very much like the function $\pi f \Delta t$, as shown in Figure 6.7. If this approximation is made and the Δt within the sine function in the numerator is ignored, then (6.47) may be easily reduced to (6.46).

The term $U_m(f)$ is periodic. That would be expected, as $S_x(f)$ in the digital definition is also periodic. The carryover to the formulation for the various windows is similar. The discrete Hann window is

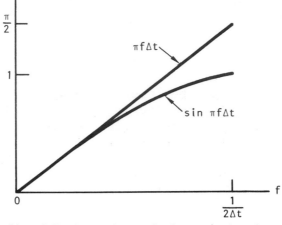

Fig. 6.7   Comparison of $\pi f \Delta t$ and $\sin \pi f \Delta t$.

$$u_{mr}^{(1)} = \begin{cases} \frac{1}{2}\left(1 + \cos \dfrac{\pi r}{m}\right) & |r| \leq m \\ 0 & |r| > m \end{cases} \qquad (6.49)$$

Using summation techniques similar to those employed to find (6.47), we find the Fourier transform of $u_{mr}^{(1)}$ to be

$$U_m^{(1)}(f) = \frac{1}{2} U_m(f) + \frac{1}{4} U_m\left(f - \frac{1}{2m\Delta t}\right) + \frac{1}{4} U_m\left(f + \frac{1}{2m\Delta t}\right)$$

$$(6.50)$$

The Hamming window is

$$u_{mr}^{(2)} = \begin{cases} 0.54 + 0.46 \cos \dfrac{\pi r}{m} & |r| < m \\ 0 & |r| > m \end{cases} \qquad (6.51)$$

Its Fourier transform is

$$U_m^{(2)}(f) = 0.54U_m(f) + 0.23U_m\left(f - \frac{1}{2m\Delta t}\right) + 0.23U_M\left(f + \frac{1}{2m\Delta t}\right)$$

(6.52)

The results for the Parzen window are not so compact. The frequency weighting function has coefficients that are approximately given by the sequence
0.75,0.493,0.123,0.006,0.000,0.000,0.002,0.000,..., as
determined by (6.41).

The question of which one of the three windows is
most appropriate is a matter best decided by the user.
The authors prefer the Hamming window for most purposes, and no smoothing at all in some special cases such
as analyzing data known to be periodic. In any event,
the general effect of the windows upon the PSD should
be understood by the user, and their action upon the
particular type of data being examined should be
weighed carefully before a final selection is made.

In the case of the analysis of cross spectral density functions, a combination of windows might be
best. The Hamming (or Hann) window can be justified
as a good choice for the power spectrum, and the Parzen window, a good choice for the cross spectrum. In
many types of data, the PSD is relatively smooth
(nearly constant) over frequency intervals on the
order of reasonable resolution bandwidths. Thus, the
oscillating side lobes of the Hamming window will tend
to give minimum leakage as discussed on page 265.

On the other hand, the real and imaginary parts of
cross spectra tend to oscillate. Thus, the oscillating
side lobes of the Hamming or Hann window might reso-
nate with the cross spectrum itself and cause excessive leakage. In this situation, the relatively constant, always positive, side lobes of the Parzen
window will allow the oscillating cross spectrum to be
given roughly equal and positive weight so that the
average will tend to be zero and leakage will be
minimized.

Blackman-Tukey Computational Procedure for PSDs

At this point, it is appropriate to sum up the formulas for computing the correlation PSD in the digital case:

1. Assume that x_i is a sequence of N points having a xero mean. (If the mean is not zero, it should be calculated and removed from the data. This step might include the removal of subharmonic terms.)

2. The sample autocorrelation function of x_i is computed for (m + 1) values (the proper choice for m as discussed in Chapter 5):

$$R_{xr} = \frac{1}{N-r} \sum_{i=1}^{N-r} x_i x_{i+r} \qquad\qquad r = 0,\ldots,m \quad (6.53)$$

3. A lag window is selected. Possible candidates are

(a) Hann

$$u_{mr}^{(1)} = \frac{1}{2}\left(1 + \cos\frac{\pi r}{m}\right)$$

(b) Hamming

$$u_{mr}^{(2)} = 0.54 + 0.46 \cos\frac{\pi r}{m}$$

(c) Parzen

$$u_{mr}^{(3)} = \begin{cases} \left(1 - 6\frac{r}{m}\right)^2\left(1 - \frac{r}{m}\right) & r < m/2 \\ \\ 2\left(1 - \frac{r}{m}\right)^3 & r > m/2 \quad (6.54) \end{cases}$$

One of these is applied to the correlation, resulting in a new correlation, $\tilde{R}_{xr}$:

$$\tilde{R}_{xr} = R_{xr} u_{mr}^{\ell} \qquad\qquad r = 0, 1, \ldots \qquad (6.55)$$

4. The PSD is calculated for various frequencies using trapezoidal integration,

$$\hat{G}_x(f) = 2\Delta t\left(\tilde{R}_{x0} + 2\sum_{r=1}^{m-1} \tilde{R}_{xr} \cos 2\pi fr\Delta t + \tilde{R}_{xm} \cos 2\pi fT\right)$$

$$(6.56)$$

A "standard" set of frequencies is

$$f_k = \frac{k}{2m\Delta t} \qquad\qquad k = 0, 1, \ldots, m \qquad (6.57)$$

This produces $(m + 1)$ equally spaced, overlapping PSD estimates. Equation (6.56) can be rewritten as

$$\hat{G}_{xk} = 2\Delta t\left(\tilde{R}_{x0} + 2\sum_{r=1}^{m-1} \tilde{R}_{xr} \cos \frac{\pi rk}{m} + \tilde{R}_{xm} \cos \pi r\right)$$

$$k = 0, 1, \ldots, m \qquad (6.58)$$

Any prewhitening would be done before step 2, and the corresponding postdarkening accomplished after step 4.

If the PSD is calculated at the frequencies $k/2m\Delta t$, $k = 0, 1, \ldots, m$, then it is possible to change the order of the computations. Step 3 in the above is deleted, and a new one is added at the end. It consists of weighting the PSD in the following manner:

$$G_{xk} = \begin{cases} D_0\tilde{G}_{x(k-1)} + D_1\tilde{G}_{xk} + D_0\tilde{G}_{x(k+1)} & k \neq 0, m \\[2mm] D_1\tilde{G}_{x0} + 2D_0\tilde{G}_{x1} & k = 0 \\[2mm] D_1\tilde{G}_{xm} + 2D_0\tilde{G}_{x(m-1)} & k = m \qquad (6.59) \end{cases}$$

The values for D_0 and D_1 are

$$D_0 = \begin{cases} \frac{1}{2} & \text{Hann} \\ 0.54 & \text{Hamming} \end{cases}$$

$$D_1 = \begin{cases} \frac{1}{4} & \text{Hann} \\ 0.23 & \text{Hamming} \end{cases} \tag{6.60}$$

There does not seem to be any real gain in doing the lag window operation in this manner. Compared with the expense of computing the autocorrelation and Fourier transform, the lag window computations require an insignificant amount of time. This formulation is therefore included only because the reader is likely to encounter it in the course of reviewing the computations as done by some organizations. That (6.59) and (6.60) are equivalent to the time plane operation can be easily verified by referring to (6.37) and (6.39).

Step 4, which is essentially that of computing the Fourier cosine transformation, could be accomplished using the FFT techniques described in Chapter 4. On the other hand, if a small number of lag values is used, the complication of the FFT may not be merited. The fact that the desired frequency spacing may not be able to be attained with the FFT can also be a disadvantage. If the FFT is not utilized, one of several recursive sine/cosine computing methods can be implemented as a cost saving procedure. A first possibility is the method described in Section 4.1. A second recursive relation takes the form

$$c_i = hc_{i-1} - c_{i-2}$$

$$h = 2 \cos 2\pi \Delta t \Delta f \tag{6.61}$$

This relation will yield either sines or cosines, depending upon what is used to start the recursion. In particular,

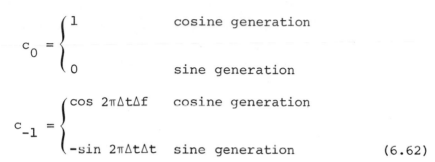

$$c_0 = \begin{cases} 1 & \text{cosine generation} \\ 0 & \text{sine generation} \end{cases}$$

$$c_{-1} = \begin{cases} \cos 2\pi\Delta t\Delta f & \text{cosine generation} \\ -\sin 2\pi\Delta t\Delta t & \text{sine generation} \end{cases} \qquad (6.62)$$

This recursion is equivalent to (3.42) with the damping terms ξ and $g(x_i)$ set to zero.

Blackman-Tukey Computational Procedure for Cross Spectra

The last topic of this section is the calculation of cross spectral density (CSD). The lag window considerations for the CSD are identical to those for the PSD, so that only the definitions and computational procedure need be discussed. In the continuous case, the cross-correlation function is

$$R_{xy}(\tau) = E[x(t)y(t + \tau)] \qquad (6.63)$$

The time average definition is

$$R_{xy}(\tau) = \lim_{T \to \infty} \frac{1}{T} \int_{-T/2}^{T/2} x(t)y(t + \tau) \, d\tau \qquad (6.64)$$

The CSD is the Fourier transform of (6.64):

$$G_{xy}(f) = 2 \int_{-\infty}^{\infty} R_{xy}(\tau) e^{-j2\pi f\tau} \, d\tau \qquad f \geq 0 \quad (6.65)$$

Another formulation in terms of real and imaginary parts is

$$G_{xy}(f) = C_{xy}(f) - jQ_{xy}(f) \qquad (6.66)$$

The C_{xy} function is the cospectral density or cospectrum, and Q_{xy} is the quadrature spectral density or quadspectrum. The definitions of these two expressions are

$$C_{xy}(f) = 2\int_0^\infty [R_{xy}(\tau) + R_{xy}(-\tau)] \cos 2\pi f\tau \; d\tau$$

$$Q_{xy}(f) = 2\int_0^\infty [R_{xy}(\tau) - R_{xy}(-\tau)] \sin 2\pi f\tau \; d\tau$$

$$f > 0 \qquad (6.67)$$

The digital procedure would be much the same as for the PSD:

1. The variables x_i and y_i are assumed to be zero mean sequences of N points. (If the means were not zero, they would be calculated and removed.)

2. Sample correlation functions are computed for (m + 1) values:

$$\hat{R}_{xyr} = \frac{1}{N-r} \sum_{i=1}^{N-r} x_i y_{i+r}$$

$$\hat{R}_{yxr} = \frac{1}{N-r} \sum_{i=1}^{N-r} x_{i+r} y_i \qquad r = 0,1,\ldots,m \quad (6.68)$$

3. An appropriate lag window is selected as in (6.55), and two new correlation functions are computed:

$$\tilde{R}_{xyr} = u_{mr}^{\ell} \hat{R}_{xyr}$$

$$\tilde{R}_{yxr} = u_{mr}^{\ell} \hat{R}_{yxr} \qquad\qquad r = 0,1,\ldots,m \quad (6.69)$$

4. The intermediate quantities A_{xyr} and B_{xyr} are computed:

$$A_{xyr} = \tilde{R}_{xyr} + \tilde{R}_{yxr}$$

$$B_{xyr} = \tilde{R}_{xyr} - \tilde{R}_{yxr} \qquad\qquad r = 0,1,\ldots,m$$

5. The cospectra and quadspectra are computed for various frequencies using trapezodial integrations:

$$\hat{C}_{xy}(f) = \Delta t \left[A_{xy0} + 2 \sum_{r=1}^{m-1} A_{xyr} \cos 2\pi f r \Delta t \right.$$

$$\left. + A_{xym} \cos 2\pi f m \Delta t \right] \qquad\qquad (6.70)$$

$$\hat{Q}_{xy}(f) = \Delta t \left[D_{xy0} + \sum_{r=1}^{m-1} B_{xyr} \sin 2\pi f r \Delta t \right.$$

$$\left. + B_{xym} \sin 2\pi f m \Delta t \right] \qquad\qquad (6.71)$$

As in the case for the PSD, a standard set of frequencies can be used:

$$f_k = \frac{k}{2m\Delta t} \qquad\qquad k = 0,1,\ldots,m \quad (6.72)$$

6. There are various ways of displaying different forms of output for $\hat{C}_{xy}(f)$ and $\hat{Q}_{xy}(f)$. Some commonly calculated additional information is the following:

(a) The absolute value of the CSD;

$$\left| \hat{G}_{xy}(f) \right| = \sqrt{\hat{C}^2_{xy}(f) + \hat{Q}^2_{xy}(f)} \qquad (6.73)$$

(b) The phase angle of the CSD (in degrees);

$$\hat{\phi}(f) = -\frac{360}{2\pi} \arctan \left[\frac{\hat{Q}_{xy}(f)}{\hat{C}_{xy}(f)} \right] \qquad (6.74)$$

Note that the quadrant is always known, so that Φ ranges over 360°. The most usual span is -180 to 180°. A test using the signs of $\hat{Q}_{xy}$ and $\hat{C}_{xy}$ has to be made to determine the proper quadrant. Many routines that compute arctangents are designed to take care of this problem.

(c) The transfer function between x and y, $\hat{H}(f)$ (see Chapter 9);

$$\hat{H}(f) = \frac{\hat{C}_{xy}(f) - j\hat{Q}_{xy}(f)}{\hat{G}_{xx}(f)} \qquad (6.75)$$

This is also usually rewritten in terms of the modulus and the phase angle. The modulus is

$$\left| \hat{H}(f) \right| = \sqrt{\frac{\hat{C}^2_{xy}(f) + \hat{Q}^2_{xy}(f)}{\hat{G}^2_{xx}(f)}} \qquad (6.76)$$

The phase angle is the same as for the CSD (6.74).

Problems

6.1 Prove that

$$A_{xy}(r) = R_{xy}(r) + R_{yx}(r)$$

is an even function and that

$$B_{xy}(r) = R_{xy}(r) - R_{yx}(r)$$

is an odd function.

6.2 Prove

$$Re[S_{xyk}] = \mathcal{F}[A_{xy}(r)] = \sum_{k=0}^{r-1} A_{xy}(r) \cos \frac{2\pi kr}{N}$$

$$Im[S_{xyk}] = \mathcal{F}[B_{xy}(r)] = \sum_{k=0}^{r-1} B_{xy}(r) \sin \frac{2\pi kr}{N}$$

i.e., the Fourier transform of an even function is a cosine transform, and the Fourier transform of an odd function is a sine transform.

6.3 Prove that the discrete Fourier transform of the Hann and Hamming lag windows gives frequency domain smoothing weights of (1/2,1/4) and (0.54, 0.23), respectively.

6.4 Show that the Fourier transform of the Parzen window is (6.41).

6.5 Prove that

$$E\left(\hat{R}_{xyr} - \frac{1}{N-r} \sum_{i=1}^{N-r} x_i y_{i+r}\right) - R_{xyr} \qquad i - 0,1,\ldots,m$$

i.e., R_{xyr} is an unbiased estimate of R_{xyr}.

6.6 From a statistical standpoint of estimators the correlation function of a hard clipped signal is biased and inefficient. Why? Why might we use such a method in practice?

6.7 Prove that the inverse discrete Fourier transform of

$$S_{xxr} = \frac{\Delta t}{N} \left| X_k \right|^2 \qquad\qquad k = 0,1,\dots,N-1$$

is

$$R^c_{xxr} = \frac{N-r}{N} \left[R_{xxr} + R_{xx(N-r)} \right] \qquad r = 0,1,\dots,N-1$$

6.8 What are the key distinctions between a convolution and a correlation? In computing a correlation via FFTs, what simple change would be necessary in the frequency domain to change the computation to convolutions?

CHAPTER 7
POWER AND CROSS SPECTRA
FROM FAST FOURIER TRANSFORMS

The computation of power and cross spectra was sys-
tematized and standardized with the methods of Blackman and Tukey (1958) which were described in the previous chapter. These methods utilize the Wiener-
Khinchin relation to obtain the spectrum as the
Fourier transform of the correlation function. One of
the major reasons for this approach was computational
efficiency, since a satisfactory spectrum could be
determined from a truncated correlation function.
Thus, with a digital time series of length N, a correlation function of length m is computed in about Nm
multiply-add operations rather than the N^2 operations
which had been previously necessary in obtaining the
spectrum from the Fourier transform of the original
data. The use of Fourier transform to obtain spectra
was not widely used due to its cumbersome computational aspects, and thus the practical problems of its
implementation were never thoroughly dealt with.

The speed of the FFT algorithms now makes the for-
merly discarded method the fastest. Although some
writers have advanced the use of the FFT to obtain the
correlation function and then proceed with the
Blackman-Tukey method, the authors can see no advantage to this. There seems to be no good reason not to
obtain the spectrum directly in the frequency domain
without ever resorting to correlation functions. One
obtains mathematically different results, but for almost all practical purposes, they are identical. A
desire to compare results exactly with existing programs might lead to a requirement to compute spectra
from correlation functions, but the spectra obtained
could hardly be considered better in any way.

279

The FFT approach requires about 4Np operations, where $N=2^p$. The number of lags for the correlation function is typically chosen to be about 0.1N to 0.05N. For N = 4096, p = 12; thus the speed advantage might range from about 100/12 to 50/12 or about 8 or 4 to 1 for this example. This is the primary reason for the direct use of the FFT, but certain other potential advantages accrue with regard to smoothing the spectrum; these will be discussed in the following sections.

The use of direct, finite, discrete Fourier transforms of time series gives rise to some relatively new problems. The Blackman-Tukey procedure of computing the smoothed transform of a correlation function has been applied for a considerable time. As discussed in Chapter 6, the limitations of that method are well-known, and much experience on a variety of types of data has been obtained. Thus, most detailed practical problems have been encountered, and accepted solutions are available.

The FFT, on the other hand, is not so well-established. In particular, there are questions with regard to good smoothing to obtain estimates with desired resolution, variability, and bias characteristics. Restrictions on the length of the sequence give rise to special problems. In principle, a program can be written to handle time series of arbitrary length N, and the computational speed will increase if N is any composite number not a prime. In practice, programs are often written for series of length $N = 2^p$. Thus, records of data of lengths that are not integral powers of two must be truncated to appropriate lengths or zeros must be attached. An alternative approach is to subdivide the time history into shorter (possibly overlapping) time histories and average the final results. In many other instances, however, digitized time histories of relatively inconvenient lengths might already be available, and discarding data might amount to throwing away expensive information. Furthermore, the requirement of collecting a certain number of data points presents an additional constraint to the data analyst.

The following sections will indicate methods for smoothing raw spectra and also the effect of augmenting the series with zeros. The problem of smoothing raw spectra via FFT computations has not been thoroughly studied, and thus the discussion is incomplete. This is partly because the potential flexibility available via the FFT is much greater than with the correlation PSD function approach.

7.1 TAPERING FUNCTIONS—DATA WINDOWS

It is usually desirable to taper a random time series at each end to enhance certain characteristics of the spectral estimates. Tapering is multiplying the time series by a "data window," analogous to multiplying the correlation function by a lag window. Thus, tapering the time series is equivalent to applying a convolution operation (see Chapter 6) to the "raw" Fourier transform. The purpose of tapering when viewed from its frequency domain effect is to suppress large side lobes in the effective filter obtained with the raw transform. When looked at from the time domain, the object of tapering is to "round off" potential discontinuities at each end of the finite segment of the time history being analyzed.

As with the correlation function, one can view a finite-length, random time series as the product of a finite-length boxcar $u_{T/2}(t)$ (Figure 7.1a) and an infinitely long time history $y(t)$ (as depicted in Figure 7.1b). Thus, the finite transform of $x(t)$ may be considered as the transform

$$X(f) = \int_{-T/2}^{T/2} x(t) \exp(-j2\pi ft) \, dt$$

$$= \int_{-\infty}^{\infty} x(t) u_{T/2} \exp(-j2\pi ft) \, dt \qquad (7.1)$$

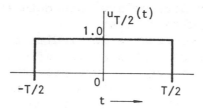

Fig. 7.1a Boxcar function for the FFT.

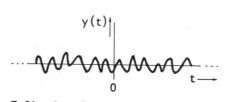

Fig. 7.1b Sample time history of length T.

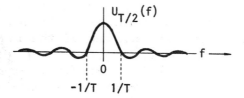

Fig. 7.2 Effective filter shape with no tapering.

Because products   transform into convolutions, we have

$$X(f) = Y(f) * U_{T/2}(f)$$

where

$$U_{T/2}(f) = \int_{-T/2}^{T/2} u_{T/2}(t) \exp(-j2\pi ft) \, dt$$

The effective filter shape with no tapering is illustrated in Figure 7.2. Note that the width of the boxcar function is T, where T is the record length, rather than the $2T_m$ as in Section 6.1, where T_m was the
maximum lag value of the autocorrelation function.
Correspondingly, the distance between zero crossings
of the principal lobe in the frequency plan is 2/T
rather than $1/T_m$. Because of the large side lobes,
power existing in the data at values other than at integral multiples of 1/T will be averaged in the value
centered at f = 0.   By sacrificing some resolution,
one can improve the side lobe characteristics.

Sloan (1969) is critical of tapering the time history (termed a "linearly modified" estimate) for
Gaussian random data. He allows merit for the "signal-
like" case for leakage suppression, but points to a
loss of degrees of freedom for the pure random case.
However, data encountered in practical problems is
often signal-like even though the data is Gaussian.
Vibration, acoustics, seismic, and much economics
data, for example, will exhibit erratically shaped
spectra in which distortion of estimates due to leakage is a severe problem. The present authors can state
that in their experience, distortion due to leakage
and finite bandwidth smearing is at least as severe
a problem as lack of available degrees of freedom in
data.   Thus, we find the opposite of Sloan's conclusion, where it is stated that "linear modification results in a decrease in resolution without a compensat-
ing decrease in variance." The decrease in variance
is almost never a problem, especially when balanced
with the valuable leakage-suppression properties.

Using a cosine taper over 1/10 of each end of the
data rather than $u_{T/2}(t)$ is suggested in Bingham et
al. (1967).   Such a tapering procedure is shown in
Figure 7.3. In equation form, $U_{T/2}^{(4)}$ is

$$
u_{T/2}^{(4)}(t) = \begin{cases} \cos^2 \dfrac{5\pi t}{T} & -\dfrac{T}{2} \le t \le -\dfrac{4T}{10} \\[2ex] 1 & -\dfrac{4T}{10} \le t \le \dfrac{4T}{10} \\[2ex] \cos^2 \dfrac{5\pi t}{T} & \dfrac{4T}{10} < t < \dfrac{T}{2} \\[2ex] 0 & \text{otherwise} \end{cases} \qquad (7.2)
$$

On the other hand, multiplying by a full cosine bell has the form

$$
u_{T/2}^{(5)}(t) = \frac{1}{2}\left(1 + \cos \frac{2\pi t}{T}\right) \qquad -\frac{T}{2} \le t \le \frac{T}{2} \quad (7.3)
$$

and can be shown to be equivalent to using discrete convolution weights $(1/4, 1/2, 1/4)$. That is, $U_{T/2}^{(5)}(f)$ is given by

$$
U_{T/2}^{(5)}\left(-\frac{1}{T}\right) = \frac{1}{4}
$$

$$
U_{T/2}^{(5)}(0) = \frac{1}{2} \qquad\qquad 0 < t < T \quad (7.4)
$$

$$
U_{T/2}^{(5)}\left(\frac{1}{T}\right) = \frac{1}{4}
$$

and is zero at all other multiples of $1/T$, which are the positions at which the finite discrete Fourier transform is evaluated. Reducing the taper to only $(1/10)T$ from each end point changes this, however. The approximate shape of the effective filter is shown in Figure 7.4.

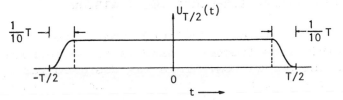

Fig. 7.3 Cosine taper data window $u_{T/2}(t)$.

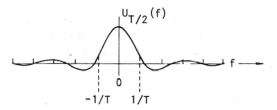

Fig. 7.4 Effective filter shape with
cosine tapering.

Sloan points out that both windows are members of a cosine-arch class given in the frequency domain by

$$U_{T/2}(\omega,m) = \frac{\sin\left(\frac{2m-1}{2m}\right)\frac{\omega T}{2}}{\left(\frac{2m-1}{2m}\right)\frac{\omega}{2}} \left\{ \frac{\left(\frac{2\pi m}{T}\right)^2}{\left[\left(\frac{2\pi m}{T}\right)^2 - \omega^2\right]} \cos\frac{T}{4m} \right\}$$

(7.5)

When $m = 5$ we have $U_{T/2}^{(4)}(\omega)$ and when $m = 1$ (7.5) gives $U_{T/2}^{(5)}(\omega)$.

The selection of a tapering function is in many respects analogous to engineering design of an electrical filter. Two special windows have been designated based on compromises between amount of allowable leakage, resolution loss, and corresponding loss in degrees of freedom. These are discussed in the following section.

The Goodman-Enochson-Otnes (GEO) Window

The first window, designed when smoothing over a reasonably wide frequency band is to be performed, is termed the GEO window. This was designed for application as a smoothing function in the frequency domain rather than as a tapering function in the time domain. From a computational expense standpoint, there seems to be little to choose between tapering in time or smoothing in frequency.

Because the smoothing will broaden the bandwidth of analysis, and to minimize computational expense, it is desirable to have the number of smoothing coefficients as small as possible. On the basis of somewhat arbitrary judgment, it was decided to use weights. This seems a reasonable compromise between computational complexity and flexibility in selection of smoothing procedures. The smoothing equation is

$$\tilde{X}_k = \sum_{\ell=-3}^{3} a_\ell \, X_{k+\ell} = X_k + \sum_{\ell=1}^{3} a_\ell (X_{k-\ell} + X_{k+\ell}) \quad (7.6)$$

where

$$a_0 = 1$$

$$a_{-3} = a_3$$

$$a_{-2} = a_2$$

$$a_{-1} = a_1 \quad\quad\quad\quad\quad\quad\quad\quad\quad\quad\quad (7.7)$$

The next constraint imposed on these weights is that they suppress the leakage. A constraint of the form

$$a_0 - 2a_1 + 2a_2 - 2a_3 = 0 \quad\quad\quad\quad\quad (7.8)$$

will reduce the power leakage from long distance in a manner proportional to $1/f^4$.

WINDOW DERIVATION

There are two more constraints that can be used to minimize the loss in degrees of freedom (d.f.) which is chosen as a figure of merit. There no doubt are numerous reasonable ways in which the remaining constraints could be selected. The method finally chosen was that of varying the zero crossing points of the derived spectral window:

$$W(f) = \sum_{\ell=-3}^{3} a_\ell \frac{\sin\left[\pi N f \left(1 - \frac{\ell}{N}\right)\right]}{N \sin\left[\pi f \left(1 - \frac{\ell}{N}\right)\right]} \qquad 0 \le f \le \frac{1}{2}$$

$$(7.9)$$

This window tends to have the form shown in Figure 7.5.

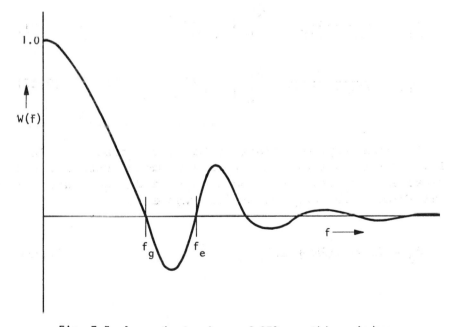

Fig. 7.5 Approximate shape of GEO smoothing window.

The frequencies f_g and f_e are, respectively, the first and second zero crossing to the right of the origin. That is,

$$W(f_g) = W(f_e) = 0 \qquad (7.10)$$

Choosing the position of these two frequencies amounts to defining the last two of the three constraints on the set a_ℓ.

The criteria for window performance which was used is based on examination of the X^2 d.f. of the transformed data before and after the smoothing has been applied and the periodogram computed.

The smoothing is applied by using (7.6). Spectral component averaging is performed also on the raw periodogram and the modified (smoothed) periodogram by:

$$G_{nk} = \frac{2}{(2M + 1)N\Delta t} \sum_{q=-M}^{M} \left| X_{k+q} \right|^2 \qquad (7.11)$$

$$\tilde{G}_{nk} = \frac{2}{(2M + 1)N\Delta t} \sum_{q=-M}^{M} \left| \tilde{X}_{k+q} \right|^2 \qquad (7.12)$$

The subscript n refers to the fact that n = (2M + 1). Assuming that $\{x_i\}$ is a zero mean uncorrelated Gaussian process, then both G_{nk} and $\tilde{G}_{nk}$ are X^2-variables. The G_{nk} has d_0 d.f. where

$$d_0 = 2n = 2(2M + 1) \qquad (7.13)$$

The number of d.f. for the modified estimates $\tilde{G}_{nk}$, denoted by d_1, is somewhat more complicated.   It turns out to be given by

$$d_1 = \frac{2n^2}{v} \tag{7.14}$$

where

$$v = n + 2(n - 1)c_0^2 + 2(n - 2)c_1^2 + \ldots + 2(1)c_{n-1}^2$$

$$\tag{7.15}$$

and

$$c_i = \frac{\Sigma a_\ell a_{\ell+1}}{\left(\Sigma a_\ell^2\right)} \tag{7.16}$$

The proof of this is left for exercise 7.3.   A figure of merit, Φ, may now be defined by

$$\Phi = \frac{d_1}{d_0} = \frac{2n^2/v}{2n}$$

$$= n/v \tag{7.17}$$

Thus, the figure of merit, Φ, is a measure of the loss of d.f. due to the tapering or transform smoothing. In order for d_1 and Φ to be meaningful, the set $\{a_\ell\}$ must be properly normalized.   This is done by constraining a_0 to be unity.
   To derive the exact form of the GEO window, the figure of merit is maximized in the following manner:

   1. A value for f_g is arbitrarily chosen to be
      (1.1)/N. This would be equivalent to having the
      W(f) window 10% wider than the natural one.

2. An arbitrary value for f_e is chosen.

3. This yields three equations in three unknowns (a_1, a_2, and a_3).

4. After solving the equations for a_1, a_2, and a_3, a value for Φ is computed based on a given n (see discussion below).

5. A new value for f_e is chosen and steps 3 and 4 are repeated. This is continued until a maximum value for Φ is determined.

6. Now holding f_e fixed, f_g is varied until a new relative maximum is found for Φ.

The above procedure was programmed on a digital computer and run for $N = 4906$ and $n = 12$. The "optimization" was done for three steps as described above, resulting in the following values:

$$a_0 = 1.0$$

$$a_1 = -0.1817$$

$$a_2 = -0.1707$$

$$a_3 = -0.1476$$

$$\Phi = 0.81715$$

$$f_e = 2.41/N$$

$$f_g = 1.17/N$$

(7.18)

Comparisons (where possible) with some of the other candidates for smoothing are illuminating. Figure 7.6 shows the basic spectral windows for GEO, Hann and cosine taper smoothing. Figure 7.7 illustrates the effective PSD window when twelve estimates are averaged (which provides 24 d.f. in a spectral estimate). Finally, Figure 7.8 shows the equivalent window operations in the time plane.

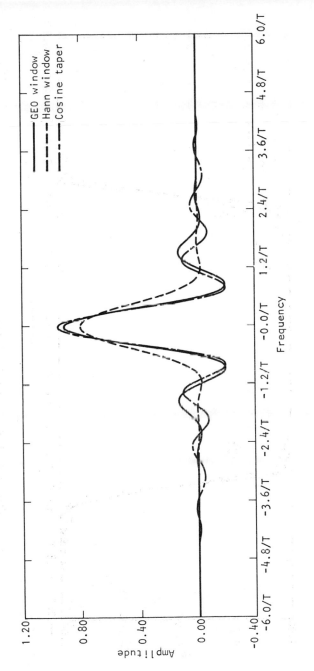

Fig. 7.6 Basic spectral window.

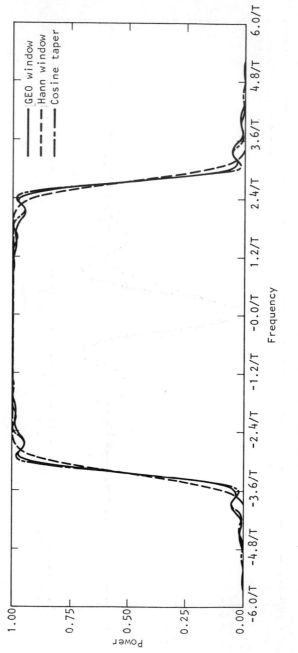

Fig. 7.7 Effective PSD window when twelve basic estimates
are averaged.

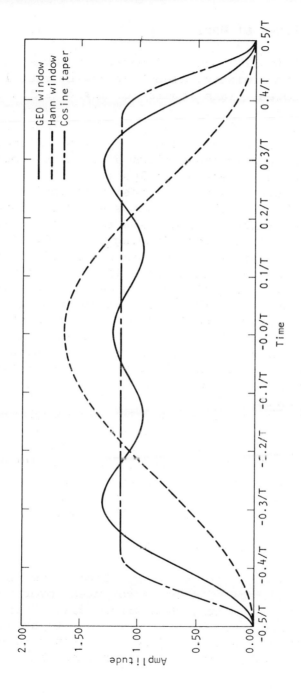

Fig. 7.8 Time plane representations of the three windows.

Leakage Figure of Merit

An additional figure of merit was investigated to estimate the relative amount of power that leaked in via side lobes. This figure of merit is the ratio of the total power in the sum of twelve spectral windows to the power in the main lobe of the composite window. The sum of 12 gives a 24 d.f. spectral estimate which is felt to be near the minimum d.f. which would occur in a reasonable spectral analysis.

This figure of merit was easily reduced to negligible values. It will only get smaller for larger d.f. spectral estimates. The value for the GEO window is 0.0073 (0.73%) and for Hanning it is 0.0022 (0.22%)

A further detail must be taken care of if the property of variance invariance is to be maintained in the results. All data windows will change the variance (or power) in the data, since unequal weight is given to different portions of the time history. In effect, data are thrown away. The result is a loss of d.f. and a decrease in variance. The magnitude of the reduction is calculated by computing the ratio in the square of the area of the data window function to the "boxcar" window. For the Hanning window the factor is 0.375, for the Tukey interim recipe the result is 0.875, and for the GEO window the factor is 1.17. The power spectrum must be multiplied by the reciprocal of the appropriate factor if the area under the power spectrum is to remain invariant. Equivalently, the time history or its Fourier transform can be multiplied by the square root of the appropriate factor.

Window for Spectrum Averaging

When a power (or cross) spectrum is to be computed from the average of spectra computed over individual time history segments, then window design criteria are somewhat different. It is now more important to reduce "nearby" leakage. This was taken care of in the previous design, since it was assumed that smoothing

over a frequency band would take place. Thus, the relatively large first two side lobes were reduced to a
very small percentage of the main lobe after smoothing. This occurs, since the main lobe broadens and becomes larger, while the side lobes retain effectively
their original size.

This does not occur when no frequency smoothing is
done. In spectrum averaging the main lobe is averaged
with the main lobe, and the side lobe is averaged with
the side lobe; the same relative magnitude is maintained. Thus we want a window design with much greater
local side lobe suppression. We will sacrifice d.f. to
obtain this and assume the d.f.   can be regained
through longer record lengths or by making the time
history segments overlapping rather than contiguous.

By overlapping the segments we use part of the data
twice, which is equivalent to multiplying by a factor
of 2.0. Suppose the tail of the data had been reduced
by a factor of 0.5 with the tapering. The factors of
2.0 and 0.5 would cancel the effect of each other, and
the loss in d.f. is therefore overcome. Of course, a
penalty in computation time is paid which may or may
not be important.

The before and after spectral windows are illustrated in Figure 7.9.

A spectral window (informally suggested by Goodman)
for time-slice averaging (to be discussed in the
following section), based on a less formal design procedure than that for the GEO window, has weights

$$b_0 = 1.0$$

$$b_1 = b_{-1} = -0.35$$

$$b_2 = b_{-2} = -0.875$$

$$b_3 = b_{-3} = -0.0625 \qquad\qquad (7.19)$$

Leakage is kept at about 2%; the coherence between
neighboring estimates is about 30%.   Local side lobes
are reduced to about 2% of the height of the main

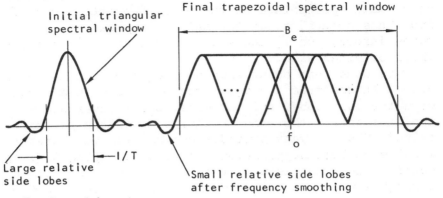

Initial triangular spectral window

Final trapezoidal spectral window

B_e

f_o

Large relative side lobes

—1/T

Small relative side lobes after frequency smoothing

T = Record length

Before and after frequency smoothing
d.f = 2ℓ, ℓ = Number of raw frequency components averaged

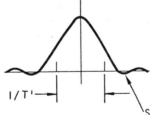 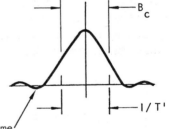

B_c

1/T'—

—1/T'

Side lobes same relative size

T' = Segment length

Before and after time-slice spectrum averaging
d.f. = 2m, m = Number of time slices averaged

Fig. 7.9 Smoothing of FFT-generated PSDs.

lobe, however. The shape of this (the Goodman window) is shown in Figure 7.10. The equivalent time domain function is given in Figure 7.11.

7.2 COMPUTATIONAL RECIPES

The computational FFT methods we will discuss here assume the number of data values transformed is $N = 2^p$. Thus, if the time history or a segment of it is not an even power of two, zero values will be used to fill out the sequence.

The spacing of discrete Fourier transform value is

$$\Delta f = 1/T = 1/N\Delta t \qquad (7.20)$$

The spacing between the first zero crossings on both sides of the main lobe for $U_{T/2}$ is $B_e = 1/T$. When zeros are attached to the sequence, nothing is contributed to the basic shape of $U_{T/2}(f)$, and hence the width of the main lobe is unchanged. However, because of the nature of the computational formula, the spacing of the estimates is based on the augmented record length and is

$$\Delta f' = \frac{1}{(N + N_z)\Delta t} \qquad (7.21)$$

where N_z is the number of zeros attached. For example, if an equal number of zeros, $N_z = N$, is attached, the spacing is halved and appears as in Figure 7.12. This change in spacing leads to problems, since the effective convolution applied to the raw Fourier transform may not lead to the desired side lobe cancellation. In fact, the side lobes might be enlarged. The problems of modifying Fourier transforms when arbitrary numbers of zeros must be added is under study. The problem is essentially that of empirical filter design. Another approach is discussed further here.

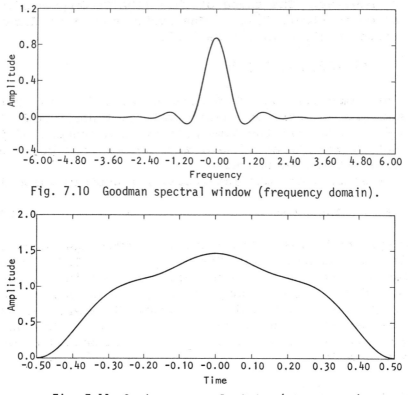

Fig. 7.10   Goodman spectral window (frequency domain).

Fig. 7.11   Goodman spectral window (time domain).

Power spectra are obtained from the Fourier transform by the formula

$$\tilde{G}_{xk} = \frac{2\Delta t}{N} \, |X_k|^2$$

$$= 2\frac{\Delta t}{N} \left\{ [\text{Re}(X_k)]^2 + [\text{Im}(X_k)]^2 \right\} \qquad (7.22)$$

Cross spectra are obtained from the more general formula

$$\tilde{G}_{xyk} = \frac{2\Delta t}{N} \, [X_k^* \, Y_k] \qquad (7.23)$$

If the number of data points $N = 2^p$, then the spacing
of the raw estimates is illustrated in Figure 7.12. In
statistical terms, the raw power spectra of G_{xk} can be
shown (as discussed in Chapter 5) to be approximately
x^2-variables with 2 d.f.   That is, if the data are
Gaussian, then each spectrum point is the sum of two
independent, squared Gaussian variables. The standard
error of the unsmoothed spectrum estimates is shown in
Chapter 5 to be

$$\varepsilon = \left(\frac{2n}{n^2}\right)^{1/2} = \left(\frac{2 \cdot 2}{2 \cdot 2}\right)^{1/2} = 1$$

or 100%.   This is not satisfactory for most purposes.
If the spectrum is locally smooth, the estimates at a
spacing of $1/T$ are approximately uncorrelated (the
correlation is the overlap between neighboring estimates as indicated in Figure 7.12a). Hence,if ℓ neighboring estimates are averaged, then the smoothed
estimate

$$\hat{G}_k = \frac{1}{\ell} \left(\tilde{G}_k + \tilde{G}_{k+1} + \cdots + \tilde{G}_{k+\ell-1} \right) \tag{7.24}$$

is a x^2-variable with roughly $2\ell n$ d.f. by the
x^2-addition theorem. The effective filter shape is
then roughly trapezoidal, since adding together tri-
angles that overlap at half-power points gives a trap-
ezoid as indicated in Figure 7.13. Note that the
effective bandwidth is now approximately

$$B_e = \ell \Delta f = \frac{\ell}{T} \tag{7.25}$$

The estimate $\hat{G}_k$ may be considered as representing the
midpoint of the frequency interval from $k\Delta f$ to
$(k + \ell - 1)\Delta f$.
    The final estimates $\hat{G}_k$ can be spaced in any manner
desired. If it is satisfactory to have final estimates
that overlap at half-power points, then one would average and decimate to obtain N/ℓ final estimates are

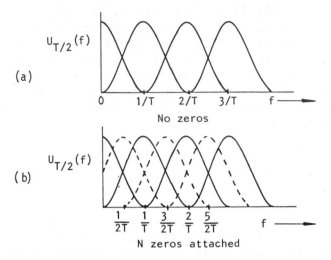

(a)

(b)

Fig. 7.12 Effect on spacing of spectral averages
when zeros are added.

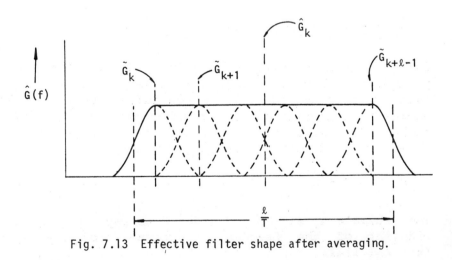

Fig. 7.13 Effective filter shape after averaging.

obtained that contain considerable correlation between
any contiguous pair of estimates.

Blackman-Tukey Spectra Via the FFT

Spectrum estimates identical to the B-T method can
be obtained using the direct Fourier transform approach (although this is by no means necessarily desirable from a statistical standpoint). A seemingly
long way around is taken which, in fact, is usually
faster than the direct correlation computation. The
procedure is as follows:

1. Compute the raw transform X_k.

2. Compute the raw spectrum $\tilde{G}_{xk} = (2\Delta t/N)|X_k|^2$.

3. Compute the inverse FFT to obtain the autocorrelation function $\hat{R}_{xr} = \mathcal{F}^{-1}[\tilde{G}_{xk}]$.

4. Multiply $\hat{R}_{xr}$ by lag window u_{mr}.

5. Compute the final smoothed spectrum $\hat{G}_k$ from the
   direct FFT of the weighted autocorrelation
   $\hat{G}_{xk} = \mathcal{F}[u_{mr}\hat{R}_{xr}]$.

As discussed in Section 6.7, this computational procedure must be modified since the usual correlation
function is not obtained at step 3. Zeros must be attached to the original data sequence (or special computational tricks applied) to obtain the desired correlation function. When this is done, spectrum spacing will be as in Figure 7.12b. The right-hand half
of the circular correlation can be discarded as discussed in Section 6.7 and the remainder used in
steps 3, 4, and 5.

The modified computational procedure is the
following:

1. Augment sequence x_i with N zeros to obtain a sequence of length 2N.

2. Compute the raw transform X_k, $k = 0,1,\ldots,2N-1$.

3. Compute the raw spectrum

$$\tilde{G}_{xk} = \frac{2\Delta t}{N} |X_k|^2 \qquad k = 0,1,\ldots,2N-1 \quad (7.26)$$

4. Compute the inverse transform of G_{xk}:

$$\tilde{R}_{xr} = \mathfrak{F}^{-1} [\tilde{G}_{xk}] \qquad r = 0,1,\ldots,2N-1 \quad (7.27)$$

5. Discard the last N value of $\hat{R}_{xr}$ and retain $\hat{R}_{xr}$, $r = 0,1,\ldots,N$.

6. Multiply $\hat{R}_{xr}$ by lag window u_{mr}.

7. Compute the direct transform of $\hat{R}_{xr}$:

$$\hat{G}_{xk} = [u_{mr}^i \hat{R}_{xr}] \qquad k = 0,1,\ldots,N \quad (7.28)$$

Note that a given sequence need be augmented with only as many zeros as lags. The number of zeros necessary to obtain sequence lengths which are a power of two and the number of lags needed or desired will dictate the final sequence length. The amount of correlation function retained need only be the smallest power of two which exceeds the number of lags to be used. Step 5 can be modified to discard as many correlation values as possible to obtain the minimum power of two larger than the number of lags desired.

Direct Spectrum Estimates Via FFT

There is no particular reason to obtain spectrum estimates via the B-T procedure other than tradition. Estimates which are as good or better from all standpoints may be obtained with less computer time, and thus more economically, directly in the frequency domain from the FFT.

Method 1. Reasonable spectral estimates can be obtained for sequences of length $N = 2^p$ by the following procedure:

1. First fill out the data sequence with zero data points to obtain 2^{p+1} total data points if this spectrum is later to be inverse-transformed to obtain a correlation function.

2. Compute the finite Fourier transform of the augmented data sequence

$$\tilde{X}_k = \sum_{i=0}^{N-1} x_i w^{ik} \qquad\qquad k = 0,1,\ldots,N-1 \quad (7.29)$$

3. Apply the GEO spectral window to the raw Fourier transform by the convolution

$$X_k = \tilde{X}_k + \sum_{i=1}^{3} a_i [\tilde{X}_{k-i} + \tilde{X}_{k+i}]$$

$$k = 0,1,\ldots,N-1; \quad a_1 = -0.1817; \quad (7.30)$$
$$a_2 = -0.1707; \quad a_3 = -0.1476$$

At the ends, use the periodicity of transform

$$\tilde{X}_{N+k} = \tilde{X}_k \qquad\qquad (7.31)$$

to define $\tilde{X}_k$ for values of the index less than zero or greater than N-1.

4. Compute the absolute value squared, scaled appropriately to obtain the "raw" power spectral estimates:

$$\tilde{G}_{xk} = \frac{2\Delta t}{N} |X_k|^2 \qquad\qquad k = 0,1,\ldots,N-1 \quad (7.32)$$

5. Adjust the estimates for the scale factor due to GEO smoothing:

$$0.856\,\tilde{G}_x(k) \rightarrow \tilde{G}_x(k) \qquad\qquad k = 0,1,\ldots,N-1$$

6. If cross spectral density functions are desired, a second Fourier transform Y_k is obtained. Then the "raw" cross spectra spectral density estimate is obtained from the equation

$$\tilde{G}_{xyk} = \frac{2\Delta t}{N} \, [X_k^* \, Y_k]$$

$$= \tilde{C}_{xyk} - j\tilde{Q}_{xyk}$$

$$k = 0,1,2,\ldots,N-1 \quad (7.33)$$

7. Smoothed estimates are then obtained by averaging ℓ contiguous raw estimates to yield

$$\hat{G}_{xk} = \frac{1}{\ell} \sum_{j=1}^{\ell} G_{xx(k+j)} \qquad\qquad (7.34)$$

or

$$\hat{G}_{xyk} = \frac{1}{\ell} \sum_{j=1}^{\ell} G_{xy(k+j)}$$

$$k = \ell, 2\ell, 3\ell, \ldots, m\ell \quad (7.35)$$

The spectrum values $\hat{G}_{xyk}$ are interpreted as being at frequency values

$$f = 0, \frac{\ell}{2}\Delta f, \frac{3}{2}\ell\Delta f, \frac{5}{2}\ell\Delta f, \ldots, \left(\frac{2m-1}{2}\right)\ell\Delta f$$

8. For cross spectra, the squared absolute value, $|\hat{G}_{xyk}|^2$, and the phase (in degrees), $\hat{\theta}_{xyk}$, will normally be the final results given by

$$|\hat{G}_{xyk}|^2 = \hat{C}_{xyk}^2 + \hat{Q}_{xyk}^2$$

$$\hat{\theta}_{xyk} = \frac{360}{2\pi} \arctan(\hat{Q}_{xyk}/\hat{C}_{xyk}) \qquad (7.36)$$

For long record lengths of data, an acceptable method is to segment the overall time history and compute an average spectrum which was referred to earlier.

A reasonable approach is to base the segment length on resolution requirements. That is, if $B_e = \Delta f$ if specified, then the segment length is $T_S = 1/\Delta f$, which is then padded with zeros to the nearest power of two. The spectral window utilized will be the Goodman window with small side lobes to account for the problem depicted in Figure 7.7. The recipe is given in Method 2.

Method 2.

1. Compute trial segment length T'_s from specified resolution:

$$T'_s = 1/\Delta f \tag{7.37}$$

Determine the smallest power of two p so that

$$\frac{T'_s}{\Delta t} = N'_s \le N_s = 2^p \tag{7.38}$$

If

$$2^{p-1} < N'_s \le 1.25\, 2^{p-1} \tag{7.39}$$

choose segment length $N_s = 2^{p-1}$; otherwise choose $N_s = 2^p$. If $N_s = 2^{p-1}$ is selected, recompute true resolution as

$$B_c = \Delta f = 1/2^{p-1} \tag{7.40}$$

2. Compute the total number of segments

$$m < [N/N_s + 1] \tag{7.41}$$

where the brackets [x] indicate the largest integer value less than x. Thus, there will usually be one "short" segment of length

$$N_m = N - (p - 1)N_s \qquad (7.42)$$

This last segment will be padded with extra
zeros as necessary to bring it to length N_s.

3. Determine weights for each spectrum in final average. The first $(m-1)$ spectra are given weight

$$w = \frac{N_s}{NN_s'} \qquad (7.43)$$

The last segment is given weight

$$w_m = \frac{N_s}{NN_m} \qquad (7.44)$$

4. Compute the finite Fourier transform of the
first N_s'-point sequence, augmented with zeros
if necessary, to bring it to length $N_S = 2^p$:

$$\tilde{x}_k(\ell) = \sum_{i=0}^{N_s-1} x_i(\ell)w^{ik} \qquad \ell = 1 \quad (7.45)$$

where ℓ indicates the segment number.

5. Apply the Goodman spectral window to the raw
Fourier transform:

$$X_k(\ell) = \tilde{x}_k + \sum_{i=1}^{3} b_i [X_{k-i}(\ell) + X_{k+i}(\ell)]$$

$$k = 0,1,2,\ldots,N_s - 1; \ b_1 = -0.35;$$
$$b_2 = -0.875; \ b_3 = -0.0625 \qquad (7.46)$$

6. Compute the absolute value squared, scaled appropriately, to obtain "raw" spectral estimates:

$$\tilde{G}_{xk} = \frac{2\Delta t}{N} \left| X_k \right|^2 \qquad k = 0,1,\ldots,N_s-1 \qquad (7.47)$$

7. Adjust the estimates for the scale factor due to Goodman smoothing:

$$(1/0.75)\ \tilde{G}_x(k) \rightarrow \tilde{G}_x(k)$$

8. Obtain cross spectra if desired as in step 6 of Method 1.

9. Repeat steps 4, 5, 6, 7, and 8 for segments $\ell = 2,3,\ldots,m$.

10. Compute final smoothed estimates by averaging the m raw spectra:

$$\hat{G}_{xk} = \frac{1}{w} \sum_{\ell=1}^{m-1} \tilde{G}_{xyk}(\ell) + \frac{1}{w_m} \tilde{G}_{xk}(m)$$

$$k = 0,1,\ldots,N_s-1 \qquad (7.48)$$

or

$$\hat{G}_{xyk} = \frac{1}{w} \sum_{\ell=1}^{m-1} \tilde{G}_{xyk}(\ell) + \frac{1}{w_m} \tilde{G}_{xk}(m) \qquad (7.49)$$

One obtains N_s spectrum estimates (possibly correlated) interpreted as located at frequency values

$$f = 0,\ \frac{\Delta f}{2},\ \frac{3\Delta f}{2},\ \frac{5\Delta f}{2},\ \ldots,(N_s - \tfrac{1}{2})\Delta f$$

each having approximately

$$n = 2m\ \text{d.f.}$$

Timing Considerations

Computational time for a correlation PSD is usually dictated almost entirely by the correlation computational time. This is about 2Nm multiply-add operations. The necessary Fourier transform time is usually not significant, because the correlation function length is so much less than the time history length. Similarly, the majority of computational time for spectra, calculated directly by FFT procedures, is the basic FFT time. The additional time for absolute value squared, smoothing, and sine-cosine generation will usually not be crucial. Thus, a fairly direct time comparison can be made, assuming 8Np operations as required for the ($N = 2^p$) type of FFT. It must be kept in mind that special techniques can reduce this time. The basic speed ratio for FFT versus B-T for a single PSD is roughly

$$SR = \text{Speed ratio} = \frac{2Nm}{8Np} = \frac{m}{4p} \qquad (7.50)$$

Consider $N = 8192$ and $p = 13$. Typically, $m = 400$ lags might be selected. Then the speed ratio is

$$SR = \frac{400}{(4)\ (13)} = 7.7 \qquad (7.51)$$

The speed advantage of the FFT approach increases when many time series are involved and cross spectra are required. If two PSDs and a cross spectrum are necessary, four times the number of operations in the B-T will be required, since two halves of the cross correlation must be computed. The FFT effort only doubles, however, since only two FFTs are required. The only new computation is the cross product of the two transforms. The speed ration therefore becomes

$$SR = \frac{2\ m}{4\ (4p)} = 15.4 \qquad (7.52)$$

Problems

7.1 Show that (7.5) gives

$$U_{T/2}^{(4)}(f)$$

for m=5 and

$$U_{T/2}^{(5)}(f)$$

when m=1.

7.2 It is stated that the smoothing weights constraint (7.8) causes "far away" leakage to be reduced by a factor proportional to

$$1/f^4$$

This statement is based upon a theorem of Fourier series that is related to approximating a function with continuous third derivatives. Relate constraint (7.8) to this theorem to explain the accuracy of the claim.

7.3 Show that the d.f. for modified spectral estimates is given by (7.14).

CHAPTER 8
FILTER METHODS FOR THE POWER
SPECTRAL DENSITY

8.1   INTRODUCTION

As discussed in Chapter 5, the basic filtering PSD
method is the following:

1. For each sample PSD value $\hat{G}_k$, a center frequency
   f_k and bandwidth B_k are chosen. It is assumed
   that $f_k < f_{k+1}$. Usually (but not always) $B_k \leq$
   B_{k+1}. These values are also chosen such that

$$ f_k + \frac{B_k}{2} = f_{k+1} - \frac{B_{k+1}}{2} \tag{8.1}$$

2. A separate bandpass filter is found for each k.
   It could be Chebyshev, Butterworth, etc., of
   either the sine or tangent variety, using 2, 4,
   6, 8,... weights. The filters have their half-
   power points at $(f_k - B_k/2)$ and $(f_k + B_k/2)$ Hz.

3. The data sequence $\{x_i\}$ is filtered using each
   of the filters. The output of the kth filter,
   $\{y_i^{(k)}\}$, is squared and summed.

4. The summation is converted to the proper units
   by multiplying by $1/B_kN$.

This procedure is shown in Figure 8.1.

One very important point which must be considered
is when to start and stop the filtering. From the
point of view of leakage, the leakage is lowest when
the following procedure is employed: Suppose that
there are N data points and that for the kth filter
the distance between the half-power points is B_k; instead of terminating at N data points, add 2 $B_k\Delta t$
zeros and continue filtering; finally, compute the expression

311

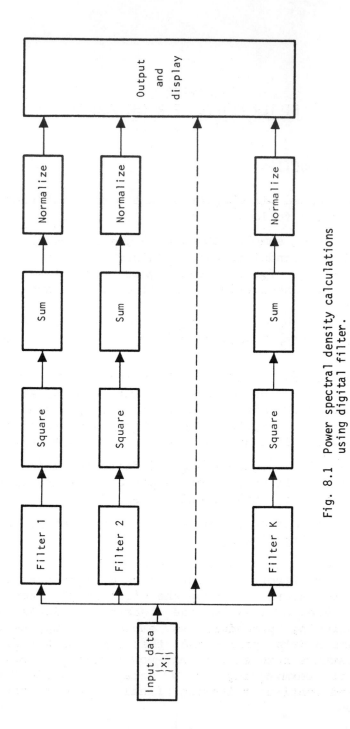

Fig. 8.1 Power spectral density calculations using digital filter.

$$G_k = \frac{1}{B_k N} \sum_{i=1}^{N'_k} \left[y_i^{(k)} \right]^2 \tag{8.2}$$

where

$$N'_k = N + \frac{2}{B_k \Delta t} \tag{8.3}$$

As shown in Figure 8.2, when a sine wave is filtered
through a bandpass filter, there are start-up and
trail-off periods, each about $2/B_k$ sec in length.
These tend to add a natural form of windowing and
leakage suppression.

Note in (8.2) that N rather than N'_k is used in the
divisor. A bias would be introduced if an N'_k were used
that would tend to lower the value for G_k. The reason
for this can be seen intuitively from Figure 8.2. The

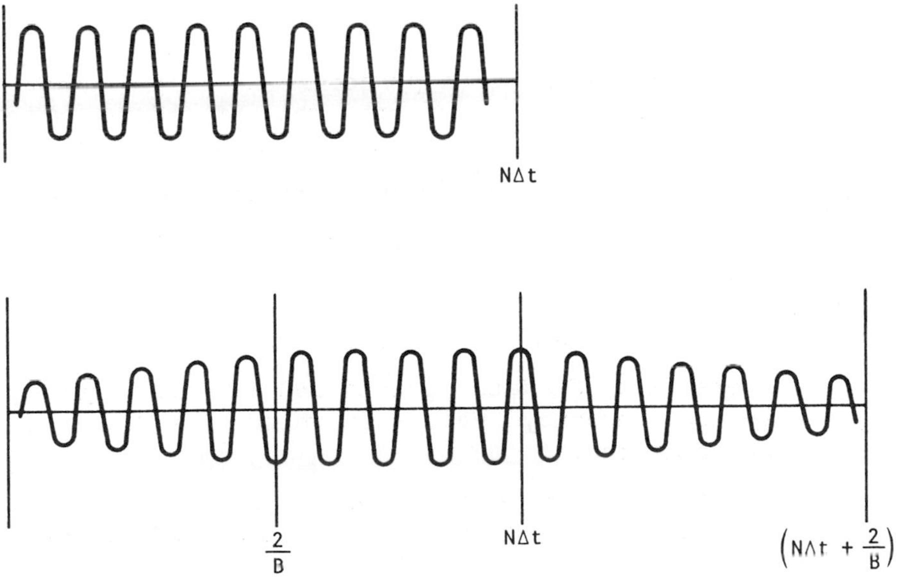

Fig. 8.2

total energy for the filtered sine wave must be the
same as for the unfiltered one; the average energy, on
the other hand, is clearly lower in the filtered case.
The result would be lower than is usually the case if
the data were divided by N_k'.

The d.f. n_k for white noise is approximately

$$n_k = 2B_k N\Delta t \tag{8.4}$$

Thus, n_k is a function of the bandwidth. If all the
bandwidths are equal, then they will of course have the
same number of d.f. Equation (8.4) is valid if the
filter form reasonably approximates the ideal bandpass
form described in Chapter 3. In any event, (8.4) may
be used to compute confidence limits in the same manner given in Chapter 5 for the Fourier PSD as long as
the same cautions are observed. Similarly, the standard error is found in Chapter 5 to be

$$\varepsilon_k = \frac{1}{\sqrt{B_k N\Delta t}} \tag{8.5}$$

The main problem with this procedure is that of cost.

It is interesting to compare this procedure with
that of the correlation PSD. Computer running time is
difficult to estimate because it involves many variables, including the individual skill of the programmer
who writes the code, a factor which is difficult to
evaluate. One thing that is known, however, is the
approximate number of purely arithmetic operations
that will be required in each case. So, assume:

1. There are N data points and (m + 1) equally
   spaced frequency values at which the PSD is to
   be estimated.

2. The correlation method uses a reasonably fast
   algorithm for computing the cosine terms recursively but does not use the FFT.

3. The filter method uses second-order filters as described in Chapter 3. Under these conditions, the number of arithmetic operations required for the two cases is (approximately)

$$\begin{array}{l}\text{Arithmetic operations} \\ \text{(correlation method)}\end{array} = (m + 1)\big[2N + 5(m + 1)\big]$$

$$\begin{array}{l}\text{Arithmetic operations} \\ \text{(filter method)}\end{array} = 7N(m + 1) \qquad (8.6)$$

The ratio of these two terms is

$$\left(\frac{\text{Correlation}}{\text{Filtering}}\right) = \frac{2N + 5(m + 1)}{7N} \qquad (8.7)$$

Thus, for evenly spaced analyses, as m < N (usually), the correlation method is the cheapest right up to the point where (m + 1) = N, which is where there are as many frequencies as there are data points. This analysis assumes that the filter approach uses the simplest of all filters. If a more complicated filter were to be used, the cost would go up even more. For example, if a six-pole sine bandpass filter were employed, then (8.6) would be

$$\begin{array}{l}\text{Floating point operations} \\ \text{(filter method, six-pole filters)}\end{array} = 13N(m + 1)$$

$$(8.8)$$

8.2 OCTAVE BAND FILTERING

The picture changes considerably if equal bandwidth estimates are not required. Many users, for example, would like the bandwidths to increase with increasing frequency in some geometrical fashion. Suppose that the bandwidth of analysis at 0 Hz is $1/m\Delta t$, and that the PSD is subdivided into n intervals, each of which is increasing multiplicatively by a factor a. The total bandwidth will be

$$\frac{1}{m\Delta t}(1 + a + \ldots + a^{n-1}) = \frac{1}{2\Delta t} \qquad (8.9)$$

This can be reduced to

$$\frac{a^n - 1}{a - 1} = \frac{m}{2} \qquad (8.10)$$

Solving for n yields

$$n = \frac{\log\left[1 + (a - 1)\frac{m}{2}\right]}{\log a} \qquad (8.11)$$

Thus, the cost of computing the variable bandwidth PSD using filters is

$$\text{Arithmetic operations} = N(3 + 2p)\frac{\log\left[1 + (a - 1)\frac{m}{2}\right]}{\log a} \qquad (8.12)$$

In (8.12), p is the number of poles in the filters. Suppose that p and a are both set equal to two, and that m is equal to N (maximum resolution). Then,

$$\text{Arithmetic operations} \approx \frac{7N \log\left(1 + \frac{N}{2}\right)}{\log a} \qquad (8.13)$$

The ratio of this expression to the similar one for the correlation method yields

$$\frac{\text{Correlation}}{\text{Filtering}} \approx \frac{N \log a}{\log\left(1 + \frac{N}{2}\right)} \qquad (8.14)$$

An even less expensive method of implementing a third-octave type of analysis is the following: A third-octave module is developed as shown in Figure 8.3. The

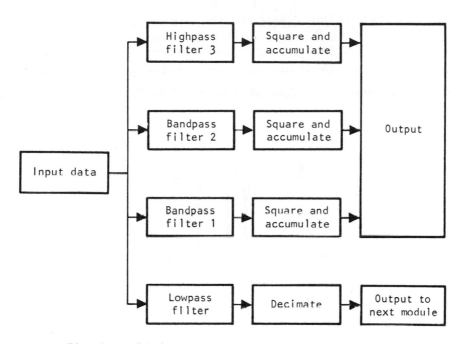

Fig. 8.3 Third-octave power spectral density module.

highpass and two bandpass filters are designed to
cover the upper one-half of the frequency interval in
the following manner (where hpp stands for half-power
point):

$$\text{Filter 1} \begin{cases} \text{Left hpp} \quad = 1/4\Delta t \\[2ex] \text{Right hpp} = \sqrt[3]{2}/4\Delta t \end{cases}$$

$$\text{Filter 2} \begin{cases} \text{Left hpp} \quad = \sqrt[3]{2}/4\Delta t \\[2ex] \text{Right hpp} = \sqrt[3]{4}/4\Delta t \end{cases}$$

$$\text{Filter 3} \begin{cases} \text{Left hpp} \quad = \sqrt[3]{4}/4\Delta t \\[2ex] \text{Right hpp} = 1/2\Delta t \end{cases} \tag{8.15}$$

The lowpass filter has its half-power point at $1/4\Delta t$. By the sampling theorem discussed in Chapter 1, every other data point is redundant and may be thrown away. This process of throwing away excess points, as described in Chapter 3, is known as decimation.

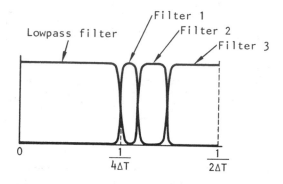

Fig. 8.4   Transfer functions of the filters in the third-octave modules.

The process for doing the decimation is as follows: Label the original sampling interval Δt_0. Call the new sampling interval Δt_1. Then the relation is

$$2\Delta t_1 = \Delta t_0 \tag{8.16}$$

The decimated data output from the module is now the input into an identical module. The output of that is as shown in Figure 8.4, except that the relative scale has changed. The combined coverage of these two modules is shown in Figure 8.5, which indicates that the procedure of putting the decimated output of a module into a new module can be carried on indefinitely. Suppose that processing all of the data using the first module requires A sec. As the first module puts out only half as many points as were continued in its input, the second module will require A/2 sec. Similarly, the third module will require only A/4 sec. Noting the fact that

$$\lim_{n \to \infty} \sum_{i=0}^{n} \frac{1}{2^i} = 2 \qquad (8.17)$$

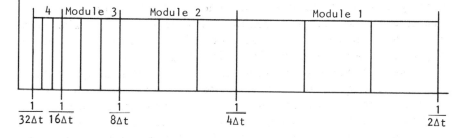

Fig. 8.5 Overall filter spacing of the third-octave
          analysis.

it is seen that a total of only 2A sec is required for
the whole analysis.

Insofar as the number of floating-point operations
is concerned, suppose that filters 1, 2, and 3 are six-
pole filters (each requiring 13 arithmetic operations)
and that the lowpass filter is a twelve-pole filter
(requiring 23 operations). Then a total of 62 operations per data point per module will be required. The
limiting operation of (8.17) shows that a total computation requires only twice as many operations. Thus,
for N original data points, 124N arithmetic operations
are required. Comparing this with the correlation procedure yields

$$\left(\frac{\text{Correlation}}{\text{Third-octave}} \right) = \frac{(m + 1)\left[2N + 5(m + 1) \right]}{124N}$$

$$\approx \frac{m}{62} \qquad (8.18)$$

Thus, any time that more than 62 autocorrelation lags are required, the third-octave filtering method is cheaper. The above procedure could be recast using other divisions of the interval instead of 1/3 oc- taves. There could be a corresponding increase in com- puting cost, of course, but the cost increase would be linear. Sine filter weights for the above procedure are given in Table 8.1. The coefficients were obtained using the methods described in Chapter 3.

Somewhat more expensive to use are the tangent fil- ters. However, they are somewhat sharper in their roll-off characteristics, so that the extra price may be well worth it. Tangent filter weights are given in Table 8.2. Their transform functions correspond to those of sine filters in the previous table insofar as half-power points, etc., are concerned.

Other filter choises are possible: Chebyshev fil- ters could well be considered; the number of weights could be varied; and the whole scheme of positioning the filters could be changed.

This last statement deserves further comment. In one sense,the filters are at their least optimal posi- tion. That is, they are relatively broad with respect to the $1/2\Delta t$ interval; if some of the higher frequen- cies could be discarded, or if the sampling interval could be decreased, then it would be possible to shift the filters further to the right causing an improve- ment in all but the highpass filter. The latter could be replaced in the first filter module with a bandpass filter of the proper bandwidth.

Table 8.1 Sine Formulation of the Third-Octave Filters

Type of filter	K	H1(K)	H2(K)	L	G(L)
Lowpass with cut-off at $\frac{1}{4\Delta t}$ Hz	1	5.10641955E-02	-5.99116440E-01	0	2.36567817E-01
	2	2.41077298E-01	-2.59084840E-01		
	3	3.80093403E-01	-1.47059093E-01		
	4	4.64205551E-01	-1.01552916E-01		
	5	5.11750397E-01	-8.10157651E-02		
	6	5.33007003E-01	-7.27518982E-02		
Bandpass with center at 0.565 $\frac{1}{2\Delta t}$ Hz	1	-4.79366260E-02	-8.20155320E-01	0	4.16720595E-02
	2	-3.18276863E-01	-6.68943218E-01		
	3	-6.62222373E-01	-8.08053772E-01		
Bandpass with center at 0.712 $\frac{1}{2\Delta t}$ Hz	1	-7.54747912E-01	-8.02421017E-01	0	3.85756409E-02
	2	-9.09404411E-01	-6.14925400E-01		
	3	-1.30574774E+00	-7.35426915E-01		
Highpass with cut-off at 0.794 $\frac{1}{2\Delta t}$ Hz	1	-1.36620793E+00	-7.07526315E-01	0	1.93640261E-02
	2	-1.14361629E+00	-4.00372098E-01		
	3	-1.07555948E+00	-2.96520518E-01		

Table 8.2 Tangent Formulation of the Third-Octave Filters

Type of filter	K	H1(K)	H2(K)	Overall scale factor*
Lowpass with cut-off at $\frac{1}{4\Delta t}$ H	1	3.17593726E-09	-7.69087717E-01	0 9.04300899E-04
	2	2.59623661E-09	-4.46462693E-01	
	3	2.23140731E-09	-2.43192412E-01	
	4	2.00172932E-09	-1.15229194E-01	
	5	1.86591939E-09	-3.95661302E-02	
	6	1.80260759E-09	-4.29594563E-03	
Bandpass with center at $0.565\,\frac{1}{2\Delta t}$ Hz	1	-4.85906681E-02	-8.11568431E-01	0 5.88143403E-03
	2	-3.43033727E-01	-6.56966270E-01	
	3	-6.82532456E-01	-8.23995996E-01	
Bandpass with center at $0.712\,\frac{1}{4\Delta t}$ Hz	1	-7.49260857E-01	-7.42619595E-01	0 1.08043386E-02
	2	-1.01090374E+00	-5.83624671E-01	
	3	-1.41961917E+00	-8.14997815E-01	
Highpass with cut-off at $0.794\,\frac{1}{2\Delta t}$ Hz	1	-1.37874686E+00	-7.29679765E-01	0 3.99625436E-04
	2	-1.11720459E+00	-4.01567045E-01	
	3	-1.00692532E+00	-2.63218323E-01	

*The nonrecursive position of the filter may be generated as shown in Chapter 3 from the scale factors given above.

CHAPTER 9
TRANSFER FUNCTION AND COHERENCE
FUNCTION COMPUTATIONS

9.1 PROPERTIES OF FREQUENCY RESPONSE FUNCTIONS

A discussion of linear systems and the computational procedures necessary for obtaining estimates of them from measured time histories is presented in this chapter. The simplest case, which has a single input and a single output, is discussed first. A generalization to the multiple-input, single-output system is then presented. Computational requirements and procedures for confidence limit evaluations are given in Sections 9.4 to 9.9. Extensions to other ideas of multivariate statistics are given in Section 9.10.

The application of these techniques lies in many physical problems including transmissibility and impedance functions in shock and vibration analysis (Barnoski, 1969) seismic data analysis (Dean et al., 1966), nuclear reactor analysis, analysis of turbulent fluid flow in an automatic transmission torque converter, the analysis of turbulent flow in jet engine turbine inlets, and the response of an aircraft while moving along a rough runway.

Consider a physically realizable linear system that does not have any time-varying parameters. As discussed in Section 3.1, the weighting function $h(\tau)$ associated with this system is defined as the response (the output) function of the system to a unit impulse input function as a function of the time τ from the occurrence of the impulse. For physically realizable systems, it is necessary that $h(\tau) = 0$ for $\tau < 0$, since the response must follow the input. The weighting function concept is useful because, for an arbitrary input $x(t)$, the system output $y(t)$ is given by the convolution integral

323

$$y(t) = \int_0^\infty h(\tau) \, x(t - \tau) \, d\tau \tag{9.1}$$

That is, the value of the output $y(t)$ at any time t is given as a weighted linear (infinite) sum over the entire past history of the input $x(t)$.

The linear system may alternatively be characterized by its frequency response or transfer function $H(f)$ which is defined as the Fourier transform of $h(\tau)$. That is,

$$H(f) = \int_0^\infty h(\tau) \, e^{-j2\pi f\tau} \, dt \tag{9.2}$$

The lower limit is zero instead of $-\infty$, since $h(\tau) = 0$ for $\tau < 0$.

The idea of physical realizability is important from the standpoint of the engineering analysis of real systems. However, from a mathematical, and sometimes also computational viewpoint, physically unrealizable versions of (9.1) and (9.2) are most useful. Instead of a finite lower limit, $-\infty$ is used. Thus,

$$y(t) = \int_{-\infty}^\infty h(\tau) \, x(t - \tau) \, d\tau \tag{9.3}$$

$$H(f) = \int_{-\infty}^\infty h(\tau) \, e^{-j2\pi f\tau} \, d\tau \tag{9.4}$$

For example, numerical filters used in a digital computer need not be realizable in this sense. It is perfectly correct to use symmetrical weighting functions and have phaseless (zero phase shift) filters (see Chapter 3). The frequency response function relates the input and output variables by the formula

$$Y(f) = H(f) \, X(f) \tag{9.5}$$

This is obtained by taking Fourier transforms of both sides of (9.3). The frequency response function is of great interest, because it contains both amplitude magnification and phase-shift information. Since H(f) is complex-valued, the complex exponential (polar) notation may be used. That is,

$$H(f) = |H(f)| e^{j\phi(f)}$$

$$|H(f)| = \sqrt{\left(Re[H(f)]\right)^2 + \left((Im[H(f)]\right)^2}$$

$$\phi(f) = arctan\left(\frac{Im[H(f)]}{Re[H(f)]}\right) \tag{9.6}$$

where the absolute value H(f) is the gain and the argument $\phi(f)$ is the phase angle.

The convention shown for the choice of the sign of the phase angle is an attempt to be consistent with control theory and other established fields utilizing the idea of a frequency response function. With this definition a negative time shift (time delay) will have a phase which is a straight line with a positive slope. Suppose y(t) is a time-delayed version of x(t). That is,

$$y(t) = x(t - \tau)$$

Then the Fourier transform of y(t) is

$$Y(f) = \int_{-\infty}^{\infty} y(t) e^{-j2\pi ft} \, dt = \int_{-\infty}^{\infty} x(t - \tau) e^{-j\pi ft} \, dt$$

$$= e^{-j2\pi f\tau} \int_{-\infty}^{\infty} x(t) e^{-j2\pi ft} \, dt = e^{-j2\pi f\tau} X(f)$$

Thus, the frequency response function, gain, and phase are

$$H(f) = exp(-j2\pi f\tau) \quad |H(f)| = 1 \quad \phi(f) = -2\pi f\tau$$

so phase is a straight line with slope $-2\pi\tau$.

9.2   SPECTRAL RELATIONSHIPS FOR SINGLE-INPUT LINEAR SYSTEMS

Assume that a linear system with a clearly defined, single input and single output is subjected to a random input x, which is a representative member from a stationary random process with a zero mean value. Then, the output y will have the same properties as shown in Bendat and Piersol (1966). Two relations between the ordinary one-sided power and the cross spectral density functions $G_x(f)$, $G_y(f)$, and $G_{xy}(f)$, defined for f greater than or equal to zero, are

$$G_y(f) \;=\; |H(f)|^2 \, G_x(f) \qquad\qquad (9.7)$$

$$G_{xy}(f) \;=\; H(f) \, G_x(f) \qquad\qquad (9.8)$$

Therefore, with knowledge of the input power spectrum and the spectrum cross power, the frequency response function for a linear system is completely determined including both gain and phase.
The coherence function $\gamma^2_{xy}(f)$ is a real-valued quantity defined as

$$\gamma^2_{xy}(f) \;=\; \frac{|G_{xy}(f)|^2}{G_x(f)\,G_y(f)} \qquad\qquad (9.9)$$

Some authors define the positive square root $\gamma_{xy}(f)$ as coherence. The cross power spectral density function $G_{xy}(f)$ may be shown to satisfy the inequality (see Jenkins and Watts, 1968, p. 467)

$$|G_{xy}(f)|^2 \;\leq\; G_x(f) \, G_y(f) \qquad\qquad (9.10)$$

which implies that

$$0 \;\leq\; \gamma^2_{xy}(f) \;\leq\; 1 \qquad\qquad (9.11)$$

Now, consider the measurement of the PSD for ideal linear systems. For this case, $\gamma_{xy}^2 = 1$. Hence, the coherence function attains a theoretical maximum of unity at all frequencies for the case of linear systems. If the coherence function is less than unity, one possible cause may be the lack of complete linear dependence between the input and the output for the system in question; that is, the system is nonlinear.

Given discrete time histories x_i and y_i, $i = 0,1$, ...,$N - 1$, (9.8) and (9.9) are directly applied to compute transfer and coherence function estimates. These might be considered as "natural" estimating formulas, but they can easily be derived from least squares considerations also (see Jenkins and Watts, 1968, p. 432, for example).

From a computational standpoint, complex quantities are involved when dealing with cross spectra and frequency response functions. This is one major contrast with time domain computations. First, the techniques of Chapters 5, 7, and 8 are applied to obtain the necessary power spectra $\hat{G}_{xk}$, $\hat{G}_{yk}$ and the cross spectrum, $\hat{G}_{xyk}$. Then if complex arithmetical operations are available in the computer software, the transfer function is obtained directly from (9.8):

$$\hat{H}_{xyk} = \frac{\hat{G}_{xyk}}{\hat{G}_{xk}} \qquad\qquad k = 0,1,\ldots,m \quad (9.12)$$

The real and imaginary parts, the cospectrum and quadspectrum, can be used in the computations individually if complex arithmetical operations are not available:

$$Re[\hat{H}_{xyk}] = \hat{C}_{xyk}/\hat{G}_{xk} \qquad\qquad k = 0,1,\ldots,m \quad (9.13a)$$

$$Im[\hat{H}_{xyk}] = -\hat{Q}_{xyk}/\hat{G}_{xk} \qquad\qquad k = 0,1,\ldots,m \quad (9.13b)$$

The final transfer function output usually desired will be gain squared $|\hat{H}_{xyk}|^2$ and phase $\hat{\phi}_{xyk}$ (in degrees):

$$|\hat{H}_{xyk}|^2 = Re^2[\hat{H}_{xyk}] + Im^2[\hat{H}_{xyk}] \quad k = 0,1,\ldots,m \quad (9.14)$$

$$\hat{\phi}_{xyk} = -\frac{180}{\pi}\tan^{-1}\frac{\hat{Q}_{xyk}}{\hat{C}_{xyk}} \quad k = 0,1,\ldots,m \quad (9.15)$$

Many possible forms of plotted and printed outputs might be desired from the transfer function computations. For all of the forms given here, the discrete frequency variable is $f = k\Delta f$, $k = 0,1,\ldots,m$:

1. $Re[\hat{H}_{xyk}]$ versus $Im[\hat{H}_{xyk}]$

2. $Re[\hat{H}_{xyk}]$ versus f

   $Im[\hat{H}_{xyk}]$ versus f

3. $|\hat{H}_{xyk}|^2$ versus f

   $\hat{\phi}_{xyk}$ versus f

4. $\log \hat{H}_{xyk}$ versus $\log f$

The plotting of the phase angle presents annoying problems as it passes from just less than 180° to just greater than 180°, assuming that these values are used for plotting limits. If the lower limit of the plot is -180° and the upper limit is $+180^\circ$, then the value 179° would appear at the top of the plot, while if the next value was 181°, it would appear at the bottom, generating a messy discontinuity. The plotting range could be extended from -360 to $+360^\circ$, for example, and sophistication could be added to the plotting program to maintain continuity. That is, if $+180^\circ$ has just been plotted, and the next value is computed at -179°, then $+181^\circ$ would be plotted instead.

A second possibility is to change the sign of a computed value each time a crossover of 180° occurs. Then an indicator would have to be plotted also to designate points that have had their sense reversed. Consider Figure 9.1, which illustrates the plotting of a linear phase that has some statistical variability attached. A sign reversal is indicated by plotting a plus (+) or minus (-) sign at the top of a plot to designate the true sign of the value.

In addition to the gain and phase, the ordinary coherence function is also obtained directly:

$$\hat{\gamma}^2_{xyk} = \frac{\left|\hat{G}_{xyk}\right|^2}{\tilde{G}_{xk}\,\tilde{G}_{yk}} = \frac{\hat{C}^2_{xyk} + \hat{Q}^2_{xyk}}{\hat{G}_{xk}\,\hat{G}_{yk}} \qquad k = 0,1,\ldots,m \qquad (9.16)$$

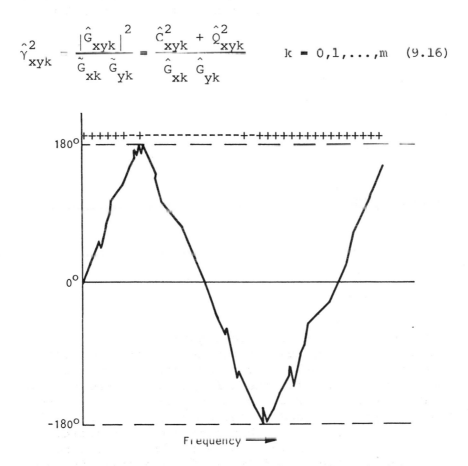

Fig. 9.1 Method of plotting phase without discontinuities.

The use of FFTs to obtain spectra suggests the application of (9.5) for transfer function estimation. The transforms of the original data are available at an intermediate state of the spectrum computations and thus H(f) can be obtained from the relation

$$\tilde{H}_k = \frac{\tilde{Y}_k}{\tilde{X}_k} \qquad k = 0,1,\ldots,m \quad (9.17)$$

where the wavy line indicates an unsmoothed estimate. It would seem that the coherence function could be obtained directly also:

$$\tilde{\gamma}^2_{xyk} = \frac{\left|\tilde{X}^*_k \tilde{Y}_k\right|^2}{\left|\tilde{X}_k\right|^2\left|\tilde{Y}_k\right|^2} \qquad k = 0,1,\ldots,m \quad (9.18)$$

Problems arise, however, since a result of unity is always obtained, as shown by

$$\tilde{\gamma}^2_{xyk} = \frac{[\tilde{X}_k {}^*\tilde{Y}_k][\tilde{X}_k {}^*\tilde{Y}_K]^*}{\tilde{X}_k {}^*\tilde{X}_k \tilde{Y}_k {}^*\tilde{Y}_k}$$

$$= \frac{\tilde{X}_k {}^*\tilde{Y}_k \tilde{X}_k \tilde{Y}_k {}^*}{\tilde{X}_k {}^*\tilde{X}_k \tilde{Y}_k {}^*\tilde{Y}_k} = 1 \qquad k = 0,1,\ldots,m \quad (9.19)$$

When the time histories are considered as samples of random processes, this reflects the fact that sample coherence is a highly biased estimator of true coherence for small d.f. The d.f. in $\tilde{\gamma}^2_{xyk}$, computed by (9.19), is n = 2. Thus, one must obtain smoothed spectra of higher d.f. and proper statistical variability before taking ratios to obtain coherence estimates.

This result regarding coherence functions tends to cast doubt on the use of (9.17) for transfer function

estimates when x_i and y_i are samples of a random process. Clearly, it is proper to use the formula when
x_i and y_i are deterministic data passed through a
truly linear system. There is considerable question
as to what is a "proper" estimation procedure for random data. At least three possibilities exist:

1. Compute $\tilde{Y}_k$ and $\tilde{X}_k$. Then compute $\tilde{H}_{xyk}$ from
   (9.17). Finally, smooth the real and imaginary
   parts of $\tilde{H}_{xyk}$ individually to obtain an estimate
   H_{xyk} of appropriate statistical reliability.

2. Compute $\tilde{Y}_k$ and $\tilde{X}_k$. Smooth $\tilde{Y}_k$ and $\tilde{X}_k$ to obtain
   $\hat{Y}_k$ and $\hat{X}_k$ of appropriate statistical reliability.
   Compute $\hat{H}_{xyk}$ from (9.17).

3. Compute $\tilde{Y}_k$ and $\tilde{X}_k$. Compute the smoothed $\tilde{G}_{xyk}$
   and G_{xk} of appropriate statistical reliability.
   Compute H_{xyk} from (9.12).

All of these procedures can give different results,
since the linear smoothing operation, the nonlinear
operations of absolute value squared, and division are
not commutative.

The first procedure can usually be eliminated from
consideration for random data. Not necessarily in all
instances, however, since (9.17) with no frequency
smoothing gives an estimate with maximum resolution
(minimum obtainable bandwidth for a finite record
length). Generally speaking, the maximum resolution
estimate will have the minimum bias due to smearing,
since no additional frequency smearing has taken place.
Thus, depending on the specific circumstances involved
in the transfer function, minimizing bias might be the
most important consideration. As a general rule of
thumb, however, when low coherence exists because of
extraneous noise in the output, then the first procedure should not be used. Nonlinearities in a system
cannot be distinguished from extraneous noise in the
output as far as the computation procedures are concerned. To prove the above statement, consider the
following:

$$\left|\tilde{H}_{xyk}\right|^2 = \frac{\left|\tilde{Y}_k\right|^2}{\left|\tilde{X}_k\right|^2} = \frac{\frac{1}{T}\left|\tilde{Y}_k\right|^2}{\frac{1}{T}\left|\tilde{Y}_k\right|^2} = \frac{\tilde{G}_{yk}}{\tilde{G}_{xk}} \qquad (9.20)$$

Thus, the absolute value squared obtained from the ratio of raw transforms is equivalent to that obtained from the ratio of raw (unsmoothed) power spectra. When extraneous noise in the output is of significant magnitude, the ratios of power spectra can be shown (Bendat and Piersol, 1966) to give highly biased results for gain factor estimates.

The first type of bias referred to, caused by smearing peaks in spectra, can also exist. It occurs when too wide a resolution bandwidth is employed. When an analysis bandwidth which is sufficiently narrow is used, additional resolution will not provide any additional help. However, it is conceivable that the smearing bias from using an excessively wide analysis bandwidth is of greater magnitude than the bias from low coherence when estimates are computed [(9.20) is used].

The recommended estimation procedure for input/output system data that occurs most typically is to use (9.12) or (9.17), in which some type of smoothing has been done on the raw Fourier transforms. Ratios of raw Fourier transforms should generally be avoided except when deterministic data are involved. Another exceptional case would be that of random data passed through a perfect linear system such as a linear numerical filter. The frequency response characteristics of a numerical filter can be conveniently evaluated by generating pseudo-random noise and operating on it with the numerical filter. Any of the frequency response estimation methods will give suitable results in this case.

9.3 SPECTRAL RELATIONSHIPS FOR MULTIPLE-INPUT LINEAR SYSTEMS

A model of a linear system responding to multiple inputs will now be considered. It will be assumed that p inputs exist, and a single output is measured. Three types of coherence functions, ordinary, multiple, and partial, play an important role in this analysis, and their evaluation is discussed.

Consider a linear system with time-invariant parameters and p inputs $x_\ell(t)$, $\ell = 1,2,\ldots,p$. That is

$$y(t) = \sum_{\ell=1}^{p} y_\ell(t) \qquad (9.21)$$

where $y_\ell(t)$ is defined as that part of the output produced by the ith input, $x_\ell(t)$, when all the other inputs are zero (see Figure 9.2). The function $h_{\ell y}$ in Figure 9.2 is defined as the weighting function associated with the linear system between the input $x_\ell(t)$ and the partial output $y_\ell(t)$. Hence, $y_\ell(t)$ is given as follows:

$$y_\ell(t) - \int_{-\infty}^{\infty} h_{\ell y}(\tau) x_\ell(t - \tau)\, d\tau \qquad (9.22)$$

The Fourier transform of (9.22) gives

$$Y_\ell(f) = H_{\ell y}(f)\, X_\ell(f) \qquad (9.23)$$

where $Y(f)$ and $X(f)$ are the Fourier transforms of $Y(t)$ and $x(t)$, respectively. Then the Fourier transform $Y(f)$ for the total output is

$$Y(f) = \sum_{\ell=1}^{p} Y_\ell(f) = \sum_{\ell=1}^{p} H_{\ell y}(f) X_\ell(f) \qquad (9.24)$$

The statistician reading this material should immediately note that (9.24) is a regression equation for zero mean variables. The dependent variable is Y, the independent variables are X_ℓ, and the regression coefficients are $H_{\ell y}$. Thus, electrical or mechanical engineering frequency domain transfer function concepts can be interpreted by the statistician via regression analysis of complex random variables. This concept is delved into in considerable detail by (Akaike, 1965). The gist of it is that we can treat each frequency band independently, and by accomplishing many complex variable regression analyses (one for each frequency band) we will obtain the entire frequency domain functions.

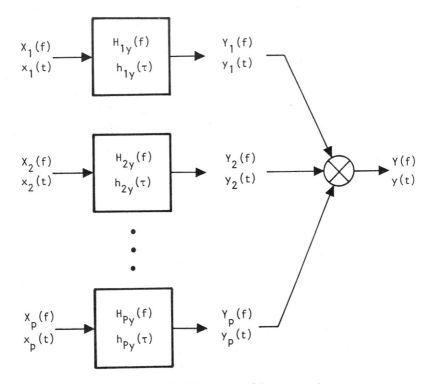

Fig. 9.2 Multiple-input linear system.

As in multiple regression analysis, the preceding relations can be expressed more concisely in matrix notation, and many results become more readily apparent. First, define a p-dimensional input column vector [the prime (') denotes transpose]

$$X(t) = [x_1(t), x_2(t), \ldots, x_p(t)]' \qquad (9.25)$$

Also define a p-dimensional transfer function vector

$$H(f) = [H_{1y}(f), H_{2y}(f), \ldots, H_{py}(f)]' \qquad (9.26)$$

Next, define a p-dimensional cross power spectrum vector of the output $y(t)$ with the inputs $x_\ell(t)$,

$$G_{xy}(f) = [G_{1y}(f), G_{2y}(f), \ldots, G_{py}(f)]' \qquad (9.27)$$

where

$$G_{\ell y}(f) = G_{x_\ell y}(f) \qquad \qquad \ell = 1, 2, \ldots, p \qquad (9.28)$$

Finally, define the $(p \times p)$ matrix of the power and cross spectra of all the inputs $x_\ell(t)$ by

$$G_{xx}(f) = \begin{bmatrix} G_{11}(f) & G_{12}(f) & \cdots & G_{1p}(f) \\ G_{21}(f) & G_{22}(f) & \cdots & G_{2p}(f) \\ \vdots & \vdots & & \vdots \\ G_{p1}(f) & G_{p2}(f) & \cdots & G_{pp}(f) \end{bmatrix} \qquad (9.29)$$

where for simplicity we adopt the notation

$$G_{ij}(f) = G_{x_i x_j}(f) \qquad \qquad i, j = 1, 2, \ldots, p \qquad (9.30)$$

The matrix $G_{xx}(f)$ is Hermitian, since it equals its conjugate transpose. This implies, for example, that the eigenvalues of $G_{xx}(f)$ are real numbers, should these parameters be of interest in an application.

The system of linear equations to obtain a least squares solution for the $H_{\ell y}(f)$ of (9.23) is the matrix equation

$$G_{xy}(f) = G_{xx}(f) H(f) \tag{9.31}$$

This is equivalent to

$$
\begin{bmatrix} G_{1y}(f) \\ G_{2y}(f) \\ \vdots \\ G_{py}(f) \end{bmatrix}
=
\begin{bmatrix} G_{11}(f) & G_{12}(f) & \cdots & G_{1p}(f) \\ G_{21}(f) & G_{22}(f) & \cdots & G_{2p}(f) \\ \vdots & \vdots & & \vdots \\ G_{p1}(f) & G_{p2}(f) & \cdots & G_{pp}(f) \end{bmatrix}
\begin{bmatrix} H_{1y}(f) \\ H_{2y}(f) \\ \vdots \\ H_{py}(f) \end{bmatrix}
\tag{9.32}
$$

The solution to this system of equations is

$$H(f) = G_{xx}^{-1}(f) \, G_{xy}(f) \tag{9.33}$$

For the practical situation, we estimate the spectra and cross spectra in (9.32) with the procedures described in Chapters 6, 7, and 8.

9.4   COMPUTATIONAL PROCEDURES

The computational procedures necessary for the solution of (9.33) subdivide into three groups:

1. Power and cross spectral density function computational routines

2. A procedure for simultaneously handling $(p + 1)$ variables to efficiently obtain the spectral density functions among all these variables

3. The complex variable arithmetical and matrix operations to compute the multidimensional linear system parameters

The spectral density functions necessary can be generated by either FFT or correlation PSD procedures. The main requirement is that all possible combinations of cross spectra are computed. Because of the Hermitian symmetry, only the diagonal and the upper right portion of the matrix need be calculated. That is,

$$G_{ij}(f) = G_{ji}^*(f) = G_{ij}(-f) \qquad (9.34)$$

The computational procedures described here are for computing parameters of a mathematical model, assuming a p-input $[x_i(t), i = 1,2,\ldots,p]$ and single-output $[y(t)]$ linear system. The system parameters to be computed are:

1. Transfer functions between each of the inputs and the output

2. Ordinary coherence functions between all pairs of variables

3. The multiple coherence function between the output and all the inputs

4. Partial (conditional) coherence functions between each input and the output while conditioning on the other inputs

In the ensuing discussion we shall not distinguish statistical estimates by the hat (⌢) notation. The notation is sufficiently complicated without introducing additional symbols. We hope no confusion will result, since in all cases the theoretical equations or those involving statistical estimates are identical anyway.

The first operation that must be performed is a sorting procedure. The spectral density functions are normally computed as a function of frequency. A program for multiple-input linear system analysis eventually must operate on the $(p + 1) \times (p + 1)$ spectral density matrices, one matrix for each frequency value.

The data operated on by the program is a set of spectral density matrices at frequencies indexed by k as follows:

$$G_{ykk} = \begin{bmatrix} G_{yyk} & G_{y1k} & G_{y2k} & \cdots & G_{yqk} \\ G_{1yk} & G_{11k} & G_{12k} & \cdots & G_{1qk} \\ \vdots & \vdots & \vdots & & \vdots \\ G_{qyk} & G_{q1k} & G_{q2k} & \cdots & G_{qqk} \end{bmatrix}$$

$$k = 0,1,\dots,m \qquad (9.35)$$

The frequency index k will usually represent special frequency values

$$f_k = \frac{kf_n}{m} \qquad\qquad k = 0,1,\dots,m \qquad (9.36)$$

where f_n is the Nyquist cut-off frequency. More generally, k can represent the frequency values

$$f_r = f_1 + k\Delta f \qquad\qquad k = 0,1,\dots,m$$

where

f_1 = Beginning frequency

Δf = Frequency increment

The m separate (p + 1) × (p + 1) spectral density matrices can be visualized in the three-dimensional form illustrated in Figure 9.3. The initial computation of any spectral density function provides a single-element (m + 1)-longitudinal column of the (p + 1) × (p + 1) × (m + 1) block in Figure 9.3. For the frequency response computations, a single slice of the block in the horizontal-vertical plane is needed. Logistical problems arise if magnetic tape is used for intermediate storage, since then the data must have been arranged in a serial fashion. Disk file storage is convenient for the necessary rearranging that has to take place.

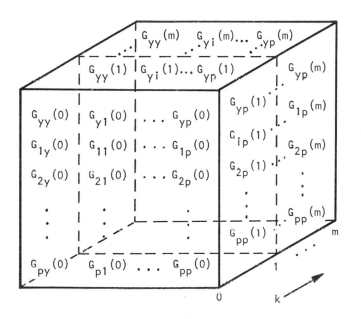

Fig. 9.3 Three-dimensional illustration of
spectral matrices.

The p input variables and the output variable are assumed to be zero mean, stationary, Gaussian processes whenever any statistical distribution results are discussed. The functions $H_{\ell y}(f)$, $\ell = 1, 2, \ldots, p$, are the frequency response function (transfer function) characteristics of the linear systems through which the variables are passing to make up $y(t)$.

The variables $x_\ell(t)$, $\ell = 1, 2, \ldots, p$, and $y(t)$ are assumed to be discrete (digitized) sequences of N points each. The notation for the N discrete points is

$$x_{1n} = x_1(n\Delta t)$$

$$x_{2n} = x_2(n\Delta t)$$

$$\vdots$$

$$x_{pn} = x_p(n\Delta t)$$

$$y_n = y(n\Delta t) \qquad\qquad n = 1,2,\ldots,N \quad (9.37)$$

where Δt is the sampling (digitizing) interval.

The matrix equation to be solved to determine the frequency response function is (9.32), where the function argument will be omitted for notational simplicity (e.g., G_{11} is written instead of G_{11k}). The matrix and vectors in (9.32) are complex-valued and hence require complex arithmetical operations for correct manipulation. In particular,

$$G_{i\ell} = C_{i\ell} - jQ_{i\ell} \qquad\qquad\qquad (9.38)$$

where C_k and Q_k are the appropriate cospectral and quadspectral density functions at index value k.

The solution to (9.32) is

$$
\begin{bmatrix} H_{1y} \\ H_{2y} \\ \vdots \\ H_{py} \end{bmatrix}
=
\begin{bmatrix}
G_{11} & G_{12} & \cdots & G_{1q} \\
G_{21} & G_{22} & \cdots & G_{2q} \\
\vdots & \vdots & & \vdots \\
G_{p1} & G_{12} & \cdots & G_{pp}
\end{bmatrix}^{-1}
\begin{bmatrix} G_{1y} \\ G_{2y} \\ \vdots \\ G_{py} \end{bmatrix}
\qquad (9.39)
$$

or, in more concise matrix notation,

$$H_{xy} = G_{xx}^{-1} G_{xy} \qquad\qquad\qquad (9.40)$$

An individual transfer function is given by

$$H_{iy} = \sum_{\ell=1}^{p} G^{i\ell} G_{\ell y} \qquad\qquad i = 1,2,\ldots,p \quad (9.41)$$

In terms of real and imaginary parts,

$$H_{iy} = \text{Re}(H_{iy}) + j\,\text{Im}(H_{iy})$$

$$= \sum_{\ell=1}^{p} [(C^{i\ell}C_{\ell y} - Q^{i\ell}Q_{\ell y}) - j(C^{i\ell}Q_{\ell y} + Q^{i\ell}C_{\ell y})]$$

$$(9.42)$$

where

$$G^{i\ell} = C^{i\ell} - jQ^{i\ell} \qquad\qquad (9.43)$$

are elements of $\|G_{i\ell}\|^{-1} = \|G^{i\ell}\|$, as required in (9.39). Equation (9.42) is the computational form implemented unless a complex arithmetic package is available, in which case (9.41) is used.

The ordinary coherence functions between the output y and each input x_i are computed by

$$\gamma_{iy}^2 = \frac{|G_{iy}|^2}{G_{ii}\,G_{yy}} = \frac{G_{iy}^2 + Q_{iy}^2}{G_{ii}\,G_{yy}} \qquad i = 1,2,\ldots,p \quad (9.44)$$

The multiple coherence function between the output y and all of the inputs $x_1, x_2, \ldots, x_p$ is computed by

$$\gamma_{y\cdot x}^2 = 1 - \left(G_{yy}\, G^{yy}\right)^{-1} \qquad\qquad (9.45)$$

where G^{yy} denotes the first diagonal element of the inverse matrix G_{yxx}^{-1} associated with G_{yxx} of (9.35).

The multiple coherence function can be obtained from the equivalent formula

$$\gamma^2_{y\cdot x} = \frac{G_{yy} - G'_{xy} G_{xx}^{-1} G_{xy}}{G_{yy}} \tag{9.46}$$

The numerator of the right side of (9.46) is the conditional (residual) output spectrum

$$G_{y|x} = G_{yy} - G'_{xy} G_{xx}^{-1} G_{xy} \tag{9.47}$$

This formula is obtained in terms of real and imaginary parts as follows: From (9.42), let the real and imaginary parts of H_{iy} be denoted by

$$A_{iy} = \text{Re}(H_{iy}) \tag{9.48a}$$

$$B_{iy} = \text{Im}(H_{iy}) \tag{9.48b}$$

Finally,

$$G_{y|x}$$

$$= G_{yy} - \sum_{i=1}^{P} [(C_{yi}A_{iy} - Q_{yi}B_{iy}) - j(C_{yi}B_{iy} + Q_{yi}A_{iy})] \tag{9.49}$$

Note that the result must be real. Thus, a convenient computational check formula is for the imaginary part of (9.49) to be zero.

The multiple coherence in terms of the conditional output spectrum is

$$\gamma^2_{y\cdot x} = 1 - \frac{G_{y|x}}{G_{yy}} \tag{9.50}$$

This formula graphically illustrates an important interpretation of the multiple coherence function. The
conditional or residual output power spectrum is the
power remaining after all power that can be accounted
for the linear filter relations is subtracted out.
Therefore, $G_{y|x}/G_{yy}$ is the fraction of power not ac-
counted for with linear relations, and one minus this
quantity is the fraction of power accounted for with
linear relations. The multiple coherence function is
the fraction of power in the output accounted for by
simultaneous linear filter relationships with all the
inputs.

This interpretation, moreover, further illustrates
transfer functions and coherence functions in terms of
regression and correlation analysis on complex variables. Power spectra may be interpreted as variances;
thus, the multiple coherence is the fraction of the
variance of the dependent variable accounted for by
the multiple regression equation.

Ordinary and multiple coherence functions for the
set of inputs x_i alone are defined by considering the
(p x p) spectral matrix of the inputs G_{xx}. The ordinary coherence function between any pair of inputs x_i
and x_ℓ is computed by

$$\gamma_{i\ell}^2 = \frac{|G_{i\ell}|^2}{G_{ii}\,G_{\ell\ell}} = \frac{c_{i\ell}^2 + Q_{i\ell}^2}{G_{ii}\,G_{\ell\ell}} \qquad (9.51)$$

The multiple coherence function between x_i and all
other inputs $x_1, x_2, \ldots, x_p$ excluding x_i, is computed by

$$\gamma_{i\cdot x}^2 = 1 - [G_{ii}\,G^{ii}]^{-1}$$

Where G^{ii} denotes the ith diagonal element of the inverse matrix $(G_{xx})^{-1}$ associated with G_{xx} of (9.29).
This quantity is convenient for understanding transfer
function confidence limits.

To obtain the partial coherence function between any input, say x_i, and the output conditioned on the remaining $(p - 1)$ inputs, one partitions G_{yxx} as indicated below:

$$
G_{yxx} =
\left[
\begin{array}{ccc|cccc}
G_{yy} & G_{y1} & & G_{y2} & \cdots & & G_{yp} \\
G_{1y} & G_{11} & & G_{12} & \cdots & & G_{1p} \\
\hline
G_{2y} & G_{21} & & G_{22} & \cdots & & G_{2p} \\
\vdots & \vdots & & \vdots & & & \vdots \\
G_{py} & G_{p1} & & G_{p2} & \cdots & & G_{pp}
\end{array}
\right]
=
\left[
\begin{array}{cc}
\Sigma_{yy} & \Sigma_{y1} \\
& \\
\Sigma_{1y} & \Sigma_{11}
\end{array}
\right]
\qquad (9.52)
$$

Then compute the conditional spectral matrix:

$$
G_{xy|p} = \Sigma_{yy} - \Sigma_{y1} \Sigma_{11}^{-1} \Sigma_{1y} \qquad (9.53)
$$

This procedure requires the inversion of the $(p - 1) \times (p - 1)$ complex-valued matrix Σ_{11}. An individual element $G_{ik|p}$ of the (2×2) matrix $G_{xy|p}$ can be written in terms of real and imaginary parts as

$$
G_{ik|p} = C_{ik|p} + jQ_{ik|p} \qquad i,k = 1,y \quad (9.54)
$$

The partial coherence function between the input x_1 and the output y, conditioned on the other $(p - 1)$ inputs, is now computed by

$$
\gamma_{1y|p}^2 = \frac{\left| G_{1y|p} \right|^2}{G_{11|p} \, G_{yy|p}} = \frac{C_{1y|p}^2 + Q_{1y|p}^2}{G_{11|p} \, G_{yy|p}} \qquad (9.55)
$$

Similar results apply for x_2 by interchanging x_2 with x_1, for x_3 by interchanging x_3 with x_2, etc.

In the special case of a single-input single-output linear system, all coherence functions are identical. This can be verified by examining (9.55) for partial coherence and (9.45) for multiple coherence. Upon substituting values when $p = 1$, these equations will both reduce to (9.44).

The equations in terms of real and imaginary parts are as follows: Let the elements of Σ_{11}^{-1} be

$$G^{hi} = U^{hi} - jV^{hi} \qquad (9.56)$$

The real and imaginary parts of an individual element $G_{\ell k}|_p$ of the (2×2) matrix $G_{xy}|_p$ are obtained in two additional steps. First define the intermediate quantity

$$C'_{ik} - jQ'_{ik}$$

$$= \sum_{h=2}^{P} [(U^{ih}C_{hk} - V^{ih}Q_{hk}) - j(U^{ih}Q_{hk} + V^{jh}C_{hk})]$$

$$j = 2,\ldots,p; \quad k = y,1 \qquad (9.57)$$

The final equation is

$$G_{\ell k}|_p$$

$$= G_{\ell k} - \sum_{i=2}^{P} [(C_{\ell i}C'_{ik} - Q_{\ell i}Q'_{ik}) - j(C_{\ell i}Q'_{ik} + Q_{\ell i}C'_{ik})]$$

$$\ell \equiv y,1; \quad k = y,1 \qquad (9.58)$$

These values are then inserted in (9.55) to obtain the partial coherence function.

9.5 COMPLEX MATRIX INVERSION AND NUMERICAL CONSIDERATIONS

Since complex-valued quantities are involved, the requirement for inversion of a complex matrix exists. Two approaches may be followed:

1. Complex arithmetic can be used to invert a matrix of complex elements directly.

2. A special procedure can be employed to reduce the complex inversion to more inversions of real matrices.

There are practical advantages to both procedures. Many library routines can be found to invert real matrices. These routines will normally make checks for the condition and rank of the matrix. Also, procedures might be included in the routine to optimize the inversion as far as numerical accuracy is concerned. There are enough definite advantages to capitalize on the effort expended in developing this kind of routine.

There are certain problems in utilizing methods involving real and imaginary parts separately. For example, consider the simple complex matrix

$$A = \begin{bmatrix} 1 & 0 \\ 0 & j \end{bmatrix} = \begin{bmatrix} 1 & 0 \\ 0 & 0 \end{bmatrix} + j \begin{bmatrix} 0 & 0 \\ 0 & 1 \end{bmatrix} = C + jD$$

The determinant of A is j; hence it has an inverse. However, the determinant of C is zero as is that of D. Thus, both C and D are singular and any inversion method based on inverting C or D could fail. However, A is nonsingular and could be inverted in terms of complex arithmetic directly. It is unlikely that a pathological matrix of the form A would ever arise in a practical physical problem. However, there is always the specter that it might.

On the other hand, efficient complex matrix conversion routines are more difficult to come by. Thus, in some instances, it is more efficient to perform the inversion in terms of real and imaginary parts separately and take the small chance that the inversion could fail. There does exist a particularly useful method for inversion termed the "escalator" method which can be implemented with a minimum of difficulty in terms of complex arithmetic. Two methods will be described, one in terms of real and imaginary parts, and the escalator method in terms of complex arithmetic.

Inversion by Real and Imaginary Parts

A method is presented in Lanczos (1956) for the inversion of a complex matrix. Write a given spectral matrix G in terms of its real and imaginary parts:

$$G = C - jQ \qquad\qquad (9.59)$$

Then the inverse of G is given by

$$G^{-1} = C_1 - jQ_1 \qquad\qquad (9.60)$$

where

$$C_1 = (C + QC^{-1}Q)^{-1} \qquad\qquad (9.61)$$

and

$$Q_1 = - C_1 QC^{-1} \qquad\qquad (9.62)$$

The computational steps are:

1. Compute the $(p \times p)$ inverse matrix C^{-1}.

2. Compute the matrix product QC^{-1} and save.

3. Compute the product $QC^{-1}Q$.

4. Compute the sum $C + QC^{-1}Q$.

5. Invert the $(p \times p)$ matrix from step 4 to obtain $C_1 = (C + QC^{-1} Q)^{-1}$.

Thus, two real matrix inversions, three matrix multiplications, and one matrix summation are required to convert the (p x p) complex spectral matrix.

A dual form of this method is easily obtained. Since

$$GG^{-1} = I \qquad (9.63)$$

we have two equations obtained from

$$(G - jQ_1) \ (C - jQ)$$

$$= (CC_1C + Q_1Q - j(Q_1C + C_1Q = I - jQ$$

or

$$C_1C - Q_1Q = I \qquad (9.64)$$

$$C_1Q + Q_1C = 0 \qquad (9.65)$$

If we solve (9.65) for Q_1 and substitute in (9.64), we obtain the form above which involves the inverse of the real part. On the other hand, we can just as well solve (9.65) for C_1 which gives

$$C_1 = - Q_1CQ^{-1} \qquad (9.66)$$

We then substitute C_1 in (9.64) and obtain

$$Q_1 = - [CQ^{-1}C - Q]^{-1} \qquad (9.67)$$

Thus, this method involves inverting the imaginary part Q of the original matrix, in contrast with the other form which involves inverting the real part. Hence, it would be possible to have a program which would attempt the second form of the method in case C was a singular matrix. Of course, it is still possible for Q to be singular in addition to C being singular and still have G^{-1} exist. Thus, this additional effort would still not guarantee being able to obtain G^{-1}.

Inversion by the Escalator Method

The escalator method is an iterative scheme whereby one proceeds from an inverse of order $(\ell - 1)$ to an inverse of order ℓ. The method has two advantages:

1. It is simple to take advantage of the complex conjugate symmetry of the spectral matrix.

2. The three orders of inverse matrix, $(p - 1)$, p, and $(p + 1)$, which are used in the computations are obtained in natural progression.

The method presented below is a special case of the one derived in (Ralston 1965). Partition a $(p \times p)$ spectral density matrix in the manner indicated:

$$G = \begin{bmatrix} G_{yy} & G_{xy} \\ G_{xy} & G_{xx} \end{bmatrix} \tag{9.68}$$

where G_{yy} is a scalar, G_{xx} is $(p - 1) \times (p - 1)$, and G_{xy} is $1 \times (p - 1)$. Let the inverse be denoted as

$$G^{-1} = \begin{bmatrix} S & T \\ T^* & U \end{bmatrix} \tag{9.69}$$

The two matrices may be multiplied and set equal to the identity matrix. The resulting equations may be solved to obtain the following formulas:

$$V = G_{xx}^{-1} G_{yx} \tag{9.70}$$

$$S = \frac{1}{G_{yy} - G_{xy} V} = \frac{1}{G_{yy} - G_{xy} G_{xx}^{-1} G_{yx}} \tag{9.71}$$

$$T* = - VS \qquad\qquad (9.72)$$

$$U = G_{xx}^{-1} - VV*S = G_{xx}^{-1} - VT \qquad (9.73)$$

Note that T need not be explicitly computed. Thus, all the elements of a (p x p) inverse matrix have been determined with knowledge of the (p - 1) x (p - 1) inverse matrix G_x^{-1} and additional matrix multiplication operations.

Equations (9.70)-(9.73) are applied recursively beginning with the (1 x 1) inverse $1/G_{xx}$. Note that at the pth stage, the inverse matrix necessary for the solution of (9.40) is available. The multiple coherence function of the output with all p inputs may be obtained from (9.70), applied at the (p + 1) stage. Namely, since

$$\frac{1}{G^{yy}} = S^{-1} = G_{yy} - G_{xy}G_{xx}^{-1} G_{yx} \qquad (9.74)$$

then

$$\gamma_{y\cdot x}^2 = 1 - \frac{S^{-1}}{G_{yy}} \qquad (9.75)$$

Also, at the (p + 1) stage, the frequency response vector is given by (9.70):

$$H_{xy} = V \qquad\qquad (9.76)$$

Thus, in computing the various quantities desired in the solution of the matrix frequency response problem, the (p + 1) x (p + 1) spectral density matrix is effectively inverted.

The partial coherence function between the output and each of the inputs may be obtained without explicitly employing the (p - 1) x (p - 1) inverse in (9.53). Once the (p x p) inverse is obtained, all of the sub-inverses are obtained. An alternate formula for an individual frequency response function (an individual element of the vector H_{xy}) is

$$H_{x_i y} = H_{iy} = \frac{G_{x_i y | p}}{G_{ii | p}} \tag{9.77}$$

The partial coherence can therefore be written as

$$\gamma^2_{iy | p} = |H_{iy}|^2 \frac{G_{ii | p}}{G_{yy | p}} \tag{9.78}$$

The two additional new quantities appearing in (9.78) are available when the (p × p) inverse G_{xx}^{-1} is obtained. First, from (9.74),

$$G_{yy | p} = 1/G^{yy} = S^{-1} \tag{9.79}$$

In general, conditional spectra are given by (9.53), and therefore $G_{ii | p}$ is the reciprocal of the ith diagonal element in the inverse matrix G_{xx}^{-1}:

$$G_{ii | p} = 1/G^{ii} \tag{9.80}$$

The partial coherence functions can then be obtained from the formula

$$\gamma^2_{iy | p} = \frac{|H_{iy}|^2}{SG^{ii}} \qquad i = 1, 2, \ldots, p \tag{9.81}$$

Thus, the escalator approach to the necessary matrix inverse unifies many of the formulas used for computing the various desired quantities.

9.6 CONFIDENCE LIMIT COMPUTATIONS FOR COHERENCE

In addition to the basic parameter estimates, the confidence limits for the different coherence functions and for the frequency response functions can be computed. Confidence limits can easily be determined for gain and phase or real and imaginary parts. Computing the coherence function limits requires a single type of formula for all three types of functions. Only the d.f. parameter need be adjusted. A Gaussian approximation was developed (Enochson and Goodman, 1965) for the distribution of sample coherence, which is valid roughly in the range $0.3 \leq \gamma^2 \leq 0.98$ and for the d.f. parameter $n \geq 20$. Benignus (1969) has improved on this result via a Monte Carlo experiment to extend the interval of validity essentially to $0 \leq \gamma^2 \leq 1.0$ and for d.f. down to about $n = 8$.

The formula for the true distribution of sample coherence is not at all conveniently evaluated. See Alexander and Vok (1963) for tables and the exact formula; the tables give the (cumulative) probability distribution function for ordinary and multiple coherence functions as a function of the number of complex d.f., n_c, and the number of variables, q. This computational difficulty is the reason for utilizing simplified approximations rather than the original formulas.

For a p-input, single-output system,

$$q = p + 1 \tag{9.82}$$

In terms of real d.f., $n = 2B_eT$, where B_e is the effective spectral resolution bandwidth and T is the effective record length:

$$n_c = \frac{n}{2} = B_eT \tag{9.83}$$

For the special case of the single-input, single-output system, $q = 2$, and the tables apply to ordinary coherence functions.

The transformation that leads to an accurate normal (Gaussian) approximation for the distribution of sample coherence functions is shown in Enochson and Goodman (1965) to be given by

$$z = \tanh^{-1}\hat{\gamma} = \frac{1}{2} \ln \left[\frac{1 + \hat{\gamma}}{1 - \hat{\gamma}} \right] \qquad (9.84)$$

where $\hat{\gamma}$ is the positive square root of the sample coherence estimate $\hat{\gamma}^2$. This transformation is valid when $n > 20$ and when the true coherence is in the range $0.3 \leq \gamma^2 \leq 0.98$. The mean value and variance associated with z are approximated by

$$\mu_z = \tanh^{-1}\gamma + \left(\frac{p}{n - 2p} \right) \qquad (9.85)$$

$$\sigma_z^2 = \frac{1}{n - 2p} \qquad (9.86)$$

where $n = 2n_c = 2B_eT$.

The improvements developed by Benignus (1969) are both bias and variability. The estimate $\hat{\gamma}^2$ of coherence can be improved by a bias correction

$$B(\gamma^2) = \frac{1}{2n} (1 - \hat{\gamma}^2) \qquad (9.87)$$

Then a corrected coherence estimate is utilized in (9.84);

$$\tilde{\gamma}^2 = \hat{\gamma}^2 - B(\hat{\gamma}^2) \qquad (9.88)$$

The correction for the variance to be utilized instead of (9.86) is based on a curve fit to improve the estimate of σ_z^2 when $\gamma^2 < 0.3$. The curve developed is

$$E(\sigma_z) = 1 - 0.004^{(1.6\,\hat{\gamma}^2 + 0.22)} \qquad (9.89)$$

Then instead of σ_z from (9.86) we use

$$\sigma_z = \left(\sqrt{\frac{1}{n - 2p}} \right) [E(\sigma_z)] \qquad (9.90)$$

From the previous equations, for measured values of γ^2 and n, one can determine $(1 - \alpha)$ confidence limits for the true value γ^2 by the following relation:

$$\tanh(z - b - \sigma_z Z_{\alpha/2}) \leq \gamma \leq \tanh(z - b + \sigma_z Z_{\alpha/2})$$

(9.91)

where Z_α is the 100α percentage point of the normal distribution, and

$$b = \frac{p}{n - 2p}$$

(9.92)

The above confidence limit formula applies either to ordinary coherence functions where $p = 1$ or to the multiple coherence functions where $p > 1$.

A simple adjustment can be made to obtain partial coherence function confidence limits. In general, one must reduce the number of d.f. in the analysis by the number of conditional variables whose effects have been subtracted out. For example, in the case where the effects of $(p - 1)$ inputs are subtracted out, one used n' real d.f. given by

$$n' = n - (p - 1)$$

(9.93)

where $n = 2B_eT$.

9.7   CONFIDENCE LIMIT COMPUTATIONS FOR TRANSFER FUNCTIONS

The confidence bands for the frequency response functions $H_{iy}(f)$, $i = 1,2,\ldots,p$, representing the model of Figure 9.2, depend upon the sample coherence function between the output and the inputs, the sample multiple coherence function between the inputs, the sample input PSD functions, and the sample frequency response functions. The basis for these results is discussed in Bendat and Piersol (1966) and Goodman (1965).

Assume negligible bias error due to smearing (discussed in Section 5.2) in the various spectral estimates involved. Let the true gain factor be $|H_{iy}|$ and the true phase factor be ϕ_{iy} so that

$$H_{iy} = |H_{iy}| \, e^{-j\phi_{iy}} \qquad (9.94)$$

Then the $(1 - \alpha)$ confidence intervals for H_{iy} and ϕ_{iy} are given simultaneously at every i and at any specified frequency f (or digitally by the frequency index k)

$$\left. \begin{cases} \hat{H}_{iy} - \hat{r}_i \leq H_{iy} \leq \hat{H}_{iy} + r_i \\[2ex] \hat{\phi}_{iy} - \hat{\Delta\phi}_i \leq \phi_{iy} \leq \hat{\phi}_{iy} + \hat{\Delta\phi}_i \end{cases} \right\} \quad i = 1,2,\ldots,p \qquad (9.95)$$

Where $\hat{H}_{iy}$ and $\hat{\phi}_{iy}$ are sample estimates. The square of the radial error, $\hat{r}_i^2 = \hat{r}_i^2(f)$, and the phase error, $\hat{\Delta\phi}_i \equiv \hat{\Delta\phi}_i(f)$, are computed for each i by

$$\hat{r}_i^2 = \frac{2q}{n - 2q} \, (F_{n_1,n_2;\alpha}) \, \frac{\left(1 - \hat{\gamma}_{y \cdot x}^2\right) \hat{G}_y}{\left(1 - \hat{\gamma}_{i \cdot x}^2\right) \hat{G}_i} \qquad (9.96)$$

$$\hat{\Delta\phi}_i = \sin^{-1}\left(\frac{\hat{r}_i}{|\hat{H}_{iy}|}\right) \qquad (9.97)$$

The various quantities in (9.96) and (9.97) are

p = Number of inputs (excluding output)

$n = 2B_eT$ = Number of d.f. in each spectral estimate

$F_{n_1,n_2;\alpha}$ = 100α percentage point of an F distribution with $n_1 = 2p$ and $n_2 = 2n - 2p$ d.f.

$\hat{\gamma}^2_{y \cdot x}$ = Sample estimate of the multiple coherence function between the output y and all the measured inputs, as defined by (9.50)

$\hat{\gamma}^2_{i \cdot x}$ = Sample estimate of the multiple coherence function between the input x_i and the other measured imputs excluding x_i, as defined by (9.55)

$\hat{G}_y$ = Power spectrum estimate for the output y

$\hat{G}_i$ = Power spectrum estimate for the input x_i

A polar diagram for the confidence region represented by (9.95) is shown in Figure 9.4 at the frequency f_0. Different confidence regions apply to each specified frequency f_0 and to each of the possible $i = 1, 2, \ldots, p$.

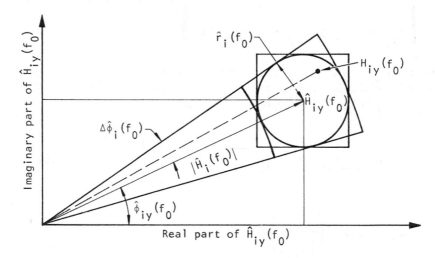

Fig. 9.4 Confidence diagram for multiple frequency response functions.

Equation (9.96) gives the radial error for the most general case of multiple coherent inputs. For special situations when the p inputs are coherent or there is only a single input $p = 1$, the square of the radial error takes the special form

$$\hat{r}_i^2 = \frac{2}{n-2} \; (F_{n_1,n_2;}\;\alpha) \; (1 - \hat{\gamma}_{yi}^2) \; \frac{\hat{G}_y}{\hat{G}_i} \tag{9.98}$$

where n, $\hat{G}_y$, and $\hat{G}_i$ are the same as before, while

$F_{n_1,n_2;\alpha}$ = 100α percentage point of an F distribution with $n_1 = 2$ and $n_2 = n - 2$ d.f.

$\hat{\gamma}_{yi}^2$ = Sample estimate of the ordinary coherence function between y abd x_i, as defined by (9.16)

The phase error $\Delta\hat{\phi}_i$ is calculated as before by (9.97); however, the $\hat{r}_i$ obtained from (9.98) instead of (9.96) is used.

9.8 CALCULATION OF F DISTRIBUTION VALUES

The necessary F distribution values may be determined to a moderate degree of accuracy with an approximation from Abramovitz and Stegun (1964, Section 26.6.1b, p. 947). If $p = (1 - \alpha)$ is the confidence band desired, then

$$F_{n_1,n_2;\alpha} = e^{2w} \tag{9.99}$$

where

$$w = \frac{p(h+\lambda)^{1/2}}{h} - \left(\frac{1}{2b-1} - \frac{1}{2\alpha-1}\right)\left(\lambda + \frac{5}{6} - \frac{2}{3h}\right) \tag{9.100}$$

$$n_1 = 2b \tag{9.101}$$

$$n_2 = 2\alpha$$

$$\lambda = \frac{p^2 - 3}{6} \tag{9.102}$$

$$h = 2 \; \frac{1}{2\alpha - 1} + \frac{1}{2b - 1} \tag{9.103}$$

The quantity z_p is the pth percentile of the normal distribution function and can be evaluated by the series approximation in Appendix B. This approximation is inaccurate for small values of n_i. An empirically determined correction is

$$F_{n_1,n_2;\alpha} = F_{n_1,n_2;\alpha} - \epsilon(n_1) \qquad (9.104)$$

where

$$\epsilon(n_1)$$

$$= 15.76003 - 16.260806n_1 + 6.675521n_1^2 - 1.3535354n_1^3$$

$$+ 0.1354177n_1^4 - 0.0053333n_1^5 \qquad (9.105)$$

9.9 FLOW CHARTS FOR TRANSFER AND COHERENCE FUNCTION COMPUTATION

A set of flow charts for the matrix frequency response function computations is given as Figure 9.5a-d. There are four stages:

1. Compute power and cross spectral density functions.

2. Rearrange into spectral density matrices.

3. Perform computations.

4. Rearrange into frequency functions for plotting.

9.10 FUNCTIONS RELATED TO EIGENVALUES AND EIGENVECTORS

More complicated multivariate statistical analysis techniques can be adapted to frequency domain spectral analysis. The authors have been closely associated with some limited excursions into these areas which are documented by Choi (1967) and Shumway (1966).

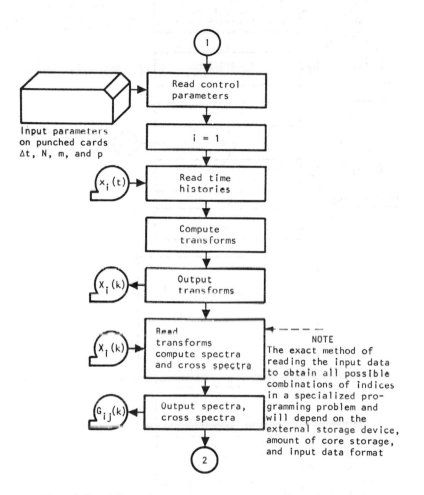

Fig. 9.5a Flow chart of computations for the matrix
frequency response function.

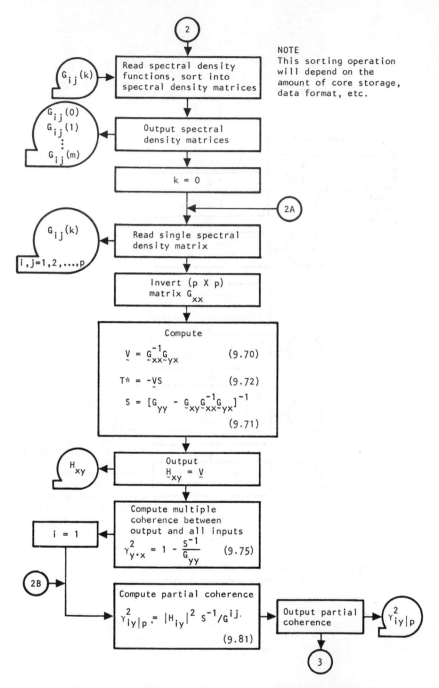

Fig. 9.5b   Continuation of flow chart of computations for
the matrix frequency response function.

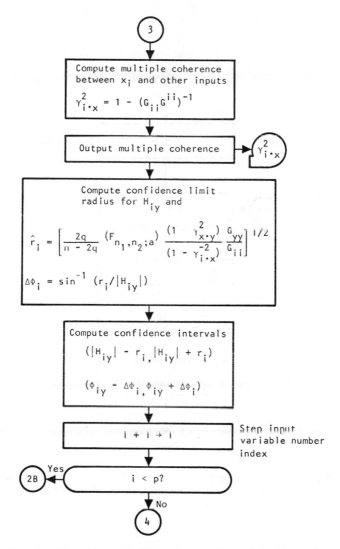

Fig. 9.5c Continuation of flow chart of computations for
the matrix frequency response function.

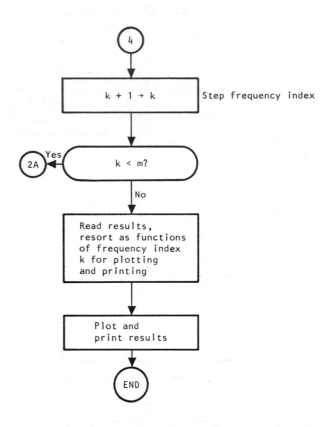

Fig. 9.5d Continuation of flow chart of computations for
the matrix frequency response function.

Advanced multivariate statistical analysis techniques such as principal component analysis, linear discriminant functions, canonical correlations, and factor analysis (see Anderson, 1958; or Kullback, 1959) all have a common mathematical thread involved in determining the eigenvalues and/or eigenvectors of the covariance matrix. As previously mentioned, the spectral density function matrix may be viewed as a covariance matrix of complex random variables; one matrix for each frequency band in the spectral analysis. The complex covariance matrix is Hermitian and leads to the study of unitary matrices which have many properties analogous to real symmetric matrices. In particular, the eigenvalues are real numbers, and in general the eigenvalue-eigenvector properties have similar interpretations. Almost all techniques discussed in Anderson (1958) or Kullback (1959) can be translated in terms of complex variables for application to the spectral density matrix. Matrix transposition must be replaced with conjugate transposition with care, but almost all operations may be interpreted directly in terms of the complex number field. We shall indicate some of the computational approaches, but practical experience with the methods is limited.

Principal Components

Generally speaking, eigenvalues and eigenvectors represent the results of certain minimum mean square transformations applied to data. For example, principal component analysis generally refers to a problem of determining a few linear combinations of the original observed data that account for most of the variance (power) in the data. The first principal component is that normalized linear combination of the original variables which accounts for a maximum fraction of the variance. The second principal component is that linear combination that is uncorrelated with (orthogonal to) the first component and accounts for the largest fraction of the remaining variance (power). This process may be continued. The underlying objective

would be to effectively reduce the number of variables
in the analysis by accounting for most of the variance
(power) in the data via a few linear combinations of
the original variables. Note that the first principal component will be a variable (input to a multiple
linear system) that has maximum multiple coherence
with the output. The second component will be the input that is incoherent with the first and has the next
largest multiple coherence with the output, etc. If
G_{xx} is a (p x p) spectral density matrix, then the solution (Choi, 1967) to the principal component problem
results in the equation

$$(G_{xx} - \lambda I)\beta = 0 \qquad\qquad (9.106)$$

This is the classic eigenvalue problem. Let the eigen-
values, in decreasing sequence, be $\lambda_1 \geq \lambda_2 \geq \ldots \geq \lambda_p$.
Further let $\beta_1, \beta_2, \ldots, \beta_p$ be the corresponding (column)
eigenvectors. The principal components are

$$C_i = \beta_i X \qquad\qquad i = 1,2,\ldots,p \quad (9.107)$$

where X is the Fourier transform vector of the original p-dimensional data. The variance of C_i may be
shown to be

$$\text{Var}[C_i] = \lambda_i \qquad\qquad i = 1,2,\ldots,p \quad (9.108)$$

Thus, the eigenvalues denote the fraction of power
being accounted for by the principal components. A
fraction of variance can be established which is sufficiently large, and then sufficient components,
$C_1, \ldots, C_s$, s < p, to account for this fraction of variance can be determined. The dimensionality of the
problem is therefore effectively reduced. Choi (1967)
suggests adapting a statistical test based on real covariance matrix analysis for testing this hypothesis.
From a computational standpoint, the determination of
the eigenvalues and eigenvectors of a complex Hermitian
matrix is the basic problem. A method for this is

given under the heading "Computational Method for Eigenvalues and Eigenvectors of a Complex Hermitian Matrix," which appears below.

Factor Analysis

Let C be the (1 x s) vector of principal components and β the matrix of eigenvectors. Then

$$C = \beta X \tag{9.109}$$

which can be solved for X as

$$X = \beta^{-1} C \tag{9.110}$$

It can be shown that the inverse matrix is the conjugate transpose of B multiplied by the eigenvalues as normalizing factors. That is, if

$$X_i = \beta^{i1} c_1 + \beta^{i2} c_2 + \ldots + \beta^{is} c_s$$

$$i = 1,2,\ldots,p \tag{9.111}$$

then

$$(\beta^{i1},\ldots,\beta^{is}) = (\beta_{i1}\sqrt{\lambda_1},\ldots,\beta_{is}\sqrt{\lambda_s}) \tag{9.112}$$

The coefficients λ^{is}, $i = i,\ldots,s$, are usually called the "factor" loadings, and an observed variable X_i is made up of the s factors $c_1,\ldots,c_s$ with weights $(\beta^{i1},\ldots,\beta^{is})$. This idea forms the basis of "factor analysis."

Computational Sequence for Principal Components

The essential aspect of the principal components determination is computing the eigenvalues and eigenvectors of the complex, Hermitian, spectral density matrix. A method for doing this is described below. The overall sequence is as follows:

1. Compute the p Fourier transforms X_{ik}, $i = 1,2,$
$\ldots,p$; $k = 1,2,\ldots,m$, of the p-dimensional set
of time histories.

2. Compute the ($p \times p$) spectral density matrix G_{xx}
$k = 1,2,\ldots,m$.

3. Compute the eigenvalues λ_{ik} and eigenvectors
β_{ik}, $i = 1,2,\ldots,p$, at each frequency value
$k = 1,2,\ldots,m$.

4. The principal components then are

$$c_i = \beta_i' x \qquad\qquad i = 1,2,\ldots,p$$

5. Compute the transpose of the matrix of the column eigenvectors for each frequency k:

$$\beta' = \begin{bmatrix} \beta_{1k}' \\ \beta_{2k}' \\ \vdots \\ \beta_{pk}' \end{bmatrix} \qquad\qquad k = 1,2,\ldots,m$$

6. Complete the inverse of β to obtain the factor
loadings by multiplying β' by the diagonal matrix of eigenvalues:

$$\beta^{-1} = \beta'\Lambda$$

where

$$\Lambda = \begin{bmatrix} \lambda_1 & 0 & \cdots & 0 \\ 0 & \lambda_2 & \cdots & 0 \\ \vdots & \vdots & \ddots & \vdots \\ 0 & 0 & \cdots & \lambda_p \end{bmatrix}$$

The row vectors of β^{-1} are then the coefficients
of the "factor loadings."

Computational Method for Eigenvalues and Eigenvectors of a Complex Hermitian Matrix

Here we describe a modified Jacobi method for determining the eigenvalues and eigenvectors of a Hermitian matrix based on a private communication from David A. Pope.

Given a square Hermitian matrix U with complex elements $\Sigma_{ik} = a_{ik} + jb_{ik}$, $i,k = 1,\ldots,n$, the Hermitian property means that $\mu_{ik} = \mu_{ki}$ (complex conjugate). The eigenvalues of U are all real, as are the diagonal elements. To find the eigenvalues, we diagonalize U using a sequence of transformations on U described below.

The first step is to select an off-diagonal element μ_{ik} of the matrix. There are several possible methods of selection, possibly the most efficient being a *threshold* method. In this method, the off-diagonal elements are looked at in sequential order, and only the ones larger in absolute value than a certain threshold value are selected. The threshold value is then periodically reduced, and the process continued until all off-diagonal elements are smaller in absolute value than some given criterion, depending on the accuracy wanted.

Each transformation of the sequence involves changing all the elements in the columns and rows in which the off-diagonal element μ_{ik} and its conjugate μ_{ki} lie. Because of the conjugate symmetry, only half of the off-diagonal elements need be looked at, and so we assume without loss of generality that $i < k$.

Let the off-diagonal element be

$$\mu_{ik} = a_{ik} + ib_{ik}$$

We define two angles Θ, ϕ, by

$$\Theta - \frac{1}{2}\arctan(b_{ik}/a_{ik})$$

$$\Theta = \frac{1}{2} \arctan\left[\frac{2(a_{ik}^2 + b_{ik}^2)^{1/2}}{a_{ii} - a_{kk}}\right]$$

Then the transformed elements, which we denote by primes on the elements, are given by

$$a'_{ii} = a_{ii} \cos^2 \Theta + (a_{ik}^2 + b_{ik}^2)^{1/2} \sin 2\Theta + a_{kk} \cos^2 \Theta$$

$$a_{kk} = a_{ii} \sin^2 \Theta + (a_{ik}^2 + b_{ik}^2)^{1/2} \sin 2\Theta + a_{kk} \cos^2 \Theta$$

$$a'_{ik} = a'_{ki} = 0$$

$$b'_{ik} = b'_{ki} = 0$$

For $\ell \neq i$ or k,

$$a'_{\ell i} = a_{\ell i} \cos \Theta \cos \phi - b_{\ell i} \cos \Theta \sin \phi$$

$$+ a_{\ell k} \sin \Theta \cos \phi + b_{\ell k} \sin \Theta \sin \phi$$

$$b'_{\ell i} = b_{\ell i} \cos \Theta \cos \phi + a_{\ell i} \cos \Theta \sin \phi$$

$$+ b_{\ell k} \sin \Theta \cos \phi - a_{\ell k} \sin \Theta \sin \phi$$

$$a'_{\ell k} = a_{\ell i} \sin \Theta \cos \phi - b_{\ell i} \sin \Theta \cos \phi$$

$$+ a_{\ell k} \cos \Theta \cos \phi + b_{\ell k} \cos \Theta \sin \phi$$

$$b'_{\ell k} = b_{\ell i} \sin \Theta \cos \phi + a_{\ell i} \sin \Theta \sin \phi$$

$$+ b_{\ell k} \cos \Theta \cos \phi - a_{\ell k} \cos \Theta \sin \phi$$

$$a'_{i\ell} = a'_{\ell i}$$

$$b'_{i\ell} = -b'_{\ell i}$$

$$a'_{k\ell} = a'_{\ell k}$$

$$b'_{k\ell} = -b'_{\ell k}$$

All other elements of the matrix are unchanged. Now a new off-diagonal element is selected, and the process is repeated. After all off-diagonal elements have been reduced to zero (to the accuracy needed), the diagonal elements of the transformed matrix are the eigenvalues of the original matrix U.

Because of the conjugate symmetry of the matrix U (which is retained through all these transformations), it is unnecessary to store the entire matrix. Instead, a convenient way of storing the matrix in the computer is as follows: Let $S(J,K)$ be a two-dimensional array in the computer storage. Then the real diagonal elements a_{jj} can be stored in $S(J,J)$. The real parts of the off-diagonal elements a_{jk}, for $j < k$, can be stored in $S(J,K)$. The imaginary parts b_{jk} can be stored in $S(K,J)$. The rest of the matrix is then implicitly defined in terms of these; that is, $a_{\ell m}$ for $\ell > m$ is found in $S(M,L)$, and $b_{\ell m}$ is the negative of the quantity in $S(L,M)$.

Problems

9.1   Derive (9.5) from (9.3) by computing the Fourier transform of (9.3). Assume that all appropriate mathematical conditions for the existence of the transforms, etc., are satisfied.

Almost all linear systems formulas can be derived by doing complex variable analogies on the Fourier-transformed variables (at each frequency value f) with classical statistics. Define variance as $E[X*X]$, and covariance as $E[X*Y]$. Let the PSD be analogous to variance and the cross spectrum to covariance. Use these facts in Problems 9.2-9.4.

9.2   Derive (9.7) as the analogy of the statistical equation

$$\sigma_y^2 = \beta^2 \sigma_x^2 \qquad\qquad y = \beta + \varepsilon$$

where ε is a zero mean independent noise.

9.3   Derive (9.8) as the analogy of the statistical equation

$$\sigma_{xy} = \beta_{xy}\, \sigma_x^2$$

where $\sigma_{xy} = \text{cov}[x,y]$.

9.4   What is the classical statistical analogy of ordinary coherence, (9.9)?

9.5   Fill in missing steps for the escalator matrix inversion method in going from (9.69) to (9.70), (9.71), (9.72), and (9.73).

9.6   Derive (9.78) for partial coherence.

9.7   Derive the special equations for a two input single output system.

CHAPTER 10

PROBABILITY DENSITY FUNCTION COMPUTATIONS

10.1 REVIEW OF BASIC STATISTICAL TERMINOLOGY— SAMPLE DENSITY FUNCTION

Definitions of the mean and variance were given in Sections 1.2 and 1.3. This section will discuss these terms more carefully, but not in the detail that will be found in a work on statistics. The precise defin- itions of the above parameters are more involved than those given earlier, and the definition of a random process would require an elaborate mathematical scaf- folding because of the variables which may be ex- amined. Fortunately, in the applications considered here, the pathological functions considered by mathe- maticians do not occur. Hence, several simplifying assumptions can be made without impairing the validity of the results. These are:

1. That the functions being considered are bounded and, before digitization, were continuous.

2. That the random process underlying the function is ergodic and stationary.

The technical definition of a random variable basical- ly requires that the variable be measurable. Assump- tion 1 guarantees this, as bounded, continuous func- tions form a subset of functions that are measurable. The remainder of this section will be spent in an in- tuitive discussion of assumption 2.

Suppose that a large number of identical noise gen- erators has been turned on at some remote time in the past and left to run. Associated with the output of all the generators is a function $f(x,t)$, the probabil- ity density function, with the following characteris- tics: For a certain time, say t_o, the probability that

371

the output of the ith signal generator $x_i(t_o)$ lies between values a and b is given by the integral

$$P[a \le x_i(t_o) < b] = \int_a^b f(x,t_o) \, dx \qquad (10.1)$$

Note that the integration is performed with respect to the range of the random variable. The expected value of any function involving x, denoted by $E[g(x)]$ where $g(x)$ is the expression whose expectation is sought, is defined to be

$$E\{g[x(t_o)]\} = \int_{-\infty}^{\infty} g[x(t_o)] \, f(x,t_o) \, dx \qquad (10.2)$$

In particular, the mean and variance are given by

$$\mu(t_o) \quad = \int_{-\infty}^{\infty} x(t_o) \, f(x,t_o) \, dx \qquad (10.3)$$

$$\sigma^2(t_o) \quad = \int_{-\infty}^{\infty} [x(t_o) - \mu(t_o)]^2 \, f(x,t_o) \, dx \qquad (10.4)$$

If the random process is stationary, the parameters $\mu(t_o)$ and $\sigma^2(t_o)$ are independent of time. That is,

$$\mu(t_o) = \mu(t_1) \equiv \mu \qquad (10.5)$$

$$\sigma^2(t_o) = \sigma^2(t_1) \equiv \sigma^2 \qquad (10.6)$$

where t_o and t_1 are arbitrary. As stationarity is assumed, the mean and variance hereafter will be written without the qualifying t_o.

The assumption of ergodicity permits ensemble averages to be replaced with time averages. In the noise

generator example,   the generators were exactly alike,
so that even if an individual generator were producing
a different, unique random function, the output of any
one of them   would be sufficient to define the statistics for all.   Thus,   the expression   for the mean in
(10.3) may be replaced with (1.2):

$$\mu = \lim_{T \to \infty} \frac{1}{2T} \int_{-T}^{T} x(t)\, dt \qquad\qquad (10.7)$$

which is the   time average based on a single record of
the process.   A similar expression for the variance is
(1.6):

$$\sigma^2 = \lim_{T \to \infty} \frac{1}{2T} \int_{-T}^{T} [x(t) - \mu]^2\, dt \qquad\qquad (10.8)$$

Because only a sample of the random variable is taken,
rather than   a record length which   is defined for infinite time,   the sample   mean and sample variance are
denoted by   symbols different from those   used for the
theoretical parameters. In particular, the sample mean
for digital data is calculated from (1.5):

$$\bar{x} = \frac{1}{N} \sum_{i=0}^{N-1} x_i \qquad\qquad (10.9)$$

The unbiased* sample   variance s^2 is   obtained from
(1.8):

---

*If the   division of   the expression   for s^2 were $1/N$
rather than $1/(N - 1)$, then the expected values of s^2
would be $[(N - 1)/N]\, \sigma^2$, so that the result would be
biased.   For large   N   the error,   however,   would be
small.

$$s^2 = \frac{1}{N-1} \sum_{i=0}^{N-1} (x_i - m)^2 \qquad (10.10)$$

Criteria exist for determining the confidence intervals for the sample mean and sample variance. Detailed formulas and tables are to be found in Bendat and Piersol (1966). For the record lengths encountered in time series data analysis, the statistical variation of these two parameters is usually low and hence not a problem.

10.2 PROBABILITY HISTOGRAM

Sample probability density functions or histograms also may be obtained from the data. The sample density functions are not unique for a given data group as are m and s^2, but depend upon the values of certain parameters used to determine them. The histogram is computed in the following manner: An interval of the range of x, say a < x < b, is subdivided into k subintervals of equal length so that the entire range of x is broken up into (k + 2) intervals. All of the data are examined, and the number of occurrences in each interval is tabulated. The histogram consists of a plot showing the number of occurrences for each of the intervals.

More formally, let $\{N_j\}$ be the set of integers obtained by counting the occurrences of $\{x_i\}$ in the jth interval. Let c = (b - a)/k, and d_j = a + jc. Then $\{N_j\}$ is defined by the table on the following page.

Figure 10.1 illustrates these terms. The $\{N_j\}$ terms are frequently called pockets. One method of doing this sorting on a digital computer is to examine each x_i, i = 1,...,N, in turn, making the following checks:

j	N_j
0	[Number of x such that x < a]
⋮	⋮
j	[Number of x such that $d_{j-1} \leq x < d_j$]
⋮	⋮
k	[Number of x such that $d_{k-1} \leq x < b$]
(k + 1)	[Number of x such that x ≥ b]

1. If $x_i < a$, add one to N_0.
2. If $x_i \geq b$, add one to N_{k+1}.
3. If neither of the two preceding requirements are met, then $a \leq x_i \leq b$; therefore, compute

$$L = \frac{x_i - a}{c} \qquad c = \frac{b - a}{k} \qquad (10.11)$$

Pick the largest integer ℓ such that $\ell \leq L$, then add one to N_ℓ. This technique turns out to be easy to implement on most digital computers.

Three forms of sequences based on the above are used. The first is the histogram, which is simply the sequence $\{N_j\}$ without change. The second sequence is $\{P_j\}$, where

$$P_j = \text{Sample probability that } [d_{j-1} \leq x < d_j]$$

$$= N_j/N \qquad\qquad j = 0,1,\ldots,k+1 \quad (10.12)$$

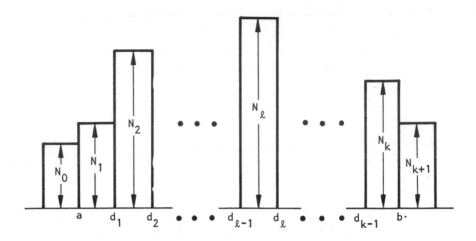

Fig. 10.1 Histogram construction.

The third is the sample probability density function (PDF) which takes the form of the sequence $\{p_j\}$, $j = 0$ ...,k+1, where

$$p_j = \frac{N_j k}{N(b - a)} \qquad (10.13)$$

This can be interpreted as the derivative of the distribution function at the midpoint of each interval.

Before the above procedure can be effected, values for a, b, and k must be chosen. The question naturally arises, what is a reasonable criterion for the choice of these three parameters? There is no good single answer to this problem. Much of the choice must rest on assumptions about the underlying distribution being examined and the manner in which the data were collected. Data obtained using a system like the hypothetical data-acquisition system of Chapter 2 have two limitations imposed on them; namely, that the data are restricted in range, and within that range there are only a finite number of possible levels. If the digitizer has only 128 levels, then it is clearly senseless

to choose a k > 128,   as   some   of   the levels must be
empty.   Also,   it is easy to visualize a situation in
which the   apportionment of ADC counts   (or their converted equivalents)   to the subintervals of the sample
PDF would cause a biasing of answers.

   Example 10.1. Suppose a digitizer with 16 levels is
used and that   the output is analyzed without any conversion   to engineering   units.   Suppose   further that
each of the levels $0, \ldots, 15$ is equally likely, so that
the a priori probability of the ith count occurring is
1/16.   If k is taken to   be 12 and a and b   are 0 and
15,   respectively,   then the following distribution of
counts would take place.

Pocket	Range	Levels contained	
1	0 - 1.25	0,1	
2	1.25 - 2.50	2	
3	2.50 - 3.75	3	
4	3.75 - 5.00	4	
5	5.00 - 6.25	5,6	
6	6.25 - 7.50	7	(10.14)
7	7.50 - 8.75	8	
8	8.75 - 10.00	9	
9	10.00 - 11.25	10,11	
10	11.25 - 12.50	12	
11	12.50 - 13.75	13	
12	13.75 - 15.00	14	

The expected contents   of pockets 1,   5, and 9 will be
twice as large as those of the other pockets,   so that
the sample PDF obtained would tend to be highly biased
at those values,   and thus, imply an incorrect result.

The above example shows that reasonable care should be exercised when setting up the calculations for the PDF and that the criteria employed should be scrutinized in order to avoid the pitfalls of biasing. One criterion for establishing the parameters arises from an attempt to determine the answer to a different but related problem; namely, that of deciding whether or not the data are Gaussian or normal in distribution.

10.3 THE CHI-SQUARE GOODNESS-OF-FIT TEST
FOR NORMALITY

The PDF for the normal distribution, denoted by ϕ, is given by (1.12):

$$\phi(x) = \frac{1}{\sqrt{2\pi\sigma^2}} \exp[-(x-\mu)^2/2\sigma^2] \qquad (10.15)$$

The PDF is the integral of the density function:

$$\text{Prob}[x \leq X] = \frac{1}{\sqrt{2\pi\sigma^2}} \int_{-\infty}^{X} \exp[-(t-\mu)^2/2\sigma^2] \; dt$$

$$= \frac{1}{\sqrt{2\pi}} \int_{-\infty}^{\frac{X-\mu}{\sigma}} \exp(-t^2/2) \; dt$$

$$= \phi\left(\frac{X-\mu}{\sigma}\right) \qquad (10.16)$$

Methods for computing this function are discussed in Appendix B.   The probability that the variable lies between α and β is given by

$$P[\alpha \leq x < \beta] = \phi\left(\frac{\beta-\mu}{\sigma}\right) - \phi\left(\frac{\alpha-\mu}{\sigma}\right) \qquad (10.17)$$

The normal distribution is assumed as a hypothesis in many analyses; and it arises naturally out of many

theoretical calculations.   It may therefore be desirable to   see if indeed the collected data appear to be
Gaussian.   One procedure   for   making a check of   the
hypothesis is known as the   chi-square goodness-of-fit
test.   The general procedure   involves the use of the
chi-square   statistic as a   measure of the discrepancy
between an   observed PDF and the   theoretical density
function.   A hypothesis of equivalence is then tested
by studying the   sampling distribution of   chi-square.
The number   of occurrences   that would be   expected to
fall within   the ith class interval,   if the   data are
Gaussian,is called the expected frequency in the class
interval and   will be denoted by F_j.   The discrepancy
between the observed frequency   and expected frequency
is $(N_j - F_j)$.   To measure the total discrepancy, each
interval must be used, since

$$\sum_{j=0}^{k+1} N_j = \sum_{j=0}^{k+1} F_j = N \qquad (10.18)$$

The sum of the   discrepancies must be zero.   Note that
F_j,   in general,   will not be an integer.   The F_j are
computed as follows:

$$F_o = N \, \Phi \left(\frac{a - m}{s} \right)$$

$$\vdots$$

$$F_j = N \left\{ \Phi \left(\frac{a + jc - m}{s} \right) - \Phi \left[\frac{a + c(j-1) - m}{s} \right] \right\}$$

$$F_{k+1} = N \left[1 - \Phi \left(\frac{b - m}{s} \right) \right] \qquad (10.19)$$

The sample chi-square is obtained as follows:

$$x^2 = \sum_{j=0}^{k+1} \frac{\left(N_j - F_j \right)^2}{F_j} \qquad (10.20)$$

Under suitable assumptions, this sample chi-square may
be compared with the theoretical chi-square distribution denoted by $\chi^2_{n;\alpha}$.

The distribution for χ^2, which was introduced in
Chapter 1, is discussed in many references, such as
Bendat and Piersol (1966). It depends upon the number
of independent squared variables in χ^2 (the number of
d.f., n). The value of n is equal to (k + 2) if all
pockets including the end ones are used, minus the number of different independent linear restrictions imposed on the observations. There is one such restriction, because once the frequencies of the first (k+1)
class intervals are known, the frequency in the last
class interval is known as their sum is N. There are
two additional restrictions caused by fitting the
theoretical normal density function to the frequency
histograms for the observed data. These arise from the
fact that the sample mean and sample variance, rather
than the true mean and variance, are used to calculate
the $\{F_j\}$. The effect of this is to subtract another
two d.f. from the data. Thus, if all $\{N_j\}$ are used,
then

$$n = (k + 2) - 3 = k - 1 \qquad\qquad (10.21)$$

The value for n actually used may be smaller than
this, as pockets for which N < 2 should be combined
with other pockets. The details of this are described
below.

Having established the proper d.f., n, for χ^2, a
hypothesis test may be performed as follows: Let it
be hypothesized that the variable x is normally distributed. After grouping the sampled observations into
the (k + 2) class intervals and computing F_j for each
interval based on the sample mean and variance, compute χ^2 as indicated in (10.20). Any deviation of the
sample PDF from the normal distribution will cause χ^2
to increase. The hypothesis that data are normally
distributed is accepted if

$$x^2 \leq \chi^2_{n;\alpha} \qquad (10.22)$$

In this case, that acceptance is at the α level of significance. If x^2 is greater than $\chi^2_{n;\alpha}$, the hypothesis is rejected at the α level of significance. Significance levels of 5, 10, and 20% (corresponding to confidence levels of 95, 90, and 80%) are commonly employed. The particular level selected is largely a matter of personal choice. The authors tend to favor α equal to 5% given no additional information.

Based on the assumption that a chi-square goodness-of-fit test for normality is to be made, an expression for the number of class intervals for a given N has been derived (Kendall and Stuart, 1961). This expression assumes that the data are uncorrelated and that $\alpha = 0.05$:

$$\text{Number of class intervals} = 1.87(N - 1)^{2/5} \qquad (10.23)$$

This function is tabulated in Table 10.1. As stated earlier, as soon as the number of class intervals becomes comparable with the number of digitizer count levels, large biases may result.

A standard rule of thumb used by statisticians when applying the chi-square test is that every interval should have at least two occupancies. This requirement enables one to determine reasonable values for a and b. The end pockets have the smallest expected occupancy. Thus, the parameter a should satisfy the following equation:

$$2 = N \left\{ \frac{1}{\sqrt{2\pi}} \int_{-\infty}^{\frac{a-m}{s}} e^{-t^2/2} \, dt \right\} \qquad (10.24)$$

This can be solved implicitly for a. After having found a value for a, the parameter b is simply

$$b = 2m - a \qquad (10.25)$$

Table 10.1 Minimum Optimum Number (k) of
Class Intervals for Sample
Size N when $\alpha = 0.05$

N	k	N	k
200	16	20,000	94
400	20	40,000	129
600	24	70,000	162
800	27	100,000	187
1,000	30	200,000	247
1,500	35	400,000	326
2,000	39	700,000	407
4,000	57	1,000,000	470
7,000	65	1,140,000	500
10,000	74		

The parameter k is given by

$$k = [\text{Number of class intervals}] - 2 \qquad (10.26)$$

After having established these three parameters, it is then possible to calculate the sample PDF and the expected normal occupancy. Before computing X^2, however, certain problems must be taken care of.   It may turn out that there are less than two occupancies in some pockets.   In such a case, the contents of both the N_j and F_j pockets must be combined with adjacent ones. While easy to do visually, it is a little harder to implement on the computer. One scheme, which has been found to be satisfactory in most cases, is the following: Find the integer p such that $F_p > F_j$ for all j. Then define the sequences $\{Q_j\}$ and $\{R_j\}$ by the following procedure where all Q_j and R_j are zero to begin with:

If $F_j \geq 2$, then $\begin{cases} N_j + Q_j \rightarrow Q_j \\ \\ F_j + R_j \rightarrow R_j \end{cases}$

If $F_j < 2$, then $\begin{cases} 0 \rightarrow Q_j, R_j \\ N_j + Q_{j+1} \rightarrow Q_{j+1} \\ F_j + R_{j+1} \rightarrow R_{j+1} \qquad j < p \end{cases}$

$\qquad$ or $\qquad \begin{cases} 0 \rightarrow Q_j, R_j \\ N_j + Q_{j-1} \rightarrow Q_{j-1} \\ F_j + R_{j-1} \rightarrow R_{j-1} \qquad j > p \quad (10.27) \end{cases}$

The sequences generated by this procedure are similar to $\{N_j\}$ and $\{F_j\}$ except that the tails have been shifted toward the center. Next, define the sequence $\{H_j\}$ by

$$H_j = \begin{cases} 1 & \text{if } Q_j \neq 0 \\ \\ 0 & \text{if } Q_j = 0 \end{cases} \qquad (10.28)$$

The quantities x^2 and n, the number of d.f., are thus given by

$$x^2 = \sum_{j=0}^{k+1} \frac{\left(Q_j - R_j\right)^2}{R_j} H_j$$

$$n = \left(\sum_{j=0}^{k+1} H_j\right) - 3 \qquad (10.29)$$

The next step is to make the comparison to see if the data are to be accepted or rejected insofar as normality is concerned. As mentioned earlier, the usual procedure for comparing x^2 with $\chi^2_{n;\alpha}$ is that of computing

α', where α' is defined by

$$\alpha' = \text{Prob}[x^2 > \chi^2_{n;\alpha'}] \tag{10.30}$$

The α' parameter is a function of x^2 and n only. Having computed it, compare it with the preselected value α and conduct the test for normality on the following basis:

$\alpha' \le \alpha$ Reject

$\tag{10.31}$

$\alpha' > \alpha$ Accept

One method for computing α' is the following:

$$\alpha' = 2\Phi(X) - 1 - \sqrt{\frac{2}{\pi}} e^{-x^2/2}$$

$$\times \left[\sum_{r=1}^{(n-1)/2} \frac{x^{2r-1}}{1\cdot3\cdot5 \ \ldots \ (2r-1)} \right]$$

for n odd   (10.32a)

or

$$\alpha' = 1 - e^{-x^2/2} \left[1 + \sum_{r=1}^{(n-2)/2} \frac{x^{2r}}{2\cdot4\cdot6 \ \ldots \ (2r)} \right]$$

for n even   (10.32b)

The computer program flow charts, Figure 10.2a-c, show one standard scheme for setting up a program. As a convenience they include the steps required to process some additional parameters not mentioned in the above discussion, such as the minimum and maximum values of x. The arithmetical expressions on the charts, e.g., $x_i^2 + x^2 \rightarrow x^2$, refer to both data values and storage

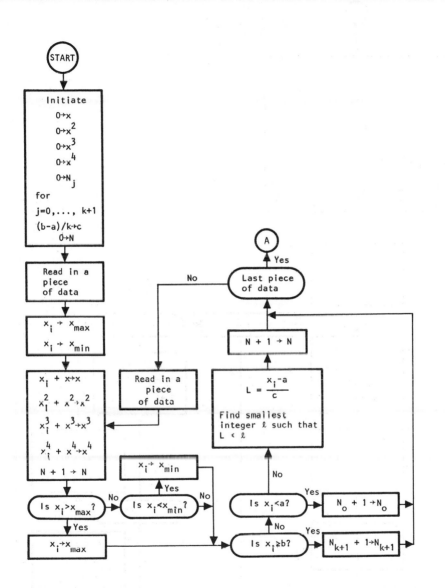

Fig. 10.2a Processing, initial phase.

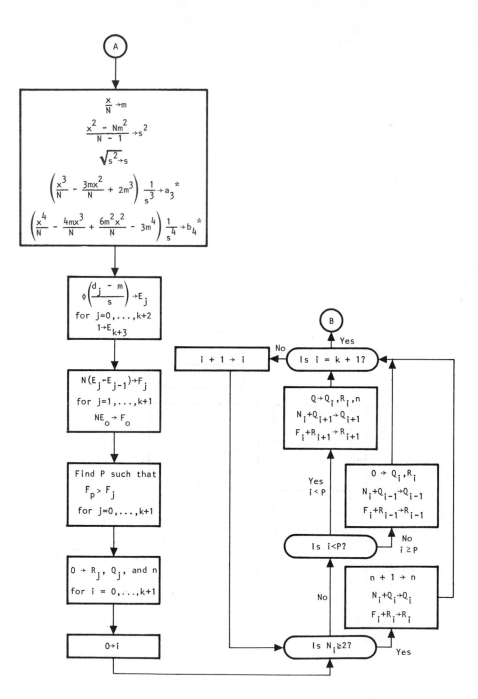

Fig. 10.2b Processing 1.

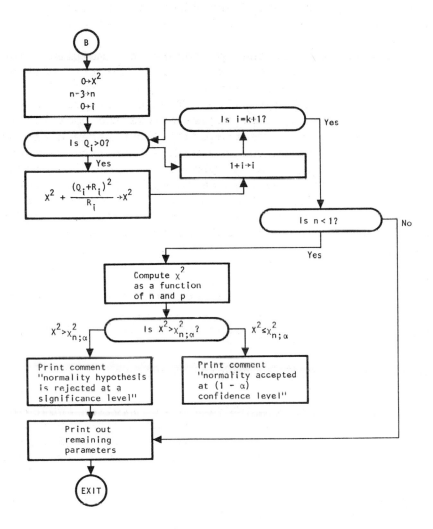

Fig. 10.2c   Processing 2.

locations. The above example would read, "The current
value of x_i is squared and added to the contents of
the running total of x^2,and the results stored in that
location."

The extension of the procedure to   multifunction
parallel processing is fairly obvious,so it is omitted
from the charts to clarify them. The overall flow of
data is shown in Figure 10.3. The form of program arrangement shown in this figure allows the user to recover some of the time frequently lost because of the
slowness of input devices.   Double buffering routines
can be employed, with the processing operating independently of the routines performing the input operations, thus allowing the input routine coding to be a
sort of universal building block, usable with other
applications or even separate parts of the same basic
data processing program.

As a final comment on the flow charts, let us note
that the boxes with printout or data input functions
will probably require the largest part of the programming effort, as these items can mushroom into large
tasks if speed of processing and clarity of output are
requirements.

10.4 PEAK PROBABILITY DENSITY FUNCTIONS

There is a serious nomenclature problem regarding
the definition of peaks, maxima, and minima. There are
at least three distinct problems that are of interest
when discussing the occurrence of extreme values in a
given record.   The three are:

1. Distribution of the largest (or smallest) value
   in a record of length T

2. Distribution of the largest value occurring
   between two zero crossings

3. Distribution of the peak values

As an example of the first type, suppose that N
values of the function $\{x_i\}$ are recorded and that they

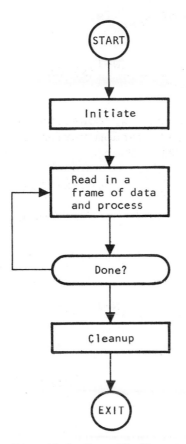

Fig. 10.3 Overall flow chart.

are independent with density function f(x) and distribution function F(x).   Then,   the density function of
the largest value of x is

$$f(x_{max},N) = Nf(x) \left[F(x)\right]^{N-1} \tag{10.33}$$

The distribution function of x_{max} is

$$F(x_{max},N) = \left[F(x)\right]^{N} \tag{10.34}$$

The expected value of x_{max} is

$$E[x_{max}] = \int_{-\infty}^{\infty} xN \, f(x) \, F^{N-1}(x) \, dx \qquad (10.35)$$

Example 10.2. Suppose x_i consists of N independent, uniformly distributed random variables with the range of x being $[-1/2, 1/2]$. Then

$$f(x_i) = \begin{cases} 1 & -1/2 \le x_i \le 1/2 \\ 0 & \text{elsewhere} \end{cases}$$

$$F(x_i) = \begin{cases} 0 & x < -1/2 \\ x + 1/2 & -1/2 \le x \le 1/2 \\ 1 & x > 1/2 \end{cases}$$

$$f(x_{max}, N) = \begin{cases} N(x + 1/2)^{N-1} & -1/2 \le x_{max} \le 1/2 \\ 0 & \text{elsewhere} \end{cases}$$

$$F(x_{max}, N) = \begin{cases} 0 & x_{max} < -1/2 \\ (x + 1/2)^N & -1/2 \le x_{max} \le 1/2 \\ 1 & x_{max} > 1/2 \end{cases}$$

$$E[x_{max}] = \int_{-1/2}^{1/2} xN(x + 1/2)^{N-1} \, dx$$

$$= \frac{N-1}{2(N+1)} \qquad (10.36)$$

For N = 1, $E[x_{max}] = 0$, as would be expected. For large N, $E[x_{max}] \to 0.5$. If N = 100, then $E[x_{max}] = 0.490099$.

While $E[x_{max}]$ as given in (10.35) may be difficult to evaluate in theory, the finding of x_{max} in a sample set of data is quite easy. Indeed, even if there is no specific interest in x_{max} or x_{min}, it is a good idea to have them found by the computer program anyway, as they frequently turn out to be useful when checking a set of data for wild points.

The second type of peak analysis encountered is the largest value between two zero crossings. These are simple to find. The following algorithm is typical of one that might be employed. As usual, it is assumed that $\{x_i\}$ has N points:

1. Compute a table of $\{I_k\}, k = 1, \ldots, K$, where I_k is in the table if

$$x_{I_k} \leq 0 \quad \text{and} \quad 0 < x_{(I_k+1)}$$

   or

$$0 < x_{I_k} \quad \text{and} \quad x_{(I_k+1)} \leq 0$$

2. If $0 < x_{I_k}$, find the minima of $x_i, i=(I_k + 1),$ $\ldots, I_{k+1}$; otherwise, find the maxima value.

3. Continuing, if $x_{I_k} < 0$, find the maxima of $x_i,$ $i=(I_k + 1), \ldots, I_{k+1}$; otherwise, find the minima of this same set.

With the minima and maxima thus found two things could be done. First, use techniques from Section 10.3 and find the separate sample PDFs for both the sets of minima and maxima. Second, set the minima positive and combine them with the maxima. Statistical properties of zero crossings are well-known for many types of data, so that the maximum (or minimum) between zero crossings is relatively amenable to analysis. A somewhat more difficult problem is presented in the third case being considered in this section—that of peak values.

In this sense, a peak value is the largest value between any two relative minima. For example, as shown in Figure 10.4, there is only one type 2 peak, but there are four type 3 peaks. The procedure for locating these values is as follows:

1. For the maxima, find all x_p such that

$$x_p - x_{p-1} > 0$$

$$x_p - x_{p+1} > 0$$

2. Similarly, for the minima, find those values x_q for which

$$x_q - x_{q-1} < 0$$

$$x_q - x_{q+1} < 0$$

As before, these sets of maxima and minima would be processed using the type of techniques outlined in Sections 10.1 and 10.3.

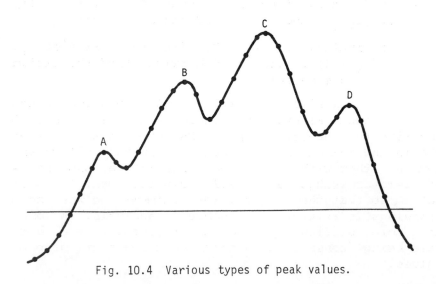

Fig. 10.4 Various types of peak values.

10.5 MULTIDIMENSIONAL DENSITY FUNCTIONS

If $\{x_i\}$ and $\{y_i\}$ are any two data functions, it is possible to compute their joint sample PDF or joint histogram. This is accomplished by dividing the range of each into k_1 and k_2 intervals, as shown in Figure 10.5. In general, more computer storage will be required for the two-dimensional than for the one-dimensional case. For example, $(k_1 + 2)$ cells would be required for $\{x_i\}$ by itself and $(k_2 + 2)$ cells for $\{y_i\}$. Thus, $(k_1 + 2)(k_2 + 2)$ cells might be a reasonable number for their joint distribution. This might very well be excessive, especially if there are more than two functions to be processed. If there are r separate functions, then there are $(r)(r - 1)/2$ ways of comparing them. Suppose that $k_1 = k_2 = \ldots = k_r = k$, then a total of

$$\frac{(r)(r - 1)}{2} (k + 2)^2$$

storage cells would be necessary. If $r = 50$ and $k = 100$, this is $12{,}744{,}900$, whereas the one-dimensional sample PDFs with the same parameter requirements would need only 5100 cells of computer memory. (See Figure 10.5.)

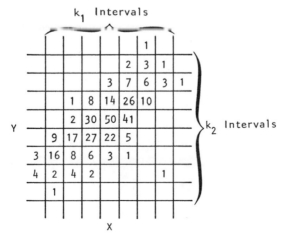

Fig. 10.5 Sample joint probability density histogram.

A meaningful display of the results may be difficult to achieve. Computer listings of the sample joint PDFs tend to be difficult to read because of the overwhelming number of digits presented to the eye. Graphic representation is also difficult. Contour plots have been used with partial success, but their generation is not trivial. New developments in three-dimensional display devices should increase the usefulness of joint PDFs. Presently, however, the lack of completely satisfactory methods to display the results severely complicates the generation of sample PDFs and impedes their interpretation.

CHAPTER 11
MISCELLANEOUS TECHNIQUES

11.1 INTRODUCTION

Several useful techniques in digital time series analysis do not fit under the general headings of correlation functions, spectral density functions, transfer functions, and probability density functions. In particular, these methods are based on the theory of stationary random processes. In this chapter we shall discuss certain elementary methods of nonstationary data analysis, plus a "zoom" PSD analysis. For other methods of transient data analysis (the shock spectrum) the reader is referred to Kelly and Richman (1970).

11.2 NONSTATIONARY DATA ANALYSIS

Before discussing nonstationarity, it is necessary to review the concept of stationarity itself. There is a hierarchy of definitions which refer to that term, as shown in Figure 11.1.

Up to this point, it has been assumed that the data samples being examined were stationary and ergodic (no modifiers), implying that the function has expectations (mean, variance, correlation, etc.) which are invariant with translations in time. Ergodicity permits time averages to be used in place of ensemble averages. When only one or a few time histories are available, it is difficult to talk about stationarity in general, which is an ensemble property. Hence, definitions in terms of time averages on a single record must be interpreted with some care. If all higher-order moments and joint moments within a record are invariant with translation, the record is strongly stationary. This is a difficult proposition to prove

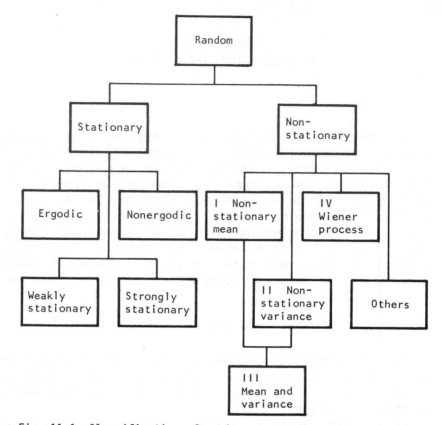

Fig. 11.1 Classification of various types of random processes.

statistically from samples of data. On the other hand, weak stationarity requires that

$$m_x(t_0) = \frac{1}{T} \int_{t_0}^{t_0+T} x(t) \; dt$$

and

$$R_x(t_0, t_0 + \tau) = \frac{1}{T} \int_{t_0}^{t_0+T} x(t) \; x(t + \tau) \; dt \qquad (11.1)$$

be invariant with translations of t_0. Clearly, T must
be sufficiently large so   that there are   no problems
with having too little data for the sample mean   and
correlation to be meaningful.   Weak stationarity is
usually assumed. Tests of the hypothesis that the record is weakly stationary are discussed in the   next
section.

What does it mean when the record is nonstationary?
There are a number of conditions for stationarity that
could be violated, and there are a variety of causes
for the violation.   Of the many possibilities,   three
have been given attention in the literature because of
their frequent occurrence in actual situations.

The first   such nonstationary process was analyzed
extensively by Wiener (1930) and generally goes by his
name.   The Wiener process can be visualized as the result of putting an ordinary stationary process into an
integrator which is turned on at time zero.   If x is
the input and y the output, then

$$y(t) = \int_0^t x(\tau) \, d\tau \tag{11.2}$$

If x has the mean μ_x, then the mean value of y varies
with time:

$$\mu_y(t) = \begin{cases} t\mu_x & t \geq 0 \\ 0 & t < 0 \end{cases} \tag{11.3}$$

Similarly, it can be shown that if $R_x(\tau)$ is the correlation of x, then the variance of y is

$$\sigma_y^2(t) = \begin{cases} \int_0^t \int_0^t R_x(t_1 - t_2) \, dt_1 \, dt_2 & t \geq 0 \\ 0 & t < 0 \end{cases} \tag{11.4}$$

For example, if

$$R_x(\tau) = \sigma_x^2 \, \delta(\tau) \tag{11.5}$$

then

$$\sigma_y^2(t) = t\sigma_x^2 \tag{11.6}$$

This is only one form of the Wiener process, which more usually is thought of as involving Brownian motion. It is referred to here because such processes do occur in some data-gathering circumstances. One instance is the integration of accelerometer data to obtain velocity. If the acceleration term has been contaminated by noise, the integration noise will give rise to terms which take the form of rambling trends.

The second nonstationary process is one in which it is assumed that $R_x(\tau)$ is stationary but $\mu_x(t)$ is not. This is most easily illustrated by again supposing that an accelerometer is used as a transducer and that its output is integrated to obtain velocity. Suppose further that the integration is digital. If the conversion is off by a constant amount, then when the constant is integrated, the trend becomes linear.

The third nonstationary process to be considered is represented by the form

$$x(t) = a(t) \, z(t) \tag{11.7}$$

By assumption, x is a zero mean process. The z function is assumed to be stationary and such that

$$E[z(t)] = 0$$

$$E[z^2(t)] = 1$$

$$E[z(t) \, z(t + \tau)] = R_z(\tau) \tag{11.8}$$

The a(t) function, however, also varies with time. The
only assumptions made about it are that it changes
fairly slowly and that

 a(t) ≥ 0   for all t   (11.9)

This definition leads to a separable correlation function of the locally stationary form (Piersol 1967).
This type of process has been discussed in Bendat and
Piersol (1966) and others.   It turns out to be a good
model for several important physical systems. One of
interest is vibration in a launch vehicle. Experience
has shown that a(t) will reach peaks at times corresponding to lift-off, maximum Q flight, and transonic
flight, while at other times the level is considerably
lower.* Another example would involve analysis of certain types of economic indices where inflation acts as
a scale factor on fluctuating fiscal parameters.

Nonstationarity Trend Test

    A useful test for trends in either mean or variance
can be adapted from Kendall and Stuart (1961). First,
one obtains a sequence of roughly uncorrelated mean
values or mean square values from a time series. This
can be done by subdividing the entire record of data
into N time slices.   From each time slice, a short-
time-averaged mean value and variance can be obtained.
One simple method of doing this is with the RC filtering procedure described in the section "Time-Varying
Mean and Variance" below.   Instead of utilizing every
output point of the filter, use only those points separated sufficiently in time so as to be considered

------

*
It should be noted that a more general type of nonstationarity occurs in that there is a tendency for
the peaks in the PSD of this type of data to move
higher in frequency as time increases, mainly because
of the depletion of fuel.

roughly uncorrelated.   For example,   the half-life of
the filter would be a reasonable choice.   This is the
time required for the response of the filter to a unit
input   (1,0,0,...) to decline to one-half of peak output from the filter.   In terms of number of digitized
time intervals, k, it is given by

$$k = - \frac{\ln 2}{\ln \alpha}$$

But $\alpha = \exp[-\Delta t / RC]$, so

$$- \frac{1}{\ln \alpha} = \frac{RC}{\Delta t}$$

and since $\ln 2 \approx 0.7$, we have

$$k = \ln 2 \, \frac{RC}{\Delta t} = 0.7 \, \frac{RC}{\Delta t}$$

The quantity   RC is the   "time constant" of the filter
in seconds,   and RC/Δt   can be considered   as the time
constant in   terms of number of digitized   time intervals.   Thus,   depending on specific circumstances, if
an RC filter is used for   computing a mean or variance
with a discrete time constant of RC/Δt, then one could
reasonably select every kth data value as being roughly uncorrelated data for use in the trend test.
     The   statistic to be considered is termed a reverse
arrangement.   Suppose the short-time-averaged mean or
mean square values are denoted by

$$x_1, x_2, x_3, \ldots, x_N$$

Define a reverse   arrangement as occurring   every time

$$x_j > x_i \qquad j > i \qquad i = 1, 2, \ldots, N-1 \qquad (11.10)$$

For a given value of the index i, denote the number of
reverse arrangements by A_j.   Then consider   the total

number of reverse arrangements

$$A = \sum_{i=1}^{N-1} A_i \tag{11.11}$$

It can be shown that the average value of A in a random sequence of integers is

$$E[A] = \frac{N(N-1)}{4} \tag{11.12}$$

This is easily seen by considering the fact that x_1 is equally likely to be larger or less than the succeeding $(N-1)$ members of a random sequence. Therefore, the average number of reverse arrangements, when considering x_1 against the remaining members, is

$$E[A_1] = (N-1)/2 \tag{11.13}$$

Now x_2 is compared against the $(N-2)$ remaining members of the sequence; hence,

$$E[A_2] = (N-2)/2 \tag{11.14}$$

Continuing the reasoning leads to

$$E[A_{N-2}] = 2/2$$

and

$$E[A_{N-1}] = 1/2 \tag{11.15}$$

The average value of A is obtained by adding up all these individual averages:

$$E[A] = \sum_{i=1}^{N-1} E(A_i) = \frac{1}{2} \sum_{i=1}^{N-1} i = \frac{N(N-1)}{4} \tag{11.16}$$

which is one-half the sum of the first (N-1) integers.
Also, the variance of A is found to be

$$Var[A] = \frac{2N^3 + 3N^2 - 5N}{72} \qquad (11.17)$$

Fortunately, for $N \geq 10$ the distribution of A may be
closely approximated by the normal distribution

$$\Phi[c] = \frac{1}{\sqrt{2\pi}} \int_{-\infty}^{c} e^{-x^2/2} \, dx \qquad (11.18)$$

where

$$c = \frac{\left[A + \frac{1}{2} - \frac{N(N-1)}{4}\right]}{\sqrt{\frac{2N^3 + 3N^2 - 5N}{72}}} \qquad (11.19)$$

Note that c in (11.19) is of the form $(x - \mu)/\sigma$; that
is, a standardized observation where $x = A + 1/2$, $\mu =$
$N(N-1)/4$, and $\sigma = $ Var[A]. The additive factor of 1/2
which appears in the numerator accounts for the fact
that A is an integer and that, in a continuous approximation, A is considered to be in the interval $[(A -$
$1/2),(A + 1/2)]$. An alternative method of defining A
is as the sum

$$A = \sum_{i < j} \sum a_{ij}$$

where

$$a_{ij} = \begin{cases} 1 & \text{if } x_i > x_j \\ 0 & \text{otherwise} \end{cases} \qquad (11.20)$$

A test of a hypothesis of the existence of a trend would proceed as follows: Note that if, for example, the mean square value of a process is rising linearly as indicated in Figure 11.2, then one would expect A to be very large.   That is, one would expect to find x_1 less than all subsequent observations except for a few cases caused by statistical sampling variations. On the other hand, an extremely small value for A would tend to indicate a decreasing trend in the mean square value.

The test is performed at a specified level of sig- nificance by use of (11.18) if A > 10 and by Table 11.1 for A < 10 to obtain the necessary probabilities of A being a given size. For example, suppose N = 8 and A = 14.   According to Table 11.1, the probability of A being less than or equal to 13 is 0.452.   The right half of the probabilities for N = 8, 9, 10 for Table 11.1 are not given explicitly, but are obtained directly since the distribution is symmetric.   That is, the entry in the table for N = 8 and A = 14 is 1 - P(13) = 0.548. Similarly, the entry for A = 15 is 1 - P(12) = 0.640, etc.

For the stated example, a hypothesis of no trend would be accepted at, say, the α = 5% level of signif- icance.   A two-tailed test would be used, which means that either too large or too small a value for A would tend to indicate a trend and require rejecting the

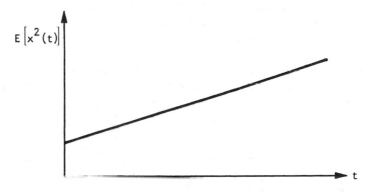

Fig. 11.2 Process with linearly increasing variance.

Table 11.1 Percentage Points of Reverse Arrangement Distribution*

	α					
N	0.99	0.975	0.95	0.05	0.025	0.01
10	9	11	13	31	33	35
12	16	18	21	44	47	49
14	24	27	30	60	63	66
16	34	38	41	78	81	85
18	45	50	54	98	102	107
20	59	64	69	120	125	130
30	152	162	171	263	272	282
40	290	305	319	460	474	489
50	473	495	514	710	729	751
60	702	731	756	1013	1038	1067
70	977	1014	1045	1369	1400	1437
80	1299	1344	1382	1777	1815	1860
90	1668	1721	1766	2238	2283	2336
100	2083	2145	2198	2751	2804	2866

*Values of $A_{N;\alpha}$ such that $[A_N > A_{N;\alpha}] = \alpha$, where N = total number of measurements.

hypothesis of no trend. For this level of significance, if the probability of obtaining the experimentally determined A is either less than 0.025 = 2.5% or larger than 0.975 = 97.5%, then the hypothesis of no trend would be rejected.

For values of N > 10, c is computed as given by (11.19), and a value for P(c) is found either by inspecting a table of the normal distribution or (in a computer) by employing the approximation in Appendix B. For the given example,

$$c = \frac{13.5 - 8(7)/4}{\sqrt{\dfrac{2(8)^3 + 3(8)^2 - 5(8)}{72}}} = \frac{13.5 - 14}{4.8} = 0.10 \tag{11.21}$$

Inspection of the normal distribution table yields $P[c = 10] = 0.460$. This value is in error by a little more than 2% from the correct value 0.452 obtained from Table 11.1, which indicates that even for N as small as 8, the Gaussian approximation is useful for some purposes.

This nonstationarity trend test will be effective against monotonic trends, but one can intuitively see that the test will have many limitations as far as certain types of nonstationary data are concerned. For example, suppose the mean square value is as indicated in Figure 11.3a. However, if the mean square value jumped as indicated, but then returned to its original level as shown in Figure 11.3b and if the test were being applied over this entire set of data, the test would probably fail. This is because, although probably too many reverse arrangements would occur over the first portion of the data, too few would most likely occur in the latter parts to obtain an overall value which was not unusual. Similarly, the test is probably effective in detecting the nonstationarity of the mean square value of the type indicated in Figure 11.4a and ineffective against the type of nonstationarities indicated in Figure 11.4b.

Nonstationary Frequency Response Test

An approach to determining stationarity of estimated filter (frequency response) relations has been applied to seismic array noise (Chiburis and Dean, 1967a-d). The idea here is as follows: Suppose an input-output relation $\hat{H}_1(f)$ is determined from measured time histories over time interval T_1. The question now arises: Is this input-output relation the same now as $\hat{H}_2(f)$ measured later over time interval T_2? The first tendency is to perform a statistical test by direct comparison of $\hat{H}_1(f)$ and $\hat{H}_2(f)$ which is possible by the confidence interval results of Chapter 9. This approach is unreasonable, as can be seen

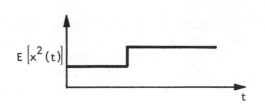

Fig. 11.3a Another nonstationary variance.

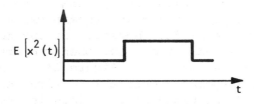

Fig. 11.3b An example the test did not detect.

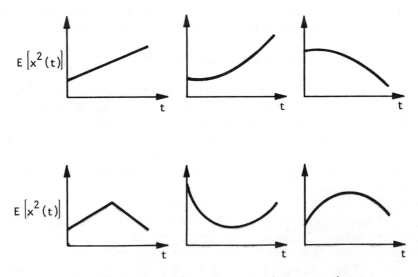

Fig. 11.4 Varieties of nonstationary variances.

by considering a case of three highly coherent variables. Suppose

$$Y(f) = H_1(f) X_1(f) + H_2(f) X_2(f) \qquad (11.22)$$

If $X_1(f)$ and $X_2(f)$ are perfectly coherent, then $X_1(f) = X_2(f)$ and

$$Y(f) = [H_1(f) + H_2(f)] X_1(f) \qquad (11.23)$$

Then, individual estimates of $H_1(f)$ and $H_2(f)$ could be
highly variable even though $[H_1(f) + H_2(f)]$ is stable.

A better question to ask is: How well do the fil-
ter relations $\hat{H}_1(f)$ and $\hat{H}_2(f)$ determined at time T_1
allow $X_1(f)$ and $X_2(f)$ to account for $Y(f)$ at a later
time T_2? The multiple coherence function can be applied to this question. It will not depend on the individual estimates $\hat{H}_1(f)$ and $\hat{H}_2(f)$, but rather on how
well the combination of the two works to predict $X(f)$.
The quantity employed to make a plausible test of this
type of stationarity is a pseudo-multiple coherence
function defined as follows: Let $\hat{\gamma}_{ij}^2(f)$ denote the
multiple coherence function using the frequency response estimates from the ith time slice applied to the
jth time slice. Let $H_{ii}(f)$ be the frequency response
function vector of p components estimated from the ith
time slice. Then $\hat{\gamma}_{ij}$ (dropping the frequency argument
for convenience) is defined by

$$\hat{\gamma}_{ij}^2 = \hat{\gamma}_{jj}^2 - \frac{(\hat{H}_{ii} - \hat{H}_{jj})^* \hat{G}_{xxj} (\hat{H}_{ii} - \hat{H}_{jj})}{\hat{G}_{yyi}} \qquad (11.24)$$

Thus, the multiple coherence $\hat{\gamma}_{ij}^2$ is the multiple coherence $\hat{\gamma}_{jj}^2$ at the jth time slice degraded by the
amount that comes from using $\hat{H}_{ii}$ instead of $\hat{H}_{jj}$. Note
that if H_{jj} is substituted for $\hat{H}_{ii}$ in (11.24), then
$\hat{\gamma}_{ij}^2$ becomes equal to $\hat{\gamma}_{jj}^2$, as it should, since the
amount of degradation goes to zero.

The statistical aspects of comparing the multiple coherence are not worked out unless time slices T_i and T_j are separated sufficiently to make the multiple coherences independent. Then the confidence limit formula of Chapter 9 is employed. Otherwise, the values of the various γ_{ij}^2 can only be compared in an approximate manner. However, it does provide a reasonable approach to evaluating stationarity of a multichannel process.

The computational sequence is:

1. Perform all spectral matrix, frequency response, and coherence function computations for a time slice T_i.

2. The parameter estimates $\hat{\gamma}_{ii}^2$, $\hat{H}_{ii}$, $\hat{S}_{xxi}$, and $\hat{S}_{xyi}$ all must be saved (on magnetic tape, for example).

3. Steps 1 and 2 are repeated for all desired time slices.

4. The pseudo-coherence $\hat{\gamma}_{ij}^2$ is computed for all values of i and j. This produces a (q x q) array, if there are q time slices, for each frequency point.

Time-Varying Mean and Variance

By far the most common test for stationarity is that of simple visual observation, usually of the smoothed data, or the output of an rms meter, using some form of analog hardware. For the mean value, the analog device may be thought of as an RC filter such as that described in Section 3.3. The time history is the input to it, and the output is plotted on an oscillograph. The equivalent sort of operation may be performed using digital filters. As is recalled from Section 3.3, the digital RC filter is

$$y_i = \alpha y_{i-1} + (1 - \alpha) x_i$$
$$\alpha = e^{-(\Delta t / RC)}$$

(11.25)

where x is the input to and y is the output from the filter. The parameter RC (and hence, α) can only be chosen from previous knowledge of the data or as the result of reruns on the same data. Experience in performing the operation will help the user in subsequent tests.

As discussed on page 400, the quantity k = 0.7 RC/Δt may be viewed as the effective number of data values being averaged. Hence, a reasonable choice would be k = 10, which implies

RC/Δt = 1.4k = 14

and in turn the value for the coefficient α is

$$\alpha = \frac{1}{\exp 14} = \frac{1}{2.54} = 0.38$$

The rms procedure is somewhat different when using a computer from that followed in using analog devices, where rectification is frequently performed in place of squaring. The digital procedure is shown in Figure 11.5. Squaring is easily done on a computer, so that this type of operation is relatively simple. The equations for $\bar{x}_i$ and s_i, the running mean and standard deviation, are

$$\bar{x}_i = \alpha x_i + (1-\alpha) \bar{x}_{i-1}$$

and

$$s_i = \sqrt{z_i - \bar{x}_i^2}$$

where

$$z_i = \alpha x_i^2 + (1-\alpha) x_{i-1}^2 \qquad (11.26)$$

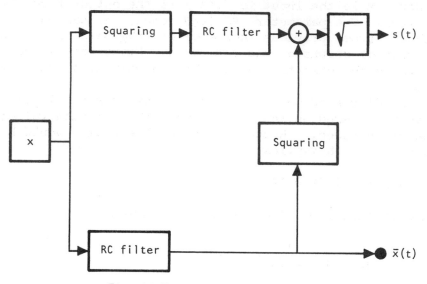

Fig. 11.5 Digital rms procedure.

Alternatively,   lowpass   filters of the   type   described in   Chapter 3   may be   used in place   of the RC
filter employed above.   There is no obvious gain from
so doing,   other than the difference in frequency response functions.

If much of this type of processing has to be done,
it may be possible to save large amounts of computer
time by decimating the data, as described in Chapter
3.   Decimation in this case would be performed before
the data are put through the rms procedure.   There is
a problem in interpreting the   information obtained
from this process.   If both s(t) and x(t) are relatively constant, the hypothesis of stationarity has
some plausibility.   On the other hand, if either of
them is varying noticeably, it would seem reasonable
to assume that x is nonstationary.

The faults of the above are fairly obvious:

   1. There are no quantitative parameters in the test
      on which a decision is based. Acceptance or re-
      jection is purely qualitative.

2. The procedure, if it tests any hypothesis at all, tests for homogeneity of mean and variance rather than stationarity. For example, suppose the first half of the record consists of a sinusoid of frequency f_0 and the second half consists of a sinusoid of frequency f_1, where $f_1 \neq f_0$, but their amplitudes are both A units. Then $\bar{x}(t)$ will be zero and s(t) will be $\sqrt{2}/2A$. On the basis of these observations, the observer would accept the data as being stationary when indeed it is not.

3. If too little smoothing is done, x_i and s_i may fluctuate considerably, perhaps leading the observer into believing that the data are nonstationary when in fact they are stationary.

Nevertheless, this procedure is probably one of the most effective in performing a preliminary analysis of a record that possibly is nonstationary.

Time-Varying Power Spectra

The concept of a time-varying PSD is a generalization of the time-varying variance. As with the standard PSD, there are three ways of performing the calculations. These are:

1. Computing the correlation function and the Fourier transform

2. Computing the Fourier transform and then taking its modulus squared

3. Using digital filters

The last two appear to be the most promising, so they will be discussed in detail.

When the Fourier transform procedure is chosen, the FFT should be employed. Some power of two, say 512, is selected. The data record is broken into segments, each containing 256 data points. The PSD is computed by taking the FFT of each pair of adjoining segments.

Label each segment as S_ℓ. Then

$$S_\ell = \{x_{\ell i}\}$$

$$= (x_{\ell 1}, x_{\ell 2}, \ldots, x_{\ell 256})$$

$$x_{\ell i} = x_{256\ell + i} \tag{11.27}$$

At time T_ℓ, where

$$T_\ell = [512\ell - 256]\Delta t \qquad\qquad \ell = 1, \ldots \tag{11.28}$$

the Fourier transform of the two segments is computed:

$$F_{\ell k} = \Delta t \left\{ \sum_{i=0}^{255} \exp\left[-\frac{j\pi ik}{512}\right] x_{\ell i} \right.$$

$$\left. + j \sum_{i=0}^{255} \exp\left[-\frac{j\pi k(i+256)}{512}\right] x_{(\ell+1)i} \right\}$$

$$k = 0, 1, \ldots, 511 \tag{11.29}$$

The PSD $\{G_{\ell k}\}$ is therefore

$$G_{\ell k} = \frac{1}{256\Delta t} \left| F_{\ell k} \right|^2 \qquad\qquad k = 0, 1, \ldots, 255 \tag{11.30}$$

Equation (11.29) looks formidable. In actual practice, the process is less difficult than it would appear. The computer program would take the following steps:

1. Initiate, including reading segment S_1 into a buffer area.

2. Transfer contents of the buffer into the upper half of the transform area. Read the next segment into the buffer area and then transfer it into the lower half of the transform area.

3. Compute the FFT of the contents of the transform area.

4. Compute the PSD from the Fourier transform and output the results.

5. Return to step 2 until all of the data have been processed.

The reason for the slight complication in step 2 is simple. Many of the computer subroutines to compute the FFT are destructive, i.e., they put the computed results back on top of the original data. This requires that the next segment be saved elsewhere in the computer. Also, the data probably will have to be moved in any event. While it is possible to compute the transform with the data scattered in various locations within the computer memory, this adds another level of complexity to the routines used to compute the FFT. On the other hand, with a fixed size of 512 points at a time, there are a number of economies which can be made in the computation with little effort. A little reflection will show that only 128 numbers are required to express all of the sines and cosines required. Thus, these can be precomputed and a short routine written to deliver the appropriate values. The 512 reverse addresses required by the FFT may also be precomputed.

Another peculiarity of the FFT procedure may be employed. As discussed in Chapter 4, the FFT is obtained from one complex or two real sequences at the same time. Therefore, as the data processes under consideration are assumed to be real, either two processes may be transformed at one time or a single one may be operated upon at double speed. The latter choice has the following steps:

1. Initiate. This includes reading segment S_1 into the buffer.

2. The contents of the buffer are moved to the upper half of the real area. The next two segments are read in. The segments are stored as follows:

```
Buffer → Upper half of real area

s_i  →  Lower half of real area
        Upper half of complex area

s_{i+1} →  Lower half of complex area
           Buffer
```

3. Compute the FFT and sort out the results corresponding to the real and imaginary parts.

4. Compute the two PSDs and output the results.

5. Return to step 2 until all of the data have been processed.

One point glossed over in the above description of the procedure is the manner and form of the output. There are a number of choices. Among the most prominent of these are plots of the following types:

1. One plot for each time at which the computations were made.

2. One plot for each frequency; each such plot would be a function of time versus power.

3. A contour plot; this would read like a topological map. One edge of the plot (usually the bottom) would be time. The side axis would be frequency. The power would be represented by a series of contours; along each contour the power would be constant. Five to ten levels would be selected, and the resulting curves would tend to be concentric and closed. This is shown in Figure 11.6a.

4. A profile plot can be made as shown in Figure 11.6b. These are somewhat easier to visualize than contour plots, but it is more difficult to make accurate readings from them.

Contour plots are probably the most expensive to generate. All of the data (or at least significant portions of it) must be readily available in storage. There is a lot of checking and interpolation to be

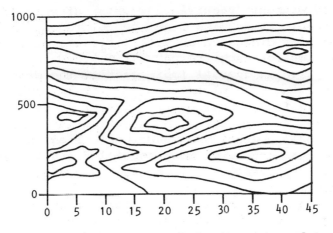

Fig. 11.6a Power spectral density contour plot.

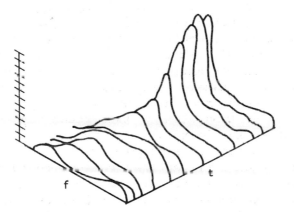

Fig. 11.6b Power spectral density profile plot.

performed, which adds to the running time, and many
people find contour plots difficult to read.

Profile plots pose a dilemma: If all the information is plotted, the graphs look confusing because of
overlapping lines. On the other hand, if portions of
data that fall behind more forward parts of the graph
are deleted in order to enhance the plot, important
results may be lost from view. Profile plots are considerably cheaper to generate, however, and may be

produced without requiring amounts of core storage. A reasonable compromise might be to produce the second type of plot discussed above, i.e., one plot of power versus time for each frequency, followed by a profile plot to give an overall impression of the process.

Generating such plots is a relatively complex operation. In fact, proprietary computer programs are now available to perform the contouring or three-dimensional operations described. These are comprehensive packages with many special features, and they consist typically of several thousand FORTRAN statements.

Bandwidth is another important consideration in setting up such an analysis. It is likely that, rather than employing the 256 equally spaced frequencies, the user would prefer a broader bandwidth analysis. Power could be combined in several ways, as discussed in Chapter 6, depending upon the application. Perhaps a more natural way of computing the time-varying PSDs is through the use of filtering. A PSD produced in this manner is a simple extension of two procedures discussed earlier, namely the direct filtering method described in Chapter 8 and the time-varying variance developed in Section 11.4. Each frequency would take the form shown in Figure 11.7. The first part of the procedure consists of a simple routine to remove the mean. The bandpass filter that follows could be of any size, but a six-pole filter is a good compromise between the sharpness of the filter and the cost of computation. The squaring and filtering that follow are exactly the same as for the variance computations described in (11.26).

The problems of display are identical to those of the FFT discussed above with one exception: The RC filter used to smooth the squared data introduces a delay, which must be accounted for when labeling the time axis. This delay is approximately

$$Delay = RC \cdot \ln 2 \qquad (11.31)$$

where RC is the filtering parameter.

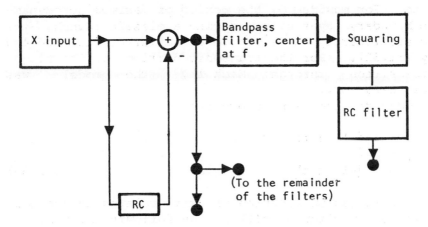

Fig. 11.7 One segment of a program designed to compute a time-varying PSD.

Clipped-Correlation Nonstationary Procedure

The relation described in Chapter 6 between the correlation function for a strongly clipped signal and the correlation function for the original signal is applied here. The relations described are not proven with any theoretical rigor. However, arguments are given for the plausibility of the methods, and they are useful in practice.

The special form of nonstationary processes to be considered are of the third type discussed in the beginning of this chapter. That is, where

$$x(t) = a(t)\ z(t) \qquad\qquad (11.32)$$

In (11.32), $z(t)$ is assumed to be a zero mean, Gaussian, stationary process. The quantity $a(t)$ is again assumed to be a slowly varying positive-valued, modulating function acting like a time-varying scale factor. It has been empirically demonstrated in Piersol (1967) that (11.32) can serve in some instances as a satisfactory model for nonstationary

data. For maximum Q, the period of maximum aerodynam-
ic boundary layer noise during a missile launch, the
nonstationarity was shown to be satisfactorily modeled
by (11.32).   For the transonic portion of the flight
(transition   through   Mach 1),   the   model   was
unsatisfactory.
   Consider the clipped process

$$y(t) = \begin{cases} 1 & x(t) > 0 \\ -1 & x(t) < 0 \end{cases} \tag{11.33}$$

The correlation function of x(t) relates to the correlation function of y(t) in the following manner:

$$\rho_x(\tau) = \sin\left[\frac{\pi}{2} R_y(\tau)\right] \tag{11.34}$$

where $\rho(\tau)$ is the normalized correlation coefficient
function.   It can be very simply argued now that the
autocorrelation function of x(t) computed by this
method is exactly the same as that of z(t) computed by
a clipping method. This is true because, when the
process is clipped, only the zero crossing information
remains. The time-varying scale factor a(t) will have
no effect on the zero crossings [assuming a(t) is non-
negative]. Hence, since the correlation function based
on clipping the x(t) time history is computed from the
identical information as the correlation function
based on the z(t) time history, ρ_x computed from
(11.34) can be used as an estimator of the stationary
autocorrelation function ρ_z. Finally, the time-varying
characteristics of ρ_x can be obtained from a separate
estimate of Var[x(t)]. The simplest approach on a digital computer is to use the squared output of a lowpass RC recursive numerical filter as discussed on
page 409a. Under the assumption that a(t) is not varying too rapidly [as compared to z(t)], then reasonably
short time-averaged estimates of Var[x(t)] can be obtained.   The selection of the RC time constant (or

equivalently, the effective averaging span) of the filter will depend on the particular type of data.

The estimation procedure for a nonstationary spectral analysis then is

1. Perform extreme clipping of $x_i = a_i z_i$:

$$y_i = \begin{cases} 1 & x_i \geq 0 \\ -1 & x_i < 0 \end{cases} \qquad (11.35)$$

2. Compute $\hat{R}_{yr}$, $r = 0, 1, \ldots, m$. Special high-speed computation procedures based on the clipped process can be employed here.

3. Perform the sin x bias correction to obtain $\hat{\rho}_{xr}$:

$$\hat{\rho}_{xr} = \sin\left[\frac{\pi}{2} \hat{R}_{yr}\right] \qquad r = 0, 1, \ldots, m \quad (11.36)$$

4. Compute the Fourier transform of $\hat{\rho}_{xr}$ tapered by a lag window to normalize spectrum to obtain $\hat{g}_{xk}$:

$$\hat{g}_{xk} = [u_{mr} \hat{\rho}_{xr}] \qquad k = 0, 1, \ldots, m \quad (11.37)$$

5. Compute estimates of $\text{Var}[x_i]$ by numerical RC filtering as illustrated in this chapter:

$$s_j^2 = \text{Var}[x_i] = \overline{x_i^2} - (\overline{x}_i)^2 \qquad (11.38)$$

where $\overline{x^2}$ and $(\overline{x_i})^2$ are the outputs from an RC numerical filter. The final plotted spectrum should be

$$\hat{G}_{xk} = s_j^2 \hat{g}_{xk} \qquad (11.39)$$

For each value of the time index j, a plot of $\hat{G}_{xk}$, $k = 0, 1, \ldots, m$ can be made.

As referred to in Chapter 6, many of the statistical aspects of spectral density estimation using
clipped time series are covered in Hinich (1967).   An
example for an ideal narrow bandwidth spectrum is presented there. It is shown that the standard deviation
of the spectrum estimated by the clipping procedure is
$(0.72\pi/2) = 1.13$ larger than with regular methods.
Thus, for this case, a 13% increase in standard deviation is experienced.   For variances, the factor is
$(0.72\pi/2)^2 = 1.28$, which is a 28% increase. A corresponding increase in record length is required to maintain equivalent statistical accuracy.

High-Frequency, High-Resolution Analysis

In many instances, a fine-resolution spectral analysis of very high frequency data is needed.   The number of data points necessary to satisfy the sampling
theorem can result in such large amounts of data that
the time and cost of processing becomes excessive,
even with the computational speed of the FFT.   In certain instances, the normally troublesome phenomena of
aliasing can be utilized to reduce the amount of data
and thus the processing cost.

The method utilizes bandpass filtering followed by
decimation and a FFT computation. With the proper
choice of filter cut-offs, relative to the sampling
interval, a high-frequency band can be effectively
processed as a much lower band, since it will fold
down by aliasing and appear at lower frequency.   The
block diagram of the method is given in Figure 11.8.
Since a frequency interval is magnified or expanded,
the effect is that of a "zoom" lens on a camera, and
we refer to the procedure as a "zoom FFT."

The specification of the method for decimation factors of a power of two is convenient. Suppose we decimate by a factor of P (keep every Pth point), where

$$P = 2^q \qquad (11.40)$$

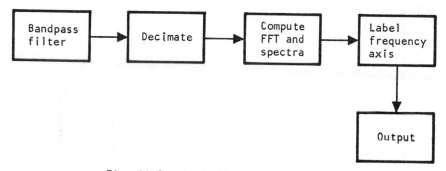

Fig. 11.8 Block diagram of zoom FFT.

In this way we will discard (2^q-1) points after filtering a block of 2^q points. The sampling interval
will increase from Δt to

$$\Delta t' = \Delta t\; 2^q \tag{11.41}$$

Let us define a "qth-order zoom." We want to place
a bandpass filter of appropriate width about the data
to take advantage of aliasing due to folding.   There
are 2^q possible bands which we might filter and analyze with the following edges:

$$f_1 = \text{Left edge} = \frac{r}{2\Delta t\; 2^q}$$

$$f_2 = \text{Right edge} = \frac{r+1}{2\Delta t\; 2^q} \qquad r = 0,1,\ldots,P-1 \tag{11.42}$$

Only one value of r will be selected, normally (P-1)
or at least one of the larger values. An example of
this is shown in Figure 11.9.
    The bandpass filter will be selected with half-
power point cut-offs that lie within the frequency interval $[f_1,f_2]$. The higher the quality of the filter
(that is, the steeper the slopes), the closer the filter cut-offs can be positioned to the band edges.

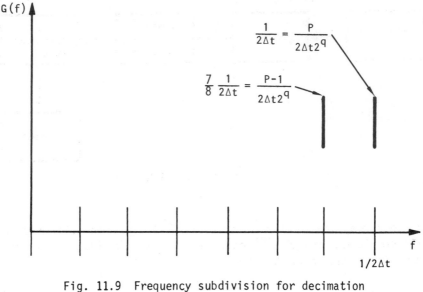

Fig. 11.9 Frequency subdivision for decimation
by factor $P = 2^3 = 8$.

After the computation of the frequency function is
complete, the frequency scale of the data analyzed in
the effective frequencies range $f_1 = 0$ to $f_2 = 1/2\Delta t'$
will actually be

$$f_1 = r/2\Delta t \; 2^q$$

$$f_2 = (r+1)/2\Delta t \; 2^q \qquad r = 0,2,4,\ldots,2^q-2 \quad (11.43)$$

$$f_1 = (r+1)/2\Delta t \; 2^q$$

$$f_2 = r/2\Delta t \; 2^q \qquad r = 1,3,5,\ldots,2^q-1 \quad (11.44)$$

That is, the frequency scale is reversed for odd values of r. An additional fact to be taken into consideration is that the sign of the imaginary part of the
Fourier transform must be changed for odd values of r;
for odd values the transformation procedure yields the
complex conjugate of the desired Fourier transform. In

the aliasing example of the stagecoach wheel in the western movie, the conjugate exhibits itself as the reversal in rotation of the wheel.

The advantage of this method is that if N data points can reasonably be processed by an available FFT, then the best resolution available is $B_1 = 1/N\Delta t$. The resolution attainable with N data points at the sampling interval $\Delta t' = P\Delta t$ is

$$B_2 = \frac{1}{N\Delta t'} = \frac{1}{P}\frac{1}{N\Delta t} = \frac{B_1}{P} \qquad (11.45)$$

Thus, resolution is increased by a factor of P, and the only increase in computing time or cost is due to the bandpass filter.

The statistical accuracy will be reduced if the effective analysis bandwidth is reduced without a corresponding increase in record length, since the number of d.f. is

$$n = 2B_e T$$

This factor must be considered if good statistical accuracy must be maintained. The importance of this depends on the problem involved. If one had very high d.f. and desired only the finer resolution, then no corresponding increase in T may be necessary. However, if the d.f. are of a borderline amount, then the record length must be increased.

The computational procedure is:

1. Select a decimation index P.

2. Generate a bandpass filter with cut-offs

$$f_{lower} = \frac{r}{2\Delta tP} > f_1 + \Delta f$$

$$f_{upper} = \frac{r+1}{2\Delta tP} < f_2 - \Delta f$$

where (f_1, f_2) is the frequency interval to be analyzed. The program user can specify the filter roll-offs and Δf.

3. Filter the data, x, with the bandpass filter, decimating the output so that only x_p, x_{2p}, x_{3p}, ... are kept.

4. Relabel the data so that

$$x_i' = x_{(i+1)P} \qquad\qquad i = 0,1,2,\ldots,N$$

5. Compute the FFT of the N-point sequence x_i':

$$X_k = \mathcal{F}[x_i']$$

6. Compute the PSD:

$$\hat{G}_k = \frac{2\Delta t}{N} \, |X_k|^2$$

7. Relabel the frequency index:

$$k' = \begin{cases} rN+k & r \text{ even} \\ (r+1)N-k & r \text{ odd} \end{cases} \qquad\qquad (11.46)$$

If cross spectra are required, then the Fourier transforms must also be complex conjugated for r odd. Note that the method does not really depend on the decimation factor being a power of two. The segment length that remains after decimation can be padded with zeros if necessary to make a power of two for the FFT routine. This is necessary, since in general it would be possible for a frequency band to overlap $f_N/2$. If this happened, it would always be aliased into itself.

CHAPTER 12
TEST CASE AND EXAMPLES

In this chapter, several plots obtained by using a package of computer programs, called the MAC/RAN* system, are presented. These plots illustrate typical results, which can be obtained from digital computer processing of data with programs that implement the methods described in the preceding chapters. Many plots of frequency response functions in various forms, power spectra, cross spectra, autocorrelation, and the various types of coherence functions, are given as figures in the following pages.

12.1 GENERATION OF TEST DATA

To produce these results, several pseudo-random time histories were generated by pseudo-random number generators. The basic procedure followed to obtain the time histories used for the test case is as follows:

1. Use a subroutine for uniformly distributed random numbers to generate a sequence of N independent pseudo-random numbers uniformly distributed on the interval -1/2 to +1/2.

2. Form the sum of each set of 12 contiguous numbers to form a new set of random numbers x_i, $i = 1,...,N/12$. The original set of uniformly distributed random numbers had a mean value $\mu = 0$ and a variance $\sigma^2 = 1/12$. The variance of the sum of independent random variables is the sum of the variances and likewise for the mean values. Thus, the random variables x_i have a

---

*MAC/RAN is a registered trademark of The University Software Systems, subsidiary of Agbabian Associates, Los Angeles, California.

425

mean value of zero and a variance of unity. By invoking the central limit term, the variable x_i will have an approximately Gaussian probability density function and lie within the range -6 to +6 and thus have a range of ±6 standard deviations. These sequences now represent approximately Gaussian band-limited white noise processes. Successive data values are very close to being independent, so the PSD function will be approximately flat and, hence, these will be white noise variables.

3. Variables generated in this manner can now be combined in various ways to construct correlated pseudo-random white noise time histories. For the example at hand, three independent processes, x_1, x_2, and x_3, were combined in the following manner:

$$x_4 = x_1 + x_2$$
$$x_5 = \frac{1}{2} x_3 + x_2$$

In this manner, the time histories x_1, x_2, and x_3 become correlated with x_4 and x_5, while x_1, x_2, and x_3 remain independent of one another.

4. These time histories are operated on by numerical filters, and time histories having specified correlation function properties or spectral density properties are generated. The numerical filtering procedure amounts to taking linear combinations of contiguous sets of the original independent random variables. Hence, the output will be sequences of data points that will be correlated and thus have a correlation function different from a spike and will in turn have a PSD function which has been given some shape. For the sample case being illustrated, new time histories were generated as follows:

x_6 = RC filtered x_1 (weights 0.8 and 0.2)

x_7 = RC filtered x_5 (weights 0.6 and 0.4)

x_8 = RC filtered x_4 (weights 0.6 and 0.4)

That is,(3.8) was utilized to generate filtered data. For example, the formula

$$x_{6i} = 0.8 x_{6(i-1)} + 0.2\, x_{1i}$$

is used to generate x_6 with similar formulas for x_7 and x_8. The number of data points is N = 2048 for each channel of data. By regarding the sampling rate (in samples per second) as f_S = 2048 sps, a Nyquist frequency of f_N = 1024 Hz is induced.

The square of the gain function for each of the three filters is (from Chapter 3)

$$\left| H_1(\omega) \right|^2 = \frac{0.04}{1.64 - 1.6\, \cos \frac{\omega}{2048}}$$

$$\left| H_2(\omega) \right|^2 = \left| H_3(\omega) \right|^2 = \frac{0.16}{1.36 - 1.2\, \cos \frac{\omega}{2048}}$$

The phase angle may be derived from the transfer function in Chapter 3 also:

$$\phi_1(\omega) = \arctan\left(\frac{-0.8 \sin \frac{\omega}{2048}}{1 - 0.8 \cos \frac{\omega}{2048}} \right)$$

$$\phi_2(\omega) = \phi_3(\omega) = \arctan\left(\frac{-0.6 \sin \frac{\omega}{2048}}{1 - 0.6 \cos \frac{\omega}{2048}} \right)$$

Plots of the gains and phases are given in Figure 12.1 so that theoretical values may be compared with the results of the test analysis performed on pseudo-random data.

5. Finally, the sum of these independent random variables is computed, which may now be thought of as the output of a three-dimensional linear system. For the case at hand, the output variable is

$$x_9 = x_6 + x_7 + x_8 + \frac{\text{White noise}}{10}$$

The white noise added is another pseudo-random time history with the same variance (power) as the other original time histories. Dividing by 10 reduces its variance by a factor of 100. Thus, the noise added simulates about 1% additive white noise at the output. Of course, since the spectrum of the output is not constant, there is proportionately more noise in the region where the output spectrum is small, and vice versa.

Figure 12.2 is a block diagram of the system generating the data for the test computations. The first stage generates the correlations in the data. It is these functions which are assumed to be the measured inputs to the bank of three RC filters. The final combination of these filtered time histories forms the output of the triple-input single-output linear system which is then corrupted with additive independent noise.

In the sample plots which follow, the test data are $N = 2048$ data points (1 sec) for each of the four time histories $x_9(t)$, $x_1(t)$, $x_4(t)$, and $x_5(t)$. We have passed the time histories through numerical filters and added extraneous noise. Thus, we are simulating a noise-contaminated output of a linear system with three correlated inputs. The squared correlations of the inputs with one another are:

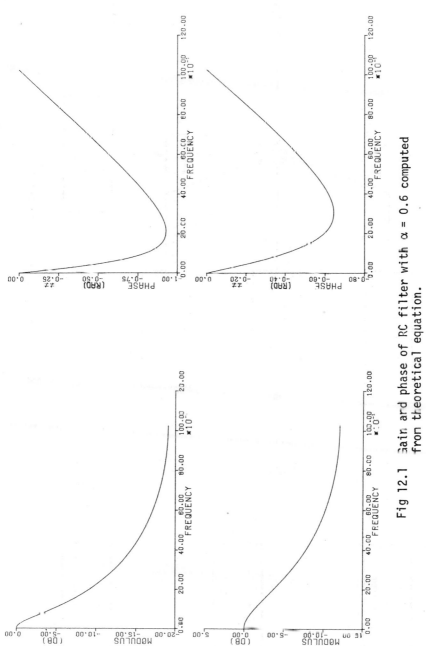

Fig 12.1 Gain and phase of RC filter with α = 0.6 computed from theoretical equation.

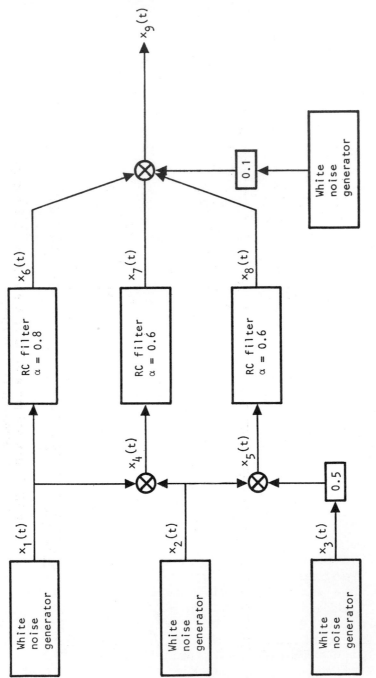

Fig. 12.2 Block diagram of test data generation.

x_1 with x_4 $1/2 = 0.50$

x_1 with x_5 0

x_4 with x_5 $4/13 \approx 0.30$

12.2 SAMPLE PLOTS

Histograms

In Figure 12.3a-d the probability histograms of the four time histories are shown; on these are superimposed the Gaussian probability density curves which have the sample mean and variance determined from the sample time histories. As one can see from inspection, these probability density functions are very close to normal probability density functions, as the central limit theorem predicts.

Autocorrelation Functions and Power Spectra

Figure 12.4a is the autocorrelation function of $x_9(t)$, the output, for m = 64 lags. Figure 12.4b is the corresponding Blackman-Tukey PSD with n $\approx$ 64 d.f. Figure 12.4c is the PSD of the same time history with n $\approx$ 64 d.f. but computed via the FFT procedure described in Chapter 6.

The Nyquist frequency is 1024, and with n $\approx$ 64 d.f. we have an effective resolution of $B_e \approx$ 32 Hz for the spectrum computations.

Figures 12.5a-c are the 64 lag autocorrelation function, 64 d.f. Blackman-Tukey PSD, and 64 d.f. fast Fourier transform PSD, respectively, for $x_4(t)$. Figures 12.6a-c are the 128 lag autocorrelation function, 32 d.f. Blackman-Tukey PSD, and 32 d.f. fast Fourier transform PSD, respectively, for $x_4(t)$. Thus, the resolution bandwidth is halved in going from Figure 12.5 to Figure 12.6 as is the number of d.f. Both PSD plots illustrate the increase in statistical variability dramatically.

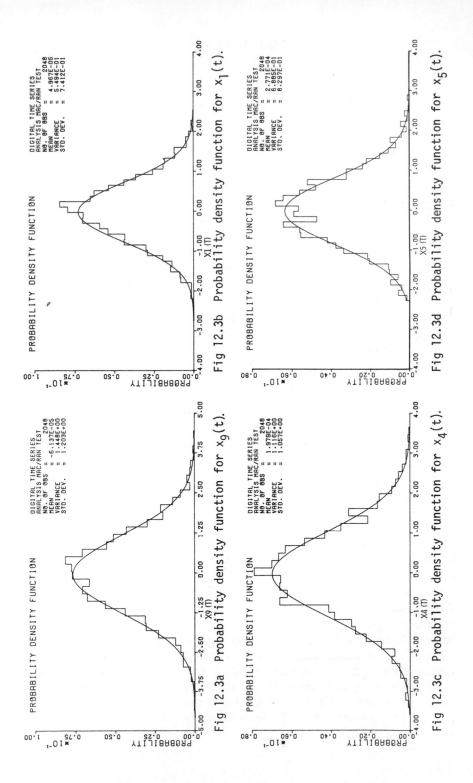

Fig 12.3a Probability density function for $x_9(t)$.

Fig 12.3b Probability density function for $x_1(t)$.

Fig 12.3c Probability density function for $x_4(t)$.

Fig 12.3d Probability density function for $x_5(t)$.

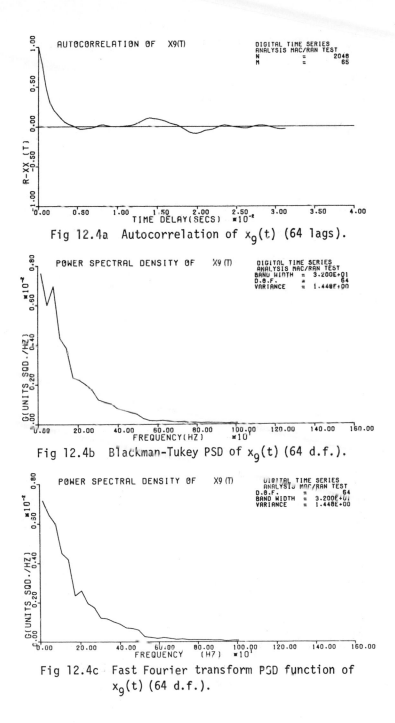

Fig 12.4a Autocorrelation of $x_9(t)$ (64 lags).

Fig 12.4b Blackman-Tukey PSD of $x_9(t)$ (64 d.f.).

Fig 12.4c Fast Fourier transform PSD function of $x_9(t)$ (64 d.f.).

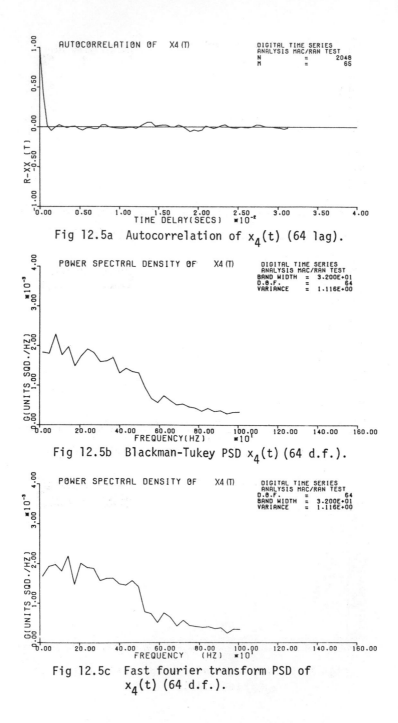

Fig 12.5a Autocorrelation of $x_4(t)$ (64 lag).

Fig 12.5b Blackman-Tukey PSD $x_4(t)$ (64 d.f.).

Fig 12.5c Fast fourier transform PSD of
$x_4(t)$ (64 d.f.).

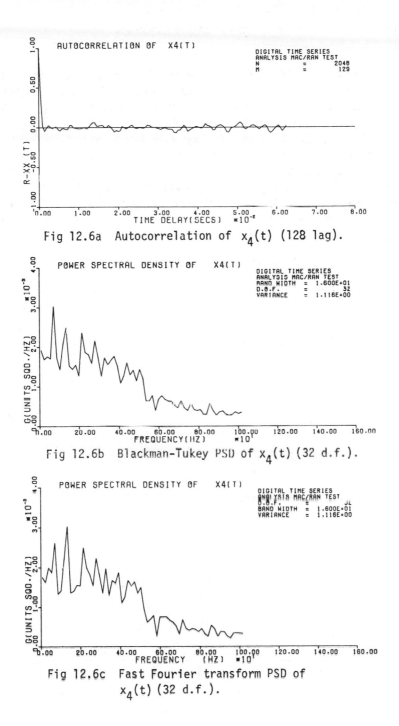

Fig 12.6a   Autocorrelation of $x_4(t)$ (128 lag).

Fig 12.6b   Blackman-Tukey PSD of $x_4(t)$ (32 d.f.).

Fig 12.6c   Fast Fourier transform PSD of
$x_4(t)$ (32 d.f.).

Figures 12.7a and b present the positive and negative delay halves of the cross-correlation function
between the output variable $x_9(t)$ and the input variable $x_1(t)$. As can be seen by the cross-correlation
function, a small time delay has been generated in the
numerical filtering of the data, since the main peak
in the cross-correlation function is not centered at
$\tau = 0$. The corresponding plots of the B-T cross spectrum absolute value and phase appear in Figures 12.8a
and b. The FFT version is shown in Figures 12.8c
and d.

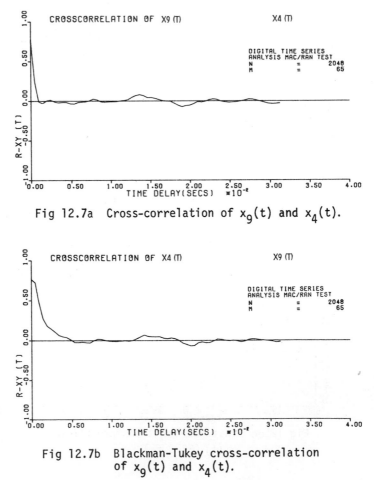

Fig 12.7a   Cross-correlation of $x_9(t)$ and $x_4(t)$.

Fig 12.7b   Blackman-Tukey cross-correlation
of $x_9(t)$ and $x_4(t)$.

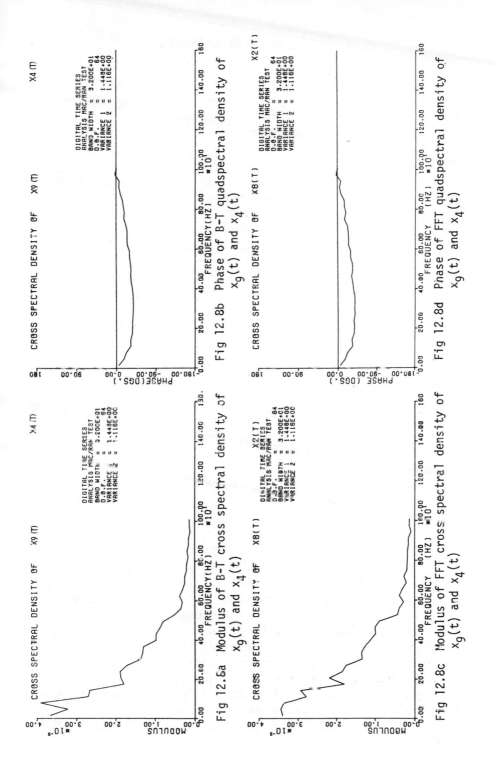

Fig 12.8a Modulus of B-T cross spectral density of $x_9(t)$ and $x_4(t)$

Fig 12.8b Phase of B-T quadspectral density of $x_9(t)$ and $x_4(t)$

Fig 12.8c Modulus of FFT cross spectral density of $x_9(t)$ and $x_4(t)$

Fig 12.8d Phase of FFT quadspectral density of $x_9(t)$ and $x_4(t)$

The corresponding frequency response function for the same input-output pair computed three different ways is given in Figures 12.9a-c and 12.10a-c. Parts a and b of the figures are plots generated utilizing the multilinear system theory of Chapter 9. The spectral matrix is generated in part a of both figures by the B-T method and in part b using spectra from FFTs. Part c is gain (in linear units) and phase generated directly from ratios of smoothed Fourier transforms. For this case of an ideal linear system and small noise in the output, the results are not all that different. However, the FFT version does have a biased gain even though it is smooth. This is due to the fact that the effect of the other correlated input is not accounted for. The gains are in Figure 12.9, which are the B-T spectral matrix version, the FFT spectral matrix version, and the FFT version computed directly from ratios of smoothed transforms. Parts a and b are dB plots, and c is in linear units. The corresponding phase angles are in Figure 12.10. The title, "Channel 2," refers to the second transmission channel, which has $x_4(t)$ as the input.

The various coherence functions generated via the two different methods make up Figures 12.11a-c and 12.12a-c. Figures 12.11a-c are the B-T version ordinary, multiple, and partial coherence functions for the transmission Channel 2 [$x_4(t)$ input]. The corresponding parts of Figure 12.12 are the FFT counterparts.

The remaining plots are presented to illustrate the improved statistical reliability obtained in frequency response estimates when the coherence is essentially unity. Figures 12.13a-b are the counterparts of the frequency response functions plotted in Figures 12.9 and 12.10. The d.f. of the estimates are the same, but a single-input, single-output system is simulated with no contaminating extraneous noise. That is, $x_4(t)$ is still the input time history, but $x_7(t)$ rather than $x_9(t)$ is now the output. As can be seen, the plots are now nearly ideal, as would be expected from a perfect, discrete, linear system. Figures 12.13a-b are the gain and the corresponding phase angle.

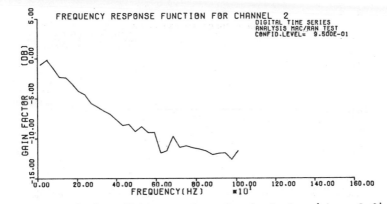

Fig 12.9a Blackman-Tukey version of gain factor (channel 2).

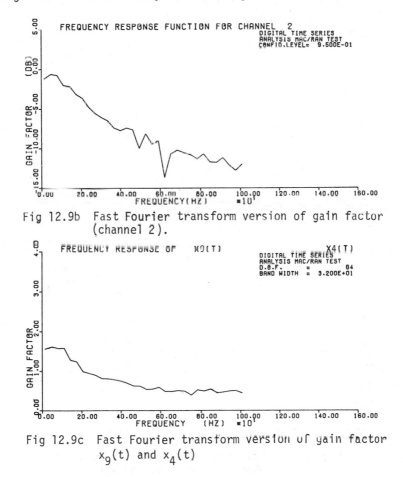

Fig 12.9b Fast Fourier transform version of gain factor
(channel 2).

Fig 12.9c Fast Fourier transform version of gain factor
$x_9(t)$ and $x_4(t)$

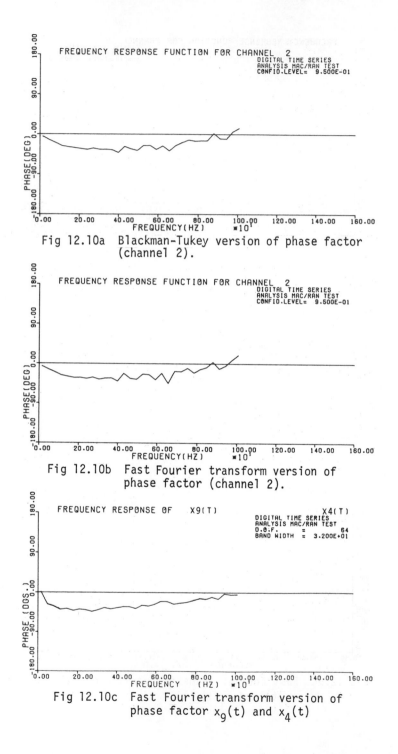

Fig 12.10a   Blackman-Tukey version of phase factor
(channel 2).

Fig 12.10b   Fast Fourier transform version of
phase factor (channel 2).

Fig 12.10c   Fast Fourier transform version of
phase factor $x_9(t)$ and $x_4(t)$

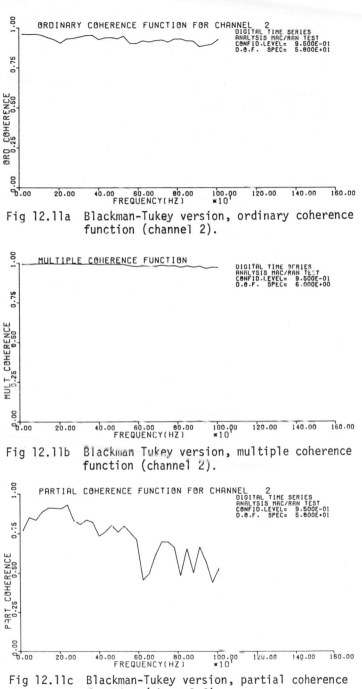

Fig 12.11a Blackman-Tukey version, ordinary coherence
function (channel 2).

Fig 12.11b Blackman-Tukey version, multiple coherence
function (channel 2).

Fig 12.11c Blackman-Tukey version, partial coherence
function (channel 2).

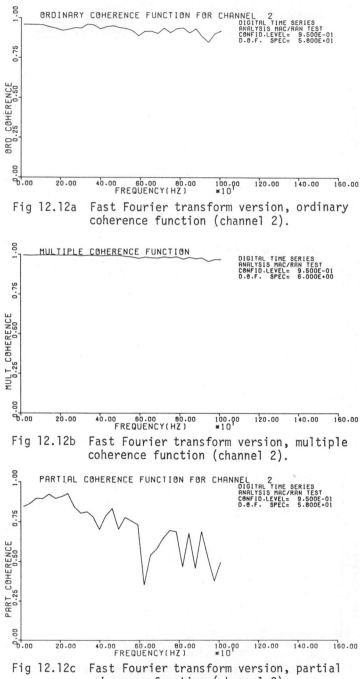

Fig 12.12a Fast Fourier transform version, ordinary
coherence function (channel 2).

Fig 12.12b Fast Fourier transform version, multiple
coherence function (channel 2).

Fig 12.12c Fast Fourier transform version, partial
coherence function (channel 2).

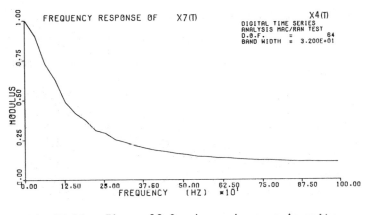

Fig 12.13a Figure 12.9a when coherence is unity.

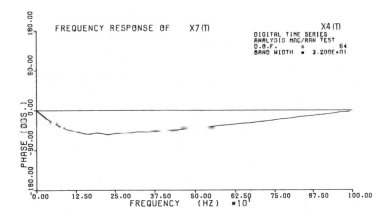

Fig 12.13b Figure 12.9b when coherence is unity.

APPENDIX A
GLOSSARY OF ABBREVIATIONS AND SYMBOLS

ADC	Analog-to-digital converter
B	Bandwidth, folding frequency
B_e	Bandwidth of analysis, effective bandwidth
B-T	Blackman-Tukey
BCD	Binary coded decimal
c	Arbitrary constant, digital filter weight
c_k	Complex coefficients of Fourier series
C	Electrical capacitance, maximum output of a limiter
$C_{xy}(f)$	One-sided cospectral density function
CSD	Cross spectral density
C-T	Cooley-Tukey; authors of an early FFT algorithm
DAS	Data-acquisition system
d.f.	Degrees of freedom
e	Voltage input
E[ ]	Expected value of
exp[ ]	e[ ],e = 2.718
f	Frequency
f(x)	Probability density function
FFT	Fast Fourier transform
F(x)	Probability distribution function
$\mathcal{F}$[ ]	Fourier transform of [ ]
$\mathcal{F}^{-1}$[ ]	Inverse Fourier transform of [ ]

445

$F_{n_1,n_2;\alpha}$	α percentage point of the F distribution with n_1 and n_2 d.f.
FM	Frequency modulation
$G_x(f)$	One-sided power spectral density
$G_{xy}(f)$	One-sided cross spectral density
G_{xk}	One-sided power spectral density at frequency $f = k\Delta f$
G_{xyk}	One-sided cross spectral density at frequency $f = k\Delta f$
$h(\tau)$	Weighting function (unit impulse response function)
h_k	Digital filter weight
$H(f)$	Frequency response function [the Fourier transform of $h(\tau)$]
$|H(f)|$	Gain
Hz	Hertz, the units of frequency
Im[ ]	Imaginary part of [ ]
i	An index
j	$\sqrt{-1}$, an index
k	An index
ℓ	An index
ln [ ]	Natural logarithm of [ ]
m	Number of lags in discrete correlation function or discrete convolution
n	Number of degrees of freedom
n(t)	Random noise function
N	Sample size or correlation of white noise correlation function
p	Number of inputs in multidimensional linear system
P	Probability

PCM	Pulse code modulation
PDF	Probability density function
PSD	Power spectral density
$Q_{xy}(f)$	One-sided quadrature spectral density
QSD	Quad (quadrature) spectral density
R	Electrical resistance
$R_x(\tau)$	Autocorrelation function
R_{xr}	Discrete autocorrelation function at lag value $\tau = r\Delta\tau$
$R_{xy}(\tau)$	Cross-correlation function
R_{xyr}	Discrete cross-correlation function at lag value $\tau = r\Delta\tau$
Re[ ]	Real part of [ ]
s	Sample standard deviation
s^2	Sample variance
$S_x(f)$	Two-sided power spectral density
sgn(x)	The sign of x
sps	Samples per second
t	Time variable
$t_{n;\alpha}$	α percentage point of statistical "t" distribution with n d.f.
T	Observation time, record length
T_m	Span of autocorrelation used (one side)
u(t)	Boxcar function (time)
U(f)	Fourier transform of the boxcar function
W	Usually $\exp[-j2\pi/N]$
W	Fourier transform matrix representation
x(t), y(t)	Time-dependent variables
x_i, y_i	Sampled function at time $t = i\Delta t$

$\hat{x}$ Estimate of x

$\bar{x}$ Sample mean value of x(t)

$\tilde{x}$ Raw estimate of x

$X(f)$ Fourier transform of x(t) or x_i

X_k Fourier transform of x_i

x^2 Sample χ^2 variable

$|[\ ]|$ Absolute value of [ ]

α A small probability, significance level, number of counts

$\gamma^2(f)$ Coherence function

γ_{ij}^2 Ordinary coherence function

γ_{ix} Multiple coherence function

$\gamma_{iy|p}^2$ Partial coherence function

$\Gamma(\ )$ Gamma function evaluated for ( )

$\delta(t)$ Delta function

Δt Interval between samples

ε Normalized standard error

ε^2 Normalized variance

ξ Damping ratio

ξ_m mth damping ratio

θ Phase angle

$\theta_{xy}(f)$ Argument of $G_{xy}(f)$, phase

λ Normalized frequency ($\lambda = 2\pi f \Delta t$)

λ_m mth natural frequency

Λ_m Complex frequency (digital)

μ Mean value

ρ Correlation coefficient

$\rho_x(\tau)$ Normalized correlation function: correlation coefficient function

σ	Standard deviation
σ^2	Variance
Σ	Indicates summation
τ	Time displacement
$\phi(f)$	Phase factor
$\Phi(x)$	Normal (Gaussian) probability distribution function
$\chi^2_{n;\alpha}$	A percentage point of statistical chi-square variable with n d.f.
ω	Frequency in radians/sec ($\omega = 2\pi f$)

APPENDIX B
MISCELLANEOUS NUMERICAL EXPRESSIONS

1. Numerical subroutine for $\phi(x)$ (normal distribution):
   By $\phi(x)$ is meant

   $$\phi(x) = \frac{1}{2\pi} \int_{-\infty}^{x} e^{-t^2/2} \, dt$$

   Approximations are readily available for erf(y), the *error* function, whose definition is

   $$\text{erf}(y) = \frac{2}{\sqrt{\pi}} \int_{0}^{y} e^{-t^2} \, dt$$

   $$\approx 1 - \frac{1}{\left[1 + \sum_{i=1}^{6} a_i y^i \right]^{16}}$$

   where

   $$a_i = 0.0705, 2307, 84$$

   $$a_2 = 0.0422, 8201, 23$$

   $$a_3 = 0.0092, 7052, 72$$

   $$a_4 = 0.0001, 5201, 43$$

   $$a_5 = 0.0002, 7656, 72$$

   $$a_6 = 0.0000, 4306, 38$$

   Thus, (x) may be calculated from

451

$$\phi(x) = \begin{cases} \dfrac{1}{2} + \dfrac{1}{2}\,\mathrm{erf}\left(\dfrac{x}{\sqrt{2}}\right) & x \geq 0 \\[3mm] \dfrac{1}{2} - \dfrac{1}{2}\,\mathrm{erf}\left(\dfrac{-x}{\sqrt{2}}\right) & x < 0 \end{cases}$$

As usual,

$$\frac{1}{\sqrt{2\pi\sigma^2}} \int_a^b e^{-\frac{(x-\mu)^2}{2\sigma^2}}\, dx = \phi\left(\frac{b-\mu}{\sigma}\right) - \phi\left(\frac{a-\mu}{\sigma}\right)$$

The approximation for erf(x) is due to Hastings, (1955).

2. Useful formulas:

$$e^{j\theta} = \cos\theta + j\sin\theta$$

$$e^{-j\theta} = \cos\theta - j\sin\theta$$

$$\cos\theta = \frac{e^{j\theta} + e^{-j\theta}}{2}$$

$$\sin\theta = \frac{e^{j\theta} - e^{-j\theta}}{2j}$$

$$1 + a + a^2 + \ldots + a^r = \frac{1 - a^{r+1}}{1-a} \qquad a \neq 1$$

$$e^{j\theta} + e^{2j\theta} + \ldots + e^{Nj\theta} = \frac{1 - e^{jN\theta}}{1 - e^{j\theta}} e^{j\theta}$$

$$\sum_{n=1}^{N} \sin n\theta = \frac{\sin\dfrac{N\theta}{2}\,\sin\dfrac{(N+1)\theta}{2}}{\sin\dfrac{\theta}{2}}$$

$$\sum_{n=1}^{N} \cos n\theta = \frac{\cos \frac{N\theta}{2} \sin \frac{(N+1)\theta}{2}}{\sin \frac{\theta}{2}}$$

$$\sum_{n=-N}^{N} e^{jn\theta} = \sum_{n=-N}^{N} \cos n\theta = \frac{\sin \left[\left(\frac{2N+1}{2} \right) \theta \right]}{\sin \frac{\theta}{2}}$$

$$\sin a \pm \sin \beta = 2 \sin \left[\frac{1}{2}(a \pm \beta) \right] \cos \left[\frac{1}{2}(a \mp \beta) \right]$$

$$\cos a + \cos \beta = 2 \cos \left[\frac{1}{2}(a + \beta) \right] \cos \left[\frac{1}{2}(a - \beta) \right]$$

$$\cos a - \cos \beta = 2 \sin \left[\frac{1}{2}(a + \beta) \right] \sin \left[\frac{1}{2}(a - \beta) \right]$$

$$\cos a \cos \beta = \frac{1}{2} \left[\cos(a - \beta) + \cos(a + \beta) \right]$$

$$\sin a \sin \beta = \frac{1}{2} \left[\cos(a - \beta) - \cos(a + \beta) \right]$$

$$\sin a \cos \beta = \frac{1}{2} \left[\sin(a + \beta) + \sin(a - \beta) \right]$$

$$1 - \cos \theta = 2 \sin^2 \frac{\theta}{2}$$

$$1 + \cos \theta = 2 \cos^2 \frac{\theta}{2}$$

$$\sin(a \pm \beta) = \sin \alpha \cos \beta \pm \cos a \sin \beta$$

$$\cos(a \pm \beta) = \cos a \cos \beta \mp \sin a \sin \beta$$

APPENDIX C
REFERENCES

Abramowitz, M., and Stegun, L. A. (1964). "Handbook of Mathematical Functions," U. S. Department of Commerce, NBS Applied Mathematics Series 55. Washington, D.C.: U. S. Government Printing Office.

Akaike, H. (1962). "On the Design of Lag Window for the Estimation of Spectra," *Ann. Inst. Stat. Math.* 14, 1-21.

Akaike, H. (1965). "On the Statistical Estimation of the Frequency Response Function of a System Having Multiple Input," *Annals of the Institute of Statistical Mathematics*, Vol. 17, No. 2.

Alexander, M. J., and Vok, C. A. (1963). "Tables of the Cumulative Distribution of Sample Multiple Coherence," Rocketdyne Division, North American Aviation, Inc., Research Memorandum 972-351 (Oct.).

Anderson, T. W. (1958). *An Introduction to Multivariate Statistical Analysis.* New York: Wiley.

Barnoski, R. L. (1969). "Ordinary Coherence Functions and Mechanical Systems, *J. Aircraft*, 6, (4).

Bendat, J. S., and Piersol, A. G. (1966). *Measurement and Analysis of Random Data.* New York: Wiley.

Benignus, V. A. (1969). "Estimation of the Coherence Spectrum and Its Confidence Interval Using the Fast Fourier Transform," *IEEE Trans. Audio Electroacoustics*, AU-17 (2).

Bergland, G. D. (1967). "The Fast Fourier Transform Recursive Equations for Arbitrary Length Records," *Math. Comput.* 21, 236.

Bingham, C., Godfrey, M. D., and Tukey, J. W. (1967). "Modern Techniques of Power Spectrum Estimation," *IEEE Trans. Audio Electroacoustics* AU-15, 56-66.

Blackman, R. B., and Tukey, J. W. (1958). *The Measurement of Power Spectra from the Point of View of Communications Engineering.* New York: Dover.

Bordner, G. W., Greaves, C. J., and Wierwille, W. W. (1964). "Research Studies of Random Process Theory and physical Applications," NASA CR-61081 (Aug.).

Brigham, E. O., and Morrow, R. E. (December 1969). "The Fast Fourier Transform," *IEEE Spectrum*.

Chiburis, E. F., and Dean, W. C. (1967a). "Multiple Coherence of Long Period Seismic Noise at LASA," Teledyne, Inc., Seismic Data Laboratory Report No. 189 (June 23).

Chiburis, E. F., and Dean, W. C. (1967b). "Multiple Coherence of Short Period Noise at LASA," Teledyne, Inc., Seismic Data Laboratory Report No. 190 (June 26).

Chiburis, E. F., and Dean, W. C. (1967c). "Multiple Coherence of Noise at Three Vertical Arrays, UBSO, GV-TX, AP-OK," Teledyne, Inc., Seismic Data Laboratory Report No. 191 (June 28).

Chiburis, E. F., and Dean, W. C. (1967d). "Multiple Coherence of Short Period Noise at UBSO and TFSO," Teledyne, Inc., Seismic Data Laboratory Report No. 192 (June 30).

Choi, S. (1967). "Principal Component Analysis of Seismic Data and Direction of the Principal Component for Seismic Record," Teledyne, Inc., Seismic Data Laboratory Report No. 181 (May).

Constantinides, A. G. (1967). "Frequency Transforms for Digital Filters," *Electronics Letters (G. B.)* (11), 487-489.

Cooley, J. W., and Tukey, J. W. (1965). "An Algorithm for the Machine Calculation of Complex Fourier Series," *Math. Comput.* 19, 297.

Cramer, H. (1946). *Mathematical Methods of Statistics*. Princeton, N.J.: Princeton University Press.

Danielson, G. C., and Lanczos, C. (1942). "Some Improvements in Practical Fourier Analysis and Their Application to X-Ray Scattering from Liquids," *J. Franklin Inst.* 233, 365-380, 435-452.

Dean, W. C., Shumway, R. L., and Enochson, L. D. (1966). "The Coherency Analysis of Seismic Noise," Earth Sciences Division, Teledyne, Inc., Seismic Data Laboratory Report No. 155 (July).

Enochson, L. D., and Goodman, N. R. (1965). "Gaussian
    Approximations to the Distribution of Sample Coher-
    ence," AFFDL TR-65-57, Research and Technology Divi-
    sion, AFSC, Wright-Patterson AFB, Ohio (Feb.).
Gentleman, W. M., and Sande, G. (1966). "Fast Fourier
    Transforms--for Fun and Profit," *AFIPS Conf. Proc.*
    29, 563-578.
Gold, B., and Rader, C. M. (1966). "Effects of Quan-
    tization Noise in Digital Filters," *1966 Spring
    Joint Comput. Conf.* 28, 213-219.
Goodman, N. R. (1965). "Measurement of Matrix Fre-
    quency Response Functions and Multiple Coherence
    Functions," AFFDL TR-65-56, Research and Technology
    Division, AFSC, Wright-Patterson AFB, Ohio (Feb.).
Guilleman, E. A. (1961). *The Mathematics of Circuit
    Analysis.* New York: Wiley.
Hannan, E. J. (1960). *Time Series Analysis.* New York:
    Wiley.
Hastings, C. (1955). *Approximations for Digital Com-
    puters.* Princeton, N.J.: Princeton University
    Press.
Hinich, M. (1967). "Estimation of Spectra After Hard
    Clipping of Gaussian Processes," *Technometrics*, 9,
    391.
Holtz, H., and Leondes, C. T. (1966). "The Synthesis
    of Recursive Digital Filters," *J. ACM* 13 (22), 262-
    280.
Jenkins, G. M., and Watts, D. G. (1968). *Spectral
    Analysis and Its Applications.* San Francisco:
    Holden-Day.
Jenkins, F. A., and White, H. E. (1950). *Fundamentals
    of Optics.* 2d ed. New York: McGraw-Hill.
Kaiser, J. F. (1965) "Some Practical Considerations in
    the Realization of Linear Digital Filters," *Proc.
    3rd Allerton Conf. Circuit Sys. Theory, Monticello.*
Kelly, R. D., and Richman, G. (1970). *Principles and
    Techniques for Shock Data Analysis.* Washington,
    D.C.: Shock and Vibration Information Center, Naval
    Research Laboratory.

Kelly, R. D., Enochson, L. D., and Rondinelli, L. A. (1966). "Techniques and Errors in Measuring Cross-Correlation and Cross-Spectral Density Functions," NASA CR-74505 (Feb.).

Kendall, M. G., and Stuart, A. G. (1961). *The Advanced Theory of Statistics*. London: Hafner.

Khinchin, A. Y. (1934). "Korrelationstheorie der stationaren stochastischen Prozesse," *Math. Ann.* 109, 604.

Knowles, J. B., and Edwards, R. (1965a). "Simplified Analysis of Computational Errors in a Feed-Back System Incorporating a Digital Computer," presented at Society of Instrument Testing Symposium on Direct Digital Control (London), April 22.

Knowles, J. B., and Edwards, R. (1965b). "Effect of a Finite-Word-Length Computer in a Sampled-Data Feedback System," *Proc. Inst. Elec. Eng.* 112, 1197-1207.

Knowles, J. B., and Edwards, R. (1965c). "Complex Cascade Programming and Associated Computational Errors," *Electronics Letters* 1, 160-161.

Knowles, J. B., and Edwards, R. (1965d). "Finite Word-Length Effects in Multirate Direct Digital Control Systems," *Proc. Inst. Elec. Eng.* 112, 2376-2384.

Knowles, J. B., and Olcayto, E. M. (1968). "Coefficient Accuracy and Digital Filter Response," *IEEE Trans. Circuit Theory* CT-15, 31-41.

Korn, G. A., and Korn, T. M. 2nd. ed. (1968). *Mathematical Handbook for Scientists and Engineers*. New York: McGraw-Hill.

Kullback, S. (1959). *Information Theory and Statistics*. New York: Wiley.

Kuo, F. F., and Kaiser, J. F., eds. (1966). *Systems Analysis by Digital Computer*. New York: Wiley.

Lanczos, C. (1956). *Applied Analysis*. Englewood Cliffs, N.J.: Prentice-Hall.

Lighthill, M. J. (1960). *Introduction to Fourier Analysis and Generalised Functions*. Cambridge: Cambridge University Press.

Liu, B., and Kaneko, T. (1969). "Error Analysis of Digital Filters Realized with Floating-Point Arithmetic," *Proc. IEEE* 57, 1735-1747.

McCowan, D. W. (1966). "Finite Fourier Transform Theory and Its Application to the Computation of Convolutions, Correlations, and Spectra," Earth Sciences Division, Teledyne, Inc., Research Department Technical Memorandum No. 8-66 (Dec.).

Magrab, E. D., and Blomquist, D. S. (1971). *The Measurement of Time-Varying Phenomena.* New York: Wiley.

Ormsby, J. F. A. (1961a). "Design of Numerical Filters with Applications to Missile Data Processing," *J. Assoc. Comput. Mach.* (July).

Otnes, R. K. (1968a). "Recursive Bandpass Digital Filters," *IEEE Proc.* 56 (2).

Otnes, R. K. (1968b). "An Elementary Design Procedure for Digital Filters," *IEEE Trans. Audio Electroacoustics* AU-16, 330-335.

Otnes, R. K., and McNamee, L. P. (1970). "Instability Thresholds in Digital Filters Due to Coefficient Rounding," *IEEE Trans. Audio Electroacoustics* AU-18.

Parzen, E. (1961). "Mathematical Considerations in the Estimation of Spectra," *Technometrics* 3, 167-190.

Parzen, E. (1962). *Stochastic Processes.* San Francisco: Holden-Day.

Piersol, A. G. (1967). "Power Spectra Measurements for Spacecraft Vibration Data," *J. Spacecraft and Rockets* 4, 1613.

Ralston, A. (1965). *A First Course in Numerical Analysis.* New York: McGraw-Hill.

Sande, G. (1965). "On An Alternative Method for Calculating Covariance Functions," Princeton Computer Memorandum, Princeton, N.J.

Schmid, L. P. (1965). "Efficient Autocorrelation," *Commun. ACM* 8, 115.

Shannon, C. E. (1949). "Communication in the Presence of Noise," *Proc. IRE* 37, 10.

Shumway, R. H. (1966). "Some Aspects of Linear Statistical Modeling for Seismic Arrays," Earth Science Division, Teledyne, Inc., Research Department Technical Memo No. 3-66 (March).

Simpson, S. M., Jr. (1961).   "Time Series Techniques Applied to Underground Nuclear Detection and Further Digitized Seismic Data," MIT Scientific Report No. 2, AFCRL 62-262, Contract AF 19(604)-7378, ARPA Order No. (80-61) (Dec.).

Sloan, E. A. (1969). "Comparison of Linearly and Quadratically Modified Spectral Estimates of Gaussian Signals," *IEEE Trans. Audio Electroacoustics* AU-17 (2).

Theilheimer, F. (1969). "A Matrix Version of the Fast Fourier Transform," *IEEE Trans. Audio Electroacoustics* AU-17 (2).

Weaver, C. S., von der Groeben, J., Mantey, P. E., Toole, J. G., Cole, C. A., Jr., Fitzgerald, J. W., and Lawrence, R. W. (1968). "Digital Filtering with Applications to Electrocardiogram Processing," *IEEE Trans. Audio Electroacoustics* AU-16, 350-391.

Weinreb, S. (1963). "A Digital Spectral Analysis Technique and Its Application to Radio Astronomy," MIT Research Laboratory of Electronics, Technical Report 412 (Aug.).

Weinstein, C., and Oppenheim, A. V. (1965).   "Some Practical Considerations in the Realization of Linear Digital Filters," *Proc. Third Allerton Conf. Circuit Syst. Theory (Monticello, Ill.)* 621-633.

Weinstein, C., and Oppenheim, A. V. (1969). "A Comparison of Roundoff Noise in Floating Point and Fixed Point Digital Filter Realizations," *Proc. IEEE (Letters)* 57, 1181-1183.

Wiener, N. (1930). "Generalized Harmonic Analysis," *Acta Math.* 55, 117.

Wiener, N. (1949). *Extrapolation, Interpolation, and Smoothing of Stationary Time Series.* Cambridge, Mass.: MIT Press.

Index